Kokota Grammar

DATE DUE

Brodart Co. Cat. # 55 137 001 Printed in USA

OCEANIC LINGUISTICS SPECIAL PUBLICATIONS

Numbers 1 through 25 and 28 are no longer available.

1. English in Hawaii: An Annotated Bibliography. Stanley M. Tsuzaki and John E. Reinecke. 1966.
2. An Ivatan Syntax. Lawrence Andrew Reid. 1966.
3. Manobo-English Dictionary. Richard E. Elkins. 1968.
4. Nguna Texts. Albert J. Schütz. 1969.
5. Nguna Grammar. Albert J. Schütz. 1969.
6. A Grammar of Kaliai-Kove. David R. Counts. 1969.
7. Chrau Grammar. David D. Thomas. 1971.
8. Philippine Minor Languages: Word Lists and Phonologies. Edited by Lawrence A. Reid. 1971.
9. Japanese Pidgin English in Hawaii: A Bilingual Description. Susumu Nagara. 1972.
10. Kapampangan Syntax. Leatrice T. Mirikitani. 1972.
11. Isneg-English Vocabulary. Morice Vanoverbergh. 1972.
12. Outline of Sre Structure. Timothy M. Manley. 1972.
13. Austroasiatic Studies, Parts I and II. Edited by Philip N. Jenner, Laurence C. Thompson, and Stanley Starosta. 1976.
14. A Bibliography of Pidgin and Creole Languages. Compiled by John E. Reinecke, Stanley M. Tsuzaki, David DeCamp, Ian F. Hancock, and Richard E. Wood. 1975.
15. A Handbook of Comparative Tai. Fang Kuei Li. 1977.
16. Syntactic Derivation of Tagalog Verbs. Videa P. De Guzman. 1978.
17. The Genetic Relationship of the Ainu Language. James Patrie. 1982.
18. A Grammar of Manam. Frantisek Lichtenberk. 1983.
19. The History of the Fijian Languages. Paul A. Geraghty. 1983.
20. For Gordon H. Fairbanks. Edited by Veneeta Z. Acson and Richard L. Leed. 1985.
21. The Causatives of Malagasy. Charles Randriamasimanana. 1986.
22. Echo of a Culture: A Grammar of Rennell and Bellona. Samuel H. Elbert. 1988.
23. A Guide to Austroasiatic Speakers and Their Languages. Robert Parkin. 1991.
24. Tonality in Austronesian Languages. Edited by Jerold A. Edmondson and Kenneth J. Gregerson. 1993.
25. Tinrin Grammar. Midori Osumi. 1995.
26. Toward a Reference Grammar of Tok Pisin: An Experiment in Corpus Linguistics. John W. M. Verhaar. 1995.
27. An Erromangan (Sye) Grammar. Terry Crowley. 1998.
28. From Ancient Cham to Modern Dialects: Two Thousand Years of Language Contact and Change. Graham Thurgood. 1999.
29. Grammatical Analysis: Morphology, Syntax, and Semantics: Studies in Honor of Stanley Starosta. Edited by Videa P. De Guzman and Byron W. Bender. 2000.
30. Nhanda: An Aboriginal Language of Western Australia. Juliette Blevins. 2001.
31. Bislama Reference Grammar. Terry Crowley. 2004.
32. Otto Dempwolff's *Grammar of the Jabêm Language in New Guinea*. Translated and edited by Joel Bradshaw and Francisc Czobor. 2005.
33. A Grammar of South Efate: An Oceanic Language of Vanuatu. Nicholas Thieberger. 2006.
34. William J. Gedney's Comparative Tai Source Book. Thomas John Hudak. 2007.
35. Kokota Grammar. Bill Palmer. 2009

Publications may be ordered electronically from www.uhpress.hawaii.edu or by mail from University of Hawai'i Press, 2840 Kolowalu Street, Honolulu, Hawai'i 96822, USA.

Oceanic Linguistics Special Publication No. 35

Kokota Grammar

Bill Palmer

University of Hawai'i Press

Honolulu

14 13 12 11 10 09   6 5 4 3 2 1

Library of Congress Cataloging-in-Publication Data

Palmer Bill, 1961–
    Kokota grammar / Bill Palmer.
       p. cm. — (Oceanic linguistics special publication ; no. 35)
    ISBN 978-0-8248-3251-3 (pbk. : alk. paper)
    1. Kokota language—Grammar. I. Title.
    PL6252.K671P36 2009
    499'.5—dc22

                                                            2008036495

Camera-ready copy for this book was prepared under
the supervision of the series editor.

Printed by Edwards Brothers, Inc.

For Sebastian

CONTENTS

LIST OF FIGURES AND TABLES

ACKNOWLEDGMENTS

My first thanks go to the people of Goveo village, among whom I lived and worked, and from whom I learned something of their language and their lives. I am particularly grateful to the late Chief Ambrose Varigutu for allowing me to live and work in Goveo, and to Chief Maro for allowing my work to continue. I am grateful to my friend, counselor and main language consultant James Tikani for his time, efforts, and considerable kindness; and to Hon. Billy Gedi for his friendship and his part in making my visit to Santa Isabel possible. I thank Edmond Belama and Peter Kodere in particular for their friendship, and to the many people who answered strange questions and who told me stories, particularly James Tikani, Ruebenson Havisade, Clement Felo Teveke, Simon Rivakato, Hugo, Mark Havilegu, Chief Varigutu, Chief Maro, and many others. *Na tageogau gau gudu.*

I am grateful to the Santa Isabel Provincial Government for permission to work in the Province and for their assistance, in particular the then office holders Hon. Billy Gedi, Speaker of the Provincial Assembly; Hon. Andrew Gedi, Minister for Education; Premier Amos Gigini; and Provincial Secretary Japhet Waipora. My thanks also go to Audrey Rusa in the Solomon Islands Ministry of Education, Honiara, for help with research permits.

Thanks to Brett Baker, Bernard Comrie, Bill Foley, Catriona Malau, John Lynch, Andy Pawley, and Malcolm Ross for comments on sections of this grammar, and to Claire Turner for formatting large parts of the manuscript.

Field research among the Kokota was funded by Bill Foley; the Faculty of Arts at the University of Sydney; the Peter Lawrence Memorial Scholarship (1992 and 1993); the Frank Coaldrake Scholarship (1994); and the Research Committee of the Faculty of Arts, University of the South Pacific. Funding from UK Arts and Humanities Research Council grant APN19365 and British Academy grant SG44063 assisted in revision of the manuscript and preparation for publication. I am pleased to acknowledge all this assistance.

GLOSSING ABBREVIATIONS

1	first person	PFV	perfective
2	second person	PL	plural
3	third person	PN	proper name
ALT	alternative	PNLOC	proper name location
CMP	comparative	PRO	pro (focused dummy argument)
CND	conditional	PRS	present
CNSM	'consumed' possessor-indexing host	PSBL	possible
CNT	continuous	PURP	purposive
CNTX	contextualizer	RD~	reduplication
CRD	cardinal	RECP	reciprocal
CS	causative	REFL	reflexive
DSDR	desiderative	RL	realis
EMPH	emphatic	S	subject
EXC	exclusive plural	SBD	subordinator
EXCLM	exclamation	SBJ	subject
EXHST	exhaustive	SEQ	sequential
FOC	focus	SG	singular
FUT	future	SPC	specifying
GENP	general possessor-indexing host	thatN	that (nearby)
IMM	immediacy	thatNV	that (not visible)
IMP	imperative	thatPV	that (potentially visible)
INC	inclusive plural	thereD	there (distal)
INIT	initiality	thereP	there (proximal)
IRR	irrealis	theseR	these (within reach)
ITR	intransitive	theseT	these (touching)
LMT	limiter	thisR	this (within reach)
LOC	locative	thisT	this (touching)
NEG	negative	thoseN	those (nearby)
NMLZ	nominalizer	thoseNV	those (not visible)
NSP	nonspecific	thosePV	those (potentially visible)
NT	neutral modality	TR	transitive
O	object	VOC	vocative
ORD	ordinal	??	function unclear
P	possessive		

CHAPTER 1: INTRODUCTION

1.1 Sociolinguistic context

Ooe Kokota ('Kokota talk') is spoken on Santa Isabel, the middle island in the northern chain of the Solomon Islands' double chain of six large islands and several smaller islands. At over 200 kilometers in length, it is the longest of these islands, but has the lowest population density in the Solomon Islands, with some 25,000 inhabitants. *Ooe Kokota* is the language of three villages: Goveo and Sisiḡa, half way along Santa Isabel's north coast, and Hurepelo at a correpsonding location on the south coast. A small number of Kokota speakers are resident in the capital Honiara and the provincial capital Buala.

Speakers refer to themselves as Kokota people, and their language as *Ooe Kokota*. The name Kokota itself refers to a currently uninhabited area of coastal Santa Isabel between Goveo and Buala, and also to a river that enters the sea at that point. The word *kota* in present day *Ooe Kokota* means 'to go ashore' or 'to land', and *Kokota* is a historically reduplicated form of that root.

Until the 19th century the mountainous interior of Santa Isabel was populated. These groups later dispersed to the coast on either side of the island, leaving most of the interior uninhabited, including the region between the Kokota villages. The relative proximity of Goveo and Sisiḡa allows regular boat contact. Travel to and from Hurepelo is a far more considerable matter, and less contact is maintained. In Kokota areas paths extend beyond the village as far as local coconut and betelnut plantations, and gardens in the hills behind the villages. People do not cross the island on foot, and travel to Hurepelo involves a boat trip of several days. Speakers from Goveo and Sisiḡa report no significant linguistic differences between those two villages, and no sound differences between these communalects and Hurepelo. Nothing else is known about Kokota dialectology.

Today the number of Kokota speakers is probably approaching 1200 individuals. Ethnologue (2005) gives a figure of 530 speakers in 1999, but Ethnologue (2000) gave a figure of 1,020 for the previous year, 1998. Palmer (1999a:1) gives a 1999 figure of "in excess of 900," based on extrapolations from 1976 and 1986 censuses. Given that the population of Santa Isabel increased by 25% between 1999 and 2007, a 2007 figure of between 1100 and 1200 is likely.

Kokota is the normal language of communication in all three Kokota villages. In the 1990s, when the present field research was carried out, it was used for all purposes except in the primary school, where English was the official medium and Solomons Pijin often used, and in church, where sermons by non-Kokota priests were given in Pijin. Outside school, children used Kokota almost exclusively. This, coupled with the rapidly increasing population, suggests that the language is not in immediate danger of disappearing, despite its low speaker numbers. Several Pijin words have been borrowed into the language, as have a number of words from the two dominant Santa Isabel languages Zabana and Cheke Holo, but this is not a new phenomenon. It is clear that borrowing between the island's languages was the norm before the arrival of Europeans.

However, Kokota is at risk from Zabana and Cheke Holo, which are spreading as their much larger populations expand and move into new areas of the island. Neighboring Hoatana, known in the literature as Laghu (Tryon and Hackman 1983), spoken between Kokota and Zabana, lost its last speaker in 1984, through intermarriage and population expansion of Zabana speakers. Kokota is similarly at risk, mainly from Cheke Holo. The inhabitants of Bolotei and Toelegu, west of Sisiḡa, and Dedeu, west of Hurepelo, are Cheke Holo speakers (Whiteman and Simons 1978:6). More recently a settlement of Cheke Holo speakers was established on the coast between Goveo and Sisiḡa. This encroachment of Cheke Holo speakers may be expected to continue. Several Kokota speakers expressed the opinion that one day everyone on Santa Isabel will speak Cheke Holo, an opinion also reported elsewhere on the island (Whiteman and Simons 1978:6).

1.2 Kokota in Oceanic

The large Oceanic branch of Austronesian has several major subgroups. With the exception of Bugotu, all Santa Isabel languages belong to Western Oceanic, a first-order subgroup displaying shared innovations. (Ross 1988:386–392; 1995:92) While some innovations are shared by more than one subgroup, none are shared by all. Western Oceanic, therefore, represents several groupings descended from a dialect network that spread slowly through the Bismarck Archipelago, coastal New Guinea, and the northwestern Solomon Islands including Bougainville, following the more rapid eastern expansion of several other first-order Oceanic subgroups.

Western Oceanic itself comprises three groups: Papuan Tip, North New Guinea (Ross 1995:89, 92–93) and Meso-Melanesian, consisting of languages of the Bismarcks and the western Solomon Islands. The Meso-Melanesian network divides into two small groups and the large New Ireland network, which in turn divides into four small groups the South New Ireland/Northwest Solomonic network. South New Ireland/Northwest Solomonic divides into seven small groups and Northwest Solomonic (NWS). (Ross 1988:257–314)

NWS comprises the Oceanic languages of Bougainville and its offshore islands (excluding Polynesian Outliers), of Choiseul, of the New Georgia group, and, excepting Bugotu, of Santa Isabel[1] (Ross 1988:213–256). The boundary with NWS Cheke Holo and Gao on one side and Bugotu on the other represents the easternmost extension of Western Oceanic.

---

[1] Although spoken on Santa Isabel, Bugotu is a South-East Solomonic language.

The roughly 37 NWS languages fall into six subgroups: Piva/Bannoni, Nehan/ North Bougainville, Mono-Uruavan, Choiseul, New Georgia, and Santa Isabel.[2] Ross (1988:224–225, 240–247) finds one shared lexical innovation and some syntactic evidence that weakly appears to link New Georgia and Isabel into a single larger subgroup. Whether or not this is ultimately demonstrated, each clearly represents a distinct subgroup at some level. Shared phonological and lexical innovations justify grouping the Isabel languages and positing a common ancestor, Proto Santa Isabel (Ross 1988:225). Members of the Isabel chain are Zabana (aka Kia), Hoatana (aka Laghu, extinct), Kokota, Blablanga (probably including Zazao [aka Kilokaka]), Cheke Holo (aka Maringe), and Gao.

1.3 Previous work on Kokota

Before the present research, Kokota was known to outsiders only from Tryon and Hackman's (1983) 320 item wordlist. A section of the Church of Melanesia Prayer Book (Church of Melanesia 1965) had also been translated into Kokota by a Zabana speaker (Church of Melanesia n.d.) and used locally, despite grammatical and lexical inaccuracies and numerous Zabana words.

In the 1990s the author began fieldwork in Goveo village. This lead to a PhD thesis (Palmer 1999a); a discussion of the phonemic status of Kokota's voiceless sonorants (Palmer 1999b); a grammatical sketch (Palmer 2002a); a discussion of the syntactic status of Oceanic indirect possessor-indexing hosts with particular reference to Kokota (Palmer and Brown 2007); and an online dictionary (Palmer 2007). In addition, at the community's request as a condition of field work, a further section of the Prayer Book, the Evening Prayer, was translated in collaboration with a local Committee and desktop published (Palmer 1998).

1.4 The present study

The present work describes the grammar of Kokota, including its phonology, and its phrase, clause, and sentence level syntax. Particular attention is paid to the system of possession; to argument structure; and to the stress regime, which is complex and in a process of change. Like many Oceanic languages Kokota has limited morphological complexity, so there is no separate chapter on morphology. Aspects of the morphology and morphosyntax are discussed in conjunction with other areas of the grammar that they relate to syntactically or functionally. The structure of the language is described up to the level of the sentence. Apart from information structure issues with syntactic implications (such as topicalization and focushood), discourse level phenomena are not discussed. Sociolinguistic phenomena and issues such as multilingualism, language mixing and code switching are beyond the scope of the work. As research was carried out in one village, Kokota dialectology is not discussed.

---

[2] This subgroup is traditionally known as the Ysabel chain, reflecting the pre-independence spelling of the island's name. Here the modern name Isabel is used.

1.5 Orthography

Kokota speakers use the standard orthography of the dominant neighboring Cheke Holo language (used by White et al. 1988, Boswell 2002, and the Cheke Holo New Testament, and for Kokota by Palmer (1998, 1999a, 1999b, 2002a).

Several Cheke Holo phonemes are not found in Kokota, and letters for these are omitted from the Kokota orthography. An exception is the apostrophe representing a glottal stop. The glottal stop is not phonemic in Kokota, but speakers often use the apostrophe to represent an epenthetic intervocalic glottal, especially in words cognate with Cheke Holo words displaying a glottal. Another anomaly is the use of both 'j' and 'z' as in Cheke Holo, where [dʒ] and [ʒ] are allophones (White et al. 1988:x). This is not true of Kokota, where the affricate is not present even phonetically. However, under the influence of Holo, cognate forms spelled with 'j' in Holo tend to be spelled with 'j' in Kokota. Finally, in line with Cheke Holo, 'w' is used in some Pijin loans, despite the absence of [w] from the Kokota phoneme inventory. The orthography used by Kokota speakers is given in Table 1.1.

Chapter 2 on phonology uses IPA throughout. In the remaining chapters all data is presented in the orthography. This orthography is treated here as a phonemic representation, and all forms, including English personal names, are spelled phonemically using the orthography. This is not representative of actual usage, as English personal names are spelled as in English by the Kokota. Thus, when the name of my informant James appears in an example, it is spelled *zemesi*, representing actual Kokota pronunciation, although no Kokota speaker would write the name in this way.

TABLE 1.1. KOKOTA ORTHOGRAPHY

phoneme	letter	phoneme	letter	phoneme	letter
/p/	p	/m/	m	/a/	a
/b/	b	/m̥/	mh	/e/	e
/t/	t	/n/	n	/i/	i
/d/	d	/n̥/	nh	/o/	o
/k/	k	/ŋ/	ñ	/u/	u, w
/g/	ḡ	/ŋ̊/	ñh		
/f/	f	/l/	l		
/v/	v	/l̥/	lh		
/s/	s	/r/	r		
/z/	z (j)	/r̥/	rh		
/h/	h	-	(')		
/ɣ/	g				

CHAPTER 2: PHONOLOGY

2.1 Segmental phonology

2.1.1 Consonants

2.1.1.1 Consonant phoneme inventory

The Kokota consonant phoneme inventory is remarkably symmetrical. Three place classes exist distinguished by the features [±labial] and [±coronal]. Each class may be characterized as follows:

(2.1) [+labial, -coronal]   (bilabials and labiodentals)
      [-labial, +coronal]   (post-alveolars)
      [-labial, -coronal]   (velars and glottals)

Five manner classes exist: two obstruent classes (plosive and fricative), and three sonorant classes (nasal, lateral, and rhotic). Of these, plosives, fricatives, and nasals occur in each of the three place classes. Laterals and rhotics occur only in [-labial, +coronal] place. Kokota is unusual in that a corresponding voice pair exists in every place/manner class: a full set of voiceless counterparts exist for each voiced consonant phoneme, including sonorants. There are thus 22 consonant phonemes in 11 place and manner pairs:

TABLE 2.1. CONSONANT PHONEMES

	[+labial, -coronal]		[-labial, +coronal]	[-labial, -coronal]	
	Bilabial	Labiodental	Post-alveolar	Velar	Glottal
Plosive	p b		t d	k g	
Fricative		f v	s z	ɣ	h
Nasal	m̥ m		n̥ n	ŋ̊ ŋ	
Lateral			l̥ l		
Rhotic			r̥ r		

TABLE 2.2. CONSONANT FEATURE MATRICES

	p, b	t, d	k, g	f, v	s, z	h, ɣ	m̥, m	n̥, n	ŋ̊, ŋ	l̥, l	r̥, r
labial	+	-	-	+	-	-	+	-	-	-	-
coronal	-	+	-	-	+	-	-	+	-	+	+
continuant	-	-	-	+	+	+	+	+	+	+	+
sonorant	-	-	-	-	-	-	+	+	+	+	+
nasal							+	+	+	-	-
lateral							-	-	-	+	-
rhotic							-	-	-	-	+

2.1.1.1.1 Evidence for phoneme status: consonants

Tables 2.3 and 2.4 demonstrate consonant phoneme contrasts by voicing status, and manner and place of articulation.

TABLE 2.3. CONTRASTIVE SETS DEMONSTRATING VOICE AND MANNER OF ARTICULATION DISTINCTIONS

	labials	coronals	nonlabial noncoronals
voice	/putu/ 'k.o. tree' /butu/ 'stomach'	/tafa/ 'encounter' /dafa/ 'burn clear'	/kulu/ 'be first' /gulu/ 'thunder'
	/fila/ 'thunderclap' /vilai/ 'knife'*	/siku/ 'lawyer cane' /ziku/ 'cone shell'	/tahina/ 'that sea' /taɣina/ 'him/herself'
	/nom̥i/ 'hear' /nomi/ 'ourEXC'	/n̥iɣo/ 'completive' /niɣo/ '2SG object'	/nan̥o/ 'k.o. in-law' /nano/ 'shadow'
	-	/bubul̥i/ 'clam sp.' /bubulo/ 'mist'*	-
	-	/r̥uta/ 'untangle' /ruta/ 'swamp taro'	-
plosive/ fricative	/popoto/ 'fish sp.' /fofoto/ 'tree sp.'	/papate/ 'k.o. crab' /papase/ 'ginger'	/ɣase/ 'girl' /gasi/ 'torch'*
	/babao/ 'be tired'* /vavau/ 'kapok tree'	/ido/ 'mother' /izo/ 'point'	/kuku/ 'defecate' /huhu/ 'question'
plosive/ nasal	/bahai/ 'tree sp.' /mahai/ 'eat'	/da/ '1INC subj.' /na/ '1EXC subj.'	/ga/ '1EXC subj.' /ŋa/ 'but'
plosive/ rhotic	-	/ade/ 'here' /are/ 'those'	-
lateral/ rhotic	-	/leleo/ 'tawny shark' /rereo/ 'shield'	-

* No minimal pair has been identified. A near minimal pair demonstrates the contrast.

2.1.1.1.2 Consonant phoneme frequencies

On the basis of a representative sample of Kokota words the relative frequencies of consonant phonemes has been calculated. The wordlist (presented along with further details in Palmer 1999a) contains 335 basic lexical items giving a total of 748 consonant phoneme tokens. The most striking findings from this analysis lie in patterns of relationship between place of articulation and sonority (Table 2.5), and voicing and sonority (Table 2.6). Table 2.5 is interesting in that while coronals are well represented as both obstruents and sonorants, the nonlabial noncoronals are the smallest class of sonorants, but the largest class of obstruents.

TABLE 2.4. CONTRASTIVE SETS DEMONSTRATING PLACE OF ARTICULATION DISTINCTIONS

	labials	coronals	nonlabial noncoronals
+voice plosives	/ba/ 'possibilitative'	/da/ '1INC subject'	/ga/ '1EXC subj. neutral'
-voice plosives	/puku/ 'be short'	/tuku/ 'wait'	/kuku/ 'defecate'
+voice fricatives	/vivivri/ 'propeller' /vilai/ 'knife'	/ziziri/ 'tree sp.'* /izo/ 'point'	/iɣo/ '2SG object' /ɣilai/ 'until'
voiceless fricatives	/fodu/ 'be full'	/sodu/ 'be tall' /soda/ 'clam'	/hoda/ 'take'*
voiced nasals	/ma/ 'father'	/na/ '1EXC subj. realis'	/ŋa/ 'but'
voiceless nasals	/m̥am̥aɣu/ 'be fearful' /m̥em̥e/ 'be difficult'	/n̥an̥aɣarai/ 'lobster'* /n̥ae/ 'be clear'	/ŋ̊eŋ̊e/ 'be separate' /ŋ̊au/ 'eat'*

* No minimal pair has been identified. A near minimal pair demonstrates the contrast.

TABLE 2.5. PROPORTION BY PLACE CLASS AND PROPORTION OF OBSTRUENTS TO SONORANTS

	[+labial]	[+coronal]	[-labial, -coronal]	Total
Obstruents	16%	21%	29%	65%
Sonorants	6%	28%	2%	35%
Total	22%	48%	31%	100%

TABLE 2.6. PROPORTION BY VOICING AND SONORITY

	Obstruents	Sonorants
Voiced	32%	89%
Voiceless	68%	11%
Total	100%	100%

The proportion of voiced to voiceless tokens overall is roughly equal (52% voiced, 48% voiceless). However, as Table 2.6 shows, this does not accurately reflect the voicing situation. Instead, there is a preference for voiceless obstruents, and a strong preference for voiced sonorants, reflecting a tendency towards a maximal contrast between obstruents and sonorants, with phoneme tokens tending to bunch at either end of the sonority hierarchy. Broadly speaking, Kokota displays a preference for nonlabial obstruents and a strong preference for anterior sonorants, along with a strong preference for voiceless obstruents and for voiced sonorants.

7

2.1.1.2 Consonant phonemes

2.1.1.2.1 Sonorants

A voiced and voiceless pair occurs in each place and manner category of sonorants. Nasals occur at each of the three place classes, with labial (bilabial), coronal (post-alveolar), and nonlabial noncoronal (velar) nasals. Laterals and rhotics occur only in post-alveolar place. The rhotics are taps. However, when immediately preceding a lateral they can be realized as rhotic approximants. This adjacency occurs in rapid speech as the result of vowel syncope:

(2.2)   /aɾe+lau/ → /aɾelau/ → /aɾlau/ → [aɹlau]

2.1.1.2.2 Plosives

Voiced and voiceless plosives ([-sonorant -continuant]) exist in each place class, produced as bilabial, post-alveolar, and velar. There is no prenasalization of voiced plosives, and voiceless plosives are unaspirated in all positions.

2.1.1.2.3 Fricatives

As with plosives, within the class [-sonorant, +continuant] voiced and voiceless counterparts exist in each place class. However, place of articulation features for fricatives are not all identical to those of the corresponding plosives, and there is less symmetry than with other categories.

2.1.1.2.3.1 Labial fricatives

The labial fricatives are labiodental and differ from each other only in voice.

2.1.1.2.3.2 Coronal fricatives

The coronal fricatives are post-alveolar, being produced further back than the English equivalents. Some variation occurs in production of the voiced phoneme. Before the high front vowel /i/ the fricative /z/ is palatalized. However, the resulting variant is not apico-palatal, like English /ʒ/. It remains apico-post-alveolar, but tongue body height is raised to position for the vowel. This only occurs under the influence of a following, not a preceding, vowel, the feature apparently only spreading within a syllable. However, it also does not occur word-initially. Thus palatalization occurs in (2.3)a., but not in (2.3)b.–c.:

(2.3)   a.   /tazi/ 'keep'   →   [tazʲi]
        b.   /ɣizu=na/ 'island'   →   [ɣizuna]
        c.   /ziku/ 'cone shell'   →   [ziku]

Some variation exists between speakers in the precise place at which /z/ is produced. It is possible this phoneme is in the process of change, perhaps from [ʒ] to [z]. Alternatively, the variation may be stable, as in several Papuan and Oceanic languages across northwest Melanesia (Ross p.c.). Similar variation is found in neighboring languages. For Zabana Fitzsimons (1989:16) reports free variation between "the voiced dental fricative [z] and the alveo-palatal fricative [ž]." Variation in Cheke Holo is regarded by White et al. (1988:x) as diachronic change in progress from /z/ to /dʒ/. However, it seems likely the reverse is true, as Isabel /z/ reflects Proto Oceanic *j (Ross 1988:221).

2.1.1.2.3.3 Nonlabial noncoronal fricatives

The largest place differentiation within a place class pair applies to the [-labial, -coronal] class of fricatives. While the voiced member of the pair is the velar /ɣ/, its voiceless counterpart is the glottal /h/. This is primarily a distinction of tongue height and backness: the tongue is raised and backed ([+high, +back]) for the voiced member, but lowered ([+low]) for the voiceless member.

This class also displays widespread lenition to zero, occuring both as regular morphophonemic deletion of /ɣ/, and as widespread phonetic deletion of both /ɣ/ and /h/, particularly in rapid speech. This appears to reflect diachronic phoneme loss in progress, at least of the voiced velar fricative.

In addition to the apparent loss of /ɣ/, a small number of examples exist of an unexplained alternation between /ɣ/ to /ŋ/, with the archaic forms /maɣava/ 'be hot' and /ɣoɣozi/ 'whistle' now normally replaced by /maŋava/ and /ŋoŋozi/. It is not clear whether these are idiosyncratic alternations, cognate borrowings, or evidence of a shift, with /ŋ/ in some other items also reflecting proto /ɣ/.

2.1.1.2.3.3.1 Surface deletion of nonlabial noncoronal fricatives

Both /ɣ/ and /h/ optionally lenite to zero in casual speech, particularly rapid speech. This may occur morpheme-medially, so, for example, /zoɣu/ 'drop' may be realized as [zou] and /glehe/ 'very' as [glee]. The greater the frequency of a word the more likely it is to display this lenition. So, for example, the ritualized greeting /gruɣu keli/ 'good night' is almost always realized as /gruu keli/. Equally, deletion occurs occasionally word-medially but morpheme-initially, for example, /n-e-ɣe/ 'RL-3S-PRS' may occur as [nee].

Deletion of this class of fricatives also occurs, though less frequently, with word-initial segments, so /ɣilai/ 'until' may be realized as [ilai], and /huhuga/ 'lie' as [uuga]. This is most common with [ɣ] before [i] and [h] before [u].

However, the most widespread phonetic deletion of these phonemes is intervocalically between identical vowels, especially the high back vowel /u/. Articulation of these phonemes between identical vowels in casual speech ranges freely from full articulation to complete deletion.

2.1.1.2.3.3.2 Morphophonemic deletion of nonlabial noncoronal fricatives

Deletion of /ɣ/ occurs regularly as phonologically conditioned allomorphic variation in at least three morphemes, all with the underlying form /ɣu/. These are in an enclitic marking verbs with continuous aspect, a suffix attaching to numeral roots to form cardinals, and the extremely high use verb 'be thus'.[3]

Phonological conditioning with the enclitic and the suffix is identical. The /ɣ/ lenites to zero in every environment except between identical vowels (in effect, except when the preceding vowel is /u/). So, for example, /zaho+ɣu/ 'go=CNT' is always realized as [zahou] and /kota+ɣu/ 'go ashore=CNT' as [kotau], but /au+ɣu/ 'be at=CNT' is normally realized as [auɣu] and /n-e-u+ɣu/ 'was being thus' as [neuɣu]. Equally, with numeral roots ending in vowels other than /u/, cardinals are formed with the suffix realized as [u]. So /tilo+ɣu/ 'three-CRD' is realized as [tilou] and /gaha+ɣu/ 'five-CRD' as [gahau], but /palu+ɣu/ 'two-CRD' is normally realized as [paluɣu].

Interestingly, when tested with non-occurring verb surface forms such as [zahoɣu] and cardinals such as [tiloɣu], with the fricative present on the surface, speakers accepted the forms, commenting that they were "very good Kokota," but observed that no one pronounced the words in that way.

When referring to the lack of /ɣ/ deletion following /u/, I have said that the unlenited forms are "normally" realized. This is because, while the morphophonemic process does not delete the segment in this environment, phonetic deletion may do so. Thus /au+ɣu/ may be realized in rapid speech as /auu/. The distinction between morphophonemic deletion and phonetic deletion is clear, however. In careful speech and in elicitation, speakers always give the full form of the suffix or enclitic when preceded by /u/, and never when not.

Phonological conditioning of /ɣ/ deletion with the verb /ɣu/ 'be thus' is similar to that of the enclitic and suffix. The form often functions as the head of a tag clause consisting of a single word made up of the verb and a cliticized preverbal modal/subject particle (see §10.4). This means the form normally does not occur word-initially. Since none of the preverbal modal/subject particles end with the

---

[3] On the basis of their respective functions it could be argued that the suffix and the enclitic actually reflect separate occurrences of a single morpheme.

vowel /u/, the fricative never occurs on the surface in these tags. Thus /n+e+ɣu/ 'it was thus' is always realized as [neu]. However, occasionally the form does occur without a modal/subject particle as a monomorphemic word. Only in this environment is the verb realized as [ɣu], with the fricative present on the surface.

Morphophonemic deletion of a more idiosyncratic nature is found with the reflexive base in one person/number category. Reflexivization is expressed using a possessor-indexed reflexive base with the underlying form /taɣi-/ (thus /taɣi-mu/ 'yourself', /taɣi-di/ 'themselves', etc.). However, in the first person singular, the normal surface form is [tai-gu]. This form is given in citation, and the unreduced form [taɣi-gu] never occurs in speech.

2.1.1.3 Phonological processes involving consonants

2.1.1.3.1 Labialization and velarization

Consonant variation occurs in Kokota when a consonant anticipates rounding and/or backness features of a following high back vowel, these features spreading from the vowel to the consonant. Consonants in all classes appear to be affected. With consonants that already have the feature [+labial] the effect is velarization, as in (2.4)a.–b. With consonants that already have the feature [+back] the effect is rounding, as in (2.4)c.–d. [4]

(2.4) a. /fufuɣo/ 'tomorrow' → [fˠufˠuɣo]
     b. /m̥um̥ui/ 'be wet' → [m̥ˠum̥ˠui]
     c. /kukuti/ 'eel' → [kʷukʷuti]
     d. /ɣura/ 'be boiling' → [ɣʷura]

The effect on coronals, which are both [-labial] and [-back], is primarily rounding, accompanied by an increase in dorsal height:

(2.5) a. /tulufulu/ 'thirty' › [tʷulʷufˠulʷu]
     b. /r̥ur̥uta/ 'untangle' → [r̥ʷur̥ʷuta]

The degree of raising of the tongue body with both labials and coronals varies depending on whether the environment also involves a preceding /u/. Consonants that occur intervocalically, where both vowels are /u/, involve a greater degree of tongue body raising than those that only precede /u/. Thus the second /f/ in (2.4)a. is produced with more dorsal height than the first.

---

[4] The preponderance of the high back vowel throughout these examples is not significant; they were chosen to maximally display the phenomenon.

Labialization appears to apply to medial consonant clusters occurring between two instances of the high back vowel. So, for example, /bubluse/ 'be easy' appears to be realized as [bʷubʷlʷuse]. It does not, however, seem to be true of initial clusters. Thus /gɾui/ appears to be realized as [gɾʷui], not [gʷɾʷui]. It is not clear what happens with medial clusters that precede but do not follow /u/.

2.1.1.3.2 Palatalization

Most consonant phonemes of the place class [-labial, -coronal] undergo palatalization under the influence of a following front vowel. It appears that the process does not occur with /h/. The process thus appears to apply to velar consonants only, not to the entire nonlabial noncoronal place class.

In this process tongue position assimilates to some extent to the position for the following front vowel by moving forward slightly. However, while tongue position on the upper articulator moves towards palatal position, the resulting allophone is very distinct from a palatal fricative since it remains dorsal. The resulting allophone is dorso-palatal, not lamino- or apico-palatal.

The degree of palatalization appears to vary on two parameters: the height of the front vowel, and whether the preceding vowel is also a front vowel. The effect of the first of these factors is that the higher the front vowel the greater the degree of palatalization. Thus a velar consonant before /i/ will tend to palatalize to a greater degree than before /e/. So, for example, the initial consonants in /ŋinoi/ 'stir', /ɣilai/ 'until', and /kilo/ 'finger, toe' are produced with the tongue fronted to a greater degree than the initial consonant in /ŋehe/ 'umbrella', /ɣeɾi/ 'beside', and /keli/ 'be good'.

The second parameter means that a velar consonant that follows as well as precedes a front vowel will palatalize to a greater degree than one that follows a non-front vowel. So, a velar consonant occurring between two front vowels will be palatalized to a greater degree than one that only precedes a front vowel. So, for example, the second /ŋ̊/ in /ŋ̊eŋ̊e/ 'be separate' is more strongly palatalized than the first, as is the second /k/ in /kekeli/ 'be pleased'.

2.1.1.3.3 Glottal epenthesis

There is no phonemic glottal stop in Kokota. However, glottal epenthesis occurs in careful speech in a number of environments.

When carefully or emphatically producing words that commence with a vowel, voiced plosive, or rhotic tap, some speakers initiate production with glottal closure. When reading a wordlist, for example, these speakers will produce ohai 'be tame' as [ʔohai], biɾo 'sleep' as [ʔbiɾo], and ɾeha 'shout' as [ʔɾeha].

In casual speech glottal epenthesis may occur intervocalically at a word or morpheme boundary, or in some circumstances morpheme-internally. Thus /eu a lao/ 'thus we go' may be realized as [eu ʔa lao], and /na ohadi/ 'I feed them' as [na ʔohadi]. This occurs frequently between a preposed particle and a vowel-initial root, for example between the causative particle /fa/ and a vowel-initial verb. Thus /fa aui/ 'cause it to be present' may be realized as [fa ʔaui], and /fa ikoai/ 'make it small' as [fa ʔikoai]. Glottal epenthesis often occurs between a prefix, proclitic or reduplicated syllable and vowel-initial roots. Thus /i+ipi/ 'be wearing clothes' (from /ipi/ 'wear [clothes]') is often realized as [iʔipi].

While intervocalic glottal epenthesis typically involves at least a morpheme boundary, it may occur between morpheme internal vowels in a syllable sequence where the second vowel is stressed. This is shown dramatically when a cliticized tag clause affects the stress so that an otherwise unstressed second vowel in a sequence becomes stressed. For example, in isolation the personal name /fáknoe/ has the stress pattern shown. However, once the tag clause /nekeu/ is cliticized, giving the sequence /faknoenekeu/ '...Faknoe, it was like that', primary stress shifts to the final vowel of the name. Glottal epenthesis may then intervene in the final vowel sequence of the name: [fàknoʔénekju].

In careful speech glottal epenthesis also occasionally occurs following a vowel when the following syllable is stressed and has an initial non-continuant (i.e., either a plosive or a nasal). Again, this typically occurs across a word or morpheme boundary, with /fa+tóli/ 'cause to be open' occasionally realized as [faʔtóli] and /ga kózei/ 'I/we sing it' as [gaʔ kózei]. Again, it also occasionally occurs morpheme-internally, but only in very careful or emphatic speech, /nakóni/ 'person', for example, occasionally realized as [naʔkóni].

2.1.1.3.4 Glides

There are no glide phonemes in Kokota. The glides [w] and [j] occur phonetically as allophones of non-low vowels (see §2.1.2.4.3). A small number of Pijin loans occur with an initial [w], including [wasi] 'wash', [wiki] 'week', [wokobaoti] 'stroll about' and possibly [wida] 'window'. Of these [wasi] has almost certainly been borrowed as an underlying /uasi/, with regular glide formation occurring on the initial segment. The extent to which this is true of the other examples is unclear. If underlying glide initial they may reflect code switching to Pijin, though this seems unlikely since [wiki] in particular occurs with high frequency. Alternatively these forms may reflect the development through borrowing of /w/ as a phoneme in Kokota, although if so this nascent phoneme is still highly marginal, occurring only in the examples cited.

2.1.2 Vowels

2.1.2.1 Vowel phoneme inventory

The vowel inventory displays the widespread Oceanic five vowel system:

TABLE 2.7. VOWEL PHONEMES

	front	central	back
high	i		u
mid	e		o
low		a	

These are primary vowels, with non-back vowels unrounded, slight rounding on the mid back vowel, and maximal rounding on the high back vowel. The system presents triangular maximal differentiation between the high and low vowels, with the mid vowels equidistant between these three points. The high vowels /i/ and /u/ are produced slightly lower than the cardinal vowels 1 and 8 (and slightly lower than their English counterparts). Within that there is a certain amount of height variation, with a further lowering of /i/ and /u/ occurring regularly in word-final position and occasionally elsewhere.

No phonemic length distinctions exist in Kokota. While it is possible to find pairs distinguished by vowel length, this represents a distinction between the presence of a single vowel and the presence of a VV sequence in which the two vowels happen to be identical, not between a short and a long vowel. Thus /ipi/ 'wear' reduplicates to form /iipi/ 'be wearing clothes'. The distinction is between a single occurrence of /i/ and a VV sequence. This is demonstrated by the fact that an optional epenthetic glottal stop may occur between the segments, giving the surface forms [iʔipi] (see §2.1.1.3.3).

Phonetic length variation does, however, occur with all vowels, with unstressed non-word-final vowels typically reducing in length. Stressed and word-final vowels may also reduce in length to a lesser degree.

2.1.2.2 Evidence for phoneme status: vowels

The following sets demonstrate the contrastive status of the vowels. Set (2.6)a. demonstrates the contrast between all vowels except /o/; (2.6)b. contrasts /o/ with /a/ and /e/; and (2.6)c.–d. contrasts /o/ with /u/ and /i/:

(2.6)   a.   /toɾu/ 'sea slug'   /toɾi/ 'open (tr)'   /toɾa/ 'open (itr)'   /toɾe/ 'ask'
         b.   /aɾa/ 'I, me'   /aɾe/ 'those (nearby)'   /aɾo/ 'these (touching)'
         c.   /hoɾe/ 'canoe'   /huɾe/ 'carry on shoulder'
         d.   /nodo/ 'stop'   /nodi/ 'their'

2.1.2.3 Vowel phoneme frequencies

The relative frequencies of vowel phonemes was calculated on the basis of the wordlist referred to in §2.1.1.1.2. The list contains a total of 797 vowel phoneme tokens. The relative frequencies of each are:

TABLE 2.8. VOWEL PHONEME FREQUENCIES

i	e	a	o	u	Total
15.3%	13.3%	35.4%	18.6%	17.4%	100%
(122)	(106)	(282)	(148)	(139)	(797)

Once the phonemes are grouped by features, either by height or on the front-back parameter, the figures are remarkably even.

TABLE 2.9. RELATIVE FREQUENCIES BY HEIGHT

[+high] (/i/ and /u/)	[-high, -low] (/e/ and /o/)	[+low] (/a/)	Total
32.7% (261)	31.9% (254)	35.4% (282)	100%
			(797)

TABLE 2.10. RELATIVE FREQUENCIES ON THE FRONT-BACK PARAMETER

[+front] (/i/ and /e/)	[-front, -back] (/a/)	[+back] (/u/ and /o/)	Total
28.6% (228)	35.4% (282)	36.0% (287)	100%
			(797)

2.1.2.4 Phonological processes involving vowels

Widespread vowel syncope occurs in Kokota. This is discussed in §2.6. Phonetic variation in vowel length and height is discussed in §2.1.2.1.

Other processes involving vowels include glide formation, and vowel devoicing. In addition, certain VV sequences are eligible for a process of diphthong formation, while in casual speech diphthongs are reduced to a single segment.

2.1.2.4.1 Diphthong formation

Kokota has no phonemic diphthongs. This is demonstrated by speaker syllabifications, in which every vowel in a sequence is syllabified separately. However, in normal speech certain non-identical VV sequences regularly undergo a process of diphthong formation. In this process the two vowels combine to form the nucleus of a single syllable, creating a heavy syllable with the structure shown in (2.18)b., but reducing overall syllable number.

2.1.2.4.1.1 Eligible sequences

A crucial criterion in the eligibility of a VV sequence to undergo diphthong formation is relative height: the second vowel in the sequence must be higher than the first. Sequences of vowels involving no increase in height are ineligible for diphthong formation. Thus /hohoa/ 'yawn', /sarie/ 'nut sp.', /beata/ 'be calm (of sea)', and /tegeo/ 'thank' are trisyllabic.

A further criterion involves movement on the front-back parameter: VV sequences involving tongue movement from front to back or back to front are ineligible. Consequently the sequences /iu/, /ui/, /eo/, /oe/, /eu/, and /oi/ are ineligible. Only sequences of front vowels, sequences of back vowels, or sequences with /a/ as the first vowel are eligible.

Diphthong formation occurs with a sequence of the low vowel /a/ plus any other vowel. Thus /hae/ 'where', /mai/ 'come', /lao/ 'go', /pau/ 'head' are all monosyllabic. It also occurs with a height-increasing sequence of vowels with the same status on the front/back parameter, with /hei/ 'who' and /dou/ 'be big' also monosyllabic. The vowel sequences that occur as diphthongs are thus /ae/, /ai/, /ao/, /au/, /ei/, and /ou/.

2.1.2.4.1.2 Diphthong frequencies

The possible diphthongs described above do not all occur with equal frequency. A total of 49 diphthongs occur in the sample wordlist. The distribution of possible diphthongs within that is:

TABLE 2.11. DIPHTHONG FREQUENCIES

ai	au	ae	ao	ei	ou	Total
16	14	9	6	3	1	49
(32.7%)	(28.6%)	(18.4%)	(12.2%)	(61%)	(2.0%)	(100%)

It is interesting that there is a very strong preference for maximal differentiation between the two vowels. The two that involve the least shared features (/ai/ and /au/)—where the height difference is the greatest and the vowels differ on the front/back parameter—account for over half (61.3%) of all diphthongs present in the list. Those where the height difference is less but there is a difference on the front/back parameter (/ae/, and /ao/) account for a smaller group (30.6%). Those where the height difference is less and there is no difference in front/back status (/ei/ and /ou/) (81%) account for the smallest group. It is also interesting to note that there is a slight preference for front V2s (57.2%).

However, while these frequency tendencies are significant, they do not necessarily correspond to occurrence in normal discourse. For example, while

/ou/ only occurs in one item in the wordlist, that item, /dou/ 'be big', is a very high use item, generating high-use of the diphthong. As a further example, an allomorph of the 3SG object enclitic is /=i/. Consequently the 3SG marked form of any verb with the final vowel /e/ has the /ei/ diphthong finally, giving a high use to this relatively low-frequency diphthong.

Overall, diphthongs occur relatively infrequently. Out of the 746 syllable nuclei present in the sample wordlist, 697 (93.4%) are monophthongs, while only 49 (6.6%) are diphthongs.

2.1.2.4.1.3 Restrictions on diphthong formation

Diphthong formation is not restricted by morpheme boundaries. Any eligible VV sequence may undergo diphthong formation, regardless of whether the vowels are adjacent in a single morpheme, or brought together by concatenation. Thus in (2.7)a. the presence of the 3SG object enclitic generates a VV sequence that is ineligible for diphthong formation and the resulting word is trisyllabic, but in (2.7)b., where diphthong formation may occur, the resulting word is disyllabic:

(2.7)   a.   /huzu=i/ 'push it'   →   [huzui]
         b.   /friŋe=i/ 'work it'   →   [friŋei]

Diphthong formation occurs in rapid speech across word boundaries. In (2.8) the final vowel of the first word in the sequence combines with the initial onsetless syllable vowel of the second word to generate a diphthong.

(2.8)   /nona uke ana/ 'that mother of his'   →   [nonaukeana]

2.1.2.4.2 Diphthong reduction

Two processes of diphthong reduction optionally occur in casual speech. In one the second vowel is deleted, in the other the two vowels in the sequence coalesce to form a single monophthong produced in a position intermediate between the positions of the two vowels in the original sequence. These processes are discussed in §2.6.8 and §2.6.9.

2.1.2.4.3 Glide formation

With certain constraints, non-low vowels are realized as glides in casual speech when they occur as the first vowel in a VV sequence that is not eligible for diphthong formation. The front vowels /e/ and /i/ are realized as the palatal glide [j], while the back vowels /o/ and /u/ are realized as the labial glide [w]. This may occur where the vowel is preceded by a single consonant. The result is a surface cluster (in which any consonant may be C3).

(2.9) a. /tegeo/ 'thank'   →   [tegjo]
       b. /ŋiaklo/ 'tree sp.'   →   [ŋjaklo]
       c. /ikoa/ 'be small'   →   [ikwa]
       d. /kuiti/ 'lie, deceive, trick'   →   [kwiti]

However, an absolute constraint exists in the language prohibiting onset clusters of more than two consonants. Consequently, where the first of the two relevant syllables already has an onset cluster, the process is blocked, as the glide would add a third consonant to the onset. Consequently, in the old form /baknoa/ 'be slow' glide formation from the /o/ is prevented, but in the new form of this lexeme, /bnakoa/, it is not:

(2.10) a. /baknoa/ 'be slow'   →   *[baknwa]
        b. /bnakoa/ 'be slow'   →   [bnakwa]

Just as glide formation may generate an onset cluster C2, it may also generate a single C onset where there is no preceding consonant. This may be because the VV sequence occurs word-initially, as in (2.11)a., or because a preceding vowel will be realized in a separate syllable.

(2.11) a. /iaɾo/ 'those (distant)'   →   [jaɾo]
        b. /ka=ia/ 'at the'   →   [kaja]
        c. /n-e-ke-u=o/ 'it was thus'   →   [nekewo]

The implication of the above environments for glide formation is that a non-low vowel will undergo glide formation if it can form an onset. The motivation for this is to reduce the prosodic complexity of the surface form, in terms of number of moras or syllables.

Glide formation is prevented where it would create a word consisting of a single light syllable, violating a word minimality constraint. So in isolation /kuo/ 'break' always occurs on the surface as a disyllable. Once the form is suffixed the risk to word minimality is removed and the process occurs.

(2.12) a. /kuo/ 'break'   →   *[kwo]
        b. /kuo=di/ 'break them' →   [kwodi]

This process applies to vowels that are adjacent morpheme-internally, as in (2.9), (2.10)b., (2.11)a., and (2.12)b., and to vowels that are adjacent as the result of affixation or cliticization, as in (2.11)b.–c. The process also occurs in rapid speech across word boundaries. In (2.13) the vowel of the object enclitic becomes a glide in the presence of the subsequent vowel-initial subject pronoun:

(2.13)   /ooeni ara/ 'I said it'   →   [ooenjara]

Where a non-low vowel occurs as the second vowel in a VV sequence that is eligible for diphthong formation it does not undergo glide formation, unless the opportunity exists for it to be realized as the onset of a subsequent vowel. Glide formation takes precedence over diphthong formation. So, for example, in /gauai/ 'be distant' the medial /u/ could potentially form a diphthong with the preceding /a/. However, it also potentially forms an onset for a syllable containing the following vowels (which do form a diphthong). It is the formation of the glide as an onset for a second syllable that occurs:

(2.14)   /gauai/ 'be distant'   →   [gawai]

The prosodic implications of glide formation are discussed in §2.6.10.

2.1.2.4.4 Interconsonantal vowel devoicing

Vowels assimilate to the voicing status of adjacent voiceless consonants when occurring between two identical voiceless consonants.

This typically occurs with the vowel of echo syllables, and may involve plosives or fricatives as the environment.

(2.15) a. /kikibolo / 'football'   →   [ki̥kibolo]
       b. /sasamala/ 'masturbate (of males)' →   [sḁsamala]
       c. /hahaglu/ 'broom'   →   [hḁhaglu]

This occurs regardless of whether the echo syllable reflects synchronic reduplication, as is the case with (2.15)c., or within a synchronically monomorphemic form, as in (2.15)a.–b. Indeed, (2.15)a. is a recent Pijin loan.

The process also occurs with vowels that are assigned secondary stress, as is the case with both (2.15)a. and b. It does not, however, appear to occur with vowels assigned primary stress.

It is not clear at this stage whether vowel devoicing occurs when the consonants that motivate the process are voiceless sonorants.

Vowel devoicing also appears to occur to a considerably lesser extent when the motivating consonants are not identical.

(2.16)   /sisikama / 'palm sp.'   →   [si̥si̥kama]

CHAPTER 2

2.2 Syllable structure

Kokota syllable structure allows an onset and a nucleus. Codas do not occur (other than in a small number of Pijin loans), so all syllables are open. Onsets may consist of a single consonant, or a cluster of two consonants in certain configurations, and syllables without onsets are permitted. Nuclei consist of a single vowel or a diphthong of certain VV sequences.

A number of phonological processes that occur in casual speech affect prosodic structure. These include vowel syncope, and the formation of glides and geminates. These processes often alter syllable structure, particularly with vowel syncope generating non-underlying consonant clusters and syllabic consonants, as well as surface codas. These effects are discussed in §2.6.

2.2.1 Onsets

Kokota permits syllables with no onset, and onset clusters of two consonants in certain configurations. However, an overwhelming majority of syllables have a single consonant onset. In a sample wordlist containing 746 syllables, 88% have a single consonant onset, 6% have no onset, and 6% have a cluster onset.[5]

2.2.1.1 Syllables with no onset

Syllables with no onset occur in only a small proportion of words. However, they occur with disproportionate frequency as a number of extremely high frequency words have an initial onsetless syllable, including the pronouns /ara/ '1SG' and /ayo/ '2SG', the locative /ade/ 'here', the articles /ia/ 'theSG' and /ira/ 'thePL', three of the four irrealis subject-indexing particles (/a/ 'first exclusive', /o/ 'second person', and /e/ 'third person'), and eight demonstratives (/ao/ 'this (holding)', /aro/ 'these (holding)', /ine/ 'this (nearby)', /ide/ 'these (nearby)', /ana/ 'that', /are/ 'those' and /iao/ 'that (distant)', /iaro/ 'those (distant)').

2.2.1.2 Onset clusters

Sequences of two consonants in Kokota form complex onsets. Speakers invariably syllabify medial CC sequences as cluster onsets, and not as coda plus onset sequences. Moreover, clusters freely occur in word-initial position,

---

[5] Only underlying clusters have been counted (casual speech surface clusters generated by vowel syncope or glide formation have not). However, underlying clusters in initial echo syllables are excluded as these never occur on the surface (see §2.4.1.2). The no-onset figures do not include vowels which undergo diphthong formation. Kokota has no phonemic diphthongs, all diphthongs being generated from underlying VV sequences. The no-onset figure represents vowels occurring on the surface as the nucleus of a syllable with no onset, but not those surfacing as the V2 of a diphthong nucleus.

eliminating the possibility that they represent a coda plus onset. Indeed, there appears to be a preference for word-initial over medial clusters.

2.2.1.2.1 Permissible onset clusters

In casual speech a number of configurations of consonant clusters occur. Most are not underlying, being generated by vowel syncope or glide formation. These surface clusters do not occur in careful speech, and are revealed as non-underlying by speaker syllabifications. However, certain other cluster onsets are underlying. These conform to the following broad constraints: C1 must be an obstruent, and C2 must be a voiced coronal sonorant.

Within this, the C1 constraints are more complex, with place class restrictions applying that differ for plosives and fricatives. With plosives only labials (/p/, /b/) and noncoronal nonlabials (/k/, /g/) occur as C1. With fricatives different constraints apply, with only labials (/f/, /v/) and coronals (/s/, /z/) occurring.

Further, not all combinations conforming to these constraints actually occur. Two of the plosives do not occur with a nasal C2, while the marginal nature of three of the fricative C1s means they do not occur with the full range of possible C2s:

TABLE 2.12. ATTESTED NON-LOAN ONSET CLUSTERS

	p	b	k	g	f	v	s	z
ɾ	pɾ	bɾ	kɾ	gɾ	fɾ	vɾ	?sɾ	zɾ
l	pl	bl	kl	gl	fl	-	-	-
n	-	bn	kn	-	fn	-	sn	zn

Although all clusters shown in Table 2.12 occur, there are clear tendencies among C1 and C2 segments. In the sample wordlist discussed above a total of 44 cluster onsets occur. Of these, 30% have /g/ as C1 and 30% have /f/. Of the rest, 16% of C1s are /k/; 11% are /p/; 11% /b/; and 2% /v/. (C1 /s/ and /z/ do not occur in the list.) Similarly strong tendencies occur with C2, with 57% of the clusters in the wordlist having /ɾ/ as C2; 32% having /l/; and 11% /n/.

As these figures show, clusters with fricative C1s other than /f/ are marginal. C1 /s/ is only attested with /n/ as C2. This occurs in four attested lexical items: the high use /snakɾe/ 'allow' and /sasna/ 'be willing', and low use /snekɾi/ 'tear fingernail, earlobe, etc.' and /nasnuɾi/ 'sea urchin sp.'. Interestingly, /s/ is the only C1 not clearly attested with /ɾ/ as C2. However, some evidence suggests that it is a possible cluster. The verb /tasuɾu/ (meaning unclear) normally occurs on the surface in casual speech as [tasɾu] through regular vowel syncope. However, for at least some younger speakers the underlying form is the disyllable, with the second syllable onset cluster /sɾ/. This may be an established but marginal cluster not yet attested. Given that /r/ occurs with all other possible C1s this seems likely. Alternatively the age variation may be evidence of a change underway in the language allowing this cluster.

The C1 /z/ is attested with both /r/ and /n/ as C2, but in only one low use item each: /zniri/ 'be tangled' and /zozozro/ 'be pouring with water'. The voiced labial fricative /v/ is only attested with /r/ as C2, and only in two relatively low use items: /vraha/ 'tree sp.' and /vivivri/ 'propeller'. It is not clear whether the unattested clusters represented by gaps in Table 2.12 do not occur, or are possible but occur in so few lexical items they have not been attested.

2.2.1.2.2 Word-level onset tendencies

In many Austronesian languages that allow consonant sequences, these only occur word-medially. This is because they do not represent onset clusters, but coda plus onset sequences. As discussed above, this is not the situation in Kokota syllable structure. Consequently there is no tendency for Kokota CC sequences to occur medially. Indeed, Kokota appears to display a crosslinguistically unusual preference for word-initial clusters over medial. This preference is evident in a diachronic shift underway in the language in which the C2 of a second syllable cluster is transferred to the initial syllable onset. Thus, in certain lexical items younger speakers have an initial cluster, while older speakers either use a medial cluster, or at least regard the medial cluster as correct Kokota and the initial cluster form as incorrect:

(2.17) a. /bakru/ → /braku/ 'liquid'
     b. /baknoa/ → /bnakoa/ 'be slow'
     c. /faklano/ → /flakano/ 'rock outcrop on beach'

It is unclear whether similarities across C1s in these examples are significant.

2.2.1.2.3 Violations of cluster constraints in loan words

A number of marginal violations of the cluster constraints outlined above occur in loan words.

2.2.1.2.3.1 A coronal C1

One cluster, /tr/, violates the constraint on coronal plosive C1s. This cluster is attested in only one item, the Pijin loan /triki/ 'lie, deceive, trick'. It is apparent that the cluster is underlying in this item for at least some speakers, as these speakers syllabify the item as a disyllable with the initial cluster.

2.2.1.2.3.2 Obstruent plus obstruent clusters

Apparently underlying obstruent plus obstruent consonant clusters are attested in four items, all Pijin or English loans. In two of these instances the cluster is initial. Both involve /s/ plus a voiceless plosive: /spika/ 'Speaker'[6] and /stiŋibili/ 'beetle sp.'[7]. That such exceptions should involve the C1 /s/ is not surprising, given its crosslinguistically common extrametrical status.

More problematic are the two attested medial obstruent plus obstruent clusters. One, /kastom/, again involves a C1 /s/. However, there is considerable variability in whether the CC sequence is treated as an onset cluster, or the /s/ is treated as a coda of the preceding syllable (in which case there is a CC sequence but no cluster). An elderly speaker consistently syllabified this word as /ka-sto-mu/, preferring an obstruent plus obstruent cluster and epenthetic final vowel to any codas. All younger speakers tested, however, displayed considerable variability, giving both the coda syllabification /kas-tom/ and the onset cluster syllabification /ka-stom/ on the same occasion. A similar situation pertained with /dokta/. An older speaker syllabified this as /do-ki-ta/, resisting both a coda and a /kt/ cluster (despite the fact that he produces the item in casual speech without the epenthetic vowel as [dokta]). Younger speakers, however, again gave the varying syllabifications /dok-ta/ and /do-kta/. For both items there is confusion among speakers as to whether to permit a normally unacceptable obstruent plus obstruent cluster, or a normally unacceptable coda.

The same confusion appears to apply to a further item, /kaspotu/ 'clam sp.'. However, the existence of this CC sequence and its consequent prosodic dilemma seems bizarre, given that it is a loan from neighboring Zabana, which does not permit clusters. The Zabana form is /kasipotu/. In Kokota older speakers seem to have that as the underlying form, though one older speaker (who regards the word as Zabana, not Kokota) syllabified it variably as /ka-si-po-tu/ and /kas-po-tu/. Younger speakers, however, regard the word as Kokota, and have the underlying form /kaspotu/ (rejecting /kasipotu/ and syllabifying the form as a trisyllable). These speakers display the same syllabification variability on this item as with /dokta/ and /kastom/, giving the syllabifications /ka-spo-tu/ and /kas-po-tu/. On the basis of regular Kokota stress assignment and vowel syncope, an underlying form /kasipotu/ would give the surface form [kaspotu] in casual speech. What seems inexplicable is that the synchronic syncope should become diachronic vowel loss, when this creates an unacceptable CC sequence in the new underlying form.

---

[6] This apparently odd loan is a relatively high frequency item in Goveo village, often used to refer to the former Speaker of the Provincial Assembly, a resident of Goveo.

[7] Presumably from 'stink beetle'.

2.2.1.2.4 Absence of /h/ and voiceless sonorants in clusters

Two facts of Kokota phonology are suggestive when taken together. First, only voiced sonorants occur in C2 position; their voiceless counterparts do not. Second, while all noncoronal plosives occur as C1, only labial noncoronal fricatives occur as C1. Nonlabial noncoronals (i.e., /h/ and /ɣ/) do not. These facts allow the hypothesis that Kokota voiceless sonorants are not phonemes but the synchronic surface coalescence of /h/ and an adjacent voiced sonorant, as is the case in some other Oceanic languages (e.g., Lenakel [Lynch 1974, 1978]).

Palmer (1999b) presents four facts as evidence against this hypothesis. Speaker judgements suggest the surface segments realize identical underlying forms. In reduplication voiceless sonorants they do not display C2 deletion (see §2.4.1.2) and therefore behave like underlying segments, not clusters. Historical evidence indicates that underlying clusters necessary to generate surface coalesced segments could not have been generated diachronically by the processes which gave rise to other underlying clusters. The constraint on noncoronal cluster C2s could not apply to clusters underlying surface voiceless sonorants. Palmer (1999b) concludes that while Kokota voiceless sonorants arose historically through diachronic coalescence, synchronically they are underlying phonemes.[8]

2.2.2 Nuclei

Kokota allows a maximum of two moras per syllable. In light syllables the nucleus consists of a single vowel (i.e., monophthong). In heavy syllables the nucleus consists of a diphthong, except for a very small number of recent loans where a coda is present and the nucleus consists of a single vowel. No forms occur with a coda following a diphthong. These, therefore, do not violate the maximal bimoraic syllable constraint. The possible syllable structures are thus:

(2.18) a. ((C)C) V   b. ((C)C) VV   c. ((C)C) VC

Structure (2.18)c. is extremely marginal. Otherwise, monophthong nuclei ([2.18]a.) occur far more frequently than diphthong nuclei, representing 93% of 746 syllables in a sample wordlist, as opposed to only 7% with a diphthong.

---

[8] Several errors crept into Palmer (1999b) after proofing: 1) Part of the final paragraph on p.77 has been lost. That paragraph should read: "Within the three broad classes, the place variation apparent in Table 1 lies with the labiodental fricatives and the glottal /h/. In addition the voiced post-alveolar fricative is palatalized medially under the influence of a following high front vowel, while its voiceless counterpart is not." 2) One member of the minimal pair in (2.2)c. is incorrect and should read [naŋo]. 3) Table 3 contains errors, most importantly *v* appearing instead of the intended *n*. The table should be identical to Table 2.12 above.

2.2.3 Codas

Apparently underlying codas occur only in a very small number of recent loans, primarily from Solomons Pijin. Some are word-final, and thus unequivocal codas, as in /kastom/. In careful speech older speakers often insert an epenthetic final vowel, giving surface forms such as [kastomu] (see §2.2.1.2.3). However, for younger speakers the form is always realized with the final coda. In other instances the possible coda is medial, in which case there is considerable variation. In examples like /kastom/ the first consonant in the medial CC sequence could potentially be a first syllable coda, or the C1 of a second syllable onset cluster. As discussed in §2.2.1.2.3, speakers typically exhibit considerable variation in this situation, with individual speakers giving both syllabifications /ka-stom/ and /kas-tom/, sometimes in a single elicitation.

Apart from in loans, codas occur only as a result of vowel syncope widespread in casual speech (see §2.6). This syncope brings together two consonants that are not adjacent underlyingly. This occurs morpheme-internally, and across morpheme boundaries and even word boundaries.

(2.19) a. /banesokeo/ 'a place name' → [bansokeo]
b. /mane dou/ 'big man' → [man dou]

Syncope of this kind generates codas in which the first of the consonants, which would otherwise be syllabified as an onset, attracts the mora associated with the syncopated vowel. It is then syllabified with the vowel of the preceding syllable to form a new, heavy syllable. So in (2.19)a. the surface form has four syllables rather than five, the first of which has a coda. In (2.19)b. the first word is realized as a monosyllable with a coda.

2.3 Word minimality

A word may consist of a single syllable. This may be a bimoraic heavy syllable with a diphthong nucleus (e.g., /mai/ 'come', /dou/ 'be big', /ao/ 'this [touching]'). A number of roots such as /su/ 'breast', /do/ 'mosquito', and /fro/ 'squeeze' are underlyingly monomoraic (i.e., the nucleus consists of a single short vowel [see §2.5]). However, stress cannot be assigned to a monomoraic form (see §2.5), so a stress-bearing word may not consist of a single light syllable. Monomoraic roots are therefore lengthened to create a heavy syllable, allowing stress assignment. Underlyingly monomoraic grammatical particles are typically not assigned stress, in which case they remain unlengthened.

The minimal Kokota word is therefore a single syllable, and the minimal stress-bearing word a single heavy syllable.

2.4 Reduplication

Kokota displays considerable evidence of historical partial reduplication and some examples of historical full reduplication of disyllabic roots. Only partial reduplication appears to occur synchronically. This section deals primarily with the formal characteristics of reduplication. The functions of reduplication are discussed briefly here, but in more detail in relevant chapters (nominal derivation in Chapter 3, verbal derivation in Chapter 6, etc.).

2.4.1 Partial reduplication

2.4.1.1 Function of partial reduplication

Derivational reduplication involving an initial echo syllable occurs extensively in Kokota. The extent to which it is productive is not entirely clear. It has a general derivation function, the nature of the derivation varying widely. Some reduplicative derivations involve change of word class. In some instances a verb is derived from a noun.

(2.20) a. /fiolo/ 'penis'   →   /fi~fiolo/ 'masturbate (of males)'
     b. /piha/ 'small parcel'   →   /pi~piha/ 'make a *piha* parcel'
     c. /puki/ 'round lump of s.th.' → /pu~puki/ 'be round'

Much more commonly, however, word class altering derivation involves the derivation of nouns from verbs, either transitive or intransitive.

(2.21) a. /siko/ 'steal'   → /si~siko/ 'thief'
     b. /lase/ 'know'   → /la~lase/ 'knowledge, cleverness'
     c. /maku/ 'be hard'   → /ma~maku/ 'leatherjacket (fish w. tough skin)'
     d. /gufu/ 'smoke s.th.' → /gu~gufu/ 's.th. for smoking (i.e., tobacco)'
     e. /kamo/ 'go across' → /ka~kamo/ 'burning stick for transferring fire'

In many instances reduplication derives a new lexeme from a root without any change of word class. Often there is little semantic predictability in the meaning of the new form. Noun-from-noun derivations include:

(2.22) a. /baɣi/ 'wing'   → /ba~baɣi/ 'side roof of porch'
     b. /buli̯/ 'cowrie'   → /bu~buli̯/ 'clam sp.'
     c. /tahi/ 'sea'   → /ta~tahi/ 'stingray'
     d. /protu/ 'distant object' → /po~protu/ 'small lump on body'

Some verb-from-verb derivations display similar semantic unpredictability:

(2.23) a. /ŋ̊au/ 'eat' → /ŋ̊a~ŋ̊au/ 'be biting (of fish)'
     b. /pɾosa/ 'slap self w. flipper (turtles)' → /po~pɾosa/ 'wash clothes'
     c. /maɾi/ 'be in pain' → /ma~maɾa/ 'be in labor'
     d. /vahe/ 'carve' → /va~vahe/ 'operate surgically'

Some verb-from-verb derivations show more predictable semantic relationship, with the derived form coding a habitual, ongoing, or diminutive event:

(2.24) a. /m̥aɣu/ 'be afraid' → /m̥a~m̥aɣu/ 'be habitually fearful'
     b. /safɾa/ 'miss' → /sa~safɾa/ 'always miss'
     c. /seha/ 'climb' → /se~seha/ 'climb all about'
     d. /fogɾa/ 'be sick' → /fo~fogɾa/ 'be a little bit sick'

However, a substantial subregularity involves the reduplication of transitive verb roots. In some instances the derived form is an unaccusative stative verb.

(2.25) a. /lage/ 'castrate' → /la~lage/ 'be castrated'
     b. /sito/ 'make hot' → /si~sito/ 'be hot to the touch'
     c. /hoti/ 'sting (tr)' → /ho~hoti/ 'be very sore and tender'

Usually, however, the derived verb is unergative. This appears to be productive to the extent that unless the reduplicated form of a transitive verb has some unpredictable (and hence lexically specified) meaning, it will be an unergative version of the root.

(2.26) a. /piɾi/ 'tie' → /pi~piɾi/ 'be tying'
     b. /kɾisu/ 'scoop liquid' → /ki~kɾisu/ 'be scooping liquid'
     c. /sofo/ 'grab' → /so~sofo/ 'be grabbing'
     d. /taho/ 'count' → /ta~taho/ 'be counting'

In some instances the reduplicated form of a root can have more than one of the possible derived meanings. For example, a number of transitive verb roots reduplicate to derive both an unergative verb and a noun.

(2.27) a. /tuɾi/ 'tell s.th.' → /tu~tuɾi/ 'chat; a story'
     b. /ɣato/ 'think (tr)' → /ɣa~ɣato/ 'think (itr); thoughts'
     c. /keɾe/ 'sting (tr)' → /ke~keɾe/ 'sting (itr); thorns'

2.4.1.2 Formal characteristics of partial reduplication

Partial reduplication involves the presence of an initial echo syllable that is underlyingly identical to the initial syllable of the root. As syllables are open in

Kokota, the effect is initial onset and nucleus reduplication. As indicated in §2.2, most Kokota syllables have a single consonant onset. Reduplication of roots with such an initial syllable formally involves reduplication of the initial CV. This generates all but three of the examples given in §2.4.1.1. However, reduplication also occurs with some roots that have an initial onsetless syllable. In the absence of an onset only the nucleus is reduplicated.[9]

(2.28)   /ipi/ 'wear (clothes)' → /i~ipi/ 'be wearing clothes'

Reduplication also occurs with roots with a first syllable onset cluster. Here the echo syllable underlyingly also has the cluster onset. However, on the surface only the initial consonant of the cluster is realized, exemplified by (2.22)d., (2.23)b., and (2.26)b. Once the entire first syllable is reduplicated, a process of reduplicated syllable cluster reduction deletes onset C2 of the echo syllable.

(2.29) a. /protu/ → /pro~protu/ → [poprotu]

     b. /prosa/ → /pro~prosa/ → [poprosa]

     c. /krisu/ → /kri~krisu/ → [kikrisu]

On the surface, even in normal careful speech, the C2 is never realized. However, it is present underlyingly. In syllabifications, speakers invariably give the echo syllable the same form as the entire first syllable of the root. In evaluating emphasized tested forms, speakers invariably judge forms with the C2 realized as correct while those with it unrealized as unacceptable, then may immediately give the unrealized C2 form in elicitation. It is apparent that speakers are unaware of, and do not 'hear', the C2 surface deletion. Similarly, where the first syllable consists of a diphthong, only the first vowel of the VV sequence is realized on the surface.

(2.30) a. /toi/ 'cook'   →   /to~toi/ 'fire'

     b. /saeko/ 'mango' → /sa~saeko/ 'liver'

     c. /ŋau/ 'eat'   → /ŋa~ŋau/ 'be biting (of fish)'

2.4.1.3 Non-synchronic echo syllables

A substantial number of lexemes have identical first and second syllables, indicating historical partial reduplication, but with no corresponding root in synchronic Kokota. Thus, for example, /mimido/ 'penis', /mamara/ 'be deep', and /rereɣi/ 'look after' are synchronically monomorphemic, there being no corresponding forms */mido/, */mara/, and *reɣi/.

---

[9] Unlike some related languages. In Simbo (New Georgia) in the absence of an initial syllable onset the second syllable onset reduplicates, so /opere/ 'spear' gives /opopere/ 'one who spears', perhaps suggesting reduplicative infixation in Simbo.

This historical reduplication was formally identical to the synchronic regime described above. Onsetless echo syllables occur (/ooe/ 'say, talk; word, language', with no synchronic */oe/), as does cluster reduction:

(2.31) a. */blata/   →   /blablata/   →   [bablata] 'bat sp.'
      b. */pɾeku/   →   /pɾepɾeku/   →   [pepɾeku] 'lip'

As with synchronic reduplicative cluster reduction, speakers have the full cluster in the underlying form of the echo syllable, with deletion occurring on the surface. As with synchronic reduplication, non-synchronic echo syllables also display loss of the second vowel in a VV sequence.

(2.32) a. */daegɾa/   →   /dadaegɾa/ 'shake with surprise'
      b. */kau/   →   /kakau/ 'crab'

2.4.2 Full reduplication

A small number of quadrisyllabic roots reflect historical full reduplication of a disyllabic root. Of thirteen attested examples of echo disyllables, two may be onomatopoeic and therefore not reflect reduplication[10]. Of the remaining 11, six have no corresponding synchronic unreduplicated form: /kilekile/ 'k.o. custom axe' but no */kile/, /kulikuli/ 'seaweed sp.' but no */kuli/, /bulobulo/ 'tree sp.'[11] but no */bulo/, /maramaɾa/ 'lagoon'[12] but no */maɾa/, /ɣiliɣili/ 'tickle' but no */ɣili/, and /fa ɣonoɣono/ 'be ready' but no */ɣono/.

The remaining 5 lexemes have semantically related unreduplicated counterparts. For four, the relationship is idiosyncratic:

(2.33) a. /seku/ 'tail'   →   /seku~seku/ 'black trevally'
      b. /ɣano/ 'smell/taste good'   →   /fa ɣano~ɣano/ 'be very good'
      c. /mane/ 'man, male'   →   /fa mane~mane/ 'be dressed up (man or woman)'
      d. /ɣase/ 'girl, female'   →   /fa ɣase~ɣase/ 'be dressed up to show off (woman only)'

One example conforms to the two subregular uses of partial reduplication: deriving unergative verbs from transitive roots, and nouns from verbs:

(2.34)   /izu/ 'read s.th.'   →   /izu~izu/ 'be reading; a reading'

---

[10] /ɲireɲire/ 'cicada'; /ŋuruŋuru/ 'make k.o. sound' (water over rocks, wake of a boat)'.

[11] Possibly cognate with /bubulo/ 'morning ground mist' and /buloma/ 'inedible betel sp.'

[12] Possibly reflecting the same now lost root as /mamaɾa/ 'be deep', /maɾakasa/ 'rainbow runner (fish)', /maɾava/ 'bluefin trevally', and /maɾafa/ 'crayfish sp.'.

Despite that one apparent subregularity, there do not seem to be any grounds for claiming synchronic full reduplication. The instances of fully reduplicated lexemes with corresponding unreduplicated forms are so few as to warrant regarding them as marginal. Of those five, three ([2.33]b., c., and d.) also display further derivational complexity with the particle /fa/ (with no corresponding */manemane/, */ɣaseɣase/, or */ɣanoɣano/). Even the apparently subregular (2.34) does not appear to suggest a synchronic process, as there is no reason why full reduplication should occur rather than the usual partial reduplication. While the vowel-initial nature of the root could suggest a motivation, it is not seen in other similar examples (such as /i~ipi/ 'be wearing clothes', from /ipi/ 'wear s.th.'; and the historical /ooe/ 'say, talk; word, language').

2.5 Stress

Stress in Kokota is characterized by considerable variation. Some words with a particular segmental structure may be assigned stress on one pattern, while others with the same structure may be assigned stress on another pattern. A single lexeme may be assigned stress on one pattern by some speakers, and on another by others. This variation occurs even to the extent that a single lexeme may be assigned stress variably by a single speaker.

There are, however, patterns to this variation. The variation results from three factors: irregular stress patterning on some lexemes resulting from the prosodic shadow of lost morphological complexity; the gradual regularization of these irregularities; and an overall shift in the language's stress regime from moraic trochees to syllabic trochees.

2.5.1 Metrical stress and moraic theory

The following discussion is couched in the framework of metrical theory (Hayes 1995:26-31) and moraic theory (Hayes 1995:48-54). This approach most adequately accounts for stress assignment in Kokota.

In this approach, stress may count syllables or moras (units of weight). In syllabic stress, syllables are assigned to feet comprised of two syllables each. In moraic stress, each vowel and coda consonant counts as one mora (onsets don't count), and moras are assigned to feet comprised of two moras each. Light syllables have a single mora, while heavy syllables have two or more. As Kokota has no codas, only vowels count as moras; light syllables have a single V nucleus (i.e., CV), heavy syllables have a diphthong nucleus (i.e., CVV).

Feet may be aligned with the left margin of the prosodic word, or with the right margin, meaning syllables or moras may be assigned to feet starting from the beginning of the word and working from left to right, or working back from the end of the word from right to left. In Kokota feet are left-aligned.

Crosslinguistically, three foot types exist: moraic trochees, syllabic trochees, and iambs. With moraic and syllabic trochees stress is asigned to the leftmost of each pair of syllables or moras in each foot. In an iambic foot stress is assigned to the righthand mora in each foot. Feet in Kokota are trochaic. Whether stress is syllabic or moraic is discussed below. In each prosodic word one foot carries primary stress while the other feet carry secondary stress. In some languages the foot carrying primary stress (called the head foot) is the leftmost foot in the word, while in others it is the rightmost. In Kokota the right foot is the head foot.

2.5.2 Foot structure and alignment

Regular Kokota stress assignment is trochaic; feet are aligned with the left margin of the word; and the rightmost foot is head foot.

Feet are aligned with the left margin of the word. Stress is then assigned to the trochee, or leftmost syllable or mora in each foot.[13] This means stress is assigned to the first syllable or mora of each word, then to every odd syllable or mora after that. In words with two light (i.e., CV) syllables, both are assigned to a single foot, and the leftmost syllable or mora is stressed:

(2.35)

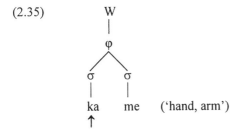

In words with three syllables/moras the first and second syllable or mora are assigned to a foot, and stress is assigned to the leftmost. The third syllable or mora is left over: it can't form a foot on it's own, so it is not assigned to a foot, and is not stressed:

(2.36)

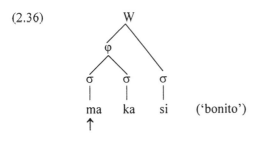

---

[13] As the language is undergoing a shift from moraic trochees to syllabic trochees, for the purposes of this section 'trochee' refers to both trochaic syllables and trochaic moras.

In roots with four syllables/moras the first and second syllable or mora are assigned to one foot. The third and fourth syllable or mora are then assigned to further foot. Stress is assigned to the leftmost syllable or mora in each foot. As the rightmost foot is the head foot, primary stress is assigned to the trochee of that foot, while secondary stress is assigned to other trochee of the other foot. This means that in words with four syllables/moras the first carries secondary stress and the third carries primary stress:

(2.37)

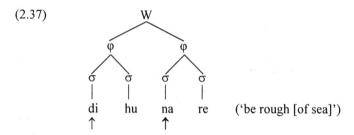

di hu na re   ('be rough [of sea]')

Roots with five syllables or moras are assigned stress in the same way as those with four syllables or moras, except that, as with three syllable/mora roots, the final syllable or mora is left over and does not participate in stress assignment:

(2.38)

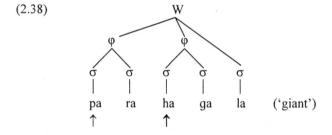

pa ra ha ga la   ('giant')

2.5.3 Moraic and syllabic stress variation

Kokota is currently undergoing a shift in its stress assignment regime from moraic trochees to syllabic trochees. This is not evident in words with only light syllables, as each syllable consists of just one mora. In most words with heavy syllables, however, the distinction results in differing stress patterns. Considerable variation exists in Kokota in this regard. Some roots with one or more heavy syllable are assigned stress on the basis of moraic trochees, and others on the basis of syllabic trochees. The majority of such roots, however, are assigned stress variably, with a strong age distinction apparent: older speakers tend to assign stress on the basis of moraic trochees, while younger speakers tend to assign on the basis of syllabic trochees. This is not apparent in words consisting of one heavy syllable followed by one light syllable (CVV.CV), as the result is the same whether the trochees are moraic ([2.39]a.) or syllabic ([2.39]b.):

(2.39) a. 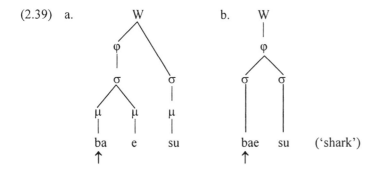 b.

bae su ('shark')

Words with the reverse structure, a light syllable followed by a heavy syllable (CV.CVV), however, display considerable variation. Here the alignment of feet with the left margin of the word creates problems in a moraic system: if the first and second moras are assigned to a left-aligned foot in a word with a heavy second syllable, a foot boundary occurs between the two moras of the heavy syllable, splitting the syllable. This is an impossible structure as the rules of foot construction may not split syllables (Hayes 1995:50). In this situation moraic feet must therefore be aligned with the leftmost *possible* pair of moras without splitting a syllable. To do so, stress assignment skips the first mora in CV.CVV words, and assigns the second and third mora (the heavy syllable) to the foot. Stress is then assigned to the second mora of the word, being the leftmost mora of the heavy syllable. This is the pattern displayed by older speakers in variably stressed words such as in (2.40)b.

However, with syllabic trochees no such problem exists. Syllables are assigned to feet with no reference to weight, so a word with two syllables will count a single complete foot, regardless of how many moras are present in each syllable. Stress is then assigned to the trochee, being the first syllable. This is the pattern displayed by younger speakers in variably stressed words ([2.40]a.):

(2.40) a. 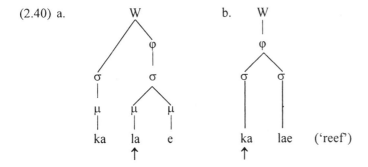 b.

ka lae ('reef')

In a representative sample of 21 historically monomorphemic roots consisting of one light followed by one heavy syllable, 2 are assigned stress on the light first syllable, 2 are assigned stress on the heavy second syllable, and the remaining 17 are assigned stress variably, with older speakers assigning stress to the heavy second syllable (as in [2.40]a.), and younger speakers assigning stress to the light first syllable (as in [2.40]b.).

The high proportion of CV.CVV words that are assigned stress variably suggests that the language is in mid change. The age distribution suggests that the preexisting stress assignment regime involved moraic trochees, now in the process of being replaced by the syllabic trochee as the preferred foot type.

A similar pattern occurs with other word types with heavy syllables. In words with two heavy syllables, older speakers assign the two moras in the first syllable to a foot, then the two moras of the second syllable to a further foot, giving two complete feet. The trochee of both feet is stressed, giving secondary stress to the first syllable and primary stress to the second syllable ([2.41]a.). Younger speakers assign the two syllables of the word to a single foot, stressing the trochee, giving stress only on the first syllable ([2.41]b.). The word in (2.41) is the only word with this structure in the data and it shows the described variation:

(2.41)

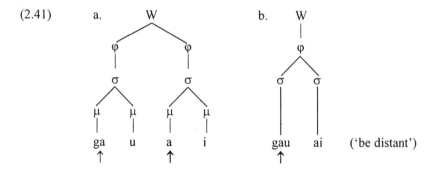

In a representative sample of five monomorphemic roots with three syllables, where the third syllable is heavy, three are assigned stress on the basis of moraic trochees. The remaing two are assigned stress variably, with the same distribution as discussed above. Older speakers assign the first and second moras to a foot, and stress the trochee (the first syllable). They then assign the third and fourth moras to a further foot, comprising the third, heavy, syllable, which is then assigned primary stress ([2.42]a.). Younger speakers also assign the first and second syllables to a single foot (both being light), but the now third syllable is not assigned to a foot and is not stressed ([2.42]b.).

Similar variation exists with trisyllabic roots where the first syllable is heavy and the second and third syllables are light. However, no roots of this shape have yet been identified where stress is assigned variably. In a representative sample of 9 roots with this segmental structure, 7 are assigned stress on the basis of moraic trochees—secondary stress is assigned to the first syllable and primary stress to the light second syllable, as with /gàepáza/ 'tree sp.' in (2.43)a. In a further 2 roots stress is assigned on the basis of syllabic trochees—stress is assigned only to the first syllable, as with /sáiɣona/ 'evening' in (2.43)b.

(2.42)   a.   b.

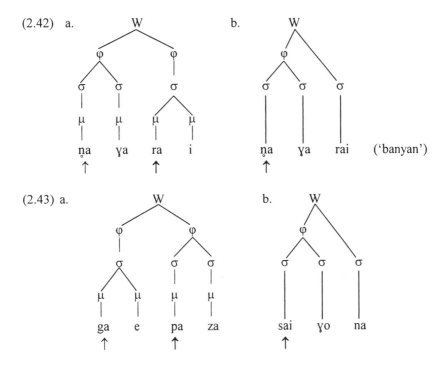

(2.43)   a.   b.

2.5.4 Irregular stress assignment in roots with light syllables only

Age-based variation also exists with certain roots with three light syllables; however, this reflects irregular assignment resulting from the prosodic shadow of lost morphological complexity.

While the regular stress assignment regime described in §2.5.2 will result in stress being assigned to the first of three light syllables, a substantial number of roots with this structure are assigned stress on the second syllable. In a representative sample of 243 of the commonest monomorphemic non-loan roots consisting of 3 light syllables:

- 182 (74.9%) are assigned stress on the first syllable;
- 25 (10.3%) are assigned stress on the second syllable;
- 36 (14.8%) are assigned stress on the first syllable by some subjects and on the second by others.

These figures alone suggest that stress on the first syllable is more regular. However, these raw figures mask further complexity. Some of these roots have an initial syllable /na/, reflecting accretion of the preposed Proto Oceanic article *na. Unlike many Oceanic languages, Kokota does not retain this form as an article (although a reflex appears to occur within the postposed demonstrative *ana* 'that'). However, *na does occur as the first syllable of a number of synchronic nouns such as *nakoni* 'person'. A further small number of roots, such as *fahega* 'be happy', possibly reflect accretion of the causative particle *fa*. In addition, a substantial number of roots, such as *fufunu* 'begin', have an initial echo syllable, in most cases reflecting historical reduplication. Roots of three light syllables occur in all of these categories. All are synchronically monomorphemic (there is, for example, no *koni, *hega, or *funu), but reflect historical morphological complexity involving a monosyllabic form attaching to the front of a root of two light syllables.

Once the 243 roots mentioned above are divided into these categories the picture becomes clearer:

TABLE 2.13. TRIMORAIC TRISYLLABLES BY HISTORICAL MORPHOLOGICAL COMPLEXITY

	σ́ σ σ	σ σ́ σ	variable	total
roots with possible accreted article	16 (76.2%)	4 (19.0%)	1 (4.8%)	21 (100%)
roots with possible accreted causative	3 (75.0%)	1 (25.0%)	0	4 (100%)
roots with initial echo syllable	58 (52.3%)	19 (17.1%)	34 (30.6%)	111 (100%)
roots without possible accretion or echo syllable	105 (98.2%)	1 (0.9%)	1 (0.9%)	107 (100%)

This categorization reveals that almost all instances of stress assigned to the second rather than first syllable occurs with roots that are historically morphologically complex. This complexity involves an initial syllable attaching to a former disyllabic root. The stressed syllable thus corresponds to the first syllable of an erstwhile root. Stress assignment on the second of three light syllables thus reflects the prosodic shadow of lost morphological complexity. This is synchronically irregular lexical stress. The large number of forms with this historical complexity that are stressed variably suggest that irregularly stressed roots are in the process of being regularized, a hypothesis supported by the fact that variably stressed roots are assigned stress irregularly by older speakers, and regularly by younger. Where variation between speakers exists, for older speakers the first syllable of the root (the former prefix or accreted particle) is extrametrical, as is synchronically the case with prefixes and proclitics. With synchronic prefixation and procliticization feet are parsed from the left margin of the root, not the word (as in [2.44]a.). This is also true of irregularly stressed roots—initially feet continue to be parsed from the left margin of the former root, despite its synchronically monomorphemic nature (as in [2.44]b.). Over time younger speakers regularize this by parsing feet from the new left margin of the synchronically monomorphemic root ([2.44]c.). Eventually this regularization occurs in the speech of all speakers. In the case of the historically polymorphemic forms in Table 2.13, the process of regularization has yet to begin for some lexemes, it is in mid process for others, and it is complete in yet others.

(2.44) a.

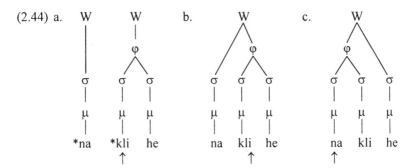

The stage illustrated by (2.44)b. represents irregular lexical stress resulting form the prosodic shadow of the lost morphological complexity represented in (2.44)a.

2.5.5 The effect of suffixes and enclitics on stress assignment

The presence of suffixes and/or enclitics simply extends the right margin of the word, adding further syllables or moras to the word to participate in stress assignment. Where a root with an even number of syllables or moras is extended by a monosyllabic or monomoraic suffix or enclitic there will be no difference in the way the root is stressed, and no stress will be assigned to the suffix or enclitic, because it remains extrametrical. Thus *hiba* 'eye' alone is assigned stress on the first syllable or mora only. With the addition of the 1SG possessor enclitic =ḡu the stress remains on the first syllable or mora of the root only, as the word is now three syllables or moras in length. The first and second syllables or moras (i.e., the root) are assigned to a single foot and the remaining syllable or mora (the enclitic) remains extrametrical. However, once a monosyllabic monomoraic demonstrative, such as =*de* 'these', is also encliticized, the word is now four syllables or moras. These are then assigned to two complete feet, both of which are assigned stress on the trochee, giving secondary stress on the first syllable or mora, and primary stress on the third, being the first of the enclitics:

(2.45)　/híba/ 'eye' → /híba=gu/ 'my eye(s)' → /hìba=gú=de/ 'these eyes of mine'

A regularly stressed root of three light syllables will be assigned stress on the first syllable only. However, the presence of a single monosyllabic/ monomoraic suffix or enclitic will provide the additional syllable or mora to allow parsing into two feet, affecting the assignment of stress—secondary stress will now be assigned to the first syllable or mora, and primary stress to the third, being the last syllable or mora of the root. A further suffix or enclitic will then be extrametrical and not affect stress assignment. In (2.46) the 3PL object enclitic creates a four syllable or mora word, affecting stress assignment. The further presence of the demonstrative enclitic causes no additional affect:

(2.46)   /tégeo/ 'thank' → /tègeó=ri/ 'thank them' → /tègeó=ri=re/
'thank those [ones]'

The same situation applies when a trisyllabic trimoraic noun root occurs with possessor and demonstrative enclitics:

(2.47)   /fíolo/ 'penis' → /fioló=na/ 'his penis' → /fioló=na=na/
'that penis of his'

A similar situation occurs when the clausal tag enclitic *nekeu* (/nekju/) 'it was thus' accompanies a root of three light syllables. As in (2.46) and (2.47), with the uncliticized root the third syllable is extrametrical and not assigned stress, but with the cliticized root that syllable then becomes the trochee of a second complete foot and thus attracts primary stress:

(2.48)   /kókota/ 'place name'   →   /kòkotá=nekju/ '…Kokota, it was thus'

When a root is assigned stress irregularly, that stress assignment irregularity extends to any words formed by attaching suffixes or enclitics to that root. For example, the root *kekredi* 'egg' is assigned stress irregularly on the basis of lost morphological complexity in the form of reduplication (see §2.5.4). The root is synchronically monomorphemic but has a prosodic structure reflecting a lost morphological structure of a reduplicated disyllabic root, **kredi*. Feet are aligned with the left margin of the historical root, not the synchronic root. The addition of two monosyllabic monomoraic suffixes or enclitics creates a five-syllable word, but feet alignment remains at the boundary between the first and second syllable of the root. As a result, the suffixes or enclitics form a foot and secondary stress is assigned to the second syllable of the word, corresponding to the second syllable of the root, and primary stress is assigned to the first of the two suffixes or enclitics. This is exemplified in (2.49), with the 3PL possessor enclitic and the demonstrative *=re* 'those'.

(2.49)   /kekrédi/ 'egg'   →   /kekrèdi=dí=re/ 'those eggs of theirs'

In some instances, however, suffixation or encliticization can trigger regular stress assignment in roots that are stressed irregularly in isolation. Thus, for example, *duduma* 'pity' is assigned stress irregularly in isolation (like many roots with an initial echo syllable). However, when a monomoraic suffix or enclitic is present, stress is assigned regularly across the resulting word. In (2.50)a. the enclitic is the 3SG possessor marker =*na*, in (2.50)b. it is the 3SG object enclitic =*i*:

(2.50) a. /dudúma/ 'pity' → /dùdumá=na/ 'his/her/its pity'
      b. /dudúma/ 'pity' → /dùdumá=i/ 'pity him/her/it'

The stress pattern in (2.50)b. is only possible in the regime based on moraic trochees, as while the inflected form in (2.50)a. is now four syllables, the infected form in (2.50)b. remains trisyllabic, the final syllable now being heavy. The inflected form in (2.50)b., therefore, has the same prosodic structure shown in (2.42)a. for the moraic trochaic version of *nhagarai*. It is not surprising that suffixation or encliticization like that in (2.50) should trigger regularization. The irregularly stressed root consists of three light syllables. In either stress regime one syllable or moras will be extrametrical. While the root's normal stress assignment is irregular, it is not prosodically more complex than a regular structure. However, once a further mora is added, this creates the possibility of parsing all moras into feet with no extrametrical mora. A dispreference for extrametrical moras makes the regular parsing into two complete feet much more appealing, triggering the regularization. This regularization, however, is not triggered by a suffix or enclitic consisting of a heavy syllable. Thus if *duduma* occurs with the first exclusive plural object enclitic =*ḡai*, stress assignment remains irregular:

(2.51) /dudúma/ 'pity' → /dudùma=gái/ 'pity him/her/it'

This remains irregular because stress is assigned to this word on the basis of moraic trochees. In that regime, if feet were parsed regularly from the right margin of the word, the boundary between the second foot and the following word-final extrametrical mora would fall in the middle of the heavy final syllable, splitting the syllable. As discussed in §2.5.3 this cannot occur. Consequently regularizing the foot parsing margin does not simplify the prosodic structure. Instead it creates new problems, so it does not occur. As indicated, however, this is only so in the regime of moraic trochees.

However, given the variation between moraic trochees and syllabic trochees discussed in §2.5.3, it is not surprising that the effects of suffixes or enclitics that create heavy syllables are varied. In some instances the regime based on moraic trochees applies. Thus, for example, when *seku* 'tail' carries the 3SG possessor enclitic =*na* the resulting word consists of three light syllables, and stress is assigned only to the initial syllable or mora of the root. When the singular nonvisible demonstrative enclitic =o is added, the two enclitics combine to form a single syllable /nao/. The resulting word still consists only of three syllables, however, the third syllable is now heavy. This creates a morphologically complex word with the same syllable structure as the root exemplified in (2.42). However, stress is normally assigned on the basis of moraic trochees, assigning secondary stress to the light first syllable and primary stress to the heavy third syllable. In other words, the two moras of the heavy syllable are assigned to a foot and assigned stress on the trochee:

(2.52)   /séku/ 'tail' → /séku=na/ 'its tail' → /sèku=ná=o/ 'that (nonvisible) tail of its'

In other instances of the creation of a heavy syllable by the addition of a suffix or enclitic, the resulting word is assigned stress on the basis of syllabic trochees. This can occur commonly when a disyllabic bimoraic verb root is accompanied by the 3SG object enclitic =i in a situation where the final vowel of the verb combines with the enclitic to form a single heavy syllable. This creates a disyllabic word with an initial light syllable and a heavy second syllable, resembling in syllabic structure the roots exemplified in (2.40). With some roots and for some speakers the resulting word is assigned stress on the basis of syllabic trochees, giving a prosodic structure like that shown for *kalae* in (2.40)b. Both syllables are assigned to a single foot regardless of the fact that the enclitic means the second syllable is now heavy. Stress is then assigned to the first syllable just as it is with the uncliticized root. In (2.53) the final vowel /e/ of *zuke* 'look for' combines with the enclitic to create a heavy syllable with as its nucleus the diphthong /ei/:

(2.53)   /zúke/ 'look for' → /zúke=i/ 'look for it/him/her'

The equally common alternative is for such words to occur with stress assigned on the basis of moraic trochees, giving a prosodic structure like that given for *kalae* in (2.40)a.:

(2.54)   /zúke/ 'look for' → /zuké=i/ 'look for it/him/her'

The presence of suffixes or enclitics that consist of a heavy syllable tends to affect stress on the basis of moraic trochees. In (2.55)a. *tulufulu* 'thirty' occurs with the cardinal suffix -*gu*. The root consists of four light syllables and is therefore assigned secondary stress on the first syllable (the trochee of the first foot) and primary stress on the third syllable (the trochee of the second foot). When the cardinal suffix occurs, being one syllable and one mora, it remains extrametrical and the stress assignment is not affected. However, when the monosyllabic suffix -*ai* (indicating a number non-final numeral) is present, as in (2.55)b., stress is affected. Although the suffix is monosyllabic it is bimoraic, allowing the parsing of a third foot (in the regime of moraic trochees, but not in the regime of syllabic trochees). The result is that the suffix forms a third foot, which being the head foot, attracts stress on its trochee:

(2.55) a. /tùlufúlu/ 'thirty' → /tùlufúlu-gu/ 'thirty (cardinal)'
       b. /tùlufúlu/ 'thirty' → /tùlufùlu-ái/ 'thirty and...'

The same is true of monosyllabic but bimoraic second elements in compounds. The second element in (2.56)b., *au* 'live' combines with the initial purposive marker *mala* to create a four mora word with the same prosodic structure as shown in (2.42)a. for the moraic trochaic version of *nhagarai*, and paralleling the stress assignment in the equivalent but quadrisyllabic compound in (2.56)a.:

(2.56) a. /màla-m̥óko/ 'bench' (lit. 'for sitting')
       b. /màlaáu/ 'village' (lit. 'for living')

However, as with heavy syllables created by the 3SG object enclitic exemplified in (2.53) and (2.54), variation exists with monosyllabic but bimoraic suffixes and enclitics, where alternative moraic and syllabic trochaic structures are possible. The first exclusive plural possessor enclitic *=mai* when attached to a root of two light syllables creates alternative possible structures. In (2.57)a. the resulting word is assigned stress on the basis of moraic trochees. The two moras of the root are assigned to one foot, and the two moras of the enclitic are assigned to a second root. Stress is then assigned accordingly. In (2.57)b., however, stress is assigned on the basis of syllabic trochees. The two syllables of the root are again assigned to a foot, but the enclitic, being monomoraic, remains extrametrical and no stress is assigned to it.

(2.57) a. /híba/ 'eye'   →   /hìba=mái/ 'our eyes'
       b. /híba/ 'eye'   →   /híba=mai/ 'our eyes'

Similar variation exists where a root with a heavy syllable is accompanied by a suffix or enclitic, where the heavy syllable of the root creates the possibility for two different stress assignments, depending on whether moraic or syllabic trochees are applying. In some instances one regime is established for the root and that regime is applied to suffixed or encliticized forms of the root. Thus *datau* 'chief', is universally assigned stress on the basis of syllabic trochees. Both syllables are assigned to a single foot ignoring the weight of the second syllable, and then stress is assigned to the trochee, being the first syllable. The prosodic structure thus resembles *kalae* in (2.40)b. When two monosyllabic monomoraic suffixes or enclitics accompany the root, the resulting word is treated as quadrisyllabic for the purposes of stress assignment, not as consisting of five moras. The effect is to create two complete feet and assigning stress to the trochee of each, being the first and third syllables, ignoring the weight of the second syllable:

(2.58) a. /dàtau/ 'chief' → /dàtau=gú=na/ 'that chief of mine'

However, in other instances variation occurs. With a root comprising a single heavy syllable, such as *pau* 'head', stress is normally assigned on the basis of moraic trochees, as this allows for the root to comprise a complete foot. Consequently, a single monosyllabic monomoraic suffix or enclitic creates a word consisting of a light first syllable and a heavy second syllable. As illustrated in (2.39), words with this prosodic structure will be assigned stress on the first syllable in both the moraic and the syllabic regimes. However, once a further suffix or enclitic is added two possibilities exist—either the resulting word will be assigned stress on the basis of moraic trochees, in which case two complete feet now exist and the first mora of the heavy first syllable is assigned secondary stress and the second syllable is assigned primary stress. The resulting prosodic structure resembles that applying to trisyllabic roots with a heavy first syllable as exemplified with *oilagi* in (2.43)a., the result being as follows:

(2.59)   /páu/ 'head' → /páu=di/ 'their heads' → /pàu=dí=ro/
'those heads of theirs'

This is the typical stress assignment for a word like *paudiro*. However, a second possibility exists. If the syllabic trochaic regime is applied the resulting word will be given the prosodic structure exemplified for *saigona* in (2.43)b. The first and second syllables are assigned to a single foot regardless of the weight of the first syllable, and stress is assigned to the trochee, being the first syllable. The third syllable is extrametrical and is not assigned stress. as in (2.60). This is not typical, but it does occur.

(2.60)   /páu/ 'head' → /páu=di/ 'their heads' → /páu=di=ro/
'those heads of theirs'

2.5.6 The effect of prefixes and proclitics on stress assignment

As feet are parsed from the left margin of the word, the presence of a prefix or proclitic has potentially considerable impact on stress assignment. Morphologically the language is largely left headed, so prefixation and proclitics are rare, being largely limited to reduplication, the causative marker *fa*, and the preposition *ka*.

2.5.6.1 Stress implications of reduplication

The form and function of reduplication is discussed in detail in §2.4. To the extent that reduplication is productive it consists of an initial echo syllable. Where the reduplicated syllable is heavy, it is always reduced in weight by the loss of the second vowel in the sequence (thus *ñhau* 'eat' is reduplicated as *ñhañhau* 'be biting (of fish)'.

Given that reduplication creates a new left margin one syllable or mora to the left of the word margin in the underived word, it might be expected that the effect on stress patterning would be to cause foot parsing to proceed from the new left margin. However, as discussed in §2.5.4, many synchronically monomorphemic roots with an initial echo syllable reflecting historical reduplication retain the prosodic shadow of that lost morphological complexity. The effect is that with many of these roots feet are parsed from the left margin of the former root, not the left margin of the word, resulting in regular stress assignment. This occurs despite the absence in the language of a semantically related unreduplicated cognate. This being so, it is hardly surprising that synchronic reduplication does not automatically cause a shift in foot parsing margin. As with the synchronically monomorphemic roots, there is considerable variation in stress assignment on reduplicated forms for which an unreduplicated cognate does exist.

A representative sample of 63 lexemes is presented in Appendix 3, §2.1.7, where the lexemes consist of three light syllables, the first of which is an echo syllable and where a semantically related unreduplicated cognate exists. Of these:

- 31 (49.2%) are assigned stress regularly on the first syllable;
- 9 (14.3%) are assigned stress irregularly on the second syllable;
- 23 (36.5%) are assigned stress on the first syllable by some subjects and on the second by others.

As with the synchronically monomorphemic roots, where variation exists it is the older speakers who assign irregularly and the younger who assign regularly. For example:

(2.61) a. /ɣáto/ 'think (TR)' → /ɣá~ɣato/ 'think (ITR); thoughts'
b. /túri/ 'tell (TR)' → /tu~túri/ 'tell stories; story'
c. /kére/ 'sting (TR)' → /ké~kere/ (younger speakers) ⎤ 'sting (ITR);
 /ke~kére/ (older speakers) ⎦ 'thorns'

Reduplication derives a new lexeme from an existing lexeme. It appears that once the derived item has entered the lexicon, it becomes eligible for regularization, a process that then gradually takes place, with some derived lexemes fully regularized, others remaining universally irregular, and others in mid change.

It appears that a reduplicated syllable does not participate in stress assignment per se. Instead, it generates a new lexeme that at least initially retains the prosodic structure of the root (from the left margin of which feet are parsed), and an initial non-participating echo syllable. Gradually the prosodic structure of the new lexeme is regularized to parse feet from the left margin of the new word.

2.5.6.2 Stress Implications of the causative particle *fa*

The causative form *fa* does not typically participate in stress assignment. Verbs that are causative-marked continue to parse feet from the left margin of the underived root. However, in a small number of causativized verbs stress assignment indicates feet are parsed from the left margin of a word, including the causative form. With a number of other causativized verbs stress is assigned variably—with feet sometimes parsed from the left margin of the root, and sometimes from the left margin of the causative form. This appears to reflect lexicalization in some instances.

Reduplication is functionally idiosyncratic with the derived meaning of each word being unpredictable. By contrast, the presence of the causative particle *fa* is functionally entirely regular. Any verb may occur with *fa*. The semantic effect is to derive a causative verb, and the argument structure is altered to introduce a new agent and reduce the A or S argument of the underived verb to object. This regular semantic and syntactic effect means that it is unlikely that every possible causativized verb is entered separately in the lexicon.

When a causativized verb is not entered in the lexicon the causative form does not participate in stress assignment. It is not clear, however, whether in words of this kind *fa* is a prefix or a preposed particle. One piece of evidence suggesting prefix status is that the form always and only immediately precedes the verb root, and can only apply to that root. It cannot, for example, apply across serialized verbs but applies only to the verb in the sequence that it immediately precedes. If *fa* is a prefix then it simply does not participate in feet parsing in the same way that per se a reduplicated echo syllable does not. Alternatively, it may be a preposed particle. This would then make its non-participation in stress assignment unproblematic—it does not participate because it does not belong to the same word. This hypothesis is also supported by the fact that speakers may pause between *fa* and the following root. Furthermore, speakers usually express the view that *fa* is a separate word, and tend to write it as such. Stronger evidence that *fa* is not a prefix lies in the fact that as well as marking verbs it may also mark the possessor-indexing host when functioning as a prehead desiderative marker (see §7.5.4.3, example [7.60]). A third possibility is that the form is a preposed particle that optionally cliticizes to the verb. Given the limited evidence on this point, I have assumed that *fa* does not form a single word with the verb unless it affects stress assignment. This strikes me as a weaker claim than that *fa* is a regular prefix that does not normally participate in stress assignment. It seems to me a weaker claim to say a morpheme does not combine with others to form a morphologically complex word unless there is direct evidence that it does. As a result of this assumption, I represent *fa* as a separate word unless it participates in stress.

This may be exemplified by most causativized verbs:

(2.62) a. /kráŋo/ 'be dry' → /fa kráŋo/ 'dry s.th.'
b. /káve/ 'descend' → /fa káve=ri/ 'lower them, drop them,
bring them down'

However, there are instances where *fa* does participate in stress assignment. Some causativized roots are always stressed in a way that indicates *fa* is attached to the beginning of the word. With these words, feet are parsed from the left margin of the causative form. A common example is *falehe* 'kill'. Stress assignment indicates that *fa* always forms a single word with the root:

(2.63) a. /léhe/ 'die, be dead' → /fà-lehé=ri/ 'kill them'

The presence of secondary stress on *fa* and primary stress on the second syllable of the root clearly indicates single word status. This is presumably the result of a process of lexicalization. It is not surprising that a form meaning 'kill' should be lexicalized even if morphologically complex (the language contains no other word simply meaning 'kill'[14]). This process is responsible for a number of synchronically monomorphemic lexemes with the initial syllable *fa*. For example, *farohi* 'strike with a long thin object (knife blade, stick, forearm, etc.)' is synchronically monomorphemic—there is no form *rohi*. However, the cognate in the neighboring Cheke Holo language is *rorohi* or *rohi* 'cut, carve into s.th.'.[15] At some point in Kokota the causative particle was accreted and the underived root lost. The difference between *farohi* and *falehe* is thus simply that with *falehe* the underived root has not been lost.

Some other causativized roots appear to be undergoing lexicalization, with variation in stress assignment, indicating that for some speakers *fa* is a preposed particle with these roots, and for others *fa* and the root form a single word. This is the case with the causativized form of *nodo* 'stop, cease', where two stress patterns exist:

(2.64) a. /nódo/ 'stop, cease' → /fa nódo-i/ 'stop him/her/it doing s.th.'
b. /nódo/ 'stop, cease' → /fà-nodó-i/ 'stop him/her/it doing s.th.'

---

[14] Two other verbs occur coding volitional events resulting in the death of another. One, *faaknu*, means to intentionally kill another person, so has the more specific meaning 'murder'. The other, *faroho* (and its archaic variant *farogoho*), is used in descriptions of battles and means 'strike', usually implying the death of the person struck. However, the resulting death is not inherent in the semantics, but an assumed consequence of the blow, and not all struck in this way die. The verb, therefore, appears to mean something like 'strike with a potentially fatal blow'. Consequently it is glossed here as 'smite'. Neither of these more specific verbs, therefore, express a general notion equivalent to *kill*.

[15] White et al. (1988:163) cryptically give an entry for *rorohi*, comment that it is from *rohi*, and then give an example with *rohi*. The entry for *rohi* simply says "see rorohi."

An alternative hypothesis is that the preposed particle optionally cliticizes to the root, always doing so with some roots, occasionally with some others, and usually not with a further group. This, however, does not so readily allow the lexicalization explanation for the variability.

If the hypothesis that *fa* is normally a preposed particle is wrong and it is in fact a prefix that simply does not normally participate in stress assignment, then the lexicalization hypothesis still holds. Just as reduplicated roots are lexicalized and gradually regularized in their prosodic structure, even if the unreduplicated root remains in the language, so too certain causativized verbs may be lexicalized, resulting in the same gradual regularization of prosodic structure. This process would presumably be complete for *falehe* but still underway for *fanodo*.

2.5.6.3 Stress implications of the preposition *ka*

While it is a possibility that the causative particle may optionally procliticize, there can be no doubt that the preposition *ka* does so. *Ka* is the only true preposition in Kokota, and its functions are described in §4.1 and §8.6. In form it occurs as an independent particle immediately preceding its complement phrase or clause, or as a proclitic attaching to the first word in the phrase or clause. This optional cliticization takes place with high frequency in casual speech, but to a lesser extent in careful speech. The distinction is visible in stress assignment. When cliticized, the particle participates in stress assignment—feet are parsed in the resulting word from the left margin of the preposition. Cliticization to articles is particularly common, giving regularly stressed disyllabic words:

(2.65) a. /ka/ + /ia/   → /ka=ia/ [kája] 'at theSG'
       b. /ka/ + /ira/   → /ka=ira/ [káira] 'at thePL'

However, cliticization occurs equally freely with nouns if they occur phrase-initially:

(2.66) a. /ka/ + /ia/ + /nau/ + /=gu/→   /ká=ia náu=gu/ 'at my house'
       b. /ka/ + /nau/ + /=gu/   →   /ká=nau=gu/ 'at my house'

As with participating echo syllables and the causative particle, by aligning feet with the procliticized ka the parsing of syllables into feet and consequent stress patterning is altered. In (2.66)b. this simply means the second of the three syllables, the former stressed first syllable of the root, is not stressed, now being the rightmost of the two syllables in the left-aligned foot. The new third syllable is extrametrical and so remains unstressed . However, in longer words additional syllables may be assigned to feet and assigned stress, for example, when a demonstrative enclitic is present:

(2.67)   /ka/ + /suli/ + /are/ → /kà=suli=áre/ [kàsuljáre] 'at those children'

The host for cliticization is not limited to nominals or nominal modifiers. *Ka* may be cliticized to whatever form occurs initially in the complement constituent. Where the complement is a clause rather than a phrase, *ka* is cliticized to the first word of the phrase, for example, a modal/subject particle (in this example it is *n-e-ke* RL-3-PFV):

(2.68)   /ka/ + /n-e-ke/   →   /ká=n-e-ke/ 'at where they did…'

It is possibile that rather than optionally cliticizing, *ka* occurs only as a proclitic. This is unlikely as it would mean it may or may not participate in stress assignment, without any distribution beyond careful versus casual speech. The fact that *ka* occurs before words of any type, as long as they fall at the beginning of the complement phrase, rules out lexicalization to explain the participation in stress assignment (it is surely implausible to suggest a lexicalized locative form of 'child'). The only plausible explanation for its optional participation in stress assignment is the optional nature of its cliticization.

2.5.6.4 Stress implications of the subordinator *ta*

The subordinating particle *ta* optionally procliticizes to words with the initial vowel /a/. This cliticization always results in the loss of one of the identical vowels. The cliticized form, therefore, simply adds the onset /t/ to the initial syllable of the host word. This, therefore, has no effect on weight or feet parsing, and consequently has no effect on stress assignment.

2.6 Prosodic processes

A number of phonological processes occur in Kokota that reduce prosodic complexity by reducing the number of moras and syllables in words. These processes include widespread vowel syncope with the effects of the generation of surface clusters, codas and geminates; and the formation of surface diphthongs, and the formation of glides from non-low vowels.

2.6.1 Word-final vowel syncope

2.6.1.1 Word-final syncope before consonants

Word-final vowels syncopate in casual speech in a number of environments. This occurs when the following word has as its initial segment a consonant belonging to the same place of articulation class as the consonant preceding the vowel. Thus in /taɾemedi tilo mane/ 'with three men' the final vowel of the first word syncopates bringing together the homorganic plosives /d/ and /t/ (as in [2.69]a.). This is not limited to plosives but may involve segments with any manner of articulation, including (but not limited to) a fricative and a plosive ([2.69]b.), a nasal and a fricative ([2.69]c.), and two nasals ([2.69]d.).

(2.69) a. /taɾeme=di tilo/   →   [taɾemed tilo] 'with three...'

     b. /gazu ta=u=na/   →   [gaz tauna] 'that tree'

     c. /mane suaɾaɣi/   →   [man suaɾaɣi] '[the] man Suaragi'

     d. /fani no-gu/   →   [fan nogu] 'used to be mine'

While this occurs most commonly with coronals, it is not limited to that place class, as (2.70) illustrates:

(2.70)   /siaɣe ga/   →   [siaɣ ga] 'and then I...'

While this process is widespread in casual speech, it occurs particularly commonly with some high frequency lexical items. *Mane* 'man' (which is not a loan word) frequently occurs in a reduced form. Object-indexed particles also commonly reduce:

(2.71)   /e=ni naŋa=na=na/ → [en naŋanna] 'did that name' (i.e., 'was called')

The reverse is also true. Final vowel deletion is particularly common before the subordinating particle *ta*, for example:

(2.72)   /nakoni ta mai/ → [nakon ta mai] 'visitors' (lit. 'people who come')

This reflects an important syntactic constraint—the word undergoing final vowel deletion and the following word must belong to the same constituent. The process, in fact, most commonly affects a head that is immediately followed by a modifier of some kind (hence the frequency of occurrence in nouns preceding a relative clause, as in [2.72]). It is in this construction that final vowel deletion is occasionally found between non-homorganic consonants:

(2.73)   /kom̥u ta mai=na/   →   [kom̥ ta maina] 'next year'

                                           (lit. 'the year that comes')

The examples in (2.72) and (2.73) are set phrases, and many of the most common occurrences of this process are in frequent collocations. It is, however, not limited to such phrases.

The prosodic effect of this process is to reduce by one the number of syllables in the affected word; however, the number of moras does not change, as the onset of the syllable that has been lost due to vowel deletion becomes the coda of the preceding syllable. The only codas found in the language are surface codas generated by vowel deletion. The prosodic change is:

(2.74)

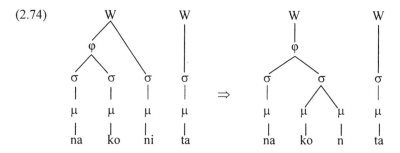

2.6.1.2 Word-final syncope before vowels

Kokota displays widespread word-final vowel syncope when the following word is vowel-initial. This usually occurs when the two vowels are identical. Although only a small number of words have no word-initial onset, several of those that do are among the highest frequency words in the language, including the articles *ia* and *ira*, the pronouns *ara* '1SG' and *ago* '2SG', and the locative *ade* 'here'.

Verb complexes with a transitive predicate often have as their final element the 3SG object enclitic =*i*~=*ni* or 3PL object enclitic =*di*~=*ri*. As a result there are frequent collocations of an /i/ final object enclitic and a noun phrase with an /i/ initial article. This creates the environment for deletion of one of the identical vowels:

(2.75) a. /friñe=ni ia/   →   [friñe nia] 'make/do the...'
      b. /duduma=di ira/   →   [dudumadira] 'feel sorry for the...'

This collocation is common and in normal casual speech always results in the deletion of one vowel.

Equally commonly, the final element of a verb phrase may be a modal or aspectual particle, many of which have the final vowel /a/.[16] Consequently there are frequent collocations of these enclitics and the /a/ initial pronouns or *ade*. Again this collocation is common, and again in normal casual speech the result is the deletion of one of the identical adjacent vowels:

(2.76) a. /a turi=ni=na ara/ → [a turininara] 'I will tell it'
      b. /ge=u=ŋa aɣo/ → [geuŋaɣo] '"..." You said.'
      c. /ta au la ade/ → [ta au lade] 'if [he] is here'

---

[16] These include the immediacy particle *ŋa*, the conditional marker *la*, the limiter *bla*, and the initial marker *fea*.

This verb complex final environment is the most common locus of the phenomenon, but the only environment where it occurs. In (2.77) the existential verb *au* collocated with an /a/ final modal/subject particle shows the same effect:

(2.77) /da au-ɣu/ → [dauɣu] 'weINC are/were staying'

Any collocation of a vowel-initial word and a preceding word with an identical vowel as its final segment is eligible for this process. Unlike the interconsonantal syncope discussed in §2.6.1.1, this is not limited to members of a single constituent, as the verb complex plus subject environments of the first two examples in (2.76) demonstrate.

The prosodic effect of this process is not only to reduce by one the number of syllables by deleting the word-final syllable, but also to reduce the number of moras. Again the syncope deletes a nucleus, leaving the former onset of that syllable unattached. However, now the initial vowel of the following word provides a replacement nucleus, the particle and the following word thus combine to form a single phonological word:

(2.78)

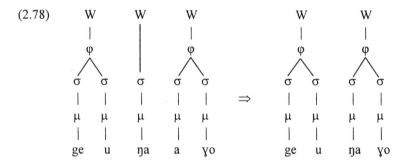

2.6.2 Vowel syncope in compounds

The behavior of identical adjacent vowels between compounded elements is the same as that between independent words. Thus a vowel-initial second element will trigger the deletion of an identical final vowel of the preceding element:

(2.79) /mala-au/ → [malau] 'inhabitable place' (purposive marker + existential verb)

2.6.3 Vowel syncope and cliticization

2.6.3.1 Syncope with enclitics

Syncope is common with vowel-initial enclitics, two classes of which occur with high frequency: demonstratives and the irrealis tag clause *eu* 'it is thus'.

Cliticization of the tag *eu* triggers vowel syncope when the host word has a front vowel in final position, be it /e/ or /i/:

(2.80) a. /ŋ̊eŋe e=u/   →   [ŋ̊eŋeu] '...is different, it's like that.'
                                             (*ñheñhe* 'be separate')

       b. /saɾe e=u/   →   [saɾeu] '...there, it's like that.'
                                               (*sare* 'there proximal')

       c. /nai e=u/   →   [naiu] '...put it, it's like that.' (*nai* 'put')

       d. /manei e=u/   →   [maneiu] '...him, it's like that.'
                                               (*manei* 'he/she/it')

Four demonstratives optionally cliticize (see §4.1.3). Once cliticized, syncope is obligatory. Syncope in this environment appears not to be an optional surface process but to be morphophonemic. All four (*ine* 'thisR', *ide* 'theseR', *ana* 'thatN', and *are* 'thoseN') have an initial vowel followed by a consonant. All delete the initial vowel regardless of the identity of the preceding vowel:

(2.81) a. /kame=gu ine/   →   [kamegune] 'this hand of mine'

       b. /mane ide/   →   [manede] 'these men'

       c. /mau ana/   →   [mauna] 'that taro'

       d. /meɾeseni aɾe/   →   [meɾeseniɾe] 'those medicines'

The prosodic effect of vowel syncope with both tag and demonstrative enclitics is to reduce the enclitic to a single mora, thus reducing the overall syllabic and moraic complexity of the surface word.

2.6.3.2 Syncope with proclitics

Two preposed particles optionally cliticize: the subordinator *ta* and the preposition *ka*.

The subordinator *ta* optionally cliticizes to the existential verb *au*, with syncope of one of the identical adjacent vowels:

(2.82)   /ta au la/   →   [tau la] 'if there is...'[17]

It is not clear whether this may also occur with other /a/ initial verbs.

Cliticization of *ta* and *au* occurs as the standard surface form in formulaic demonstrative clauses. These demonstrative clauses frequently also reflect demonstrative cliticization with its commensurate syncope:[18]

---

[17] The particle *la* marks conditional clauses.

[18] For a discussion of clausal demonstratives, see §3.1.3.3.

(2.83) a. /mane ta au ana/ → [mane tauna] 'the man who is that one'
(i.e., 'that man')
  b. /suga ta au ide/ → [suga taude] 'the houses that are these ones'
(i.e., 'these houses')

The preposition *ka* optionally cliticizes to the first word of the constituent to which it is head (see §2.5.6.3). Where the initial segment of the host word is /a/, vowel syncope of one of the adjacent identical vowels occurs. This happens very frequently with the first and second person singular pronouns *ara* and *ago*, to the extent that the non-cliticized, non-syncopated forms are heard only in careful speech:

(2.84) a. /ka aɾa/   →   [kaɾa] 'at me'
  b. /ka aɣo/   →   [kaɣo] 'at you'

Again, the prosodic effect of this encliticization and syncope is to reduce by one the number both of moras and syllables in the surface form.

2.6.4 Suffixed demonstrative vowel syncope

Demonstratives typically undergo syncope of the final vowel when one of a set of suffixes is attached. Demonstratives frequently occur with one of a number of pragmatic and modal suffixes and enclitics, most commonly the limiter =*blau*, emphatic -*hi*, and specifying -*lau*. When followed by one of these suffixes the unstressed final vowel of the demonstrative typically syncopates in normal casual speech:

(2.85) a. /ao-hi/   →   [ahi] 'this!'
  b. /iao-hi/   →   [jahi] 'that!'
  c. /ana=blau/   →   [anblau] 'just that'
  d. /aɾe-lau/   →   [aɾlau] 'those ones'
  e. /ana-lau/   →   [anlau] 'that one'[19]

In this situation there is no restriction on the consonants that may be brought together by this syncope, as all demonstrative forms trigger the process. As with word-final syncope, the process has the effect of reducing the number of moras by one when the syncopated vowel is preceded by a vowel, as in (2.85)a.–b. However, unlike word-final syncope, in (2.85)a.–b. the syncopated vowel is the second vowel of a diphthong sequence. Here the effect is diphthong reduction, so while the number of moras is reduced by one, the number of syllables remains the same:

---

[19] The exact semantic distinctions between these demonstratives are described in §3.1.3.

(2.86)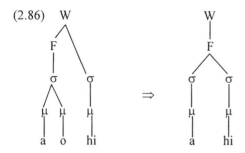

Conversely, as with word-final syncope, when the syncopated vowel represents a separate syllable with its own onset, syllable number is reduced by one, but the number of moras remains the same, the onset of the syncopated syllable becoming the coda of the preceding syllable:

(2.87)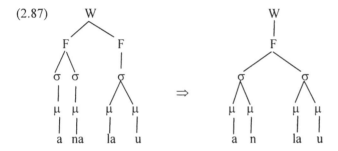

Reduced forms such as this are assigned stress on the basis of syllabic trochees. Thus the reduced form in (2.87) is assigned stress on the first syllable only, although both syllables are heavy.

2.6.5 Word internal syncope between non-identical consonants

Vowel syncope occurs word-internally between homorganic consonants. This is very widespread between identical consonants. However, it also occurs occasionally between non-identical homorganic consonants, particularly in high frequency items. Between non-identical homorganic consonants the vowel of an unstressed syllable may syncopate, apparently without restrictions based on features other than place class:

(2.88) a. /salenaboko/ → [salnaboko] 'place name'
b. /banesokeo/ → [bansokeo] 'place name'
c. /varedake/ → [vardake] 'twenty'
d. /fa leheŋaunau/ → [fa lehŋaunau] 'make me hungry'
e. /mane-dou/ → [mandou] 'big man'

In (2.88) consonants with a range of voicing and manner features are brought together as a result of vowel syncope. Interestingly, the collocation of /h/ and /ŋ̊/ in (2.88)d. provides evidence of the status of [-labial, -coronal] as a broad place class in Kokota (see §2.1.1). The restriction by place classes is demonstrated by the behavior of numerals with the suffix *salai*, indicating multiples of ten:

(2.89) a. /fitusalai/   →   [fitsalai] 'seventy'
      b. /hanasalai/   →   [hansalai] 'eighty'
      c. /n̥evasalai/   →   *[n̥evsalai] 'ninety'

In (2.89)a.–b. syncope occurs between the homorganic final syllable onset of the numeral and the initial consonant of the suffix. In (2.89)c. this is blocked by the fact that the relevant consonants belong to separate place classes.

As with word-final and demonstrative-final syncope, interconsonantal syncope reduces syllable numbers by one but does not reduce moras number as the onset of the syncopated syllable becomes the coda of the preceding syllable.

2.6.6 Geminate consonant formation

Vowel syncope of unstressed vowels between identical consonants is very widespread in normal casual speech, and results in the formation of geminates. This typically occurs in a number of high frequency collocations, and frequently occurs in reduplication, and with some suffixes and enclitics.

2.6.6.1 Geminates in suffixes and enclitics

The presence of one or more suffixes or enclitics may create an environment in which vowel syncope may occur. This may occur when a cliticized demonstrative occurs with a root where the onset of the final syllable of the root is homorganic with the initial consonant of the enclitic. For example, when *mane* 'man' carries the demonstrative enclitic =*de* 'this', the vowel of the second syllable becomes eligible for syncope:

(2.90)   /mane=de/   →   [mande] 'this man'

Here the cliticized word has three light syllables, the first and second of which are assigned to a single foot, the third syllable remaining extrametrical. Consequently, only the first syllable is stressed. The vowel of the second syllable is unstressed and occurs between the homorganic /n/ and /d/. It is therefore eligible for syncope. The mora of the lost syllable then transfers to the former onset of that syllable, which becomes the coda of the preceding syllable. The prosodic effect of this is to simplify the prosodic structure of the word by removing the extrametrical syllable and reducing the word to a single complete syllabic trochaic foot:

(2.91)

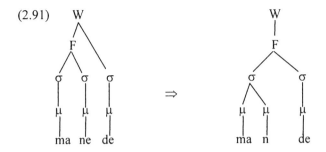

A number of the most commonly occurring enclitics have identical initial consonants. These include the 3SG possessor-indexing marker =*na*, and the 3SG object enclitic, one allomorph of which is =*ni*. The cliticized demonstrative =*na* 'that (nearby)' also commonly occurs. Consequently the sequences /na=na/ '3SGP=thatN', and /ni=na/ '3SGO=thatN' are common. Where the first syllable in each sequence is not stressed, the vowel may syncopate, leaving a geminate consonant. In (2.92) a trisyllabic root is marked with the 3SG possessor marker and demonstrative. Stress is assigned regularly, leaving both enclitics unstressed, the first because it is not a trochee, and the second because it is extrametrical. As the first is not stressed, the vowel may syncopate, leaving a geminate:

(2.92)   /nanafa=na=na/   →   [nànafánna] 'that heart of his/hers/its'

The same process occurs in (2.93) when the sequence /nina/ is cliticized to a regularly stressed trisyllabic verb root:

(2.93)   /tavihi=ni=na/   →   [tàvihínna] 'hunt that'

This syncope reduces the number of syllables in the word by one. However, the number of moras remains the same. The mora associated with the syncopated vowel is transferred to the consonant that was formerly the onset of the reduced syllable. That consonant then becomes the coda of the preceding syllable:

(2.94)

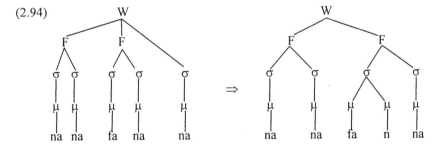

Again stress is assigned on the basis of syllabic trochees. The syncope and consequent coda formation simplify the prosodic structure of the complex word by removing the extrametrical syllable and reducing the word to two complete feet. Primary stress has been assigned to the third syllable of the root, being the trochee of the rightmost foot. The onset of the reduced syllable becomes part of that third syllable, and the former extrametrical syllable becomes the unstressed syllable of the rightmost foot.

2.6.6.2 Geminates in synchronic reduplication

The most common locus of geminate formation is in reduplication. Apart from a small number of lexemes displaying historical full reduplication (see §2.4), reduplication involves an echo syllable identical to the initial syllable of the reduplicated root. To the extent that reduplication is synchronic, only this partial reduplication occurs. Thus *turi* 'tell (TR)' is reduplicated as *tuturi* 'tell stories, chat; a story'. However, a restriction applies where the onset of the reduplicated syllable is a consonant cluster. In this situation the C2 of the onset of the reduplicated syllable is deleted on the surface. For example, *knusu* 'break (ITR)' is reduplicated as *kuknusu* 'a broken piece of s.th.'.[20]

Consequently, whether the unreduplicated first syllable onset is a cluster or not, reduplication creates a situation in which a vowel is flanked by two identical consonants. In addition, until a process of regularization moves the foot boundary to the left margin of the echo syllable, the echo syllable is extrametrical and thus unstressed.[21] This is precisely the environment in which vowel syncope normally occurs in Kokota, and in casual speech reduplicated syllables typically appear on the surface as geminates. However, unlike geminates resulting from suffixation or encliticization, reduplicative geminates are word-initial. Consequently, the former onset of the reduced syllable cannot be reanalyzed as the coda of the preceding syllable. A reduplicative geminate therefore adds a segment to the onset of the subsequent syllable:

(2.95) a.

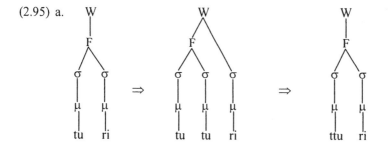

---

[20] See §2.4.1.2 for a discussion of this C2 deletion.
[21] See §2.5.6.1 for the prosodic effects of reduplication and the regularization of irregular prosodic structure in reduplicated lexemes.

b.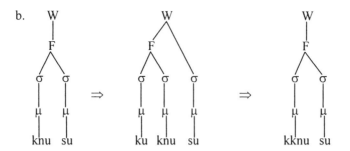

Again the effect is to simplify the prosodic structure of the reduplicated words by removing an extrametrical syllable. In this case the effect is also one of regularization by removing an extrametrical syllable that is irregularly to the left of the complete foot, rather than to the right of it.

2.6.6.3 Geminates in non-synchronic reduplication

As discussed in §2.5.4, numerous Kokota roots have identical first and second syllables, without a corresponding semantically related unreduplicated root existing in the language. For example, *fufunu* 'begin' has no corresponding **funu*. Almost all such roots reflect historical reduplication, and although no unreduplicated cognate exists, many such lexemes are stressed irregularly reflecting the prosodic shadow of the lost morphological complexity.

As with synchronic reduplication, the vowel of the initial syllable is flanked by two identical consonants, and again vowel syncope is common. For example:

(2.96) a. /fufunu/ → [ffunu] 'begin'
b. /huhuɾaŋi/ → [hhuɾaŋi] 'place name'
c. /titili/ → [ttili] 'tabu stone circle'
d. /m̥um̥ui/ → [m̥m̥ui] 'be wet'

The prosodic implications of this are the same as for synchronic reduplication.

2.6.7 Compensatory lengthening

In some instances geminates are created, not by two identical consonants brought together as a result of vowel syncope, but by a single consonant lengthening to compensate for a mora lost through syncope. What makes this process remarkable is that the geminate compensates to the right to replace the mora of a vowel following the consonant that becomes geminate.

This may occur when a root final vowel has syncopated before an object enclitic with an identical initial vowel:

(2.97) a. /kati=iɣo/ → [kàttíɣo] 'bite you'

     b. /huhi=iɣo/ → [hùhhíɣo] 'ask you'

     c. /tufa=au/ → [tùffáu] 'give me'

Here the final vowel of the root syncopates in the environment of the identical following vowel. The former onset of the reduced syllable attracts the mora of the lost syllable and becomes the coda of the preceding syllable. The right compensating consonant then becomes the onset of the second syllable. This has the prosodic effect of allowing a reduction in the number of syllables, while retaining two complete feet (in this case moraic):

(2.98)

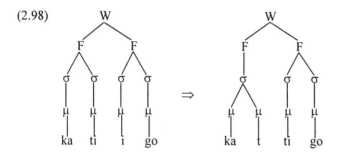

2.6.8 Reduction of diphthong weight by V2 deletion

Two processes reduce prosodic complexity by reducing the weight of diphthong nuclei. Consisting of a sequence of two vowels, these nuclei are bimoraic, and such syllables are heavy. Two processes reduce this weight to one mora, one by deleting the second of the two vowels, the other by coalescing the features of both vowels into a single vowel.

Monosyllabic roots that have a diphthong as their nucleus occur in casual speech in reduced form in which the second vowel is deleted when a single monomoraic suffix or enclitic is present. This reduces the heavy syllable to a light syllable, creating a bimoraic disyllabic word. This simplifies the prosodic structure of the word by allowing for a single complete moraic foot.

(2.99) a. /ŋau=di/ → [ŋadi] 'eat them'

     b. /lao=bo/ → [labo] 'go ahead!'[22]

2.6.9 Vowel coalescence

Diphthongs may also be reduced by a process of vowel coalescence. Features of the two vowels in the VV sequence coalesce to form a single monophthong

---

[22] It is worth noting that while speakers routinely produce these reduced variants in casual speech, when tested they are regarded as being acceptable but not good Kokota.

produced in a position intermediate between the positions of the two vowels in the original sequence. This is most evident with low + high sequences. The resulting monophthong is the mid vowel with the same front/back features as the high vowel. Thus /au/ is reduced as /o/ and /ai/ is reduced as /e/:

(2.100) a. /vilai/   →   [vile] 'knife'
       b. /bula=nau/   →   [bulano] 'I'm angry'

This process also applies to sequences of mid + high vowels, the resulting monophthong being in an intermediate position between the two vowel positions. Thus *manei* 'he, him', for example, typically occurs with a monophthong that is intermediate between the mid front and high front vowel positions, equivalent to a reduced height variant of /i/.

Coalescence is, however, not limited to the reduction of diphthongs, but may occur across morpheme boundaries with other VV sequences in high frequency collocations. A collocation of /u/ and /a/, for example, may surface as [ɔ]:

(2.101)   /kame=mu ana/   →   [kamemɔna] 'that hand/arm of his/hers/its'

This has the effect of reducing the word to four light syllables, allowing the parsing of syllables or moras into two complete feet.

2.6.10 Glide formation

Kokota has no underlying glides (see §2.1.1.3.4). However, as discussed in §2.2.4.3, non-low vowels form glides in certain environments: the front non-low vowels /e/ and /i/ becoming the palatal glide [j], the non-low back vowels /o/ and /u/ the labiovelar [w]. As discussed in §2.2.4.1, diphthong formation reduces syllable number by combining a sequence of two vowels into a single heavy syllable. However, diphthong formation only occurs with certain VV sequences. Other VV sequences also undergo a process that reduces not only syllable number, but also moras number, by changing one of the vowels into a glide.

This process of glide formation only affects the first vowel in a VV sequence, turning that vowel into an onset consonant. One environment where this occurs is where it will create an onset for a syllable that would otherwise be onsetless. In a sequence of three vowels, if the middle vowel is eligible for glide formation that will take place. For example, the clausal tag *nekeuo* 'that was thus' is quadrisyllabic in slow careful speech, each vowel realized as a separate syllable. However, the middle vowel in the VVV sequence is eligible for glide formation. This occurs, creating a word that has only three syllables (and moras), the /u/ becoming a glide onset for the /o/:

(2.102)   /ne-ke-u=o/   →   [nekewo] 'that was thus'

The vowel /e/ in that sequence is also eligible for glide formation in some circumstances. If that vowel underwent glide formation instead of the /u/ the resulting word would be *[nekjuo], which is trisyllabic. However, this involves the acceptable, but not preferred, syllable structure CV CCV V. Instead the preferred structure CV CV CV is generated.

A similar situation pertains in (2.103). Unlike the underlying form in (2.102), the first and second vowel in the VVV(V) sequence are eligible for diphthong formation. However, the diphthong is not formed. Instead of forming a diphthong with the preceding vowel, the middle vowel forms the onset of a syllable containing the following vowel(s):

(2.103) a. /gauai/ → [gawai] 'be distant'
b. /koṃu ta mai ana/ → [koṃu ta majana] 'that week that is coming'
(i.e., 'next week')

The fact that the vowel that undergoes glide formation would also be eligible for diphthong formation if it did not immediately precede a vowel means that the effect of glide formation in this situation does not reduce syllable numbers. It does, however, reduce mora numbers. As in (2.102), it also creates a sequence of two syllables each with an onset, the first of which is light, rather than a dispreferred sequence of two syllables, the second of which has no onset and the first of which is heavy. This shows that CV-CV is preferred to CVV-V. Example (2.103) demonstrates that diphthong formation occurs after glide formation.

It will be noted that the surface form of *gauai* [gawai] consists of a light followed by a heavy syllable. Words with this structure are the locus of considerable variation (see §2.5.3). This variation, reflecting a shift from moraic to syllabic trochees, is seen in this surface form, with syllabic stress assignment [gáwai] and moraic [gawái] both occurring, with younger speakers tending to use the former and older speakers the latter. As this occurs in a surface form after another phonological process has modified the prosodic structure, it suggests that both moraic and syllabic trochees are operating synchronically. However, glide onset formation is not limited to the second vowel in a VVV(V) sequence. The first vowel in a VV sequence can undergo glide formation, even if an onset is already present, creating an onset cluster

(2.104) a. /n-e-ke-u/ → [nekju] 'it was thus'
b. /ikoa/ → [ikwa] 'be small'

This reduces the number of moras and syllables, simplifying the prosodic structure from one complete foot plus an extrametrical syllable or mora into the preferred root shape of a single foot consisting of two light syllables. The resulting onset clusters in (2.104) conform to the language's constraints on underlying clusters described in §2.3.1.2, broadly that C1 must be an obstruent and C2 a voiced sonorant. However, there is no restriction that a C1 in a cluster resulting from glide formation conform to those constraints. Glide formation freely occurs where the resulting cluster C1 is a sonorant, as (2.105) illustrates.

(2.105)   /prepreku=mu-are/ →   [peprekumware] 'those lips of yours'[23]

Glide formation generating a surface cluster may occur only when the existing onset consists of a single consonant. A constraint exists in the language, on onset clusters of more than two consonants. This prevents glide formation where the glide would add a third consonant to a syllable onset.

Stress assignment occurs after glide formation, as (2.104)b. and (2.105) illustrate. When produced in slow careful speech *ikoa* is realized as a trisyllable, with stress assigned irregularly to the second syllable vowel /o/. However, it is this vowel that undergoes glide formation, creating a disyllabic word that is assigned stress on the first syllable, both syllables being assigned to a single foot, resulting in the stress assignment [íkwa].

In isolation, *pepreku* is also irregularly stressed on the second syllable. In this case syllables two and three (/preku/) are assigned to one foot (the first syllable being extrametrical). With the addition of the enclitics =*mu* and =*are*, syllables five and six (/mu-a/) would normally be assigned to a second foot. The remaining syllable [re] would be extrametrical. Primary stress would then be assigned to the trochee of the rightmost foot, being the syllable /mu/. However, it is the vowel of this syllable that undergoes glide formation. In the surface word the second and third syllables remain assigned to a foot. The third and fourth syllables are also assigned to a foot, but the third and fourth syllables are now [mware]. Consequently primary stress is assigned to [mwa], no word-final extrametrical syllable now occurring. Stress assignment is thus [peprèkumwáre].

While glide onset formation occurs widely, word minimality constraints prevent glide formation if the resulting word would consist only of a single light syllable. For example, the first vowel in *kue* 'grandfather' is eligible for glide formation, generating a cluster onset like that in (2.104)b. However, when the word occurs without any affixes or clitics this may not occur, as it would generate a word consisting of a single light syllable. Word minimality constraints preclude stress-bearing words of less than two moras. Glide formation is thus blocked in that environment. However, if an enclitic is present, glide formation does not violate that constraint and so takes place:

---

[23] The sequence =*mu* plus a demonstrative with initial /a/ here undergoes glide onset formation, the segments /ua/ occurring on the surface as [wa]. However, in §2.6.9 (example [2.101]) a phonologically and morphological similar sequence undergoes vowel coalescence (/ua/ occurring on the surface as [ɔ]). No basis for determining choice of these rival strategies has been identified.

(2.106) a. /kue/   →   [kúe] 'grandfather' (not *[kwe])

     b. /kue=gu/   →   [kwégu] 'my grandfather'

In summary, glide onset formation occurs when a non-low vowel precedes another vowel, except when it will generate an onset of more that two consonants or a subminimal word. It occurs before either diphthong formation or stress assignment.

CHAPTER 3: NOUN PHRASES

3.1 Nominal forms

3.1.1 Nominal derivation

Most phonologically unitary nominal forms consist of a single nominal root morpheme. However, two kinds of morphologically complex nominals exist: compounds, and forms derived by reduplication.

3.1.1.1 Nominal compounding

Nominal compounding involves the concatenation of exactly two normally independent words. Both endocentric and exocentric compounds occur.

3.1.1.1.1 Endocentric compounds

Nouns may be modified by, among other things, another noun or a stative verb (see §3.3.1.2). These are not compounds as they do not constitute a single phonological word. However, many nominal compounds appear to be the result of the morphological concatenation of a nominal head plus modifier. Such compounds are left headed and endocentric. Some have a nominal root as the second element (having the structure N+N=N), with the second element identifying the domain that the head belongs to:

(3.1) a. *mane-vaka*   'white/Asian man' ('man-ship')[24]
      b. *hobo-ḡazu*   'tree branch' ('branch-wood')
      c. *hiba-mautu* 'right eye' ('eye-right.side')
      d. *kala-mhata* 'bush leaves' ('leaf/hair-bush')

Others have a verb as the second element, identifying a state ($N+V_{stative}=N$) or action ($N+V_{active}=N$) that is characteristic of the head:

(3.2) a. *mane-dou*   'important man' ('man-be.big')
      b. *vaka-flalo* 'aircraft' ('ship-fly')

The presence of the active verb in (3.2)b. illustrates that not all endocentric nominal compounds are the result of the head plus modifier concatenation, as active verbs may not modify a noun directly, but do so within a relative clause. The compound in (3.1)d. also is not the result of head plus modifier

---

[24] *Vaka* 'ship' occurs in several nominal compounds, indicating that the referent of the head nominal is non-indigenous. These include *gase-vaka* ('woman-ship') 'white/Asian woman' and *ooe-vaka* ('talk-ship') 'English, Pijin'. *Vaka* also occurs widely as a modifying nominal (see §3.2.3).

concatenation as the noun *mhata* 'bush' does not occur as a modifier, there being a corresponding adjective (see §3.2.3.1.1).

Given the fact that some roots function as either a verb or a noun it is not always possible to identify whether the modifying root is a verb or noun, or is perhaps underspecified. For example, as an independent form, *pamu* can refer to the act of pumping a tilly lamp, or the pump itself. It is not clear which applies in (3.3). Note that *pamu* is a Pijin loan, indicating the recent formation of this compound and demonstrating the productivity of this kind of nominal compounding.

(3.3)   *zuta-pamu*   'tilly lamp' ('lamp-pump')

3.1.1.1.2 Exocentric compounds

Kokota exocentric compounds usually reflect the morphological concatenation of two items that would otherwise be adjacent in a syntactic structure. Many consist of a verb root plus a noun root.

(3.4)   a. *deke-tatala*   'tree sp.' ('step-butterfly/moth')
        b. *siko-ḡia*   'bird sp.' ('steal-lime')

Example (3.4)a. is so named because it is a tree that butterflies like to land on, while the avian raptor in (3.4)b. has a white head accounted for by a custom story in which the bird tries to steal white lime powder (for chewing with betel nut) by putting its head into the lime pot. These compounds reflect the pragmatically unmarked syntactic constituent order of VSO, with the verb and first argument nominal concatenated. In (3.4)a. the noun root represents the subject of the verb root, while in (3.4)b. it represents the object. In (3.4)b. the syntactic position for agent is unfilled; however, in normal discourse agents rarely receive a full mention, the participant being indicated by zero anaphora. No compounds have been identified that involve the concatenation of a transitive verb root and a noun root representing the agent. Verb plus nominal compounds thus appear to be absolutive in character. It will also be noted that in both examples the verb root is an active verb. No stative verbs have been found in V+N nominal compounds. These compounds are thus $V_{active}+N=N$.

A small number of compounds concatenate an active verb with a stative verb ($V_{active}+V_{stative}=N$). All compounds of this type identified so far have *blahi* 'be sacred' as the second element. It is not clear whether others may occur.

(3.5)   a. *ika-blahi*   'Baptism' ('wash-be.sacred')
        b. *ñhau-blahi*   'Holy Communion' ('eat-be.sacred')

The Christian senses in (3.5) are less than a century old. It is not clear whether these compounds are recently formed or semantic adaptations of existing forms.

A small number of compounds have a noun root as the leftmost element but are exocentric (i.e., the referent of the compound is not a hyponym of the referent category of the left element):

(3.6)   *zagi-maha*   'stone adze' ('bird.sp.-eat')

The visual similarity between the bird pecking at the ground and an adze in use is readily apparent. The reasons for the nominal plus verb structure, the reverse of that in (3.4), is less apparent, reflecting perhaps the pragmatically marked syntactic constituent order of argument plus verb.

One compound exists in which the second element is a local noun:

(3.7)   *riñi-ḡilu*   'room' ('?wall-inside')

A formal difference exists between *riñi* and its independent counterpart *ririñi* 'wall', in that the latter demonstrates frozen reduplication (no independent root **riñi* exists in synchronic Kokota). However, loss of an echo syllable in forms displaying historical but not synchronic reduplication is common in Kokota and may explain this divergence. Alternatively the independent root may have acquired its echo syllable after the compound was formed. Either way, the compound is semantically transparent to speakers and demonstrates the potential for local nouns occurring as the second element in compounds of this type.

A large and highly productive subclass of exocentric compounds are those in which the first element is the preverbal purposive marker *mala*. The second element in such compounds is always an active verb, and the compound referent is always an entity that plays a crucial non-agentive role in the event, either as an instrument of some kind (as in [3.8]a., b., and c.) or an undergoer ([3.8]d.). This PURP+V_{active}=N pattern is a highly favored compound type in Kokota, with the resulting forms preferred over monomorphemic synonyms (the root *tañano* 'food', for example, is rarely used in place of [3.8]d.). These compounds directly reflect the structure of purposive predicates. For example, a speaker will indicate whether something is edible by saying it is *mala ñhau* 'for eating'.

(3.8)   a. *mala-mhoko*   'bench' ('PURP-sit')
        b. *mala-kuku*   'anus' ('PURP-defecate')
        c. *mal-au*   'inhabited place' ('PURP-exist')
        d. *mala-ñhau*   'food' ('PURP-eat')

3.1.1.2 Nominal derivation by reduplication

Reduplication is discussed in detail in §2.4. Reduplication in Kokota has a general derivational function, but two major subregularities exist: the derivation of intransitive verbs from transitive roots, and the derivation of nouns from verbs. Some nouns involve the reduplication of an intransitive verb root, typically unergative, as in (3.9), but occasionally unaccusative (3.10). Reduplicated unergative roots have as their referent an instrument that enables the event expressed by the verb to occur or a locus at which it occurs.

(3.9) a. *deke* 'step'   → *de~deke* 'stairs'
　　　b. *kamo* 'go across' → *ka~kamo* 'smouldering stick for transferring fire'
　　　c. *rata* 'walk on sand/beach' → *ra~rata* 'sand, beach'

A very small number of nominals are derived by reduplication from unaccusative roots. The resulting meaning has a more idiosyncratic relationship with the verb meaning. However, the referent always has the verb meaning as a prominent characteristic. The reduplicated verb root may be active or stative:

(3.10) a. *nuge* 'shake'   → *nu~nuge* 'earthquake'
　　　 b. *maku* 'be hard' → *ma~maku* 'leatherjacket (fish sp. w. hard skin)'

A larger number of nominals are derived by the reduplication of transitive roots. The resulting form may relate to the underived verb as an actor (again with meaning of the verb as a prominent characteristic), as in (3.11)a.–c. Alternatively the nominal referent may be an instrument ([3.11]d.–e.), an effective theme ([3.11]f.–g.) or other theme ([3.11]h.), or possibly as some kind of patient ([3.11]i.) (though it is possible this may also be an instrument).

(3.11) a. *siko* 'steal'   → *si~siko* 'thief'
　　　 b. *kaflo* 'beckon'   → *ka~kaflo* 'crab (w. waving claw)'
　　　 c. *tako* 'catch s.th. in air' → *ta~tako* 'bird sp.'
　　　 d. *haḡlu* 'sweep'   → *ha~haḡlu* 'broom'
　　　 e. *kere* 'sting'   → *ke~kere* 'thorns'
　　　 f. *gato* 'thinkTR'   → *ga~gato* 'thought'
　　　 g. *lase* 'know'   → *la~lase* 'knowledge, cleverness'
　　　 h. *turi* 'tell (a story)' → *tu~turi* 'story'
　　　 i. *ḡufu* 'smokeTR'   → *ḡu~ḡufu* 's.th. to smoke (i.e., tobacco)'[25]

Reduplication may also derive a noun from a nominal root. The semantic relationships between the derived and underived forms are idiosyncratic, but the referent of the derived form typically resembles in some way ([3.12]a.–b.) or is associated with ([3.12]c.–d.) the referent of the underived root.

---

[25] This is largely synonymous with *viri* 'tobacco', but tends to be used when it is about to be, or is being, smoked, while *viri* is used when the smoking is less immediate, for example, when buying tobacco at a store.

(3.12) a. *bagi* 'wing, fin'   →   *ba~bagi* 'side roofs of porch'
     b. *bulhi* 'cowrie'   →   *bu~bulhi* 'clam sp.'
     c. *tahi* 'sea'   →   *ta~tahi* 'stingray'
     d. *komhu* 'year, crop'   →   *ko~komhu* 'bush apple'

3.1.2 Pronouns

Four sets of pronominal forms exist: independent pronouns, possessor-indexing, postverbal object-indexing, and preverbal subject-indexed particles.

3.1.2.1 Non-independent pronominal categories

All pronominal forms distinguish four person categories: first person exclusive, first person inclusive, second person, and third person. The preverbal subject-indexing particles do not distinguish number,[26] while possessor and postverbal 'object' indexing distinguish singular and plural, except in first person inclusive.

TABLE 3.1. SUBJECT-INDEXING

1EXC	1INC	2	3
a	*da*	*o*	*e*

TABLE 3.2. 'OBJECT'-INDEXING

	1EXC	1INC	2	3
SG	*=au ~ =nau*	-	*=igo ~ =nigo*	*=i ~ =ni ~ Ø*
PL	*=ḡai*	*=gita*	*=ḡau*	*=di ~ =ri*

TABLE 3.3. POSSESSOR-INDEXING

	1EXC	1INC	2	3
SG	*-ḡu*	-	*-mu ~ -u*	*-na*
PL	*-mai*	*-da*	*-mi*	*-di*

The function of these forms and distribution of allophones are discussed elsewhere: subject-indexing in §7.5.2.2; object-indexing in §6.1.2.2; and possessor-indexing in §5.2.

3.1.2.2 Independent pronouns

Table 3.4 shows the independent focal pronoun forms. The two third person singular forms distinguish gender (see §3.1.2.2.2).

---

[26] The formal and functional characteristics of preverbal subject-indexing are discussed in §7.5.2.

TABLE 3.4. INDEPENDENT PRONOUNS

	1EXC	1INC	2	3
SG	*ara*	-	*ago*	*manei / nai*
DL	*gai-palu*	*gita-palu*	*gau-palu*	*rei-palu*
TR	*gai-tilo* ~	*gita-tilo* ~	*gau-tilo* ~	*rei-tilo* ~
	gai+NUM	*gita*+NUM	*gau*+NUM	*rei*+NUM
PL	*gai* (+NUM)	*gita* (+NUM)	*gau* (+NUM)	*maneri* ~
				rei+NUM

3.1.2.2.1 Pronominal number marking

The numerical specification of plural pronouns involves cardinal numeral forms. Cardinals (see §3.2.2.2.1.4) are derived from most numeral roots by marking the root with the suffix *-gu* ~ *-u*. Thus 'you four' is expressed as *gau fnoto-u*.

The non-third person plural forms freely occur with or without numerical specification. Two third person plural forms exist: *maneri* and *rei*. Only *maneri* may occur independently as a numerically unspecified pronoun. *Rei* can only occur in association with a cardinal numeral. Numerically specified groups up to one hundred may be expressed by either, thus 'they four' can be *maneri fnoto-u* or *rei fnoto-u*. However, the larger the group the greater the tendency to use *maneri*. Thus while *rei fnoto-u* is more common than *maneri fnoto-u*, *maneri naboto-u* 'they ten' is much more common than *rei naboto-u*. Speakers will accept *rei* with numbers up to 99; however, for numbers of a hundred or greater, only *maneri* is acceptable.

Dual pronouns are formed by concatenating the plural pronoun and *palu* 'two' without the cardinal suffix. Thus **gau palu-gu* 'you two' is ungrammatical. In the third person this concatenation must involve the form *rei*. Groups of three may be referred to by either a special trial pronoun, or following the normal plural pattern. The trial pronoun follows the pattern of the dual, with a concatenated trial pronoun involving the numeral root (e.g., *rei-tilo* 'they three'). The normal numerically specified plural form involves the plural pronoun marked with the cardinal form in the normal way (e.g., *rei tilo-u* 'they three').

The trial pronouns are also used with a paucal function. This may occur to refer to a small group whose precise numbers are either not known or not important. It is also used commonly as a vocative to address small groups:

(3.13)   *gure*   *foro*   *ḡ-e=u=gu*   *ade titili=o*
          nut.paste coconut.paste NT-3S=be.thus=CNT here *titili*=thatNV
          'They made nut and coconut paste here at those standing stones,[27]

---

[27] A *titili* is a group of standing stones with pre-Christian spiritual significance.

> *maneri* **gaha** *mane* *e=u...*
> they   five   man   3S=be.thus
> they the five men....

> *"tilo* **mane**, *n-o* *friñhe heve* *gau"*
> three man   RL-2S work what youPL
> "Three men, what are you doing?"

> *ḡ-e* *mai* *manei* *e=u*
> NT-3S come he   3S=be.thus
> He came like [i.e., saying] that [to them].'

Pronouns occur with cardinal number forms, which are themselves nominals. These follow the pronoun, not precede it as numerals do with other nominal heads. This suggests that numerically specified pronominals have the number as the head, with person and number information given by modifying pronouns.

Diphthongs frequently coalesce in casual speech. The frequency with which dual and trial pronoun forms occur in discourse makes them prime candidates for this coalescence, consequently the first exclusive and second person dual and trial pronouns are normally reduced on the surface to [ɣepalu], [ɣotilo], and so on.

3.1.2.2.2 Third person singular gender distinctions

Some Isabel languages distinguish gender in third person singular pronouns. In Kokota a residual gender distinction exists in the pronoun *nai* 'she':

(3.14) *ta* *fakae=ni* *la* **nai**,
        SBD see=3SGO CND she
        'If she sees it,

> **nai** *ginai torai* *dia-nanafa=na* *ḡlehe*
> she FUT definitely be.bad-heart=thatN very
> she will be very upset.'

Nai is now used rarely and only by older speakers. The non-feminine pronoun *manei* is now standard for all third singular referents, including females:

(3.15) **manei** *n-e-ge* *nakodou*
        she   RL-3S-PRS old.woman
        'She is an old woman.'

The substantial homonymy between *manei* and *mane* 'man' may provide clues to the origin of this gender distinction, with the final [i] perhaps reflecting an accreted and reduced *ine* 'this', or a reduced form of the pragmatic particle *hi*.

Entities referred to with *manei* are typically human, or at least animate. Proform reference to inanimate objects typically involves demonstratives, reflecting a preference in Kokota for the use of demonstratives over alternatives such as pronouns; however, while speakers express a dispreference for it, *manei* does occur with inanimates:

(3.16)   *n-e-ge*   *la*   *maku=ña*   **manei** *ge,*
            RL-3S-PRS go   be.hard=IMM it   SEQ
            'It (the tap on the stove gas pipe) becomes firm,

            ao   *bla*   *lehe=na=na*   *e=u*
            thisT LMT   die=3SGP=thatN 3S=be.thus
            and then it's off.'

3.1.2.2.3 Indefinite pronoun

In addition to the inherently definite independent focal pronouns shown in Table 3.4, Kokota has two indefinite independent pronoun, *ihei* and *iheri*. These are clearly related to the interrogative proform *hei* 'who' (see §9.2.2.1.1). Unlike the interrogative, which appears to occur only as *hei*, the most common (and apparantly standard) forms of the indefinite pronouns have the initial vowel /i/, but this may be elided.[28] The indefinite pronouns are used to refer to a participant whose identity is uncertain.

(3.17) a. *...mala* *hoda* *fa* *mhañai=di*   *nhave=di=ro*   **iheiri**
          PURP take CS ??=3PLO   sin=3PLP=thoseNV whoeverPL
          '...in order to take away those sins of whoever [has them].'

      b. *...nafu=na* *teo*   **ihei**   *mane*
          base=3SGP not.exist whoeverSG man
          '...because there isn't anyone

          ta   *torai*   *mai*   *reregi=ni=na*   *ia*   *vetula=na*
          SBD definitely come look.after=3SGO=thatN theSG law=3SGP
          who actually looks after the law of

          ḡavana   *ka=ia*   *ḡilu=na*   *nau* *gai*
          government LOC=theSG inside=3SGP place weEXC
          the government in our village.'

---

[28] Cheke Holo (White et al. 1988:69–70), has an identical form *ihei* with the same initial vowel elision. In Cheke Holo, however, the most common variant appears to be *hei*. The initial /i/ is presumably connected to the initial vowel in the Cheke Holo first and second person independent pronouns *iara* and *iago*, corresponding to the Kokota *ara* and *ago*, presumably reflecting the Proto Oceanic personal article *i*.

c. *e   teo   kaike **ihei***
   3S not.exist one   whoeverSG
   'There is not anyone

   ta   aḡe boka   fa-lehe=i=na   ia   to~toi
   SBD go   be.able CS-die=3SGO=thatN theSG RD~cook
   who can kill the fire.'

d. *...**heiri**   ana   n-e   keha ñheñhe   si   za~zaho=na=na.*
   whoeverPL thatN RL-3S NSP be.separate FOC   RD~go=3SGP=thatN
   '...such things have a different way.'

e. *a   boka   ke   fa keli=ni   bo*
   1EXCS   be.able PFV   CS be.good=3SGO   CNT
   'We can make good

   ihei   *ia   ta   toke=i=na*   *ia   malaria...*
   whoeverSG   theSG   SBD   arrive=3SGO=thatN   theSG   malaria
   whoever [is] the one who catches malaria...'

Indefinite pronouns may function as a nominal head and may be modified by a relative clause ([3.17]c.), an embedded NP ([3.17]b. and e.), a quantifier ([3.17]b.), or a demonstrative ([3.17]d.). NPs with an indefinite pronoun head may function as the subject (as in [3.17]b.–d.) or object ([3.17]e.) of a clause, or as an embedded possessor NP ([3.17]a.).

As (3.18) shows, a NP with the indefinite pronoun as head may also itself occur as an adnominal modifier.

(3.18) *mane **hei***   *ta   mhoko fa-lehe=i=**na***   *to~toi=ne,*
      man   whoeverSG SBD   sit   CS-die=3SGO=thatN   RD~cook=thisR
      'Whichever man sits and kills this fire,

      an=bla   mane=na
      thatN=LMT   man=thatN
      that is that [true] man.'

In its function as an indefinite proform, and its relationship with the semantically corresponding interrogative form, *ihei* resembles the corresponding indefinite locative proform *hae* (see §4.2.2).

3.1.2.3 Reflexive forms

Reflexive arguments are expressed in Kokota by a reflexive base that is marked with direct possessor-indexing to the referent. This base has the form *tagi-*;

however, in the first person singular category the normal surface form is *tai-*. This reflects a process of loss of the phoneme /ɣ/ widespread in the language. The first singular form with the full *tagi-* is, however, occasionally given in careful speech or as citation form. The reflexive forms are:

TABLE 3.5. REFLEXIVE FORMS

	1EXC	1INC	2	3
SG	*tai-ḡu ~ tagi-ḡu*	-	*tagi-mu*	*tagi-na*
PL	*tagi-mai*	*tagi-da*	*tagi-mi*	*tagi-di*

3.1.3 Demonstratives

3.1.3.1 Demonstrative forms and categories

Demonstratives distinguish two number categories, singular and plural, and five categories of relationship with deictic center. The five deictic categories are: touching, within reach, out of reach but nearby, further away but potentially visible, and out of sight. The first four of these categories are expressed using independent particles, while the remaining category is expressed by enclitics.

TABLE 3.6. DEMONSTRATIVE FORMS

	touching	within reach	nearby	potentially visible	not visible
SG	*ao*	*ine ~ =ne*	*ana ~ =na*	*iao*	*=o ~ =no*
PL	*aro*	*ide ~ =de*	*are ~ =re*	*iaro*	*=ro*

The terms 'proximal' and 'distal' have been avoided in Table 3.6 for several reasons. First, these five categories do not fall into two groups that correspond to those notions. Second, the actual distance involved, indeed the actual physical relationship in space with the speaker, depends on a range of factors, primarily to do with the nature of the referent. For example, if a knife is being held it will be referred to with *ao*, while if it is within reach but not in the hand it will be *ine*. A house, on the other hand, may be *ao* or *ine* if the speaker is inside it, since they are making contact with it, and it is within reach. If a speaker is outside a house within reach but not touching it, only *ine* is possible.

Furthermore, the distinction between the nearby and distant but potentially visible categories is dependent on context. A house at the far end of the village might be *ana* if the speaker is thinking in a scale greater than the village, but *iao* if the speaker is just thinking of houses within the village. It may also be *=o* if it is not within view of the speaker. The category *iao* may also be used if the speaker is not seeing the house at the time of speaking, but if it is normally visible from the speaker's location or nearby. So *iao* may be used at night to refer to a house that is visible during the day from the speaker's location, or indoors to refer to a house that is visible from just outside. In either situation =*o* may also be used if the speaker is thinking of the house as out of view, or perhaps outside the scope of the discourse context. However, a house in a neighboring village that is never visible from anywhere near the speaker can only be referred to with =*o*. The potentially visible can be used for very distant objects, as long as they can be seen. Thus a child may call out *iao, iao* when finally locating visually a very distant aeroplane.[29] In addition to these demonstrative meanings, all the demonstratives may function anaphorically.

The allomorphy in the singular 'not visible' category is phonologically motivated: the allomorph =*no* occurs when the enclitic is attached to an /o/ final word, while =*o* occurs in all other environments (e.g., *suḡa*=*o* 'thatNV house' and *raro*=*no* 'thatNV pot'). The bound allomorphs in the 'within reach' and 'nearby' categories are encliticized forms occurring following a word with the same final vowel as is initial in the demonstrative. The independent forms in those categories, along with the forms in the 'touching' category, also optionally cliticize to a preceding word in casual speech.

Demonstratives in the 'within reach' and 'nearby' categories (and possibly the 'touching' category) also cliticize to direct possessor-indexing enclitics in casual speech, without necessarily involving the reduced forms. Thus, for example, *ine* 'this (within reach)' may attach to a possessor-indexed noun such as *nene*=*ḡu* 'my leg', giving the single word *nene*=*ḡu*=*ine* 'this leg of mine'. Demonstratives in the 'touching', 'within reach', and 'nearby' categories obligatorily cliticize to the verb *au* 'exist' in clausal demonstratives (see §3.1.3.3). This may involve either the reduced clitic forms, or the full independent forms. Finally, independent demonstratives in these three catgeories also optionally cliticize in casual speech in normal adnominal contexts.

3.1.3.2 Temporal distance

Certain of the deictic categories discussed in §3.1.3.1 are used to express temporal as well as spatial distance. All time that is passed is treated as belonging to the non-visible category. While temporal locations in the future may not be 'seen' at the time of speaking, they are treated as being potentially 'visible'. The past, on the other hand, is treated as time that will never be 'seen' again. This suggests that the Kokota regard time as involving facing towards the future and away from the past, unlike some other cultures that regard time as involving facing towards what has been (and is thus visible) and away from what has yet to occur (and is thus invisible). For the Kokota, past temporal locations are marked with the non-visible determiners:

---

[29] The following glossing abbreviations will be used: touching - T; within reach - R; nearby but out of reach - N; distant but potentially visible - PV; and non-visible - NV.

(3.19) a. *wiki*   *ta*   *aḡe=o*   b. *wiki*   *ta*   *salupu=o*
      week SBD proceed=thatNV   week SBD pass=thatNV
      'last week'   'last week'

Temporal locations in the future are referred to using the 'within reach' category if the temporal unit is the one adjacent to the unit during which the speech event takes place (e.g., the immediately forthcoming week or year).

(3.20) a. *wiki*   *ta*   *mai=ne*   b. *komhu* *ta*   *mai=ne*
      week SBD come=thisR   year   SBD come=thisR
      'next week'   'next year'

Periods further away than the immediately forthcoming period are referred to using the 'nearby but out of reach' category.

(3.21) a. *ara ginai pulo mai   ka fa-palu wiki **ana***
      I   FUT   return come LOC CS-two week thatN
      'I will return in two weeks.' [lit. '…on that second week']

     b. *ara ginai lao ka   keha   nare   **are***
        I   FUT   go LOC NSP   day   thoseN
        'I'll go on another day.' [lit. '…on one of those other days']

It is not clear at this stage whether all future non-adjacent temporal periods are referred to using the nearby category, or whether the distant but visible category can be used for periods further away in time. No examples exist in the collected texts of demonstratives in that category marking temporal locations.

3.1.3.3 Clausal demonstratives

In addition to the monomorphemic demonstrative forms outlined in Table 3.6, a corresponding set of demonstratives exist that are syntactically single word subordinate clauses. These consist of the subordinator *ta* procliticized to the existential verb *au*, followed by any one of the demonstratives shown in Table 3.6. For example, *t=au=ao* 'thisT' and *t=au=are* 'thoseN', literally translate as 'that which is this' and 'that which are those'. Clausal demonstratives can function as any kind of argument, as in (3.22), or adnominally (3.23). The demonstrative forms are optionally reduced in this construction by the loss of the initial vowel (as in [3.22]c. and [3.23]c.).

(3.22) a. *e salupu **t=au=aro***
        3S pass   SBD=exist=theseT
        'These [events] are over.'

b. *ḡ-o   tahe=i=ña*   ***t=au=ana***   *ba*
   NT-2S tell=3SGO=IMM   SBD=exist=thatN   ALT
   'You tell [them] that.'

c. *fa ka~kave=di=ña*   ***t=au=de***
   CS RD~descend=3PLO=IMM   SBD=exist=theseR
   '[He] took them down.'

d. *e=u   n-e-ke   hoda=ña=bla   ka=t=au=aro*
   3S=be.thus   RL-3S-PFV   take=IMM=LMT   LOC=SBD=exist=theseT
   'So, they can take from these.'

(3.23) a. *naitu toke   n-e   lao ka   mane t=au=ine...*
   devil arrive RL-3S   go   LOC   man   SBD=exist=thisR
   'The arriving devils who went to this man'

b. *teo   ḡ-e   au=gu   kokolo ga~gato   t=au=are*
   not.exist NT-3S exist=CNT class   RD~think SBD=exist=thoseN
   'Those kinds of thoughts won't come true.' [lit. '...won't be.']

c. *ḡ-a   la hod-i=Ø   gai   kala=na ḡazu   t=au=na*
   NT-1EXCS go take-TR=3SGO   weEXC leaf=3SGP woods SBD=exist=thatN
   'We take the leaves of that tree.'

d. *guanha e=ni   bla nañha=na=na   ḡazu t=au=ao*
   guanha 3S=3SGO LMT name=3PLP=thatN wood   SBD=exist-thisT
   '*Guanha* is just the name of this tree.'

Clausal demonstratives occur infrequently with direct possessor-indexing.

(3.24) *ginai e=u   nau t=au=di=de*
   FUT   3S=be.thus   place SBD=exist=3PLP=theseR
   'These places will be like that.' [lit. 'These of the places...']

Clausal demonstratives may occur with an article:

(3.25) *...ira   foro, ira   gure, **ira**   t=au=ro*
   thePL   *foro* thePL   *gure* thePL   SBD=exist=thoseNV
   '...[they took] the *foro*, the *gure*, those.'

A functional distinction between monomorphemic demonstratives and clausal demonstrative forms is not apparent at this stage.

3.1.4 Suffixes on deictic forms

3.1.4.1 Emphatic -*hi*

The suffix -*hi* marks certain deictic forms with contrastive emphasis. This has the effect of contrasting the referent with other possible participants. It occurs with all eight of the independent demonstratives, both as arguments ([3.26]a.–c.) and adnominals ([3.26]e.), and with the three deictic spatial locatives *ade* 'here', *sare* 'there proximal', and *sara* 'there distal' (3.27). It also occurs with pronouns, but only with the first and second person singular pronouns (3.28).

(3.26) a.   ara   teo   *ḡ-a*   manahagi   friñhe=i   **ao-hi**
        I   not.exist   NT-1EXCS   want   work=3SGO   thisT-EMPH
        'I don't want to do this [work].'

     b.   **ine-hi**   bla   botolo   fa   nhi~nhigo=na
         thisR-EMPH LMT   bottle   CS   RD~be.finished=3SGO
         'This is the last bottle.'

     c.   ke   kota   bla   **ia-hi**
         PFV   go.ashore LMT   thatPV-EMPH
         '[They] came ashore at that [place].'

     d.   peleta   **a-hi**   t=au   ka   ara
         plate   thisT-EMPH SBD=exist   LOC   I
         'This plate is mine.'

(3.27)   ...ge   au   fa   puhi   **ade-hi**   selena   t=au=na   gau
         SEQ   exist CS   way   here-EMPH   PNLOC   SBD=exist=thatN youPL
         '...then you can all live together here at Selena'

(3.28) a.   ara   n-a   taḡeo=nigo   **ago-hi**
        I   RL-1EXCS thank=2SGO   youSG-EMPH
        'I thank you

        ka   n-o-ke   toga=nau
        LOC   RL-2S-PFV   help=1SGO
        for you helping me.'

     b.   **ara-hi**   a-ti-ke   fufunu=di   bo   t=au=de
         I-EMPH   1EXCS-NEG-PFV   begin=3PLO   CNT   SBD=exist=theseR
         'I didn't start these [arguments].'

Deictics with -*hi* may only be used indicatively, and not anaphorically.

Due to widespread diphthong reduction, the normal surface forms of *ao-hi* and *iao-hi* in casual speech are [ahi] and [iahi]. While *-hi* occurs with all independent demonstratives, it is most common with the 'touching' category forms *ao* and *aro*. These occur more frequently with the suffix than without it.

3.1.4.2 Specifying *-lau*

The suffix *-lau* is a pragmatic marker primarily (and very commonly) suffixed to demonstratives and deictic locatives. Its function is to provide emphasis in a way that indicates that the referent is exactly the entity at issue. How this is manifested varies widely depending on context. It has something of the sense of English *one* in expressions such as *that one*, in contrast with *that*. Often it occurs with demonstratives referring to information that is prominent in the discourse, emphasizing that it is exactly that information that is being referred to. In (3.29) the speaker is discussing details omitted from the telling of a story.

(3.29) **are-lau**   ago   n-e-ge   turi salupu=di=ro   bla   ago
        thoseN-SPC youSG RL-3S-PRS tell pass=3PLO=thoseNV LMT youSG
        'Those ones [parts of the story] you're leaving out.

        teo   *ḡe lao=di*   *ago*   ***t=au=are-lau***
        not.exist   NT go=3PLO   youSG   SBD=exist=thoseN-SPC
        You didn't tell those ones.'

Similarly, demonstratives marked with *-lau* are frequently used as discourse sequencers, emphasizing that the event in the subsequent clause follows in a sequence of events from the event of the preceding clause.

(3.30) *kulu*   *friñhe=ni* *fea*   *ia*   *suḡa*
        be.first work=3SGO   INIT   theSG house
        'First they build the house.

        friñhe=ni *ia*   *suḡa* *n-e*   *nhigo=u*
        work=3SGO theSG house RL-3S   be.finished=CNT
        Making the house is finished.

        an-lau   *ge*   *kata* *n-e=u*   *suli*   *ana*
        thatN-SPC SEQ bite   RL-3S=be.thus child   thatN
        That, then that child bites [i.e., labor pains start]

        an-lau   *ge*   *ḡ-e*   *lao=ña*   *ka=ia*   *suḡa*
        thatN-SPC SEQ NT-3S go=IMM   LOC=theSG house
        That, then she goes to the house.'

Adnominally, it has the effect of emphasizing that the referent of the head is the specific participant referred to earlier.

(3.31) ḡ-a   kaike fa-lehe=ri gudu   ña   gai   teḡe   **are-lau**
        NT-3S   one   CS-die=3PLO EXHST IMM   weEXC turtle thoseN-SPC
        'We kill every one of those turtles.'

The suffix also attaches to spatial deictic locatives, emphasizing that the location in question is exactly the location indicated by the locative, with something of the sense of the English locative specifier *right* (as in *right here*).

(3.32) ḡ-e   la   posa=u   **sare-lau**   ka   nau   fitupoḡu
        NT-3S go   emerge=CNT   thereP-SPC   LOC place PNLOC
        'They came out right there at the place Fitupoḡu...'

In the examples above -*lau* occurs with root and clausal demonstratives and deictic locatives. Speakers express a dispreference for -*lau* occurring with other forms; however, it does occasionally occur in discourse marking other proforms, including pronouns and interrogatives.

(3.33) a. ka   **gai-lau**   ta   aḡe e=u   la
           LOC weEXC-SPC   SBD   go   3S=be.thus CND
           'With us if it's

           ka=ia   ḡilu=na   tahi... e   no-mai   mhemhe=ni
           LOC=theSG inside=3SGP sea   3S GENP-1EXCP   be.difficult=3SGO
           in the sea...it's hard to do.

       b. **hei-lau**   nañha=na=na   mane ana-lau
           who-SPC   name=3SGP=thatN   man   thatN-SPC
           'What is the name of that man?'

The suffix *lau* may cooccur with the emphatic suffix -*hi*:

(3.34) **a-hi-lau**   fa   ḡaha=na=na
        thisT-EMPH-SPC   CS   five=3SGP=thatN
        'This one is the fifth one.'

The suffix occurs most commonly with the 'nearby' demonstratives *ana* 'thatN' and *are* 'thoseN'. Vowel syncope typically reduces the resulting forms to [anlau] and [arlau], with the former often reducing further to [ālau].

3.1.5 Proper nouns

Any object or entity, animate or inanimate, may be assigned a specific name, including people, spirits, locations, buildings, boats, sacred stones, etc.

Kokota individuals have two personal names. The first is often an English borrowing, particularly among men. Many 'custom' (i.e., non-loan) personal names are semantically opaque, but some are not (e.g., *Belama* 'frigate bird'). For individuals with two custom names, the first name is normally used in the community. For individuals with an English name, the second (custom) name is normally used, with the English name usually reserved for dealing with Westerners.[30] Reduction of long custom names to two syllables as the normal form of address and reference is common. Quadrisyllabic names always appear to be reducible (*Rivakato* to *Riva*). Trisyllabic names are also reducible, particularly quadrimoraic ones (*Dilauna* to *Dilau*), but also some trimoraic (*Belama* to *Bela*).

Nicknames are common to avoid ambiguity between similarly named individuals. These typically reflect some characteristic of the individual. Of the two men named *Hugo* (pronounced [huɣo]) in Goveo village, one was affected by polio as a child and was usually referred to as *Polio*, although the two have different custom names. In another example, an adoptive father and son both named Ruebenson Havisade were normally referred to as *Havidou* 'big Havi' and *Havi Ikoa* 'little Havi', and so on.

The coast of Santa Isabel is a seamless chain of named locations, as is some or all of the interior. Place names vary in semantic transparency, some apparently assigned in other languages or prior to lexical change. Some are entirely opaque. Others, such as *Koilolehe* 'dead coconut', are entirely transparent. Still others are partially transparent: in *Fitupoḡu*, *fitu* means 'seven' in synchronic Kokota, while *poḡu* is identified by some speakers as "a word for hill in the time before".

3.2 Adnominal modifiers

Nominal heads may be modified by a range of modifiers including relative clauses, embedded phrases, possessor NPs, and adnominal modifier forms of various kinds. Relative clauses are discussed in §10.2.3; embedded phrases in §3.3; and possession in Chapter 5.

Other forms of adnominal modification are discussed here. These include articles, demonstratives, an unspecified class-member marker, quantifiers (including numerals), an exhaustive marker, and adnominal locatives.

---

[30] However, children in the village school are addressed by their English name, even by teachers who are close relatives and who use their custom names outside school.

3.2.1 Markers of specificity and definiteness

3.2.1.1 Adnominal demonstratives

Demonstratives may function either as a nominal head or an adnominal modifier. They assign definiteness to the referent or modified nominal, and typically refer to or modify a participant whose identity has been established in the discourse, is assumed by the speaker to be known to the hearer, or is indicated by gesture. Demonstrative forms and categories are discussed in §3.1.3. Their syntactic behavior is discussed in §3.3.

3.2.1.2 Articles

Two articles exist: singular *ia* and plural *ira*. These occur in pre-head position.

(3.35) a. ...*korho*   *ma=di*   ***ira***   *lholhoḡuai=na*
            pull   come=3PLO thePL   coil=3SGP
            '...[he] pulled his coils towards him.'

     b. ***ia***   *puku* *ba,* ***ia***   *do*   *ba, n-e*   *kati=nau*   *ara*
        theSG fly   ALT theSG mosquito ALT RL-3S bite=1SGO I
        'A fly or a mosquito bit me.'

The articles assign specificity to the nominal they modify. They occur most frequently modifying newly introduced participants, indicating that the speaker has a specific participant in mind. This participant may be definite ([3.35]a.), or indefinite ([3.35]b.). While the marked participants in (3.35)b. are not definite, (i.e., they have not been established in the discourse and are not assumed to be known to the hearer), they are specific, in the sense that the speaker has the specific insect that bit him in mind, not just any fly or mosquito.

Subsequent mentions of an introduced participant are typically accompanied not by an article, but by a demonstrative, indicating the definiteness of the referent, and therefore its identity as the previously mentioned participant. As well as modifying newly introduced participants, however, articles may also modify an established participant when its specificity is limited to that resulting from its status as an established participant, rather than because it is known to the hearer outside the context of the discourse. In the text fragment in (3.30), for example, the first line introduces a new participant to the discourse—a house that is constructed to function as a confining house for childbirth. This is marked with an article because although the house is hypothetical, the speaker has a specific house in mind: one that has been constructed for use by a participant already established in the discourse. However, being hypothetical, not definite (in the sense of an actual building known to the hearer), in subsequent mentions (in lines 2 and 4 of [3.30]) the house is again marked with an article.

3.2.1.3 Cooccurrence of articles and demonstratives

Articles precede the nominal they modify, while demonstratives follow the
nominal. The two do not commonly cooccur, because the specificity expressed
by the articles is implicit in the definite status assigned by a demonstrative.
However, such cooccurrences are grammatical and may occur:

(3.36) a.   *...ira   suli   ta   au   ka **ia**   nau **ana***
          thePL child SBD exist LOC theSG place thatN
          '...the children who live in that village'

     b. ***ira   naitu toke aro   bo***
          thePL devil arrive theseT CNT
          'These arriving devils

          ta   au   kuru   nañha=di=re
          SBD exist possess name=3PLP=thoseN
          have names.'

     c. *...tana boro ḡ-e   lao **ira**   palu tati=ro*
          then *boro* NT-3S go thePL two mother&baby=thoseNV
          '...then the two mother and baby stay *boro*.'[31]

As well as modifying nouns that are also modified by a demonstrative, articles
may modify demonstratives themselves as nominal heads, as in (3.25).

3.2.1.4 Nonspecific marker *keha*

The pre-head particle *keha* indicates that the referent of the NP is a nonspecific
member of the class of entities indicated by the head.[32] In (3.37) the speaker
does not have a particular day in mind, simply an unspecified day in the future.

(3.37)   *ka **keha** nare are bo   ge*
        LOC NSP   day thoseN CNT SEQ
        '[Wait for] some other day before

        ke   e=ni   ñ=ago   an-lau
        PFV 3S=3SGO IMM=youSG thatN-SPC
        you tell that one.'

---

[31] *Boro* refers to the practice of a mother and newly born infant remaining lying in
seclusion for a period after the birth.
[32] Ross (pers. com.) points out that both *keha* and the numeral *kaike* 'one' appear to
reflect Proto Oceanic terms for 'one'. In synchronic Kokota *keha* is non-specific and
kaike specific.

As well as being unspecified for identity, *keha* does not specify number. In some situations number specification is assigned by the context. In (3.38) the demonstratives indicate whether the unspecified part(s) are singular or plural.

Number can be indicated with *keha* by the use of a quantifier such as a numeral or *huḡru* 'all', or by *tehi* 'many', as in (3.39).

(3.38) a. **keha**   *pile=di=re*   *no-na*   *bla*   *tagi-na*
        NSP   part=3PLP=thoseN GENP-3SGP LMT REFL-3SGP
        'Some copies will just belong to him.'

     b. *ke*   *la* *nai* **keha** *lholhoḡuai=na=o* *ade*
        PFV go put NSP   coil=3SGP=thatNV here
        '[He] went and put another of his coils here.'

(3.39) a. *n-e*   *ñha=di*   **keha** **palu** *namhari*
        RL-3S eat=3PLO NSP   two   fish
        'He ate two more fish.'

     b. *ara* *n-a*   *fakae=di* **keha** **huḡru** *nakoni*
        I   RL-1EXCS see=3PLO NSP all   person
        'I saw a whole group of people.'

     c. *ara* *n-a*   *oha=di*   **keha** **tehi** *zora*
        I   RL-1EXCS keep=3PLO NSP   many pig
        'I keep many pigs.'[33]

Keha also occurs with mass nouns:

(3.40)   *ara* *n-a-ke*   *manahagi=di* **keha** *no-ḡu*   *kareseni*
        I   RL-1EXCS-PFV want=3PLO   NSP   GENP-1SGP kerosene
        'I needed some kerosene.'

Keha indicates that an entity is a nonspecific member of a class of entities. This often results in a meaning similar to English *some*. However, when the form marks a nominal belonging to a class a member of which has already appeared in the discourse, the effect is to indicate that the entity is a further member of the class. In this sense the meaning is more akin to the English *another*. Example (3.41) is taken from a text about the treatment of a sickness called *naitu tahi* 'sea devil'. The speaker turns to the implications of the presence of another sickness in the patient. The identity of the additional sickness is not relevant, and the speaker has no particular sickness in mind, so the sickness is marked with *keha*:

---

[33] The verb *ohai* means 'keep' only in the sense of animal husbandry.

(3.41)   *ña   e-ke   **keha** foḡra ñheñhe   bo   ta=ke   au*
            but   3S-PFV NSP   sick be.separate   CNT SBD=PFV exist
            'But some other sickness that is

            tareme=na=na   naitu tahi ana   ge...
            with=3SGP=thatN devil sea   thatN SEQ
            with that sea devil

            teo   ña gai   boka=i=na   e=u.
            not.exist IMM weEXC be.able=3SGO=thatN   3S=be.thus
            we can't do [cure it].

            ḡ-e-la   dokta baiu ge   ḡ-e age   boka=i   ña
            NT-3S-go doctor PSBL SEQ NT-3S proceed be.able=3SGO IMM
            I think doctors are able [to cure]

            *ta=ḡ-e   tareme=na   **ia**   **keha** foḡra ñheñhe*
            SBD=NT-3S with=3SGP   theSG NSP sick be.separate
            what's with the other different sickness'

The function of *keha* as a nonspecific marker would seem to rule out its cooccurrence with the articles, which assign specificity to a participant. However, as the last line of (3.41) illustrates, such cooccurrences do occur. This is not a paradox. Such cooccurrences only occur in contexts like (3.41), where the modified nominal is already established in the discourse as a nonspecific entity. In (3.41) an unspecified sickness is established in line 1. It is relevant only because it cooccurs with the sickness under discussion. The identity of this additional sickness is not specified, and the speaker has no particular sickness in mind. When it is mentioned again in line 4, an article also occurs, indicating that the nonspecific sickness referred to is the one previously mentioned. If the article were absent, this line would refer to yet another sickness. The article assigns specificity to the referent in terms of the discourse, while *keha* indicates that the participant is nonspecific in a discourse external sense.

In addition to modifying nouns, *keha* also occurs as a nominal head. In (3.42)a. *keha* is modified by a demonstrative, and in (3.42)b. by a relative clause.

(3.42) a. *ḡ-e=u=gu   ña gai   ira   legu   nakoni ña...*
            NT-3S=be.thus=CNT IMM weEXC thePL every person IMM
            'It's like that with us all the people

            *zaho ḡ-e   la   au   iaro   hurepelo **keha=re**...*
            go   NT-3S go   exist thosePV PNLOC   NSP=thoseN
            some went and lived over at Hurepelo

     ḡ-e   *mai*   *au=gu*   *gai*   **keha**   **ide**
     NT-3S   come   exist=CNT   weEXC   NSP   theseR
     some of us came and lived [here].'

  b. *ka*   *ia*   *fai*   *dokta*   *e*   *au=i*   *la*   *bla*
      LOC   theSG   part   doctor   3S   exist=3SGO   ??   LMT
      'On the part of doctors they have

      keha   *ta*   *fakilo=ni*   *tritmenti*   *ka*   *ia*   *ooe-vaka*
      NSP   SBD   call=3SGO   treatment   LOC   theSG   talk-ship
      what's called 'treatment' in English/Pijin.'

Note that when *keha* modifies the demonstratives *ana* 'thatN' or *are* 'thoseN'
cliticization occurs, as illustrated in the second line of (3.42)a.

Example (3.42)a. illustrates the cooccurrence of demonstratives and *keha*,
reflecting an interaction of the parameters of specificity and definiteness. In
(3.42)a. a group of people is established in line 1. Lines 2 and 3 refer to
subgroups of these people, the identity of the members of which are unspecified.
In this instance, *keha* is used to refer to an unspecified member or members of
the group referred to in line 1. The use of the demonstratives indicate that
definite subgroups known to the hearer are intended (i.e., the subgroups that live
in Hurepelo and Goveo). The subgroups themselves are definite, while the actual
membership of each subgroup remains unspecified simply as members of the
overall group established in line 1.

3.2.2 Quantification

3.2.2.1 Number marking

There are no specific number marking morphemes. Instead, articles and
demonstratives assign singular or plural status to the head nominal, while
numerals and other quantifiers provide more specific enumeration. Kokota
distinguishes count and mass nouns. The class of count nouns can be
characterized as singular or plural, and includes relatively small objects:

(3.43) a. *kame=ḡu=**ine/ide***   b. *kala=ḡu=**ine***
        arm=1SGP=thisR/theseR   leaf/hair=1SGP=thisR
        'this/these hand(s) of mine'   'this hair of mine [one/all of my hair]'

Mass nouns consist of substances that are regarded as non-individuatable, and
these are marked as plural. However, many, perhaps all, mass nouns also allow
singular marking to indicate an individuated unit of the substance:

(3.44) a. *no-ḡu*   *kareseni* **ide**   b. *no-ḡu*   *kareseni* **ine**
       GENP-1SGP kerosene theseR   GENP-1SGP kerosene thisR
       'this kerosene of mine'   'this kerosene of mine'
       (an undifferentiated amount)   (a drum or bottle of kerosene)

     c. *ira*   *raisi* **are**   b. *ia*   *raisi* **ana**
       thePL rice thoseN   theSG rice thatN
       'that rice'   'that rice'
       (an undifferentiated amount)   (a plate of rice)

Some substances appear to allow singular marking without implying an individuated unit. For example, *dadara* 'blood' may be modified by a singular or plural demonstrative. Equally, some apparently countable objects (such as *pau* 'head' in [3.45]b.–c.) may also be modified by a singular or plural demonstrative. It is not clear at this stage what difference in meaning is carried by this distinction.

(3.45) a. *dadara=ḡu=**ine/ide***
       blood=1SGP=thisR/theseR
       'this blood of mine'

     b. ...*ḡ-e pogah-i=Ø*   *pau=na=**na***   *sala* *n-e-ke=u*
       NT-3S break-TR=3SGO   head=3SGP=thatN PN   RL-3S-PFV=be.thus
       '...he broke Sala's head'

     c. *marh-i=di*   *pau=ḡu=**de***   *n-a=u*
       hurt-TR=3PLO head=1SGP=theseR RL-1EXCS=be.thus
       'My head hurts.'

3.2.2.2 Quantifiers

3.2.2.2.1 Numbers

3.2.2.2.1.1 Numerals and complex number forms

The Kokota use a decimal counting system, with lexical items for numerals one to nine, for multiples of ten from ten to ninety, and for hundred and thousand. These numeral forms function adnominally. There is no dedicated lexical item meaning zero. The numerals are presented in Table 3.7. Most numeral lexemes are monomorphemic. The forms for thirty and sixty are synchronically monomorphemic, but demonstrate frozen historical compounding. Interestingly, the first element of *tulufulu* 'thirty' is a reflex of the same protoform from which *tilo* 'three' derives. The corresponding element of *limafulu* 'fifty' is the only reflex of Proto-Oceanic **lima* 'five', 'hand'.

TABLE 3.7. NUMERAL ROOTS

1	*kaike*	10	*naboto*
2	*palu*	20	*varedake*
3	*tilo*	30	*tulufulu*
4	*fnoto*	40	*palu-tutu*
5	*ǧaha*	50	*limafulu*
6	*nablo*	60	*tilo-tutu*
7	*fitu*	70	*fitu-salai*
8	*hana*	80	*hana-salai*
9	*nheva*	90	*nheva-salai*
		100	*ǧobi*
		1000	*toga*

Several other forms for multiples of ten are bimorphemic, right-headed compounds. The forms for forty and sixty compound the roots for two and three with -*tutu*, which occurs only in these two lexical items, and corresponds to the English 'score', as in 'three score' for sixty. The forms for seventy, eighty, and ninety compound the roots for seven, eight, and nine with -*salai*. Numbers other than those realized by numeral lexemes are realized by complex number forms:

(3.46)   *kaike   ǧobi   tilo-tutu*
          one   hundred   three-score
          'one hundred and sixty'

In complex number forms some multiple of ten-forms take the suffix -*ai* when in non-final position. The exceptions are the forms with -*salai*, and *varedake* 'twenty'. The lexemes for one to nine, 'hundred', and 'thousand' also do not take the suffix. For example:

(3.47)   *kaike   ǧobi   tilo-tutu-**ai**   ǧaha*
          one   hundred   three-score-plus   five
          'one hundred and sixty five'

TABLE 3.8. MULTIPLES OF TEN WITH AND WITHOUT -*ai*

10	*naboto-**ai***	60	*tilo-tutu-**ai***
20	*varedake*	70	*fitu-salai*
30	*tulufulu-**ai***	80	*hana-salai*
40	*palu-tutu-**ai***	90	*nheva-salai*
50	*limafulu-**ai***		

Numerals function in three main ways: adnominally as either numeric quantifiers or as ordinals, and nominally (as cardinals). In addition, *kaike* 'one' also functions as a unitative adverb (see §7.5.5).

3.2.2.2.1.2 Adnominal numeric quantifiers

In their unmarked forms numerals and complex numbers occur prenominally to quantify count nouns. Demonstrates, numerals, and articles may cooccur:

(3.48) a. *ira*   **tilo**   *tomoko*   b. **naboto** *gase*
       thePL   three   war.canoe   ten   woman
       'the three war canoes'   'ten women'

The adnominal use of *kaike* 'one' typically assigns indefinite status to the head nominal, similar to the function of indefinite articles in languages like English:

(3.49)   *da*   *friñhe=ni*   **kaike** *visi*   *ade*
          1INCS work=3SGO   one   play   here
          'You and I will play a game here.'

Toga 'thousand' and *ḡobi* 'hundred' are typically preceded by a numeral indicating multiples, and only occur without a numeral if an article is present.

(3.50) a. *naitu toi-kame* *ña,*   **kaike** *ḡobi*   *kilo=na...*
       devil   cook-arm IMM   one   hundred digit=3SGP
       'Centipede devil, one hundred fingers'

     b. *hage*   *bla* ***ira***   *ḡobi*   *kolu*
         ascend LMT thePL hundred snake
         'The hundred snakes rose up.'

As discussed in §3.1.2, pronouns are an exception to the numeral-nominal relationship of an adnominal numeral preceding a head nominal. Instead, the number is head, preceded by pronominal modification.

3.2.2.2.1.3 Ordinal numbers

Ordinals except for 'first' are formed by preposing the appropriate numeral with the particle *fa*. Numbers of any size, such as *fa ḡobi* 'hundredth', or complexity, such as *fa fitu-salai gahau* 'seventy fifth', can form ordinals.

(3.51) a. *ara* ***fa*** **palu**   *mane n-a-ke*   *ooe=na*
       I   ORD two   man   RL-1EXCS-PFV talk=thatN
       'I was the second person who spoke.'

     b. ***fa*** **fnoto** *koze* *a-hi*
         ORD four   sing   thisT-EMPH
         'This is the fourth song.'

The particle *fa* is formally identical to the causative particle *fa* marking verbs. The ordinal forms presumably originated as a predicate construction involving a causative marked numeral with the sense of 'making' a certain number, and it is noteworthy that there is a strong tendency for ordinal marked NPs to function as the predicate of equative constructions. However, synchronically ordinals function attributively as well as predicatively and are thus adnominal modifiers.

(3.52)   *ara*   *ginai*   *fakae=nigo*   *ago*   *ka*   ***fa***   ***palu***   *wiki*   *ana*
            I   FUT   see=2SGO   youSG   LOC   ORD   two   week   thatN
            'I'll see you in two weeks.' [lit. '…in that second week.']

The notion 'first' is not realized by an ordinal but by the verbs *kusu* ~ *kulu* 'be first' and *fufunu* 'begin':

(3.53) a. *zosea wud*   *n-e-ke*   ***kusu***   *hedmasta=na*
         PN   RL-3S-PFV   be.first   headmaster=thatN
         'Josaiah Wood was that first headmaster

         ka   *sikolu*   *ine*   *goveo*
         LOC   school   thisR   PNLOC
         of this school in Goveo.'

     b. *zosea wud*   *n-e-ke*   ***fufunu***   *hedmasta=na...*
         PN   RL-3S-PFV   begin   headmaster=thatN
         'Josaiah Wood was that first headmaster…'

Ordinals may be nominalized by a possessor-indexing enclitic. In (3.54)a. the possessor complement is present, while in (3.54)b. the nominalized ordinal is modified only by a demonstrative:

(3.54) a. *ḡ-e*   *lao*   *ña*   ***fa***   ***palu=na***   *ḡazu=na*   *e=u*
         NT-3S   go   IMM   ORD   two=3SGP   wood=thatN   3S=be.thus
         'Go for the second [part] of that tree.'

     b. *u*   *heve*   *ba=ine*   *ara*
         be.thus   what   ALT=thisR   I
         'What will I say

         ta   *la=i=na*   ***fa***   ***palu=na=na***
         SBD   go=3SGO=thatN   ORD   two=3SGP=thatN
         to give that second one?'

3.2.2.2.1.4 Cardinal numbers

Numerals may function as nominal heads. The polymorphemic numerals (for 'forty', 'sixty', 'seventy', 'eighty', and 'ninety') form cardinals without any formal derivation, as do the forms for 'hundred' and 'thousand'. The monomorphemic numerals other than 'hundred' and 'thousand' form cardinals with the nominalizing suffix *-gu ~ -u*. The cardinal forms are as follows:

TABLE 3.9. CARDINAL FORMS

1	*kaike-u*	10	*naboto-u*	100	*ḡobi*
2	*palu-gu*	20	*varedake-u*	1000	*toga*
3	*tilo-u*	30	*tulufulu-gu*		
4	*fnoto-u*	40	*palu-tutu*		
5	*ḡaha-u*	50	*limafulu-gu*		
6	*nablo-u*	60	*tilo-tutu*		
7	*fitu-gu*	70	*fitu-salai*		
8	*hana-u*	80	*hana-salai*		
9	*nheva-u*	90	*nheva-salai*		

The suffix is underlyingly *-gu*, with the consonant deleting in environments resulting in the adjacency of dissimilar vowels. This follows a pattern of synchronic loss of [ɣ] in Kokota (see §2.1.1.2.3.3). Complex numbers form cardinals by suffixing the final element (if applicable). Thus the cardinal form of *varedake gaha* 'twenty five' is *varedake gaha-u*.

Cardinals are nominals with two functions: in counting, and as nominal heads. Counting numbers (rather than items) involves listing cardinal forms. Some speakers report a variant counting system used by old men. The numerals above ten in this system are claimed to be standard. Table 3.10 highlights the variation, other than the (possibly misreported) absence of the cardinal suffix.

TABLE 3.10. COUNTING SYSTEM

Numeral	Standard counting	"Old man counting"
1	*kaike-u*	*taho*
2	*palu-gu*	*palu*
3	*tilo-u*	*tilo*
4	*fnoto-u*	*fnoto*
5	*gaha-u*	*fagaha*
6	*nablo-u*	*fanablo*
7	*fitu-gu*	*fitu*
8	*hana-u*	*hana*
9	*nheva-u*	*nheva*
10	*naboto-u*	*boto*

Cardinal numbers also function as the head of a NP, indicating a specific number of some unspecified object, typically one that is already established in the discourse or understood from context:

(3.55) a. *lao   la   tehi   n-e=u   tēge   ana,*
go   CND   many   RL-3S=be.thus   turtle   thatN
'If there are many turtles,

          *ḡ-e-la   **naboto-u** ba,   **varedake-u**   ba,   tulufulu   tēge*
          NT-3S-go   ten-CRD   ALT   twenty-CRD   ALT   thirty   turtle
          it might be ten, or twenty, or thirty turtles

          ta   la   hod-i=di=re   gai
          SBD   go   take-TR=3PLO=thoseN   weEXC
          that we take."

As nominals, cardinals have two slightly different functions. Like the cardinals in (3.55), in (3.56)a. the cardinal *palugu* 'two' refers to two examples of some unspecified object. In (3.56)b., however, it indicates number two in a series of objects, with a commensurate distinction in the verb's object agreement enclitic.

(3.56) a. *ara   n-a-ke   tabara=di **palu-gu***
I   RL-1EXCS-PFV   buy=3PLO   two-CRD
'I bought two.'

     b. *...fa kave=i   kaike-u,   fa kave=i   **palu-gu**...*
        CS descend=3SGO   one-CRD   CS descend=3SGO   two-CRD
        '...[he] took off one, took off number two...'

See §3.4.6 for modification of numeral heads, and structure of numeral phrases.

3.2.2.2.1.5 Small indeterminate number specification

The non-specific marker *keha*, discussed in §3.2.1.4, often has the effect of suggesting a smallish group. Small quantities can also be indicated by a string involving *tilo* 'three' preceded by either *kaike* 'one' or *palu* 'two', sometimes marked with the 'alternative' marker *ba*.

(3.57) a. *gita   da-ke   koze=ri   **palu   tilo**   koze*
weINC   1INCS-PFV   sing=3PLO   two   three   sing
'We sang two or three songs.'

     b. *...da   koze=i   **kaike** ba   **tilo**   koze*
        1INCS   sing=3SGO   one   ALT   three   sing
        '...we'll sing one or three songs.'

3.2.2.2.1.6 A lexicalized phrase

The numeral modified phrase *palu mane* 'two man' is a semantically bleached exclamation used to express emotions ranging from surprise to pain.

3.2.2.2.2 Non-numerical quantifiers

Two quantifiers occur in complementary distribution with numerals. These are *huḡru* 'all', and *legu* ~ *lelegu* 'every'.

3.2.2.2.2.1 *Huḡru* 'all'

The quantifier *huḡru* 'all' forms a syntactic class of quantifiers with numbers and *(le)legu* 'every', and may not cooccur with either. It cooccurs with articles, the nonspecific marker *keha*, *tehi* 'many', and the exhaustive modifier *gudu*:

(3.58) a.   *...tana mai   ḡ-e=u=ña   ira   huḡru gase*
         then come NT-3S=be.thus=IMM thePL all   woman
         '...then all the women come.'

    b. *ara n-a   fakae=di   keha huḡru   nakoni*
        I   RL-1EXCS see=3PLO NSP   all   person
        'I saw all a group of people.'

    c. *ara n-a   fakae=di   huḡru tehi   nakoni*
        I   RL-1EXCS see=3PLO all   many person
        'I saw all the many people.'

    d. *a   turi=di=ra   huḡru tu~turi gudu t=au=ro*
        1EXCS tell=3PLO=thePL all   RD~tell EXHST SBD=exist=thoseNV
        'I tell all of those stories.'

3.2.2.2.2.2 *Legu* and *le~legu* 'every'

The form *legu* has three distinct but semantically related functions, all with meanings based on the underlying sense of 'follow'. It functions as a verb meaning 'follow', a relational noun meaning 'behind' and 'after', and an adnominal quantifier meaning 'every'. The quantifier sense is discussed here.

As an adnominal quantifier, *legu* differs semantically from *huḡru* 'all' in that it indicates each individual in a group or series of nominal referents, having a sense of 'each and every', rather than 'all'. It typically modifies temporal locatives, but may also modify non-temporal nominals:

(3.59) *ḡ-e=u–gu–ña*   *gai*   *ira*   **legu**   *nakoni=ña*
NT-3S=be.thus=CNT=IMM   weEXC   thePL   every   person=IMM
'We were like that, every person

n-a-ke   *kapru=ro*   *sare*
RL-1EXCS-PFV   gather=thoseNV   thereP
who was gathered there.'

A reduplicated version, *le~legu*, modifies temporal locatives (a function not also performed by *huḡru*).

(3.60) *ara n-a   lao ka sitoa le~legu   nare*
I   RL-1EXCS go   LOC store RD~every   day
'I go to the store every day.'

(Le)legu forms a single syntactic class of quantifiers with numbers and *huḡru*. Its cooccurrence possibilities are identical to those described for *huḡru*.

3.2.2.3 "Multitude" markers *tehi* and *toga-tehi*

Two modifiers, *tehi* 'many' and *toga-tehi* 'very many' (lit. 'thousand-many'), form a single class of pre-head adnominals.

The form *tehi* functions in three syntactically distinct but semantically related ways. It is a noun meaning 'a large quantity or number of', and a main verb meaning 'be numerous', but it primarily functions as an adnominal quantifier meaning 'many'. As an adnominal quantifier *tehi* indicates a large number or quantity of the referent of the head nominal:

(3.61) a. *manei "tehi tu~turi"   n-e=u   sini*
he   many RD~tell   RL-3S=be.thus FOC
'There are many stories, he says.'

b. *gai   n-a   toḡla=di   tehi   zora*
weEXC   RL-1EXCS chase=3PLO   many   pig
'We chased many pigs.'

c. *n-a-ke   lao buala   tehi   fata*
RL-1EXCS-PFV   go   PNLOC   many   occasion
'I went to Buala many times.'

Tehi may not cooccur with a numeral, but may occur with articles (as in [3.62]), and with *keha* (see §3.2.1.4 and exemplified in [3.39]).

(3.62)   *ira*   **tehi**   *parahaḡala*
        thePL many giant
        'the many giants'

Toga-tehi is a compound of *toga* 'thousand' and *tehi* 'many', and indicates a greater number than *tehi*. Its syntactic behavior is identical to that of *tehi* with its adnominal function.

(3.63)   *ara n-a*   *ñha=di*   **toga-tehi**   *meruku*   *ide*
        I   RL-1EXCS eat=3PLO thousand-many flying.fox theseR
        'I ate these very many flying foxes.'

3.2.2.4 *Gudu* 'Exhaustive'

The form *gudu* is a post-head exhaustive marker that functions most commonly to modify predicates, but that may also modify nominals. With its adverbial function it indicates that the action encoded by the verb was carried out exhaustively (see §7.6.9). With its adnominal function it indicates every possible member of the class of entities expressed by the modified nominal.

(3.64) a. *n-a*   *duduma=di=ra*   *teḡe*   **gudu**
        RL-1EXCS pity=3PLO=thePL turtle EXHST
        'I feel sorry for all the turtles.'

      b. *gita*   **gudu**   *n-a-ke*   *fakae=ni*   *mane ana*
         weINC EXHST RL-1EXCS-PFV see=3SGO man thatN
         'We all saw that man.'

      c. *are-lau*   **gudu**
         thoseN-SPC EXHST
         'All of those [things you just mentioned]!'

As discussed in §3.2.2.2.2.1, the exhaustive marker may cooccur with *huḡru* 'every'. Cooccurrence of *gudu* with numerals or *tehi* is not also possible, presumably for semantic reasons. Exhaustive marking of an object NP often cooccurs with exhaustive aspect marking of the verb:

(3.65)   *n-a*   *manahagi=di* **gudu**   *ara namhari* **gudu**
        RL-1EXCS want=3PLO   EXHST I   fish   EXHST
        'I want every one of the fish.'

Like cardinal numerals and *tehi*, *gudu* may be nominalized by suffix *-gu*, and function as a nominal head:

(3.66) *belo e-ti=u   da   nomh-i=Ø   **gudu-gu***
        bell 3S-NEG=be.thus 1INCS   hear-TR=3SGO EXHST-NMLZ
        'It's not a bell that we can hear it all.'[34]

3.2.3 Adjectives

The assignment of attributes to the referent of a nominal is largely performed by
a stative verb modifying the noun. Thus (3.67)a. corresponds to (3.67)b.

(3.67) a. *kaike namhari **dou***
           one   fish   be.big
           'a big fish'

     b. *namhari ine   n-e   **dou***
         fish   thisR   RL-3S   be.big
         'This fish is big.'

These verbs ('adjectival verbs' in Ross's [1998] terminology) modify the noun
directly, not as a relative clause. This is demonstrated by the fact that
modification by a relative clause consisting of a stative verb with a
subordinating particle is also possible, although this occurs infrequently.

(3.68) *o la hoda mai=ni=u   ia   raro **ta dou***
        2S go take come=3SGO=CNT   theSG   pot   SBD be.big
        'Go and bring the pot that is big.'

Most stative verbs can function adnominally. The exceptions are those for which
there is a corresponding adjective. Nouns may also function attributively:

(3.69) a. *raḡi **boñihehe*** b. *misikete **koilo*** c. *ñehe   **vaka***[35]
           dance heathen   biscuit coconut   umbrella ship
           'pre-Christian dance'   'coconut biscuit'   'manufactured umbrella'

The adjectival use of nouns and verbs is discussed in more detail in §3.3.1.2.

Color terms are stative verbs, not adjectives. This is illustrated by the fact that,
as well as occurring predicatively, they may occur adnominally without any
special marking (as in [3.70]a.), or within a relative clause ([3.70]b.):

---

[34] This is an expression meaning it is not possible to know what is going on in private.

[35] *Vaka* 'ship' occurs frequently as a modifier indicating that the referent is of a type
introduced since European contact, not of a traditional type. Manufactured umbrellas are
ñehe-vaka ('umbrella-ship') while the traditional leaf umbrella, *kaku-vaka* ('banana-
ship') refers to a banana species identical to those normally grown commercially in
Australia and thus presumably introduced, and so on. The opposite, traditional as opposed
to introduced, is expressed by use of the adjective *mata* 'bush' (see §3.2.3.1.1.)

(3.70) a. *gai   nakoni **zuzufra***
weEXC person black
'we black people'

    b. *palu   kaklatu **ta   vega**   are*
two   testicle SBD   white thoseN
'those two testicles that are white'

In addition to the use of stative verbs and nouns as adnominal modifiers, a very small number of true adjectives exist in the language. Some of these forms only function as adjectives. Others function as an adjective and as a verb, but not a stative verb. In addition, there is a small class of forms that carry direct possessive marking indexed to the possessor of the attribute, but that are either not nouns or are derived in some way, and that follow the modified noun rather than precede it as in a possessive construction.

3.2.3.1 Formally underived adjectives

Only three formally underived adjectives have been identified:

(3.71) a. *mata*   'bush, wild'
    b. *ohai*   'domesticated, tame'
    c. *tove*   'old'

3.2.3.1.1 *Mata* 'bush'

The form *mata* occurs only as an adjective. It is clearly related to the noun *mhata* 'bush', but no systematic derivation is involved. This is the only instance where corresponding voiced and voiceless phonemes occur in a minimal pair distinguished only by word class. It is possible that borrowing is involved with the adjective. White et al. (1988:116, 120) report both *mata* and *mhata* as variant forms in neighboring Cheke Holo. They give no examples for *mhata*, but their *mata* examples suggest it functions as a noun and an adjective. My own Cheke Holo informant is unfamiliar with the form *mhata*.

The Kokota adjective *mata* has two closely connected senses. One indicates that the referent of the modified nominal is prototypically associated with the bush.

(3.72)   *kaike naitu **mata***
one   devil bush
'a bush devil'

This prototypical association is often used to distinguish wild from domesticated plants or animals, as in (3.73)a., and to distinguish things associated with the land rather than the sea ([3.73]b.).

(3.73) a. *zora* ***mata***   b. *kakau* ***mata***
       pig   bush   crab   bush
       'bush [i.e., wild] pig'   'land crab' (descriptive, not specific variety)

The second sense distinguishes traditional artifacts from introduced goods. In this respect it is the antonym of *vaka* 'ship' (see §3.1.1.1.1). Introduced manufactured goods have completely replaced many traditional artifacts, such as lamps. Others, such as umbrellas, coexist with the traditional goods. *Mata* indicates that the referent is an object made from locally available materials:

(3.74) a. *zuta* ***mata***   b. *ñehe*   ***mata***   c. *pohe*   ***mata***
       lamp   bush   umbrella bush   clothing   bush
       'bush lamp'   'bush umbrella'   'bush clothes'

3.2.3.1.2 *Ohai* 'tame'

As an adjective, the form *ohai* indicates that the referent is domesticated or tame. It distinguishes animals that are farmed, such as pigs (whether they are particularly tame by nature), from their wild equivalent; and characterizes animals (or birds) that are normally wild but that have been caught and tamed as pets. It is the antonym of the first sense of *mata* discussed above.

(3.75)   *zora* ***ohai***
       pig   tame
       'domesticated pig'

In addition to its adjectival function, *ohai* is a transitive verb meaning 'to keep' (as in animal husbandry). However, this is not an instance of a verb occurring adnominally, similar to example (3.67)a. *Ohai* cannot occur as a stative verb:

(3.76)   **zora ine ne ohai*   'This pig is tame.'

3.2.3.1.3 *Tove* 'old'

Like *mata* 'bush', *tove* 'old' occurs only as an adjective:

(3.77) a. *n-e-ke*   *mai*   *velepuhi=na...*   *ka*   *ira*   *mane-dou*   ***tove***
       RL-3S-PFV   come   right.way=thatN   LOC   thePL   man-be.big   old
       'That catechist came... to the old big men.'

     b. *ine-hi*   *kaike*   *suḡa*   ***tove**=na*
       thisR-EMPH   one   house   old=thatN
       'This is an old house.'

The assignment of the attribute 'old' to an entity may be expressed using an equative construction like that in (3.77)b. However, the actual referent may function as the subject, in which case a particular equative construction is used where the existential verb is subordinate and functions as a clausal nominal, which is then modified by *tove*.

(3.78) | ia | faiba | n-e-ke | kokopo | e | t=au | **tove**=na |
|---|---|---|---|---|---|---|
| theSG | dinghy | RL-3S-PFV | capsize | 3S | SBD=exist | old=thatN |

'The boat that capsized was old.'

The literal meaning of (3.78) is actually closer to something like: "The boat that capsized equated to an old existence". These are the only ways of assigning this attribute to an entity—*tove* does not occur as a stative verb:

(3.79) *suḡa ine ne tove*   'This house is old.'

Tove does occur in the compound verb *tu~turi-tove* 'tell custom stories'.

3.2.3.2 Possessor-indexed adjectival forms

A small class of forms exists that function adjectivally and have a derivational relationship with non-adjectival roots, but that do not behave morphosyntactically in the same way as either verbs or nouns. Like adjectival verbs and nouns, these adjectival forms immediately follow the head noun; however, they are marked with possessor agreement enclitics. The forms in this class (marked for third person singular possessor) include:

(3.80) a. *ma~mane-na*   'male' (of animals)
       b. *ga~gase-na*   'female' (of animals)
       c. *lehe-na*   'dead' (of creatures)
       d. *le~lehe-na*   'dead' (of plants)
       e. *doli-na*   'alive' (of creatures)
       f. *do~doli-na*   'alive' (of plants)
       g. *foforu-na*   'new'
       h. *kenu-na*   'first'

The possessor-indexing agrees with the entity that the attribute applies to. This is most commonly third person, but any person or number category may occur, as (3.82)b. illustrates.

3.2.3.2.1 Gender

The adjectives *ma~mane-na* 'male' and *ga~gase-na* 'female' are derived by reduplication from the nouns *mane* 'man' and *gase* 'woman', and are used to assign gender to animals, but may not be used with human referents.

(3.81) a. *ine   kaike zora   **ma~mane=na***
      thisR   one   pig   RD~man=3SGP
      'This is a male pig.'

   b. *taio   n-e   pusi   **ga~gase=na***
      PN   RL-3S cat   RD~woman=3SGP
      'Taiyo is a female cat.'

3.2.3.2.2 Alive and dead

The states of being alive or dead, and the events of being born and dying, are expressed using verbs that differ depending on whether the subject is a creature (person, animal, bird, fish, etc.) or a plant. For both, an underived root is used in relation to creatures, while a reduplicated derivation is used with plants:

TABLE 3.11. VERBS OF EXISTENTIAL STATUS

	creatures	plants
'be alive; be born'	*doli*	*dodoli*
'be dead; die'	*lehe*	*lelehe*

This distinction carries over into the adjectival function. Although the four verb forms are stative (as well as dynamic), in their adjectival function they do not behave as other stative verbs, but carry possessor-indexing in the same way as the gender adjectives above. Although no other derivational process is involved, the differing morphological behavior of the verbal and adjectival uses justifies regarding these as adjectives as well as verbs, not mere adjectival verbs.

(3.82) a. *ine   kaike zora   **doli=na***
      thisR   one   pig   be.live=3SGP
      'This is a live pig.'

   b. *ago   kaike zora   **lehe=mu***
      youSG one   pig   be.dead=2SGP
      'You are a dead pig.'

   c. *ḡazu   are   e   ḡazu   **le~lehe=di***
      wood   thoseN 3S   wood   RD~be.dead=3PLP
      'Those trees are dead trees.'

3.2.3.2.3 *Foforu=na* 'new'

As with verbs of existential status, *foforu* 'be new' is a stative verb that cannot function adnominally, but the form also occurs with possessor-indexing as an adjective:

(3.83)   *suḡa   are   palu suḡa   **foforu=di***
         house thoseN two house be.new=3PLP
         'These are two new houses.'

3.2.3.2.4 *Kenu=na* 'first'

The form *kenu* has a number of functions with related meanings. It is a relational noun meaning 'front' or 'first'. As an intransitive verb it means to be ahead or in the forefront, and as a transitive verb means to be ahead of someone in a competition or comparison. Reduplicated it occurs as a noun meaning 'the first one'. In addition, it functions as an adjective:

(3.84)   *ine-hi   bla   botolo   **kenu=na=na***
         thisR-EMPH   LMT   bottle   first=3SGP=thatN
         'This is the first bottle

         ta   kulu   kumai=ni=na   gita
         SBD be.first drink=3SGO=thatN weINC
         that we will drink.'

The possessor-indexing shows this is not stative verb functioning adnominally, while the postverbal position indicates that the form is not functioning as a relational noun. The same meaning can be expressed with the form preceding the noun. However, in (3.85) the form is functioning as a relational noun, giving the sentence the more literal meaning "this is the first of the bottles".

(3.85)   *ine-hi   bla   **kenu=na**   botolo=na*
         thisR-EMPH   LMT   front=3SGP   bottle=thatN
         'This is the first bottle.'

3.3 Structure of Noun Phrases with common noun head

Several structural NP types occur, depending on the lexical category of the head. This section will discuss the structure of NPs with an ordinary nominal head. Other NP types include those whose heads are pronouns, reflexives, personal and location names, local nouns, demonstratives, and numerals (see §3.4). In addition a subordinated clause may function as an argument (see §10.2.4).

NPs with a noun as head consist of a nominal core, and a series of optional outer modifiers. The nominal core consists of a noun, an optional pre-head core modifier, an optional post-head core modifier, and possessor-indexing. The noun and the core modifiers form the structural and semantic core of the NP. It is this core that is modified by any outer modifiers that may be present. Nouns may also be modified by a relative clause, as discussed also in §10.2.3.

3.3.1 NP core

A clear distinction exists between the core and non-core components of a NP. The constituent status of the NP core is evident in incorporation: the NP core is that part of a NP that may participate in incorporation. Consequently the diagnostic for whether an adnominal modifier is core or non-core is whether that modifier participates in incorporation or not. This is discussed in detail in §6.4.

The nominal head and its optional core modifiers form the semantic and structural core of a NP. The head consists of a nominal form that is either an underlying noun, or a member of another word class that has been nominalized or is functioning as a nominal. Core modifiers include a small closed class of pre-head core modifiers, several open classes of lexical post-head core modifiers, and possessor-indexing.

3.3.1.1 Pre-head core modifiers

An immediate pre-head core modifier position may be filled by the modifiers *tehi* 'many' and *toga-tehi* 'very many'. Details of the functions of these modifiers are discussed in §3.2.2.3. In both examples in (3.86) the modifier and noun are incorporated, neither verb being in its transitive form.

(3.86) a. *ago   n-o   hoda **tehi**   kaku*
        youSG RL-2S take many banana
        'You took many bananas.'

     b. *ara n-a   korho **toga-tehi**   namhari*
        I   RL-1EXCS pull   thousand-many fish
        'I caught very many fish.'

3.3.1.2 Post-head core modifiers

An immediate post-head core modifier position also exists. This may be filled by almost any member of an open word class, including nouns (including local nouns), proper nouns (personal or locative), stative verbs, or adjectives, or by a member of a small class of spatial locatives. It appears that a very limited type of relative clause may also occur in this post-head core position. Core modification by nouns, stative verbs, and adjectives is discussed below.

3.3.1.2.1 Nouns as post-head core modifier

Lexical nouns may occur as the core modifier. This may specify what kind of entity the referent is, within a class identified by the head nominal:

(3.87) a. *ke   la toke   ka   palu **mane vave**=ro   ñ=ago*
　　　　PFV go arrive LOC two man in.law=thoseNV IMM=youSG
　　　　'You go to those two in-laws.'

　　b. *ia   **pike mau**=ḡu n-e-ke   hod-i=Ø=o...*
　　　　theSG piece taro=1SGP RL-3S-PFV take-TR=3SGO=thatNV
　　　　'My piece of taro [they] brought...'

　　c. *ara a   tu~turi=ni   ia   **naitu parahaḡala***
　　　　I   1EXCS RD~tell=3SGO theSG devil giant
　　　　'I will tell a story about the giant devil.'

　　d. *ka **nare sade** ḡ-e lao=u   ḡ-e la tarai=u*
　　　　LOC day   Sunday NT-3S go=CNT NT-3S go pray=CNT
　　　　'On Sundays they were going and praying.'

There are numerous kinds of men, pieces and devils, and several days of the week, and the core modifiers in (3.87) serve to specify a subclass of each entity. Noun core modifiers may be even more specific, indicating a single member of the class expressed by the head:

(3.88) *ia   mane n-e-ke   lehe e fani **mane premie** e=u*
　　　　theSG man RL-3S-PFV die 3S often man Premier 3S=be.thus
　　　　'The man who died used to be Premier.'

In some cases the core modifier noun provides additional information about the referent, rather than specifying a subclass. In (3.89) *kumai* is not specifying a subclass of cups. Instead it provides information about the contents of the cups.

(3.89) *palu **panikine kumai** ide*
　　　　two cup   water theseR
　　　　'these two cups of water'

Because a noun may occur as the core modifier, two nouns may occur in either order in the core, with variation in meaning commensurate with the change in the head-modifier relationship:

(3.90) a. *ira no-mai   **kastom mereseni** tagi-mai*
　　　　thePL GENP-1INCP custom medicine REFL-1INCP
　　　　'our own medicine customs'

　　b. *ira no-mai   **mereseni kastom** gai*
　　　　thePL GENP-1INCP medicine custom weINC
　　　　'our custom medicines'

The phrase in (3.90)a. refers to the speaker's community's traditions, specifically, traditions relating to medicine, while in (3.90)b. the reference is to medicine, specifically, medicines within the community's tradition.

Nominal compounds themselves consist of two elements. However, being lexical words, they may occur with a core modifier, or as a core modifier:

(3.91)   *ia*   ***mereseni mane-vaka***
         theSG medicine man-ship
         'the white man's medicine'

3.3.1.2.2 Personal name core modifiers

The degree of specificity exhibited by the core modifier in (3.88) is taken a step further by the use of personal names to identify a specific individual or entity:

(3.92) a. *kai*   *bo*   *au*   *ia*   *pirisi* ***hugo hebala***...
          later CNT exist theSG priest PN
          'Later there was the priest Hugo Hebala.'

   b. ...*ḡ-e=u=ña*   *mane* ***havisade*** *ine*
       NT-3S=be.thus=IMM man PN   thisR
       '"..." thought this man Havisade.'

   c. *ḡahipa* ***sagetolu*** *ine,*   *hod-i=Ø*
       stone   PN   thisR   take-TR=3SGO
       'This stone Sagetolu, take it

       aḡe nai=ni   *ka*   *suḡa*   *tarai=ne*
       go put=3SGO LOC house   pray=thisR
       and put it in the church.'

The position of the PNs in relation to the demonstratives in (3.92)b.–c. demonstrate that the PNs are functioning as core modifiers and not as phrasal adjuncts in these examples.

Conjoined personal names can modify a single head:

(3.93)   *mane* ***sala ge ruruboñi*** *n-e-ke*   *namha* *mai*   *ka*   *suaragi*
         man   PN and PN   RL-3S-PFV love   come LOC PN
         'Sala and Ruruboñi were kind to Suaragi.'

This demonstrates that it is PN' that occurs as a core modifier, not merely PN.

3.3.1.2.3 Location name core modifiers

Locative proper nouns may occur as outer modifiers, corresponding syntactically to locative prepositional phrases. They may also function as a core modifier, specifying the head by associating it with a particular location, as in (3.94).

(3.94) a. *ḡ-e   aḡe=u* **mane huhurañi=de** *haidu maneri sare=u*
     NT-3S go=CNT man   PNLOC=theseR meet   they   thereP=be.thus
     'These Huhurangi people were going and they held a meeting there.'

   b. *ara n-a-ge   fufunu lase=i   **ooe kokota***
     I   RL-1EXCS-PRSbegin   know=3SGOtalk PNLOC
     'I am starting to understand the Kokota language.'

   c. *ḡ-e   mai=ña   ia   velepuhi ka gai*
     NT-3S come=IMM theSG right.way LOC weEXC
     'Then the catechist came to us,

     *ka   **nau   kokota   ine***
     LOC place PNLOC   thisR
     to this Kokota place.'

3.3.1.2.4 Local nouns as core modifiers

Local nouns, both intrinsic (as in [3.95]a.–b.) and absolute ([3.95]c.–d.) occur as core modifiers assigning specific locative information to the referent.

(3.95) a. *pile **mairi**   b. *pile **hotai**   c. *pile **rhuku**   d. *pile **paka***
     side left   side between   side landward   side east
     'left side'   'middle side'   'landward side'   'east side'

The exception is the relational noun *kenu* 'front', which occurs as an adjective with possessor marking (see §3.2.3.2.4).

3.3.1.2.5 Stative verb core modifiers

Ross (1998:98) defines an 'adjectival verb' as a member of a subclass of stative verbs that have the predicate syntax of a stative verb, but that modify nouns without relative marking. Almost all stative verbs in Kokota function adnominally without subordinate marking, although such marking is possible, as a comparison of (3.67)a. and (3.68) above demonstrates.

It appears that almost all stative verbs behave in this way. The exceptions include stative verbs that correspond semantically to an adjective. That aside, stative verbs freely occur as the core modifier, assigning a state to the referent:

(3.96) a. *n-e-ke*   *mai=u*   ***puhi***   ***keli=ro***
RL-3S-PFV   come=CNT   way   be.good=thoseNV
'Those good ways came.'

    b. *ine-hi*   *ia*   ***buka blahi***
thisR-EMPH   theSG   book   be.sacred
'This is the Bible.'

    c. ***soda   maku***
clam   be.hard
'hard clam' (a subtaxon of clams)

3.3.1.2.6 Adjectives

Adjectives occur as core modifiers. Adjectival forms and meanings are discussed in detail in §3.2.3.

3.3.1.2.7 Reflexive core modifiers

An indexed reflexive base may occur as a core modifier:

(3.97)   *korho=u tagi-di*   *ka*   *nau*   *fai*   *kokota*   *a-hi,*
pull=CNT REFL-3PLPLOC place side PNLOC thisT-EMPH
'They pulled themselves to this Kokota place,

    la bla   ***ira***   ***mane tagi-di***
go LMT thePL   man   REFL-3PLP
the people themselves.'

The adnominal function of reflexives is to contrastively emphasize the identity of the referent. In (3.97), for example, emphasis is being placed on the fact that the people came of their own volition, rather than being brought or instructed to come. Reflexive forms are discussed in §3.1.2.3.

3.3.1.3 Direct possessor-indexing

Possession is discussed in detail in Chapter 5. However, this section locates possessor-indexing within the overall structure of a common noun NP. Kokota displays direct and indirect possessor-indexing. With direct possessor-indexing the indexing occurs within a NP which has as its head the possessum noun. Indirect possessor-indexing in Kokota involves a distinct NP type which has as its head the indirect possessor-indexing host. That NP$_{POSS}$, is discussed in §3.4.2. The possessor NP is an outer modifier and is discussed in §3.3.2.2.2.

Direct possessor-indexing involves a core-final enclitic that is the most peripheral rightmost component of the NP core and represents the core's outermost boundary. As such, the indexing form attaches to the otherwise final constituent in the core, whether or not that constituent is the head nominal. Direct enclitics do not commonly occur with one of the post-head core modifiers discussed in §3.3.1.2, so the enclitic usually attaches directly to the head nominal. However, the two may cooccur, in which case it is the modifier that carries the enclitic, demonstrating that the indexing forms are enclitics not suffixes, as in (3.87)b. and (3.98):

(3.98) *n-e*   *hure*   *ña*   *tilo*   **tomoko**   **dou=di**   *wistin*
       RL-3S carry IMM three war.canoe be.big=3PLP western
       'They carried the three big war canoes of the westerners.'[36]

3.3.1.4 NP core structure

The pre-head core modifiers *tehi* and *toga-tehi* form a single class glossed here as MULT(iplicity). They are shown to be a part of the NP core by their participation in incorporation, as illustrated by (3.86). Members of a number of word classes may occur in a single post-head modifier position. This is followed by direct possessor-indexing, as shown in (3.98).

The NP core forms a single constituent within the NP, and lacks a specifier, so is represented here as a N'. The NP core has the following structure:

$$(3.99) \quad N' \rightarrow (MULT) + N + \begin{Bmatrix} (ADJ) \\ (V_{STATIVE}) \\ (N) \\ (PN) \\ (PN_{LOC}) \\ (N_{LOC}) \\ (N_{RFLX}) \end{Bmatrix} + (PSSR)$$

3.3.2 NP non-core modifier structure

The forms and functions of adnominal outer modifiers are discussed in §3.2. The syntactic behavior of these modifiers within the NP is discussed here.

3.3.2.1 Pre-core modifier structure

Pre-core adnominal modifiers include articles, the nonspecific marker *keha*, enumerative (NUM) and ordinal (ORD) numbers, and the quantifiers *hugru* 'all' and *(le)legu* 'every'. Of these, *hugru*, *(le)legu*, the enumeratives, and apparently

---

[36] *Wistin* refers to the Solomon Islands' Western Province and to people from that area.

the ordinals, cannot cooccur and constitute a single quantifier position class. Three pre-core positions thus exist, in the following order:

(3.100)   (ART)   +   (NSP) + (QUANT)

The quantifier position with its range of possible forms expands as:

(3.101)   QUANT → $\left\{\begin{array}{l} \text{NUM} \\ \text{ORD} \\ \textit{hu\={g}ru} \\ \textit{(le)legu} \end{array}\right.$

The category NUM may contain more than one numeral combining to form a complex number. The manner in which complex numbers are formed is discussed in §3.2.2.2.1.1. As discussed in §3.2.2.2.1.3, ordinals are formed by marking a number of any complexity with the preposed particle *fa*. The category ordinal thus expands as:

(3.102)   ORD   →   *fa* + NUM

The non-core status of the modifiers in (3.100) is shown by the fact that *hu\={g}ru*, occurring in the rightmost QUANT position, cannot participate in incorporation:

(3.103)   **n-a*   *ñhau* **hu\={g}ru**   *namhari*
          RL-1EXCS eat   all   fish
          'I ate all the fish.'

3.3.2.2 Post-core modifiers

Post-core adnominal modifiers include demonstratives, the exhaustive marker *gudu*, the possessor NP, various adnominal adjuncts, and relative clauses.

3.3.2.2.1 Post-core outer modifiers

Two post-core modifier positions exist (other than complement and adjunct positions). One may be filled by the exhaustive marker *gudu*, discussed in §3.2.2.4. The other may be filled by a demonstrative.

The innermost of the post-core modifiers is the exhaustive marker. This is shown to be a non-core modifier as it does not participate in incorporation. It follows the possessor-indexing enclitic, which is the outermost core modifier:

(3.104)   *e* *palu* *\={g}azu=di*   **gudu**   *bla*   *are-lau*
          3S two   wood=3PLP   EXHST   LMT   thoseN-SPC
          'Those [treatments] are both trees [of treatments].'

Demonstrative forms and functions are discussed in §3.1.3. Demonstratives occupy the final modifier position other than complements or adjuncts. If both occur, the exhaustive marker and a demonstrative occur in that order:

(3.105) *ira   huḡru suḡa* **gudu   are**
         thePL all   house EXHST thoseN
         'every one of those houses'

In the absence of *gudu* and any post-head core modifiers the demonstrative may be cliticized directly onto the head itself, as in (3.106)a. If a lexical post-head modifier is present the demonstrative may be cliticized onto that, as occurs twice in (3.106)b.: in the first NP the clitic is attached to a personal name functioning as a post-head core modifier, and in the second to an adjective. If a direct possessor enclitic is present then the demonstrative is cliticized to that ([3.106)c.). Demonstratives do not appear to cliticize to *gudu*.

(3.106)a. *ḡ-e   tu~turi=ña   palu   **mane=de**   sala ge   tikilave*
          NT-3S RD~tell=IMM   two   man=theseR   PN   and PN
          'These two men Sala and Tikilave talked.'

   b. **mane suaragi=ne** *ḡ-e   tufa=ri=u*   **pohe   mata=de**
      man PN=thisR   NT-3S affect=3PLO=CNT   clothes bush=theseR
      'This man Suaragi was giving them these bush clothes.'

   c. *zaho si=ago   ka   ta   muni=ro   **hiba=ḡu=de**   ara*
      go   FOC=youSG LOC   SBD   hide=thoseNV eye=1SGP=theseR I
      'You go, to where you're hidden from these eyes of mine.'

3.3.2.2.2 Possessor complement

NPs in which the head carries possessor-indexing may contain a NP that expresses the possessor. This is subcategorized for by the possessor-indexing, so is a complement. A possessor complement occurs immediately following the demonstrative if one is present in the phrase. Any kind of NP may occur as a possessor. The possessor NPs in (3.107) include as heads personal names, an ordinary nominal, a pronoun, a reflexive, and a location name.

(3.107)a. *e=u   ao   bla   tu~turi=na   **sala   ge   ruruboñi**,*
          3S=be.thus   thisT LMT   RD~tell=3SGP   PN   and   PN
          'So that's the story of Sala and Ruruboñi,

          *tu~turi=di=re   **palu mane ta=u=de***
          RD~tell=3PLP=thoseN   two   man SBD=exist=theseR
          those stories of these two men.'

b. *ia   kolu-seku=na=o   **manei***
theSG snake-tail=3SGP=thatNV he
'that snake's tail of his'

c. *ira   no-mai   kastom mereseni **tagi-mai***
thePL GENP-1INCP custom medicine REFL-1INCP
'our own medicine customs'

d. *n-e-ge   mai   toke=ña   kaike mane=na   **koromata***
RL-3S-PRS come   arrive=IMM   one   man=3SGP   PNLOC
'A man from Koromata was arriving.'

Possessors may be expressed by prepositional adjuncts instead of nominal complements, with no possessor-indexing. This is discussed in §3.3.2.2.3.1.

3.3.2.2.3 Adnominal adjuncts

The NP may contain an adjunct. This may be a prepositional phrase, a deictic locative, a place name, a personal name, or a relative clause. The adjunct position follows that of the possessor complement.

3.3.2.2.3.1 Adnominal prepositional adjuncts

A NP may be modified by a prepositional phrase. Only one true preposition, *ka*, exists in Kokota, with a very broad locative function. PPs may function as adverbial or sentential modifiers, or adnominally. As an adnominal adjunct its functions range from identifying a physical location to identifying a possessor. An adnominal PP may locate the head noun in a particular physical location:

(3.108) *ia   mavitu   **ka ia   ḡilu=na   nau***
theSG community LOC theSG inside=3SGP place
'the community within the village'

More commonly it indicates the possessor of the NP head.

(3.109)a. *padagi=ne **ka gai***   *e   keha   za~zaho=na=na   bo*
shrine=thisR LOC weEXC 3S NSP RD~go=3SGP=thatN   CNT
'Our shrine has a different way.'

b. *t=au=la   ke   nhogi   ia   lehe **ka suaragi**...*
SBD=exist=CND PFV payback theSG die LOC PN...
'If that is so we will payback the death of Suaragi...'

As (3.109)b. demonstrates, the possessed head does not need to be a physical object. Prepositional possession is discussed in §5.7.

3.3.2.2.3.2 Deictic locatives as adnominal adjunct

An adverbial phrase with a deictic locative head (AP$_{DLOC}$) may occur as an adnominal adjunct. In (3.110) the nominal head *ḡahipa* is modified by a deictic locative phrase with the head *sarelau* (itself modified by a location name). Deictic locatives are discussed in detail in §4.2.1.

(3.110) *mala=na=re*   *au*   *ka*   **ḡahipa sare-lau**   **lego**
footprint=3SGP=thoseN exist   LOC stone   thereP-SPC   PNLOC
'Those footprints of his are in the stone there at Lego.'

3.3.2.2.3.3 Location names as adnominal adjunct

Place names may occur in post-head core modifier position. However, locative modification of a NP may also occur by means of a locative adjunct consisting of a location name. The syntactic behavior of a location name with an adnominal adjunct function, as with the adverbial construction, directly parallels that of a locative prepositional phrase, but does not involve a preposition. A locative adjunct of this kind may function as a pseudo-locative possessor, as in (3.111)a. (see §5.7), or the actual name of a location, as in (3.111)b.

(3.111)a. *e=u*   *mane ide*   **kokota** *n-e-ke*   *kulu*   *tarai*
3S=be.thus man   theseR   PNLOC   RL-3S-PFV   be.first   pray
'So these Kokota people were the first to start prayer.'

   b. *zemesi* *e*   *au*   *ka*   *nau*   *ine*   **goveo**
PN   3S exist LOC place thisR   PNLOC
'James lives in this village Goveo.'

In (3.111) the location names can be seen to be adjuncts, not core modifiers, as they follow the demonstratives. Demonstratives are outer modifiers, so locative core modifiers precede any demonstrative present (as [3.94]a. and c. show).

3.3.2.2.3.4 Local noun adjuncts

Local nouns (see §4.4) primarily function as a locative adjunct. However, they may function as a NP core modifier (see §3.3.1.2.4):

(3.112)a. *ḡ-e*   *la*   *toke=na*   *ka*   *titili*   *are-lau*   **fate**   *e=u*
NT-3S go   arrive=thatN LOC *titili*   thoseN-SPC   above   3S=be.thus
'They arrived at those standing stones up there.'

   b. *da*   *mala rereo=u...*   *ka*   *nau*   *ao-hi*   **pari**
1INCS PURP shield=CNT   LOC place thisT-EMPH   below
'We will be the shield... in this place below.'

It appears that as an adnominal adjunct a NLOC occurs alone, without any modifiers of its own.

3.3.2.2.3.5 Personal name adjuncts

Like location names, personal names typically occur as core modifiers, but may also occur as an adnominal adjunct.

(3.113) *palu   mane   aro   **sala ge ruruboñi***
         two   man   theseT PN   and   PN
         'those two men Sala and Ruruboñi'

Again the relative positions of the demonstrative *aro* and the personal name demonstrate that in this example the PN′ is outside the NP core.

3.3.2.2.3.6 Relative clauses

The internal structure of relative clauses is discussed in §10.2.3.4. However, their location within the NP can be usefully discussed here. Reduced relative clauses consisting of a single stative verb, including the existential verb *au*, the subject of which is the head noun, occur as an immediate post-core modifier. Relative clauses are discussed in §10.2.3, but broadly two kinds of relative clauses exist: those marked with the subordinator *ta* (as in [3.114]b. line 3), and those that are zero marked but have a modal/subject particle ([3.114]b. line 2).

(3.114) ...*nafu=na   are   bla   ḡ-e-la   ge-mai   mitia*
         base=3SGP thoseN LMT NT-3S-go CNSM-1EXCP meat
         '...because only those were those meats

         n-e-ke=u=re   *gai   ira   nakoni zuzufra*
         RL-3S-PFV=be.thus=thoseN   weEXC thePL person black
         that were like that of us black people,

         ta   aḡe   hod-i=Ø   fakamo=na   gai
         SBD go   take-TR=3SGO   always=thatN weEXC
         that we would always take.'

In (3.114)b. line 1 the relative clause precedes, not follows, the demonstrative, and the demonstrative is cliticized to the relative clause. However, the nominal head *mitia* in line 1 is in fact modified by two relative clauses, the second occurring in line 3. This second, full, relative clause contrasts syntactically with the reduced relative clause in line 1. Instead of occurring before the demonstrative it occurs as the final modifier in the NP, following not only the demonstrative, but also a complement possessor NP.

The clausal demonstratives discussed in §3.1.3.3 are syntactically, though perhaps not functionally, reduced relative clauses (i.e., RELCs of the immediate post-core type). In (3.115) the head *mane* 'man' is modified by a reduced relative clause consisting of the subordinator *ta* cliticized to the existential verb *au*, with the demonstrative *ine* also cliticized to the verb.

(3.115) *naitu toke n-e   lao ka   mane t=au=ine*
         devil arrive RL-3S go   LOC man   SBD=exist=thisR
         'the arriving devils of this man'

Reduced relative clauses functioning as demonstratives occur frequently in discourse. Such forms are clearly a ritualized and somewhat semantically bleached use of this reduced relative clause type.

Reduced relative clauses are limited to those consisting of a single subordinated lexeme. Relative clauses of greater internal complexity may only occur in NP final position. In (3.116)a. the relative clause follows both a demonstrative, and the limiter *bla*. In (3.116)b. line 2 two conjoined full relative clauses follow the clausal demonstrative in line 1 and modify a single head (*ḡazu*). In line 4 a full relative clause again occurs NP-finally and follows a clausal demonstrative.

(3.116)a. *teo   mereseni tehi-u   ara,*
           not.exist medicine many-CRD I
           'I don't have many medicines,

           marha-pau ana   bla ta   tahe aḡe=i=na
           hurt-head thatN LMT SBD tell go=3SGO=thatN
           just that headache that I will tell.'

        b. *ta   la hod-i=∅=la   gai   ḡazu   t=au=o*
           SBD go take-TR=3SGO=CND weEXC wood   SBD=exist=thatNV
           'If we take that tree

           ta   fa ku~kumai=ni=u   ba   ta   fa siri la=i=u
           SBD CS RD~drink=3SGO=CNT   ALT SBD CS smell go=3SGO=CNT
           that is to drink or to smell

           ka   nakoni t=au=o
           LOC person SBD=exist=thatNV
           to that person

           ta   toke=i   t=au=o   malaria,
           SBD arrive=3SGO SBD=exist=thatNV malaria
           who has got that malaria,

> *boka   ke   aḡe keli   bo   bla*
> be.able PFV   go   be.good   CNT   LMT
> they are simply able to get well.'

No examples exist in my corpus of a reduced relative clause modifying a head that is also modified by the exhaustive marker *gudu*. There is no immediately apparent reason why they should not cooccur, but as no examples are available it is not clear whether they may, and if so, in what order.

3.3.2.2.4 Post-core modifier structure

The possessor NP, being a complement, is closer to the core than, and therefore precedes, any adjuncts. In (3.117) three post-core modifiers are present. The innermost is the demonstrative *aro*. This is followed by the possessor complement (in this case a PN$_{LOC}$), with the PN' adjunct occurring phrase finally.

(3.117)   ...*mane=di   **aro   fitupoḡu sala ge   ruruboñi***
           man=3PLP theseT PNLOC   PN   and   PN
           '...these men of Fitupoḡu, Sala and Ruruboñi'

As (3.114)b. shows, a full relative clause also follows a possessor complement if one is present. In (3.118) a full relative clause follows an adjunct (a local noun).

(3.118)   *n-e-ke   au=gu   parahaḡala ade ka   vuhuku   **ine   fate***
           RL-3S-PFV exist=CNT giant   here LOC mountain thisR   above
           'The giant was living here on this mountain above,

           n-e-ke   au=na=u   nhagarai dou=na
           RL-3S-PFV exist=thatN=CNT banyan   be.big=thatN
           where there was that big banyan tree.'

The evidence of (3.114)b., (3.117), and (3.118) reveals that adjuncts follow the possessor complement, while full relative clauses follow both. The sequence of post-core modifiers is therefore as shown in (3.119). Note that the order of the exhaustive marker and inner of the two relative clause positions is not known.

(3.119)   (RELC)/(EXHST) + (DEM) + (NP$_{PSSR}$) + $\begin{cases} \text{(PP)} \\ \text{(AP}_{DLOC}) + \text{(RELC)} \\ \text{(PN}_{LOC}) \\ \text{(PN)} \end{cases}$

3.3.3 Multiple head NPs

A series of nominal heads with modifiers can be linked to form a complex NP:

(3.120)a. *ḡ-e   mai   la   keha mane mariñi keha mane hoḡrano*
NT-3S come CND NSP man PNLOC NSP man PNLOC
'If some Maringe man [or] some Hograno man came,

ta   mhagu=i=na   an-lau
SBD fear=3SGO=thatN thatN-SPC
that you might be afraid of.'

b. *la hure kota=i   n-e=u   hinage*
go carry go.ashore=3SGO RL-3S=be.thus boat
'...they carried the canoe ashore,

mane mariñi   ge   mane ḡao
man PNLOC and man PNLOC
the Maringe people and the Gao people.'

Typically no conjunction links such constituents; however, the conjunction *ge* may intervene, as in (3.120)b. Full relative clauses have scope over all constituents in strings like these. In (3.121) the relative clause in the first line has scope over all three of the preceding nouns.

(3.121)   *ira   mavitu,   ira   nakoni, ira   suli*
thePL community thePL person thePL child
'The community, the people, the children

ta   au   ka=ia   nau   ana
SBD exist LOC=theSG place thatN
that live in that village...'

The scope of the relative clauses in sentences such as this, coupled with the presence of non-core modifiers modifying each head noun, indicate that a NP may consist of one or more constituents smaller than a NP, but larger than a N', i.e., a N''. Consequently the post-core modifier sequence given in (3.119) does not accurately reflect syntactic structure, as the final RELC is not present in the same level of the hierarchy. The structure of a NP is thus:

(3.122)   NP →   N'' + ([CONJ] + N'')* + (RELC)

3.3.4 Summary of NP structure

A NP with a lexical nominal head may consist minimally of a core consisting of a single noun with no modifiers, and maximally of a sequence of N''s, each consisting of a core containing a head plus several pre- and post-head modifiers, along with a number of pre- and post-core modifier particles, a possessor complement, and an adjunct, all modified by a full relative clause. In summary:

113

(3.123)a. NP → N″ + ([CONJ] + N″)* + (RELC)

    b. N″ → (ART) + (NSP) + (QUANT) + N′ + (RELC)/(EXHST)

$$+ (DEM) + (NP_{PSSR}) + \begin{cases} (PP) \\ (AP_{DLOC}) \\ (PN_{LOC}) \\ (PN) \end{cases}$$

    c. QUANT → $\begin{cases} NUM \\ ORD \\ \textit{huḡru} \\ \textit{(le)legu} \end{cases}$

    d. N′ → (MULT) + N + $\begin{cases} (ADJ) \\ (V_{STATIVE)} \\ (N) \\ (PN) \\ (PN_{LOC}) \\ (N_{LOC}) \\ (N_{RFLX}) \end{cases}$ + (PSSR)

    e. ORD → $\textit{fa}$ + NUM

3.4 Minor NP types

3.4.1 NPs with pronominal heads

Within clause-level syntax, NPs with a pronominal head behave in the same way as NPs with other nominal heads. However, the internal structure of pronominal headed NPs differs from that of other NP types. Consequently a subtype of the NP in Kokota is the NP_{PRO}.

A NP_{PRO} consists of a pronoun head and one modifier position. This modifier position may be filled by a numerical specifier, the exhaustive marker $gudu$, an embedded NP specifying the identity of the pronominal referent, or a deictic locative phrase.

3.4.1.1 Pronominal head

The head of a NP_{PRO} is a single pronoun lexeme, the forms and categories of which are discussed in detail in §3.1.2. Pronoun lexemes distinguish the person categories first exclusive, first inclusive, second and third persons, and the number categories singular, dual, trial, and plural. Other numerical specification is made by modification of the phrasal head.

3.4.1.2 Pronominal number specification

Pronominal number marking is discussed in detail in §3.1.2.2.1. Unlike in nominal-headed NPs, number specification in a NP$_{PRO}$ follows the head, not precedes it. Furthermore, specification involves numbers in their cardinal (and thus nominal) form. NP$_{PRO}$ number specification therefore involves modifying the pronominal head with a post-head nominal.

(3.124) gai **fnoto-u** n-a birho
we four-CRD RL-1EXCS sleep
'We four are sleeping.'

For obvious semantic reasons number specification above three does not occur with singular, dual, or trial pronoun forms. A constraint on redundancy in pronoun number marking prohibits the marking of dual pronouns with the number specifier for 'two'. As noted in §3.1.2.2.1, numerical specification of three is possible as an alternative to a trial pronoun, but again redundancy prohibits cooccurrence of a trial pronoun with number specification for 'three'.

3.4.1.3 Exhaustive marking

The exhaustive marker *gudu* may modify pronouns, indicating that the referent group includes all potential members:

(3.125) gai **gudu** n-a-ke fakae=ni mane ana
weEXC all RL-1EXCS-PFV see=3SGO man thatN
'We all saw that man.'

In third person, *gudu* may only occur with the plural form *maneri*, and not with the form *rei*. The distinction between *maneri* and *rei* is discussed in §3.1.2.2.1.

3.4.1.4 NP specification of pronouns

An ordinary nominal NP can be embedded in a NP$_{PRO}$, specifying details of the referent. While such a NP may consist of a single noun, as in (3.126)a., NPs of any complexity may occur, including pre- or post-head, core, or outer modifiers.

(3.126)a. ...ta=ke hoda toke=ḡai=ña gai-palu **tati**
SBD=PFV take arrive=1EXCO=IMM weEXC-two mother&baby
'...that [you] will take us back, mother and baby.'

b. ka gai **ira** **nakoni zuzufra**
LOC weINC thePL person black
'With us black people,

115

> *tana   nogoi naitu tahi ke   aḡe=u=ni=u*
> then   VOC   devil sea PFV   go=be.thus=3SGO=CNT
> then man!, 'sea devil' is what it's called.'

c. *gau   **mane huhurañi=de**   zaho koko=ni   huhurañi*
   youPL man   PNLOC=theseR   go   leave=3SGO PNLOC
   'You Huhurangi people leave Huhurangi.'

d. *n-e-ke   kave   mai=ña   fate,*
   RL-3S-PFV   descend come=IMM above
   'He came down from heaven,

   *gu=da   gita   **ira   huḡru nakoni***
   CNTX=1INCP weINC   thePL all   person
   for all us people.'

e. *tana aḡe=na   hage=ni=ña   sare-lau   ia   hinage*
   then go=thatN ascend=3SGO=IMM thereP-SPC theSG boat
   'Then they brought up the canoe there,

   *maneri **gaha   mane=de***
   they   five   man=theseR
   these five men.'

3.4.1.5 Personal name specification of pronouns

A dual or trial pronoun may be modified by a personal name to indicate that the named individual is included in the pronominal reference. This only occurs when the named individual is not present at the time of speaking.

(3.127)a. *gai-palu   **belama***   b. *gita-tilo   **hugo***
        weEXC-two PN   weINC-three PN
        'we, Belama and I'   'we three, you and I and Hugo'

With trial pronouns two individuals can be named if neither is present, demonstrating that NP_PRO is modified by a PN', as shown in (3.128).

(3.128)   *gau-tilo   **riva ge   hugo***
        youPL-three PN   and PN
        'you three, [you,] Riva, and Hugo'

Personal name specification of NP_PRO only occurs where the group includes the addressee and/or speaker. It does not appear to apply to third person categories:

(3.129)   *rei-palu   riva   ge   hugo*
'they two Riva and Hugo'

3.4.1.6 Locative specification of pronouns

Pronouns may be modified by a deictic spatial locative phrase (see §4.2.1).

(3.130)a.   *...keha   mereseni   ka   gai   **ade   kokota***
            NSP   medicine   LOC   weINC here   PNLOC
            '...some medicines of us here in Kokota'

   b.   *gau   **ade paka**, fafra   mai   gau*
        youPL   here   west   be.quick come   youPL
        'You here in the west, come quickly.'

3.4.1.7 NP$_{PRO}$ structure

Unlike nominal-headed NPs, only one modifier position exists in the NP$_{PRO}$. All the NP$_{PRO}$ modifiers discussed above occur in this position:

(3.131)   NP$_{PRO}$ →   PRO + $\begin{cases} \text{(CRD)} \\ \text{(EXHST)} \\ \text{(NP)} \\ \text{(PN}') \\ \text{(AP}_{DLOC}) \end{cases}$

3.4.2 Indirect possessor-indexing NPs

Possession is discussed in Chapter 5. The syntactic status of NPs with indirect possessor-indexing are discussed here.

3.4.2.1 Indirect possessor-indexing host as head

Indirect possessor-indexing hosts in Oceanic languages are often described as classifiers. However, these hosts in Kokota do not satisfy criteria for classifier status. They occur with almost any common noun (subject to pragmatic or semantic compatibility), comprise a small closed class of items, do not function primarily to individuate referents, and may occur in non-referential NPs (see [5.65] below), each conflicting with key criteria for classifier status (Palmer and Brown 2007:201–205). The indirect hosts do, however, satisfy key criteria for headhood: morphosyntactic locushood, obligatoriness, category determinance, and distributional equivalence (Palmer and Brown 2007:205–207).

By hosting possessor-indexing, indirect hosts are the morphosyntactic locus of the NP in which they occur, in the same way as directly possessor-indexing

117

nouns, as they mark the relation between that NP and the external possessor. Moreover, indirect possessor-indexing hosts in Kokota are obligatory, while the adjacent fully specified possessum noun is optional, as in (3.132)b. This does not simply involve elision of a possessum noun. Instead, the object NP can be fully interpreted without recourse to a recoverable nominal referent. No possessum noun occurs in (3.132)b. because the NP is non-referential.

(3.132)a. *n-e*   *ñha=di*   *manei*   **ge-ḡu**   *kaku=ro*
        RL-3S eat=3PLO he   CNSM-1SGP banana=thoseNV
        'He ate my bananas.'

     b. *n-e*   *ñha=di*   *manei*   **ge-ḡu=ro**
        RL-3S eat=3PLO he   CNSM-1SGP=thoseNV
        'He ate my food.'

     c. *n-e*   *ñha=di*   *manei*   **mala-ñhau=ro**
        RL-3S eat=3PLO he   PURP-eat=thoseNV
        'He ate that food.'

Because indirect possessor-indexing hosts are the only obligatory element in phrases in which they occur, they must logically also be the category determinants for those phrases.

They are also distributionally equivalent to nouns. The indexed host in (3.132)b. has the same distribution as the object noun in (3.132)c., as both occur as the sole overt form in an object NP. In addition, an indexed host may be followed by a bare N specifiying the nature of the referent, as in (3.133)a., directly paralleling the modification of lexical nouns with a single bare N specifying in more detail the nature of the head's referent, as in (3.133)b. (See §3.3.1.2.1).

(3.133)a. **ge-ḡu**   **kaku=ro**
        CNSM-1SGP   banana=thoseNV
        'my bananas'

     b. **mane**   **vave=ro**
        man   in.law=thoseNV
        'those in-laws'

Finally, possessor-indexing hosts are distributionally equivalent to lexical nouns in their participation in incorporation. In (3.132) the object is not incorporated, as shown by the object enclitic on the verb and VSO order. In (3.134)a. the noun is incorporated, as shown by the VOS order and lack of object enclitic. As (3.134)b.–c. show, an indexed host can participate in incorporation, with or without a possessum noun. The host in (3.134)c. is distributionally equivalent to the noun in (3.134)a. (See §6.4.2 on incorporation of possessor-indexed forms.)

(3.134)a. *n-a   ñhau   **kaku**   ara*
        3S-RL eat   banana I
        'I'm eating bananas.'

    b. *n-a   ñhau   **ge-ḡu**   **kaku**   ara*
        3S-RL eat   CNSM-1SGP banana   I
        'I'm eating my bananas.'

    c. *n-a   ñhau   **ge-ḡu**   ara*
        3S-RL eat   CNSM-1SGP I
        'I'm eating my food.'

In NPs displaying indirect possession it is therefore the possessor-indexing host that is the syntactic head. The phrase is a NP$_{POSS}$.

3.4.2.2 NP$_{POSS}$ structure

In phrases displaying indirect possessor-indexing the lexical possessum noun is an adjunct specifying the exact nature of the possessed item, in the same way as the bare N adjunct on a lexical noun head in (3.133)b. The possessor NP, however, is a complement of the possessor-indexing morphology (see §5.9.2). The structure of a NP$_{POSS}$ is, therefore, a highly simplified version of the common noun NP structure in (3.123):

(3.135)a. NP$_{POSS}$ →   N'$_{POSS}$ + (NP$_{PSSR}$)
     b. N'$_{POSS}$ →   N + (N)

3.4.3 NPs with reflexive head

A reflexive argument is expressed by a possessor-indexed reflexive base (see §3.1.2.3). While reflexives typically occur without any modification, a NP adjunct may occur. This may have a nominal or pronominal head:

(3.136)a. *ira   mereseni ka   tagi-mai **gai**   **nakoni zuzufra***
        thePL medicine LOC REFL-1EXCP weINC person black
        'the medicine of ourselves we black people'

    b. *ira   mereseni ka   tagi-mai **nakoni zuzufra***
        thePL medicine LOC REFL-1EXCP person black
        'the medicine of ourselves we black people'

The reflexive base with a modifier adjunct forms a NP$_{REFL}$:

(3.137)   NP$_{REFL}$ →   REFL + (NP)

3.4.4 NPs with demonstrative head

In addition to their adnominal role, independent demonstratives may function as a clausal argument. In this nominal role they typically occur without any modifiers (other than the suffixed emphatic *-hi*, the specific marker *-lau*, and limiter *=blau*). However, demonstratives may be modified by a single spatial locative form. This may be a deictic locative ([3.138]a.), a local noun ([3.138]b.), or a location name ([3.138]c.). The effect of this modification is to give the demonstrative a locative referent.

(3.138)a.　...*kuru　nakoni　ña　　n-e-ke=u　　　　　ña*
　　　　　　have　person　IMM　RL-3S-PFV=be.thus　IMM

　　　　　aro-hi　　　ade-hi
　　　　　theseT-EMPH　here-EMPH
　　　　　'...these [places] here have people.'

　　　b.　*fa-lehe=ri　mane n-e　mai　au　n-e=u*
　　　　　CS-die=3PLO man　RL-3S　come　exist　RL-3S=be.thus
　　　　　'He killed some of those men who came and were

　　　　　are　　fate　ḡ-e-gu　　　n-e-ke=u
　　　　　thoseN　above　NT-3S=be.thus　NT-3S-PFV=be.thus
　　　　　in those [places] on top.'

　　　c.　...*zaho　ḡ-e　　la　au　　iaro　　hurepelo keha=re*
　　　　　　go　NT-3S　go exist　thosePV　PNLOC　　NSP=thoseN
　　　　　'...some of those went and lived at those Hurepelo [places].'

While the NP$_{DEM}$ typically functions as a locative adjunct, it may function as an argument, as the subject demonstrative in (3.138)a. illustrates. The structure of a demonstrative NP is as follows:

$$
(3.139)\quad NP_{DEM}\ \rightarrow\ DEM + \left\{ \begin{array}{l} (DLOC) \\ (N_{LOC}) \\ (PN_{LOC}) \end{array} \right.
$$

3.4.5 NPs with personal name as head

Personal names occur as the head of a NP consisting of a PN head, optionally modified by a NP adjunct.

(3.140)a.　...*ḡ-e　lisi=ni=u...　　　ka　nomana witili ia　　mane-vaka*
　　　　　　NT-3S　lease=3SGO=CNT　LOC　PN　　　　　　theSG　man-ship
　　　　　'...he leased it...to Norman Wheatley, the white man.'

b. *ia*   *dadara=na*   *zesas* *ia*   **no-mai**   **lod**
  theSG   blood=3SGP   PN   theSG GENP-1EXCP Lord
  'the blood of Jesus our Lord'

A NP$_{PN}$ head may consist of more than one conjoined PN. Either conjunction *ge* or *n-e=u* may link PNs, but *ge* is by far the more common in this context.

(3.141) *...n-e-ke*   *hod-i=Ø=o*   **sala ge** **ruruboñi** *bla...*
        RL-3S-PFV take-TR=3SGO=thatNV PN and PN   LMT
        'Sala and Ruruboñi brought it...'

The operation of conjoined PNs as a single constituent NP$_{PN}$ head involves a N$'_{PN}$ level between PN and NP$_{PN}$. The structure of a NP$_{PN}$ is thus:

(3.142)a. NP$_{PN}$ →   N$'_{PN}$ + (NP)
      b. N$'_{PN}$ →   PN + (CNJ + PN)

3.4.6 NPs with numeral head

Numbers function primarily as pre-head adnominal modifiers. However, as discussed in §3.2.2.2.1.4, numerals may be nominalized as cardinals, and function as a nominal, and typically occur without any modification, as in (3.143)a. However, a single post-head modifier position exists in which a noun may occur, specifying the class of entities the numerical referent belongs to, as in (3.143)b.

(3.143)a. **kaike-u** *ara* *ñhau=ni,* **kaike-u** *n-e*   *au*   *blau*
         one-CRD I   eat=3SGO one-CRD RL-3S exist LMT
         'One I ate, one remains.'

      b. *ara* *manahagi=di* **palu-gu** *namhari*
         I   want=3PLO   two-CRD fish
         'I want two fish.'

In (3.143)b. the cardinal is the head, while *namhari* 'fish' indicates the class of entities the speaker wants two of. A more literal translation would be something like "I want two of fish" or "I want a pair of fish". This only superficially resembles the less marked sentence in (3.144), in which the noun is head, and the numeral a pre-head modifier indicating simply the number of referents of the head that the speaker wants.

(3.144) *ara* *manahagi=di* **palu** *namhari*
        I   want=3PLO   two   fish
        'I want two fish.'

The structure of phrases with a cardinal head is:

(3.145)   NP$_{CRD}$ →   CRD + (N)

Ordinals also may function as nominal head (see §3.2.2.2.1.3), once nominalized by direct possessor-indexing. Nominalized ordinals may occur with modifiers in two positions, a post-head noun modifier, and a demonstrative, as in (3.146) where both occur, with the demonstrative cliticized to the noun modifier.

(3.146)   ḡ-e   lao   ña   *fa   palu=na*   ḡazu=na   e=u
          NT-3S   go   IMM   ORD   two=3SGP   wood=thatN   3S=be.thus
          'Go for that second tree.'

Nominalized ordinals typically occur with a demonstrative, particularly when no noun modifier is present; however, it is not obligatory:

(3.147)a. u   heve   ba=ine   ara
           be.thus   what   ALT=thisR   I
           'What will I say

           ta   la=i=na   *fa   palu=na=na*
           SBD   go=3SGO=thatN   ORD   two=3SGP=thatN
           to give that second one?'

       b. *fa   palu=na,*   naitu   sasapu   e=ni
          ORD   two=3SGP   devil   pass   3S=3SGO
          'The second, "passing devil" it's called.'

A phrase with an ordinal head involves an ordinal number plus a direct possessor enclitic as the phrasal core, followed by an optional complement noun (a bare N not a full NP or N′), and demonstrative:

(3.148)a. NP$_{ORD}$ →   N′$_{ORD}$ + (N) + (DEM)
       b. N′$_{ORD}$ →   ORD + PSSR

3.5 Nominal adjunct types

Proper nouns naming physical locations may function as core arguments. Typically, however, they function as adjuncts. They are not phrasal heads, and no modification of PN$_{LOC}$s occurs. Location names are discussed further in §4.3.

Contextualizer and associative nouns function only as clausal adjuncts, and in the case of the contextualizer *yu-*, as a prepositional complement. Contextualizer nouns are discussed in §4.5 and the associative noun in §4.6.

CHAPTER 4: OBLIQUES AND CLAUSE-LEVEL ADJUNCTS

The clausal and sentential functions and syntactic behavior of PPs and adjuncts are discussed in §6.7.1, §8.2.2 and §8.6. This chapter discusses the internal structure of constituents that primarily express adjuncts, including PPs, deictic locatives, location names, and local, contextualizer, and associative noun.

4.1 Prepositional phrases

Only one true preposition, *ka*, exists in Kokota, with a general locative function. Prepositional phrases have a variety of adverbial and adnominal functions, discussed in §6.7.1 and §3.3.2.2.3.1 respectively. A prepositional phrase consists of a preposition as head, followed by a phrase or subordinated clause as its complement. The prepositional complement may be a NP with as head a common noun head ([4.1]a.), pronoun ([4.1]b.), reflexive ([4.1]c.), personal name ([4.1]d.), local noun ([4.1]e.–f.), or contextualiser ([4.1]g.), or may be a subordinate clause ([4.1]h.):

(4.1) a. *ḡ-e   fa-lehe=i=u   **ka=ia**   **pike   mau=na***
       NT-3S CS-die=3SGO=CNT LOC=theSG piece taro=thatN
       'They killed with that small piece of taro.'

    b. ***ka   gai   ira   nakoni   zuzufra***
       LOC weINC thePL person black
       'With us black people,

       tana   nogoi naitu tahi ke   aḡe=u=ni=u
       then   VOC devil sea PFV   go=be.thus=3SGO=CNT
       then, man!, 'sea devil' is what it's called.'

    c. *ira   mereseni   **ka   tagi-mai   gai   nakoni   zuzufra***
       thePL medicine   LOC REFL-1EXCP weINC person   black
       'the medicine of ourselves we black people'

    d. *kelokolo   ḡ-e   lisi=ni=u   selana...*
       PN   NT-3S   lease=3SGO=CNT PNLOC...
       'Kelokolo leased Selana...

       ka   nomana witili   ia   mane-vaka
       LOC PN   theSG man-ship
       to Norman Wheatley, the white man.'

    e. *manei   n-e   au   **ka   kota=na   suḡa=na***
       he   RL-3S exist LOC outside=3SGP house=thatN
       'He is outside that house.'

f. *ḡ-a   mai=ña   gai   ade   ka   ia   rhuku*
NT-1EXCS come=IMM weEXC here   LOC theSG landward
'We come here to the shore side.'

g. *ara manahagi turi tufa=nigo   ago*
I   want   tell affect=2SGO youSG
'I want to tell you

   ka   gu=na   ia   au   ka   gai...
LOC CNTX=3SGP theSG exist LOC weEXC
about our living...'

h. *zaho si=ago   ka   ta   muni=ro   hiba=ḡu=de   ara*
go FOC=youSG LOC SBD   hide=thoseNV eye=1SGP=theseR I
'You go, to where you're hidden from these eyes of mine.'

Deictic locatives, location names, associative nouns, and NPs with a
demonstrative or cardinal or ordinal numeral as head do not occur as
prepositional complements. The structure of the Prepositional Phrase is thus:

(4.2)   PP   →   P   + $\begin{cases} \text{NP} \\ \text{NP}_{\text{PRO}} \\ \text{NP}_{\text{REFL}} \\ \text{NP}_{\text{PN}} \\ \text{NP}_{\text{LOC}} \\ \text{NP}_{\text{CNTX}} \\ \text{S} \end{cases}$

Ka optionally procliticizes to the first word of its complement. This occurs
commonly with the pronouns *ara* 'I' and *ago* 'youSG'. With these, as with other
forms with an initial /a/, the preposition reduces to *k=*, giving *k=ara* and *k=ago*.

(4.3)   *gai   teo   ḡ-a   mai=u   k=ago   nogoi sala*
weEXC not.exist NT-3S come=CNT LOC=youSG VOC   PN
'We are not coming to you, Sala.'

This cliticization occurs elsewhere, affecting stress assignment (see §2.5.6.3):

(4.4)   *suli=ana   n-e   faroh-i=Ø   mheke=na ká=nihau   ḡazu*
child=thatN RL-3S smite-TR=3SGO dog=thatN LOC=how.many wood
'That child hit that dog with how many sticks?'

The cliticization occurs not only with nominal forms, but also with the first word
in complement clauses. In (4.5) the subordinate clause has no subordinating
particle, and the preposition is cliticized to the modal/subject particle.

(4.5)   *ke pulo e=u   tana   zelu*
           PFV return be.thus then   PNLOC
           'They went back to Zelu,

           ká=n-e-ke   *hure=ro*   *ira*   *tilo*   *tomoko*
           LOC=RL-3S-PFV carry=thoseNV thePL three war.canoe
           to where they had carried the three canoes.'

4.2 Locative adverbs

4.2.1 Deictic spatial locatives

Three deictic spatial locatives exist in the language:

(4.6) a. *ade*   'here'
       b. *sare*   'there (proximal)'
       c. *sara*   'there (distal)'

These occur with a variety of locative modifiers including intrinsic local nouns ([4.7]a.), absolute locatives ([4.7]b.), the locative interrogative ([4.7]c.), location names ([4.7]d.), prepositional phrases ([4.7]e.), and ordinary NPs ([4.7]f.):

(4.7) a. *e la   fufunu ka n-e-ke   au=o   rei-palu **ade fate***
         3S go   begin LOC RL-3S-PFV exist=thatNV they-two here above
         'Start where they two stayed here on top.'

       b. *ḡ-e   koko la=ni=n̄a   **sara   rauru***
         NT-3S leave go=3SGO=IMM thereD   seaward
         'He threw him there seaward.'

       c. ***sara hae*** *manei n-e lisa=i=na   no-ḡu   vilai ana*
         thereD where he   RL-3S put=3SGO=thatN GENP-1SGP knifethatN
         'Where did he put that knife of mine?'

       d. *n-e   au=gu   **ade goveo***
         RL-3S   exist=CNT here PNLOC
         'He's living here in Goveo.'

       e. *n-e-ke   au=gu   parahaḡala **ade ka vuhuku ine***
         RL-3S-PFV exist=CNT giant   here LOC mountain thisR
         'The giant was living here on this mountain

         fate n-e-ke   ***au=na=u***   *nhagarai   dou=na*
         above RL-3S-PFV exist=thatN=CNT banyan   be.big=thatN
         above where there was that big banyan tree.'

f. *gure*   *foro*   *ḡ-e=u=gu*   **ade titili=o**
nut.paste coconut.paste NT-3S=be.thus=CNT here *titili*=thatNV
'[They] made nut and coconut paste here at those standing stones.'

Deictic spatial locatives can therefore be modified by an individual locative form, or by a PP or NP. The structure of the spatial locative phrase is thus:

(4.8)

$$\text{ADVP}_{\text{SLOC}} \rightarrow \text{SLOC} + \left\{ \begin{array}{l} \text{N}_{\text{LOC}} \\ \text{PN}_{\text{LOC}} \\ \text{INTRRG}_{\text{LOC}} \\ \text{NP} \\ \text{PP} \end{array} \right\}$$

Spatial deictic locatives may also be modified morphologically by the emphatic suffix *-hi* or the specific suffix *-lau* (see §3.1.4):

(4.9) a.   ...*kaike*   *mai*   *au*   *gudu*   **ade-hi**   *kokota*
     one   come   exist   EXHST   here-EMPH   PNLOC
     '...together come and all live here at Kokota'

b.   *ḡ-e*   *la posa=u*   **sare-lau**   *ka*   *nau*   *fitupoḡu...*
     NT-3S   go emerge=CNT   thereP-SPCLOC   place   PNLOC
     'They emerged there at the place Fitupoḡu....'

4.2.2 Indefinite spatial locative proform *hae*

The form *hae* functions primarily as a locative interrogative pronoun (see §9.2.2.1.4). However, it also functions as an indefinite spatial locative:

(4.10) a.   *buka are-lau*   *e-ti-ke*   *mala fa za~zaho* **hae**   *ge*   **hae**
      book thoseN-EMPH   3S-NEG-PFV   PURP   CS   RD~go   where   and   where
      'These books will not be for sending just anywhere.'

b.   *ña*   *teo*   *ḡ-a*   *lehe* **hae**
     but   not.exist   NT-1EXCS   die   where
     'But I'm not dying [because of people from] just anywhere.'

When unmodified, as in (4.10), *hae* refers to any unspecified location, somewhat akin to English *just anywhere*. However, *hae* may also be modified to identify in some way the location referred to, as in (4.11). In this context *hae* refers to a specific place, but is indefinite because the actual location of the place is unknown. *Hae* can refer to a single location (as in [4.11]b.) or multiple locations ([4.11]a.), as the postverbal agreement enclitics on the main verbs reveal.

(4.11) a. *da   aḡe   kae=di=u*
      1INCS go see=3PLO=CNT
      'Let's go and see

      hae ta au=re   n-e hure=ri   hinage=re maneri
      where SBD exist=thoseN RL-3S carry=3PLO boat=thoseN they
      where it is that they carried the boats!'

    b. *ara   teo   ḡ-a   lase=i=u*
       I   not.exist NT-1EXCS know=3SGO=CNT
       'I don't know

       hae ta au=na   sitoa=na
       where SBD exist=thatN store=thatN
       where the store is.'

The transparent semantic relationship between *hae*'s functions as an indefinite locative and as a locative interrogative suggests that both represent instances of a single lexical item. In its function as an indefinite proform, and it's relationship (or identity) with the corresponding interrogative form, *hae* resembles the corresponding indefinite personal proform *ihei* (see §3.1.2.2.3).

4.2.3 Deictic temporal locatives

Seven deictic temporal locative forms exist:

(4.12) a. *goino(de)* 'today (realis)'   e. *nariha* 'the day after tomorrow'
     b. *ginai*   'today (irrealis)' f. *narihao* 'the day before yesterday'
     c. *fufugo*   'tomorrow'   g. *tifaro* 'the distant past'
     d. *nhorao* 'yesterday'

The distinction between the two forms glossed as 'today' corresponds to the realis/irrealis distinction. The Kokota day begins and ends with sunrise. *Goinode* (and its optionally shortened version *goino*) refer to the period since the beginning of the day of speaking, up to and including the time of speaking. Thus it equates to what in a tense system would be the recent past (within that day) and the present. The latter component of its meaning often gives it a sense equivalent to 'now', both in the sense of 'right at this moment' ([4.13]a.), and in the broader sense of 'at the present time' as opposed to some other period ([4.13]b.–c.). However, it also covers the past within the same day ([4.13]d.):

(4.13) a. *goinode   n-e   nahani*
      todayRL RL-3S rain
      'It's raining now.'

b. *ḡ-a*   *mai*   *au=gu*   *gai*   **goinode**   *ade*
    NT-1EXCS come   exist=CNT weEXC   todayRL   here
    'So now we come and are living here today.'

c. **tifaro** *ara*   *a*   *lao*   *tarai*   *fakamo le~legu*   *sade*
    before I   1EXCS go   pray   always   RD~follow   Sunday
    'I used to always go to prayer every Sunday,

    ña   **goinode**   *teo*
    but   todayRL   not.exist
    but now I don't.'

d. *turi*   *n-e-ke*   *la=i=o*   *ago*   **goino**
    tell   RL-3S-PFV   go=3SGO=thatNV   youSG   todayRL
    '...that story you told [earlier] today'

The form *ginai* has two functions. It occurs inside the verb complex as a future tense marker, referring to any point in the future no matter how distant. Outside the verb complex the form behaves syntactically in the same way as the other temporal locatives, and refers to the period after the time of speaking within the temporal frame of the day of speaking ([4.14]a.). In this function it often has a sense equivalent to 'later', as in (4.14)b. However, it can also mean 'immediately', with a sense of an about to be realized 'now' ([4.14]c.):

(4.14) a. **ginai**   *ara*   *a*   *lao*   *buala*   *baiu*
       todayIRR   I   1EXCS go   PNLOC   PSBL
       'Today I might go to Buala.'

      b. **ginai**   *fea*   *da*   *toi=ña*
       todayIRR   INIT   1INCS   cook=IMM
       '[Later] today [must come] first before we cook.'

      c. *ai*   *lehe=ña* *gita*   **ginai**
       EXCLM   die=IMM   weINC   todayIRR
       'Oh! We're going to die now.'

Fufugo 'tomorrow' reflects historical reduplication. The unreduplicated form does not occur independently, but occurs in the compound *fugo-nare* 'morning' (*nare* 'day'). In *nhorao* 'yesterday' and *narihao* 'day before yesterday' the final /o/ reflects a fused 'nonvisible' demonstrative clitic *=o*, as *nariha* 'day after tomorrow' suggests. The 'nonvisible' demonstrative often indicates entities that are not visible due to their location in the past, rather than geographic distance. *Tifaro* indicates any time prior to the day before yesterday, although it usually suggests a long time ago. Depending on context this can range from earlier in a person's life ([4.13]c.), to the legendary, historical, or pre-Christian past:

(4.15)   *ka=ira*   *boñihehe* **tifaro**...
        LOC=thePL heathen   before
        'In the heathen time before...'

4.3 Location names

Proper nouns naming physical locations may function as core arguments:

(4.16)   *n-e-ge*   *mai*   *fa nhigo=i=u*
        RL-3S-PRS come CS be.finished=3SGO=CNT
        'He came and finished

        lao   *tabar-i=Ø=na*   **banesokeo**
        go   buy-TR=3SGO=thatN PNLOC
        buying Banesokeo.'

Typically, however, location names function as adjuncts. In that function they do not occur in a PP, instead they occur independently, paralleling an entire PP.

(4.17) a. *n-a-ge*   *zaho* *koko=di*
         RL-1EXCS-PRSgo   leave=3PLO
         'We will be leaving behind

         ira   *ge-mai*   *no-mai*   *e=u*   **huhurañi**
         thePL CNSM-1EXCP GENP-1EXCP 3S=be.thus PNLOC
         our food and our things at Huhurangi.'

    b. *aḡe* *da*   *hage=u*   **fitupoḡu**
         go   1INCS ascend=CNT PNLOC
         'Let's go up to Fitupoḡu.'

Location names are not phrasal heads, and no modification of PN$_{LOC}$s occurs:

(4.18)   *goveo ine/ide*   'this/these Goveo (village)'

Similarly two location names cannot be linked by the conjunction *ge*, which only links forms at the same level of syntactic structure. Location names may be linked by *n-e=u*, but in this context this forms a second clause: (4.19)a. consists of two clauses, literal meaning 'I went to Buala and like that also to Popoheo'.

(4.19) a. *ara n-a-ke*   *lao buala* **n-e=u**   *popoheo*
         I   RL-1EXCS-PFV go   PNLOC RL-3S=be.thus PNLOC
         'I went to Buala and Popoheo.'

    b. *ara nake lao buala **ge** popoheo*

4.4 Local nouns

Local nouns are a subclass of nouns that may be distinguished from other nouns in Kokota in two ways. First, they only function as locative adjuncts, never as core arguments. Second, while ordinary nouns may only function as an oblique within a PP, local nouns may do so without the presence of the preposition.

Two types of local noun occur. One encodes intrinsic and relative spatial relations, the other absolute relations. Intrinsic relations locate the referent in relation to an intrinsic facet of another entity. In *the cat is in front of the TV* the cat is located in relation to the facet of the TV regarded as its front. Relative relations involve a third participant: a viewpoint. The referent of the head is located in relation to another entity from the perspective of a viewpoint. In *the cat is in front of the tree*, the location of the cat depends on the location of the viewer. Absolute relations invoke an independent coordinate system imposed on the referent and entity to which is is related. In *the cat is east of the tree* the cat is located on the basis of the cardinal system, without reference to the location of a viewer or any internal characteristics of the referent (Palmer 2002b:109–110).

4.4.1 Intrinsic and relative locatives

The local nouns in (4.20) express intrinsic and relative spatial relations.

(4.20) a. *pari* 'below, underneath' g. *hotai* 'in the middle'
  b. *fate* 'above, on top' h. *fari hotai* 'between'
  c. *kenu* 'in front' i. *geri* 'beside'
  d. *legu* 'behind'[37] j. *mairi* 'left'
  e. *ḡilu* 'inside' k. *mautu* 'right'
  f. *kota* 'outside'

All local nouns are monomorphemic except for *fari hotai*, which consists of the local noun *hotai* 'middle' preceded by the preposed reciprocal particle. Local nouns may occur alone as an oblique without a preposition. They may indicate a location ([4.21]a.–c.), or a direction ([4.21]d.–e.).

(4.21) a. *t=au=ana*   *n-e*   *au*   **mautu**   *bo*
  SBD=exist=thatN RL-3S exist   right   CNT
  'That's on the right.'

  b. *tana*   *kave*   *mai*   *ka=ia*   *riñata,*   *naboto gase*   **kenu**,
  then   descend come LOC=theSG doorway   ten   woman front
  'Then they come out the door, ten women in front,

---

[37] Some speakers say *legu* 'behind' is a recent term, and that *bete* is the true Kokota term, still used by old people. I did not encounter *bete* in use and it is not in my corpus.

<table>
<tr><td>naboto</td><td>gase</td><td>legu,</td><td>hotai</td><td>rei-palu</td><td>tati</td></tr>
<tr><td>ten</td><td>woman</td><td>behind</td><td>middle</td><td>they-two</td><td>mother&baby</td></tr>
</table>

ten women behind, in the middle the mother and baby.'

c. *manei n-e   ri~riso   **mairi***
   he   RL-3S   RD~write   left
   'He writes left.' [i.e., He is left handed.]

d. *n-e   lao=u   **fate***
   RL-3S   go=CNT   above
   'He's going up on top.'

e. *ara n-a   kave   **kota***
   I   RL-1EXCS descend outside
   'I went outside [the house].'

Local nouns may occur with possessor-indexing as an adjunct without a preposition. When possessor-indexing is present a possessor NP is also usually present, but is not obligatory if the possessor is understood, as in (4.22)b.

(4.22) a. *ara n-a   korho namhari **kenu=mu** ago*
          I   RL-1EXCS pull fish   front=2SGP youSG
          'I caught fish in front of you.' [i.e., sitting in front of you in a boat]

       b. *manei n-e   lao **mairi=na** bo*
          he   RL-3S   go   left=3SGP   CNT
          'He went to the left side [of it].'

       c. *n-e   fike=u   manei **ḡilu=na**   kaike komhu*
          RL-3S   cut.wood=CNT he   inside=3SGPone year
          'He cut firewood for a year.'

       d. *mama pita   n-e-ke   ooe=na   **legu=na**   rodoki*
          father PN   RL-3S-PFV   talk=thatN behind=3SGP   PN
          'Father Peter spoke after Rodoki.'

Legu 'behind' and *ḡilu* 'inside' have a temporal as well as spatial function. In (4.22)c. *ḡilu* has a durational function, while in (4.22)d. *legu* means 'after' in time, not space. This creates potential ambiguity. In (4.22)d. the first clause sets up a temporal framework, so *legu* can only be interpreted with its temporal function. However, in (4.23) temporal and spatial readings are both possible.

(4.23)   *n-e   pulo   mai   **legu=ḡu**   ara*
         RL-3S   return come behind=1SGP   I
         'He came back after me [in time]/behind me [in space].'

Although local nouns freely occur as the head of a locative adjunct, they occur equally freely with the same functions, as a complement of the preposition *ka*.

(4.24) a. *e-ke   au   ka hotai   gegere=ro*
3S-PFV exist LOC middle forest=thoseNV
'They lived in the middle of the forest.'

    b. *e teo   ḡ-e-ke   au   ka geri   tahi=de*
3S not.exist NT-3S-PFV exist LOC beside sea=theseR
'They didn't live beside the sea.'

    c. *t=au=o   ka pari   ḡazu=o*
SBD=exist=thatNV LOC below wood=thatNV
'It's under that tree.'

    d. *ta mai la naitu tahi, ta mai ka ia   hotai   tahi...*
SBD come CND devil sea SBD come LOC theSG middle sea
'If a sea devil comes, if it comes from the middle of the sea...'

As with prepositionless local nouns, possessor-indexing may be present:

(4.25) a. *n-e   au   ka mairi=ḡu   ara*
RL-3S exist LOC left=1SGP   I
'It's at my left [must be immediately to hand].'

    b. *manei n-e   au ka kota=na   suḡa=na*
he   RL-3S exist LOC outside=3SGP house=thatN
'He is outside that house.'

    c. *toi-kame ana n-e   au ka fari   hotai=di   buti   are*
cook-arm thatN RL-3S exist LOC RECP middle=3PLP shoe thoseN
'That centipede is between those shoes.'

    d. *ta aḡe e=u   la ka=ia   ḡilu=na   tahi...*
SBD go 3S=be.thus CND LOC=theSG inside=3SGP sea
'If it goes into the sea...'

The difference in usage between local noun locatives with and without the preposition seems to be stylistic. Syntactically the preposition adds an additional layer to the structure in which the preposition functions as the head of a PP, with as its complement a phrase with a NLOC head. Whether it occurs within a PP or independently, a NLOC phrase has the same structure with the exception that in a PP the NLOC may be preceded by an article (as in [4.24]d. and [4.25]d.). No other modification is possible. The NP$_{LOC}$ has the following structure:

(4.26)   NP$_{LOC}$ →   (ART)   +   N'$_{LOC}$
           N'$_{LOC}$ →   N$_{LOC}$ +   (PSSR   +   [NP$_{PSSR}$])

The article cannot occur when the N$_{LOC}$ is a sentential adjunct, only when it is a prepositional complement. This means that the prepositional complement is a NP$_{LOC}$, while the sentential adjunct is not a NP but a N'$_{LOC}$.

Several local noun forms occur with other semantically related functions. *Legu* ('behind') also functions as a verb meaning 'follow' and a quantifier meaning 'every'; and *kenu* ('front') is also a verb meaning 'be foremost, be in front'. *Kota* ('outside') also functions as a verb, usually translated by speakers as 'go ashore'. However, it also occurs meaning 'get out of [a tree]', and possibly 'go out of [a house]' (the occurrence in [4.21]e. may, in fact, be a serial verb, although this verb could not occur alone with that meaning—the usual verb for going out of a house [or boat] is *kave* 'descend'). These have a unifying semantic sense of moving onto land (houses are raised on stilts so one climbs down out of them onto the ground). However, they also appear to have a unifying sense of moving outside something (a body of water, a tree), but the verb does not appear to be used to simply mean 'go outside'. The other local nouns appear to function only as local nouns.

Related to the temporal function in (4.22)c.–d. and (4.23), *legu* and *ḡilu* differ from other local nouns in that they may have as complement a nominalized clause. Like other local nouns the complement of *legu* or *ḡilu* may be a NP (as shown above). However, while other local nouns subcategorize only for a NP complement, *legu* and *ḡilu* subcategorize for a NP or nominalized clause complement. With a complement clause, the reading is always temporal, not spatial. With *legu* the subordinate clause expresses an event that precedes the main clause event, revealing the semantic relationship between the local noun and the verbal function of *legu* 'follow'. With *ḡilu* the complement clause expresses an event during which the main clause event occurs.

(4.27) a. ***legu=na***   *toka kave*   *ana*   *gita*   *ḡazu*   *ana*   *ge*
           behind=3SGP chop descend thatN weINC wood thatN SEQ
           'After we have cut down the tree,

           ḡ-o   *fike*   *no-u*   *ḡazu=n̄a*   *ago*
           NT-2S cut.firewood GENP-2SGP wood=IMM youSG
           you can make your firewood.'

       b. *ara*   *n-a*   *tehi*   *ta*   *marhi=au=re*
           I   RL-1EXCS be.many   SBD hurt=1SGO=thoseN
           'I have many pains

133

> ka **legu=na**   *faroho=nau=o*   *maneri*
> LOC behind=3SGP   smite=1SGO=thatNV   they
> since they were hitting me.'

    c. *fufunu*   *ka*   *keli-kava=o*   *n-e*   *la*   *mai=u*
       begin   LOC be.good-earth=thatNV   RL-3S go   come=CNT
       'Start from the peace [and] it [the story] comes

> ka **ḡilu=na**   *toke=i=a*   *ta*   *dia*
> LOC inside=3SGP   arrive=3SGO=theSG   SBD be.bad
> to reaching the badness.'

4.4.2 Absolute locatives

Four absolute locative terms relating to the horizontal domain exist in Kokota:

(4.28) a. *rauru*   'seaward'
       b. *rhuku*   'landward'
       c. *paka*   'west'⎫ The east-west axis runs northwest-southeast
       d. *fona*   'east' ⎭ slightly less than 45° off cardinal East-West

These lexify directions on a pair of crossed axes. Kokota is spoken on roughly straight coastline running northwest to southeast on both sides of Santa Isabel. The *paka-fona* axis corresponds to a line parallel to a regularized coastal line, the *rhuku-rauru* axis to a line crossing the coast at right angles. *Rauru* lexifies a direction from the mountainous interior towards the coast, from the village to the shore, and away from the shore out to sea. The opposite, *rhuku*, lexifies a direction from the sea towards land and then on into the interior. The *paka-fona* axis crosses that at right angles: *fona* being the direction closest to the location of the rising sun, and *paka* the direction closest to that of the setting sun. This system was schematized for Goveo village by an informant, James Tikani.

FIGURE 1: KOKOTA ABSOLUTE DIRECTIONAL SCHEMA.

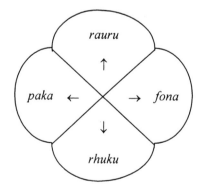

This shows that these directional terms refer to quadrants not vectors (Palmer 2002b:123–125), meaning that each direction refers to a 45° chunk of the horizontal domain (which the 'axis' bisects). Directions on the *paka-fona* axis are unbounded: *paka* continues beyond Santa Isbel to Choiseul, Bougainville, and beyond, and *fona* to Malaita and beyond. The direction expressed by *rauru* is also unbounded, crossing the coast and continuing out to sea indefinitely. *Rhuku*, however, appears to be bounded, continuing inland to a point somewhere in the center of the island. Once that point is reached and a descent towards the other side of the island begins, the direction would again be *rauru* 'seaward'. Figure 1 represents the absolute spatial system as it applies in Goveo and Sisiga, on the northwest coast. The system as it applies in Hurepelo on the southwest coast, on the opposite side of the island, differs, as the relationship between the axes differs. In Goveo and Sisiga southwest is landward and northwest seaward. In Hurepelo the opposite is the case. As a result, the *rauru-rhuku* axis interacts with the *paka-fona* axis in Hurepelo in a way that is a direct mirror image of that shown in Figure 1. In Goveo when one is facing *rauru*, *fona* is on your right. In Hurepelo it is on your left. This is not a dialect difference, but the effect of environmental constraints on an environmentally sensitive directional system.

These absolute directional terms may indicate location (as in [4.29]), or direction of motion (4.30):

(4.29)   *da   la   au=gu   **rhuku***
           1INCS go   exist=CNT landward
           'We are living on the shore side [i.e., in the bush].'

      b.   *ana   **rauru**   bo*
           thatN   seaward   CNT
           'It's (on the) seaward (side of the house).'
           [Response to the question 'Where is your cookhouse?']

(4.30) a. *gai   lao   **fona**   buala*
           weEXCgo   east   PNLOC
           'We're going east to Buala.'

      b.   *kamo   **rauru**   bo   s=ago*
           go.across seaward   CNT   FOC=youSG
           'Paddle-turn seaward, you.' [Instruction to paddle so a canoe that is moving westward will change course and move directly out to sea.]

They may also indicate the location of motion, rather than its direction:

(4.31)   *bili   n-e-ke   mai   **rauru**   bo,*
           PN   RL-3S-PFV   come   seaward   CNT
           'Billy came on the sea side,

> ago   n-e-ke   lao **rhuku**   bo
> youSG RL-3S-PFV   go   landward CNT
> you went on the land side.'

In (4.31) my informant James explains how Billy and I missed each other. I went to Billy's house from James's house, which faces seaward, by exiting on the seaward side but going around the back (the landward side) of the house and passed along the back (landward side) of the row of houses to Billy's house. At the same time Billy went from his house to James's house along the front (seaward side) of the row of houses. Here the absolute terms do not indicate the direction of the motion, but its location in the village in relation to the side of the row of houses. Both Billy's coming and my going took place parallel to the coast, along the *paka-fona* axis, not along the *rhuku-rauru* axis.

Although the four absolute terms under discussion here apply only in the horizontal domain, the verbs *hage* 'ascend', and *kave* 'descend' are used systematically in association with the directions expressed by the absolute terms. In fact, *hage* and *kave* each has a meaning applicable in each of the two horizontal and one vertical axes:

TABLE 4.1. "ASCENDING" AND "DESCENDING" ON HORIZONTAL AXES

	vertical axis	landward-seaward	east-west
hage	'ascend'	' go landward'	'go east'
kave	'descend'	'go seaward'	'go west'

These absolute terms are local nouns with the same syntactic characteristics as intrinsic local nouns (see §4.4.1). They typically occur on their own as locative or directional obliques, as in (4.29) to (4.31). However, they may occur with possessor-indexing and a possessor complement, or in a prepositional phrase:

(4.32) a. *n-e   au   fona=na   suḡa=o*
          RL-3S   exist   east=3SGP   house=thatNV
          'It [the new cookhouse] is at the east of the house.'

   b. *ḡ-a   mai=ña   gai   ade   **ka**   **ia**   **rhuku**
       NT-1EXCS come=IMM   weEXC   here   LOC   theSG   landward
       'We come here to the shore side.'

While both of these constructions are possible, they occur much less commonly with absolute locatives than with intrinsic locatives. As absolute locatives are local nouns, the phrasal structure given in (4.26) applies. Of these absolute locative forms only one, *rauru*, has another function, also occurring as a verb meaning 'to go seaward'.

4.5 Contextualizer nouns

Two bound nouns exist that function as adjuncts introducing contextual information. These contextual nouns resemble local nouns in that they possessor-index a complement. However, unlike local nouns the possessor-indexing and possessor complement are obligatory. The two contextualizer nouns, *gu-* and *nafu-*, are functionally identical. The choice between them appears to be stylistic, and a matter of speaker preference. Both introduce an adjunct expressing the context in which the main clause predication holds. Often this indicates that the adjunct is the cause of the main clause event.

(4.33) a. ***gu=na***   *bia=na*   *ne*   *fa kalahohoa=nau=na*   *ara*
        CNTX=3SGP beer=thatN RL   CS burp=1SGO=thatN   I
        'Because of that beer I am burping.'

     b. *n-e=u*   *bo* *ge* *teo*   *boka=di=na,*
        RL-3S=be.thus CNT SEQ not.exist be.able=3PLO=thatN
        'So they weren't able to

        n-e=u   ***nafu=na*** *ia*   *parahağala* *bla=u*
        RL-3S=be.thus base=3SGP theSG giant   LMT=be.thus
        because it was a giant.'

In other cases the contextual oblique is interpreted as one on whose behalf the predication holds, as in (4.34), or as the subject matter of a story, etc. ([4.35]).

(4.34) a. *n-e-ke*   *kave*   *mai=ña*   *fate,*
        RL-3S-PFV descend   come=IMM above
        'He came down from heaven

        gu=da   *gita*   *ira*   *huğru nakoni*
        CNTX=1INCP weINC thePL every person
        for we the people.'

     b. *ti-ke*   *mai* ***gu=ğu***   *bo*   *tai-ğu*
        NEG-PFV come CNTX=1SGP CNT REFL-1SGP
        'I haven't come on my own behalf.'

(4.35) a. *buka* *ine*   ***gu=di***   *palu* *gizu=di*
        book thisR CNTX=3PLP two   island=3PLP
        'The book is about the two islands.'

     b. *manahagi tu~turi=di=u*   *no-mai*   *kastom* *mereseni=re...*
        want   RD~tell=3PLO=CNT GENP-1EXCP custom medicine=thoseN
        'I want to tell some of our medicine customs

> *nafu=na*   *kaike*   *ḡlepo*   *ka*   *tahi=ne...*
> base=3SGP   one   thing   LOC   sea=thisR
> about one thing in the sea....'

The interpretation of the exact role of the contextual oblique proceeds from the semantics of the predicate. In the examples above the complement of the contextualizer nouns is a NP. However, both contextualizer nouns also subcategorize for complement clauses, and occur frequently with such clauses:

(4.36) a.   *ara*   *n-a*   *lao,*   ***gu=na***   *zemesi n-e-ke*   *tore=nau ara*
        I   RL-1EXCS   go   CNTX=3SGP PN   RL-3S-PFV   ask=1SGO I
        'I went because James asked me to.'

      b.   *e=u*   *teo*   *ḡ-e*   *boka*   *turi=di*   *manei...*
          3S=be.thus   not.exist   NT-3S   be.able   tell=3PLO   he
          'He can't tell [those things]...

          nafu=na   *n-e-ke*   *blahi*   *ka*   *gai*   *t=au=are*
          base=3SGP   RL-3S-PFV   be.tabu   LOC   weEXC   SBD=exist=thoseN
          because those are tabu for us.'

Contextualizing subordinate clauses are discussed further in §10.2.5.1.

In addition to obligatory possessor-indexing, the forms may carry a cliticized demonstrative:

(4.37)   *manei n-e*   *lao buala*   ***gu=ḡu=na***   *ara*
        he   RL-3S   go   PNLOC   CNTX=1SGP=thatN   I
        'He went to Buala because of me.'

Contextualizer nouns occur as the head of a N$'_{CNTX}$, consisting of a contextualizer noun with the possessor enclitic, with an optional demonstrative, and a NP or clausal complement. No article occurs with a contextualizer noun, so it does not project a full NP but a N'.

(4.38)   N$'_{CNTX}$ →   CNTX + PSSR + (DEM) + $\begin{cases} \text{(NP}_{PSSR}) \\ \text{(S)} \end{cases}$

A NP$_{CNTX}$ typically occurs directly modifying the predication. However, occasionally phrases with *gu-* occur in a PP, adding an additional layer to the structure, with the NP$_{CNTX}$ as the complement of the preposition.

(4.39)   *ara manahagi turi tufa=nigo*   *ago*   *ka*   ***gu=na***   *ia*
        I   want   tell   affect =2SGO   youSG   LOC   CNTX=3SGP theSG
        'I want to tell you a story about

au	*ka*	*gai*	*ka=ia*	*fufunu*	*mai=na*	*ia*	*velepuhi*
exist	LOC	weINC	LOC=theSG	begin	come=3SGP	theSG	right.way

our living when Christianity first came.'

As well as functioning as a contextual noun, *nafu* also functions as a common noun meaning 'base'. As such it is inalienably possessed. However, like all inalienably possessed common nouns in Kokota, it may occur independently:

(4.40) a. *n-e-ge*   *au=gu*   *ka*   **nafu**   *ḡazu*   *ine*
        RL-3S-PRS   exist=CNT   LOC   base   wood   thisR
        'He stayed at this tree base.'

    b. *ka*   **nafu=na**   *ḡazu*   *ana*
        LOC   base=3SGP   wood   thatN
        'at the base of that tree'

This does not indicate that *nafu* is a local noun, as unlike local nouns it cannot occur as an oblique without a preposition or direct possessor complement.

4.6 Associative noun

The noun *tareme-* occurs only as an adjunct, assigning an associative role to a participant. It occurs with obligatory direct possessor-indexing and a possessor complement, whose referent is the associated participant. It marks adjuncts that are participants in the event by virtue of association with another participant.

(4.41) a. *ara*   *n-a-ke*   *turi*   **tareme=na**   *gase*   *ana*
        I   RL-3S-PFV   talk   with=3SGP   woman   thatN
        'I have talked with that woman

        ka   *kaike*   *fata*   *bla*
        LOC   one   occasion   LMT
        on only one occasion.'

    b. *n-e-ke*   *aḡe-re-u*   *ku*   *hinage=ne*
        RL-3S-PFV   go=thoseN=CNT   LOC   boat=thisR
        'He went in the canoe

        tareme=di   *tilo*   *mane=u*
        with=3PLP   three   man=be.thus
        with three men.'

The associated participant is typically human or at least animate; however, it can be inanimate, or even not a physical object.

(4.42) a. *ia   mane n-e   lao   ka=ia   sitoa   **tareme=na** ḡasi*
      theSG man   RL-3S go   LOC=theSG store   with=3SGP   torch
      'The man went to the store with a torch.'

    b. *manei n-e   za~zaho **tareme=na** mhagu*
       he   RL-3S RD~go   with=3SGP   fear
       'He walked in fear.'

The associative noun may carry a cliticized demonstrative:

(4.43)   *e-ke   keha   foḡra ñheñhe   bo*
        3S-PFV NSP   sick   be.separate CNT
        '[But if] there is some other sickness

        *ta=ke   au   **tareme=na=na**   naitu tahi ana...*
        SBD=PFV   exist   with=3SGP=thatN   devil sea   thatN
        that is with that sea devil...'

As an extension of its associative meaning, *tareme-* has a more specific meaning of 'wantok', 'relative', or 'friend'. This may be referential, as in (4.44)a., but occurs more typically with a vocative function, stressing the existence of a community relationship with the speaker, as in (4.44)b (starting a sign in a store). In this vocative role a cliticized demonstrative is obligatory.

(4.44) a. *ara n-a   fakae=ni   **tareme=mi=na**   gau*
      I   RL-1EXCS see=3SGO   with=2PLP=thatN   youPL
      'I saw your wantok.'

    b. *ehe **tareme=ḡu=ro**,*
       yes with=1SGP=thoseNV
       'Yes my friends,

       ke   nodo fea ke   mai   tore kaoni   t=au=o
       PFV stop INIT PFV come ask   account SBD=exist=thatNV
       stop coming and asking for credit....'

The associative noun occurs as the head of a N'ASSC, consisting of the associative noun with the possessor enclitic, with an optional demonstrative, and an obligatory complement possessor NP. Complement clauses do not occur with *tareme-*. No article occurs with the associative noun, so it does not project a full NP but a N'.

(4.45)   N'ASSC → NASSC + PSSR + (DEM) +   (NPPSSR)

CHAPTER 5: POSSESSION

5.1 Overview of possession

Kokota expresses possessive relations by head-marking the possessum to index the possessor. Typically for an Oceanic language, Kokota has both direct and indirect marking, broadly encoding semantic categories of inalienable and alienable possession. Two forms of indirect marking encode a semantic distinction between general and 'consumed' alienable possession. With both direct and indirect possessor-marked NPs the possessor may be omitted if the context precludes ambiguity.

In addition, to this system of possessor-indexing, possession may also be expressed by realizing the possessor as a pseudo-locative prepositional phrase. Finally, within highly restricted parameters a possessor may be expressed without indexing on the possessum and without a prepositional head.

5.2 Direct possessor-indexing

Direct possession involves possessor-indexing enclitics attached to the nominal core of the possessum NP. The enclitic status of these forms is discussed in §3.3.1.3. The forms recognize the same person and number categories as the pronominal system described in §3.1.2.

TABLE 5.1. DIRECT POSSESSOR-INDEXING ENCLITICS

	1EXC	1INC	2	3
SG	=ḡu	-	=mu	=na
PL	=mai	=da	=mi	-di

Direct possessor-indexing encodes the semantic category of inalienable possession.

5.3 Indirect possessor-indexing

Indirect possession involves a possessor-indexing host that is syntactically the head of the NP in which it occurs (see §5.9.2). Two possessor-indexing hosts occur: ge-, marking possession of anything consumed by mouth (food, drink, tobacco, etc.); and no-, encoding a general category including all indirectly possessed items other than those qualifying for the consumed category.

Indirect possessor suffixes recognize the same person and number categories as the direct possessive enclitics, and are formally identical except for the second person singular form.

TABLE 5.2. INDIRECT GENERAL POSSESSOR-INDEXING

	1EXC	1INC	2	3
SG	*no-g̃u*	-	*no-u*	*no-na*
PL	*no-mai*	*no-da*	*no-mi*	*no-di*

TABLE 5.3. INDIRECT 'CONSUMED' POSSESSOR-INDEXING

	1EXC	1INC	2	3
SG	*ge-g̃u*	-	*ge-u*	*ge-na*
PL	*ge-mai*	*ge-da*	*ge-mi*	*ge-di*

5.4 The semantics of Kokota direct possession

5.4.1 Inalienably possessed items

A number of types of items are typically treated as being in an inalienably possessed relationship with their possessor. Unlike in many Oceanic languages, almost all inalienably possessed nouns may be realized in isolation, without possessor-indexing, the exceptions being the contextualizer and associative nouns discussed in §4.5 and §4.6.

Possessive relationships typically treated as inalienable include certain kin relationships; part-whole relationships (including body parts, bodily matter, bodily states, and inanimate part-whole relationships); the impression of parts; non-physical parts; divisions of time; intrinsic characteristics; possession by a location (including local nouns and location names); contextual and associative relationships; and the possession of events. In addition, a class of adjectives expressing gender, existential status, and status as new or first, are treated as being in an inalienable relationship with the noun they modify (see §3.2.3.2).

5.4.1.1 Inalienable kin

In Kokota some kin terms are treated as inalienably possessed while others are treated as alienable. The distinction is based primarily on age: kin who are younger than the possessor are inalienably possessed. Apart from members of certain culturally highly salient relationships, older kin are alienably possessed.

The younger kin category includes *tu-* 'child' and *tamo-* 'younger sibling, grandchild':

(5.1) a. *ara n-a   fakae=ni   **tamo=mu**=na   ago*
       I   RL-1EXCS see=3SGO   younger.sibling=2SGP=thatN   youSG
       'I saw your younger brother.'

b. ***tu=mai***   *ana*   *gai*
child=1EXCP thatN weEXC
'that child of ours'

The category of highly salient relationships consists of spouses, a tabu reciprocal in-law relationship between parent-in-law and son-in-law or daughter-in-law, and the relationship between a man and his sister's sons. This latter relationship is the primary relationship of authority and discipline an individual has with a member of a previous generation. These relationship categories are treated as inalienably possessed regardless of age. They include:

(5.2) a. *nafe*   'spouse'
       b. *nañho*   'parent-in-law/child's spouse
       c. *mageha* 'maternal uncle'
       d. *ḡlegu*   'sororal nephew'

While *nafe* 'spouse' is inalienably possessed, *nakrupe* 'wife' may be inalienably or alienably possessed. There is no specific term for husband. The term *kue* 'grandfather' may also be inalienably or alienably possessed.

5.4.1.2 Physical part-whole relationships

5.4.1.2.1 Body parts and bodily matter

A range of items involved in part-whole relationships are inalienably possessed. This includes external body parts (5.3), and internal body matter and organs (5.4):

(5.3) a. *ara n-a*   *marhi=nau*   ***nene=ḡu=ine***
        I   RL-1EXCS be.in.pain=1SGO   leg=1SGP=thisR
        'This leg of mine hurts.'

       b. *...ḡ-e age tob-i=ri*   *ka* ***poto=di=re***
         NT-3S go kick-TR=3PLO LOC arse=3PLP=thoseN
         '...he went [and] kicked them in the arse.'

       c. *n-e*   *la piri=ni=u*
         RL-3S go bind=3SGO=CNT
         'He tied him up

         ka=ia   ***kolu-seku=na=o***   *manei*
         LOC=theSG snake-tail=3SGP=thatNV he
         with his snake tail.'

(5.4) a. *n-e   dou   lao   n-e=u   nanafa=ḡu=ine   ara*
           RL-3S be.big go   RL-3S=be.thus heart=1SGP=thisR I
           'It is big in my heart.' [i.e., 'I am thinking about it a lot.']

    b. *numha=mai=de   gai*
        bone=1EXCP=theseR   weEXC
        'our bones'

    c. *dadara=na=ro   naitu   t=au=o   toke   goinode*
        blood=3SGP=thoseNV devil   SBD=exist=thatNV arrive todayRL
        'That devil's blood is still there today.'

This category also includes matter that may be separated from the body, such as hair, fingernails, and teeth, and matter emanating from the body:

(5.5) a. *kala=ḡu=de   ara*   b. *bi=mu=de   ago*
           hair/leaf=1SGP=theseR   I   fart=2SGP=theseR youSG
           'my hair'   'these farts of yours'

    c. *soso=na=re   manei*   d. *kekredi=di   kokorako*
        piss=3SGP=thoseN he   egg=3PLP   chicken
        'his piss'   'chicken's eggs'

5.4.1.2.2 Bodily states

Body states, even temporary ones, are inalienably possessed. For example, the compound noun *dia-tini* 'fever', is inalienably possessed by the sufferer:

(5.6) *ara n-a   mhoto=u   gu=na=na   dia-tini=ḡu*
       I   RL-1EXCS sweat=CNT CNTX=3SGP=thatN be.bad-body=1SGP
       'I am sweating because of my fever.'

5.4.1.2.3 Inanimate part-whole relationships

Part-whole relationships involving inanimate objects are also treated as inalienable possession:

(5.7) a. *ia   hobo=na   ḡazu*   b. *ia   wili=na   tarake*
           theSG branch=3SGP wood   theSG wheel=3SGP   truck
           'the branch of the tree'   'the wheel of the truck'

    c. *ago n-o   tiki   kikilova=na   suḡa=o*
        youSG RL-2S construct ridge.cap=3SGP house=thatNV
        'You are making the ridge cap of the house.'

d. *...ta ḡ-e ku~knusu=o **papari=na** to~toi=ne*
   SBD NT-3S RD~break=thatNV wood.stack=3SGP RD~cook=thisR
   '...that broke the fire's wood stack.'

e. *...kolodadara ka **pau**=na kumai=na*
   PNLOC LOC head=3SGP water=thatN
   '...at Kolodadara at the head of that river'

f. *ta moita la raisi ana*
   SBD be.cooked CND rice thatN
   'If the rice is cooked,

   *zikra koko=ni **bakru=na=na***
   pour.out leave=3SGO liquid=3SGP=thatN
   pour out its liquid.'

Just as inalienable possession with animates extends to separable bodily matter, emanations of inanimate objects are treated as inalienably possessed:

(5.8)   *ia **komhu=na** koilo*
       theSG fruit=3SGP coconut
       'the fruit of the coconut tree'

5.4.1.3 Impressions of parts

Impressions such as footprints and other imprints are inalienably possessed by the entity that made the impression:

(5.9)   ***mala=na**=re*
       footprint=3SGP=thoseN
       'those footprints of his'

5.4.1.4 Possession of non-physical 'parts'

Certain non-physical items are treated as parts of a whole and are inalienably possessed, including shadows, spiritual elements, sounds caused by the possessor, and names:

(5.10) a. ***naño=ḡu** ara*   b. *ia **oḡla=na** ḡita*
       shadow=1SGP I   theSG sound=3SGP guitar
       'my shadow'   'the sound of the guitar'

    c. *e-ke fa heta legu=gita=u manei*
       3S-PFV CS be.strong follow=1INCO=CNT he
       'He will make us strong

> ira   huḡru   **matirihi=da**
> thePL   every   spirit=1INCP
> in all our spirits.'

d. *fahega   ira   **nanafa=mai**   gai*
   be.happy thePL heart=1EXCP   weEXC
   'Our hearts are happy

   *ta   mala tihi   koko=di   ira   **nhave=mai***
   SBD   PURP wash leave=3PLO   thePL sin=1EXCP
   to wash out our sins.'

e. *...fa lehe=ri   lao fa kave=i   ia   **nañha=na** ruruboñi*
   CS die=3PLO go   CS descend=3SGO theSG name=3SGP PN
   '...[they] killed them and put down the name of Ruruboñi.'

This is not limited to personal names, as in (5.10)e., but includes the relationship
between any noun and its referent:

(5.11) *ḡuanha e=ni   bla **nañha=na=na**   ḡazu t=au=ao*
        ḡuanha 3S=3SGO LMT name=3SGP=thatN wood SBD=exist-thisT
        '*Ḡuanha* is the name of that tree.'

Parts of non-physical items are treated as inalienably possesed:

(5.12) ***fufunu=na=na***   *e=u*   *ade* *n-e=u*
        begin=3SGP=thatN 3S=be.thus here   RL-3S=be.thus
        'That start of it [the story] will be like this here, he says.'

Significant roles within groups or organizations are treated as participating in a
part-whole relationship and are inalienably possessed:

(5.13) a. *zemesi   **velepuhi=na** sikolu*
          James   teacher=3SGP school
          'James is the teacher at the school.'

    b. *t=au=na   **pau=na**   solomoni tikilave*
       SBD=exist=thatN head=3SGP PN
       'That [group]'s leader was Solomon Tikilave.'

5.4.1.5 Divisions of time and stages in temporal frames

Units of time are in a part-whole relationship with larger units and are treated as
inalienably possessed:

(5.14)   *hage   ka   **saigona=na**   sarere   ana...*
          ascend   LOC   evening=3SGP   Saturday   thatN
          '[They would] go up in the evening of that Saturday...'

Phases in processes or large periods of time are inalienably possessed, including beginnings and ends:

(5.15) a. *gai   a   boka   ñha=di   gudu...*
          weEXC   1EXCS   be.able   eat=3PLO   EXHST
          'We could eat them all

          *ka=ia   **fufunu=na**   ia   kastom   ka   gai*
          LOC=theSG   begin=3SGP   theSG   custom   LOC   weEXC
          at the beginning of our custom.' [i.e., '...in our original custom.']

     b. *goinode   ka   **nhigo=na**   nare*
          todayRL   LOC   be.finished=3SGP   day
          'Now it's the end of the day.'

5.4.1.6 Intrinsic characteristics

A wide range of relationships are treated as the inalienable possession of an intrinsic characteristic. This typically applies where there is a perceived inseparable and unique relationship between the possessor and the possessum.

Membership of a class of objects is treated as an intrinsic characteristic. *Kokolo* means 'class of', or 'category of', and 'clan' when applied to humans:

(5.16) a. *kaike-u   **kokolo=na**   namhari   ka   solomon*
          one-CRD   class=3SGP   fish   LOC   Solomons
          '(It is) one kind of fish from the Solomons.'

     b. *boboe   **kokolo=ḡu**=ne   ara*
          dugong   class=1SGP=thisR   I
          '"Dugong" is my clan.'

Similarly, any intrinsic association involves inalienable possession. In (5.17), for example, a church is inalienably possessed by the saint for whom it is named:

(5.17)   *zesas   n-e   kave   mai   ka   **suḡa=na**   sin meri*[38]
          PN   RL-3S   descend   come   LOC   house=3SGP   PN
          'Jesus came down, to the house [i.e., church] of Saint Mary.'

---

[38] The local orthography is used here phonemically. The Kokota spell introduced names as in English, and would never write 'Jesus', 'Saint', or 'Mary' as shown here.

Several nouns capture notions of intrinsic character. These 'ways' refer to the characteristic behavior of an entity, or behavior perceived to be inherently associated with an entity. These 'ways' are, therefore, treated as inalienably possessed by the relevant entity. The nouns are *hana*, *puhi*, and *zazaho*.

(5.18) a. *e=u*   *bla*   *za~zaho=di=re*   *palu*   *naitu*
        3S=be.thus   LMT   RD~go=3PLP=thoseN   two   devil
        'So they're the ways of the two devils.'

     b. *ira*   **puhi=di**   *fa ku~kumai*   *mereseni*
        thePL   way=3PLP   CS RD~drink   medicine
        'the way of drinking medicine'

     c. *tana*   *nogoi*   *nhigo*   *n-e=u*   *ia*   *ḡrui*
        then   VOC   be.finished   RL-3S=be.thus   theSG   garden
        'Then, man!, it's finished, the garden,

        ira   *toka*   *legu-kava=di=ña,*   **hana=di=re=ña**
        thePL   chop   follow-ground=3PLP=IMM   way=3PLP=thoseN=IMM
        their [the trees'] chopping to the ground, those ways of them.'

In (5.18)a. the characteristic behavior is the behavior of the possessor entity itself, while in the remaining examples it is behavior that is characteristically associated with it: the procedures for preparing certain custom medicines, and for clearing ground to make a garden. All three terms are used in both ways.

Zazaho is a reduplicated version of the verb *zaho* 'go'. Kokota reduplication has a general derivational function, with two subregularities: the derivation of intransitive verbs from transitive roots, and nouns from verbs. Two forms are derived by reduplication from *zaho*. One, *zazaho* 'walk', is the idiosyncratic derivation of a specific (perhaps prototypical) way of going. The other, *zazaho* 'way', derives a noun from the verb root, with a general sense of 'way of going'. The semantic distinction between *zazaho*, the widely used *puhi*, and the rarely used *hana* is unclear.

Other such intrinsic characteristics treated as inalienably possessed include personal characteristics such as a person's age or handwriting:

(5.19) a. *nihau*   **komhu=mu=na**   *ago*
        how.many   year=2SGP=thatN   youSG
        'How old are you?' [lit. 'How many are your years?']

     b. *ara n-a*   *mhemhe*   *izu=ri*   **ririso=mu=re**   *ago*
        I   RL-1EXCS   be.difficult   read=3PLO   writing=2SGP=thoseN   youSG
        'I find it hard to read your writing.'

Certain nouns expressing quantities may be possessed by the nominal they quantify. These include *tehi* 'a large quantity (of)' and *kata-* 'a modicum (of)'.

(5.20) a. **tehi=di**   *mane=re*   *n-e*   *kaike*   *isi*   *hage*   *ka*   *ḡuku ana*
        many=3PLP man=thoseN RL-3S one   flee ascend LOC path thatN
        'Many of those men ran away together up the road.'

   b. *fa loga*   *mai*   **kata=na**   *karoseni*   *ña*   *bo*
      CS pour   come   modicum=3SGP kerosene   IMM   CNT
      'Pour a little bit more kerosene.'

Tehi has three syntactically distinct semantically related functions. Its primary function is as an adnominal quantifier (see §3.2.2.3). It also has the nominal function shown above, and a verb function with the meaning 'be many'. It is unclear whether *kata* also occurs independently, and with other functions.

Forms expressing a place in a sequence are inalienably possessed, including ordinal numbers (see §3.2.2.2.1.3), and the adjective/local noun *kenu* 'front':

(5.21) a. *ḡ-e*   *lao*   *ña*   **fa**   **palu=na**   *ḡazu=na*   *e=u*
        NT-3S go   IMM   ORD two=3SGP   wood=thatN   3S=be.thus
        'Go for the second of that tree.'

   b. *ide-hi*   *bla*   **kenu=di**   *botolo=re*
      theseR-EMPH LMT   front=3PLP bottle=thoseN
      'These are the first bottles.'

Ordinals are not obligatorily possessor-indexed, occurring frequently as adnominal modifiers with no possessor-indexing:

(5.22)   *ara* **fa** **palu**   *mane* *n-a-ke*   *ooe=na*
         I   ORD two   man   RL-1EXCS-PFV   talk=thatN
         'I was the second person who spoke.'

5.4.1.7 Possession of adjectives

A small number of adjectives exist in Kokota. One subclass (see §3.2.3.1) are formally underived and occur with no possessor-indexing A further subclass are derived by direct possessor-indexing, including forms assigning gender, existential status, newness, and 'first' (see §3.2.3.2). One example is repeated:

(5.23)   *ḡazu*   *are*   *e*   *ḡazu*   **le~lehe=di**
         wood   thoseN   3S   wood   RD~be.dead=3PLP
         'These trees are dead trees.'

5.4.1.8 Possession of local nouns

Local nouns (see §4.4) identify a location in relation to an item that is either specified or understood. Locations of this kind are treated as parts of the item they relate to, and are thus inalienably possessed. In effect, spaces adjacent to (including enclosed by) items are treated as a part of the item.

(5.24) a. *n-e*   *au*   *ka*   **mairi=ḡu**   *ara*
       RL-3S exist LOC left=1SGP   I
       'It's at my left.' [must be immediately to hand]

     b. *manei n-e*   *au*   *ka*   **kota=na**   *suḡa=na*
        he   RL-3S exist LOC outside=3SGP house=thatN
        'He is outside that house.'

Local nouns in Kokota are not bound nominals, and may occur without possessor-indexing, when the item the location relates to is understood:

(5.25)   *...ḡ-e lao=ña*   *sare*   **ḡilu**   *n-e-ke=u*
       NT-3S go=IMM thereP inside RL-3S-PFV=be.thus
       '...they went there inside, it was like that.'

5.4.1.9 Possession of contextualizer and associative nouns

Three nominals introduce an adjunct and identify its relationship with the event. One, *tareme-*, is associative, indicating that the possessor is associated with the event in some way, while two others, *gu-* and *nafu*, indicate that the possessor is the context of the main clause event. All three are inalienably possessed.

(5.26) a. *ago*   *ginai*   *aḡe*   *ka*   *rarata=o*   **tareme=ḡu** *ara*
       youSG FUT   go   LOC sand=thatNV with=1SGP I
       'You will go to the beach with me.'

     b. *manei*   *n-e*   *turi tufa=di*   *maneri* **gu=ḡu**   *ara*
        he   RL-3S tell affect=3PLO they   CNTX=1SGP I
        'He told them about me.'

     c. *... n-e=u*   **nafu=na**   *ia*   *parahaḡala*   *blau*
        RL-3S=be.thus base=3SGP theSG giant   LMT
        '...it was like that simply because [it was] a giant.'

The associative and the contextualizer *gu-* are obligatorily possessed. *Nafu* is obligatorily possessed as a contextualizer noun. However, the form also occurs as an ordinary noun meaning 'base'. As such it is inalienably possessed, but may also occur without possessor-indexing (see §5.4.2). Contextualizer nouns are discussed further in §4.5, and the associative in §4.6.

5.4.1.10 Possession by location names

The relationship between an item and a location with which the item is characteristically associated may be expressed by a location name occurring as an adnominal core modifier (see §3.3.1.2.3). However, this relationship may also be expressed as an inalienable possessive relationship:

(5.27)　　*ago　kaike **mane=na**　ostrelia*
　　　　　youSG one　man=3SGP　PNLOC
　　　　　'You are a man from Australia.'

Just as significant roles within groups or organizations are inalienably possessed (see §5.4.1.4), so are significant roles associated with locations:

(5.28) a.　*bili ḡedi **spika=na**　　isabel*
　　　　　　PN　　　Speaker=3SGP　PNLOC
　　　　　　'Billy Gedi is the Speaker of Santa Isabel.'[39]

　　　　b.　*manei　**man-datau=na=na**　　goveo*
　　　　　　he　　　man-chief=3SGP=thatN　PNLOC
　　　　　　'He is that chief of Goveo.'

5.4.1.11 Possession of events

A clause may be inalienably possessed by its absolutive argument. An intransitive clause may be inalienably possessed by its sole core argument, either unaccusative (as in [5.29]) or unergative (5.30):

(5.29) a.　*n-e-ke　　kaike au　　nakoni=di=ña*
　　　　　　RL-3S-PFV　one　exist person=3PLP=IMM
　　　　　　'People continued to live,

　　　　　ka　　lehe=na=na　　　naitu　ta=au=ne
　　　　　LOC　die=3SGP=thatN　devil　SBD=exist=thisR
　　　　　due to that death of this devil.'

　　　　b.　*ka　**la au　fufunu foḡra=na**　　manei*
　　　　　　LOC　go exist begin　be.sick=3SGP　he
　　　　　　'[It is] at that starting to get sick of his

---

[39] I.e., the Provincial Assembly. Note the inalienable possession of loan words (see [5.46]).

151

> ta=ke   fufunu=na   ara
> SBD=PFV begin=thatN I
> that I will start [the story].'

(5.30) a. ka **mhoko aḡe=na=na**   manei...
>   LOC sit   go=3SGP=thatN   he
>   'At that sitting down of his...' [i.e., 'When he sat down...']

   b. ka **mai=ḡu=o**   ara ginai, ara fahega
>   LOC come=1SGP=thatNV I   FUT   I   be.happy
>   'At that coming of mine [again] I will be happy.'

Transitive clauses may not be possessed by their agent, but may be inalienably possessed by their undergoer ('passive possession'). In (5.31)a. trees possess the event of their being chopped down; in (5.31)b. a child possesses its baptism:

(5.31) a. ..nhigo   n-e=u...   ira   toka   legu-kava=di=ña...
>   be.finished RL-3S=be.thus   thePL chop   follow-ground=3PLP=IMM
>   '...it's finished... their [the trees'] chopping to the ground...'

   b. ...toke ia   nare mala **sugitabu=na** suli=ana   e=u
>   arrive theSG day   PURP baptism=3SGP   child=thatN 3S=be.thus
>   '...the day for the baptism of that child arrives.'

Clauses functioning as arguments are discussed in detail in §10.2.4.

5.4.2 Optional nature of direct possessor-indexing

Unlike many Oceanic languages, direct possessive marking in Kokota is not obligatory. Almost any noun that typically occurs with direct possessor-indexing may occur without it in certain circumstances. This is apparent in citation forms, which are always given without possessor-indexing. In many Oceanic languages, in the absence of any clear possessor, inalienably possessed forms are given with third person singular possessor marking. This is not the case in Kokota, even for nouns that have an apparently inseparably close relationship with their possessor, such as body parts or intrinsic characteristics. This may occur if the specific possessor is not apparent or is not relevant. In (5.32)a. the speaker is discussing the custom medicine treatment for headaches, and has no particular individual's head in mind. However, as (5.32)b. shows, it is not limited to such non-specific contexts:

(5.32) a. e au   ka **pau** ine   marha-pau ana
>   3S exist LOC head thisR pain-head thatN
>   'That headache is in the head.'

b. *n-e-ge*   *au=gu*   *ka*   **nafu**   *ḡazu*   *ine*
   RL-3S-PRS   exist=CNT   LOC   base   wood   thisR
   'He stays at this tree base.'

Intrinsic characteristics such as class membership and characteristic ways (see §5.4.1.6) may also occur without possessor-indexing:

(5.33) a. *teo*   *ḡ-e*   *au=gu*   **kokolo**   *ga~gato*   *t=au=are*
         not.exist   NT-3S   exist=CNT   class   RD~think   SBD=exist=thoseN
         'Those kinds of thoughts won't be [i.e., won't eventuate].'

      b. *n-e-ke*   *mai=u*   **puhi** *keli=ro*   *ka*   *tilo*   *mane=re*
         RL-3S-PFV come=CNT   way   be.good=thoseNV LOC   three man=thoseN
         'Those good ways came with those three men.'

A small number of exceptions exist that cannot occur without direct possessor-indexing. None are ordinary nouns. They include the kin terms *tu-* 'offspring' and *tamo-* 'younger sibling', possessor-indexed adjectives (see §3.2.3.2), the contextualizer noun *gu-* (see §3.5.4), and the associative noun *tareme-* (3.5.5). These require possessor-indexing, and, apart from the kin terms, may not occur without an overt mention of the item being indexed. In the case of the adjectives this item occurs as the nominal head the adjective modifies. In the case of the contextualizer and associative nouns it is the noun's own complement. All other nouns may occur without possessor-indexing.

5.5 The semantics of indirect possession

Two classes of indirect possession are recognized in Kokota: that of consumed items, and that of all alienable items not eligible for the consumed class.

5.5.1 Possession of consumed items

The possession of any item that has been, is being, or will be consumed by mouth is treated as alienable possession and is expressed using the 'consumed' indirect possessor-indexing host *ge-*. Anything consumed by mouth is treated in this way, including food, drink, and tobacco:

(5.34) a. **ge-ḡu**   **bia**   *are*
         CNSM-1SGP beer   thoseN
         'those beers of mine'

      b. **ge-na**   **viri**   *havi*
         CNSM-3SGP tobacco PN
         'Havi's tobacco'

c. *ḡ-e   la   fa   manemane=ri*   *ira*   **ge-mai**   **teḡe**
NT-3S go   CS   be.very.happy=3PLO   thePL   CNSM-1EXCP turtle
'We are very happy about our turtles

ta   mala   ñhau   ia   mavitu
SBD   PURP   eat   theSG community
for the community to eat.'

Items that may in some forms not be consumed by mouth are marked with the 'consumed' host when in a form that is consumed by mouth. For example, medicine is possessed using *ge-* if it is to be taken orally, but not otherwise:

(5.35)   *mereseni ine*   **ge-ḡu**   **mereseni**   *ara*
medicine thisR   CNSM-1SGP medicine   I
'This medicine is my medicine (to eat or drink).'

Other items not typically consumed are possessed using *ge-* if for some reason they are being consumed. Thus *pepa* 'paper' is not normally thought of as consumed, but when used for rolling cigarettes is possessed using *ge-*:

(5.36)   **ge-ḡu**   **pepa**
CNSM-1SGP   paper
'my paper (for rolling cigarettes)'

5.5.2 Non-consumed indirect possession

5.5.2.1 Alienably possessed kin

As indicated in §5.4.1.1, some kinship terms are treated as inalienably possessed. Others are normally treated as participants in an alienable possessive relationship. With the exception of the culturally salient relationships discussed in §5.4.1.1, kin terms referring to older relatives are treated as alienably possessed. This includes those occupying positions in previous generations (parents, grandparents) and older siblings. In-laws other than those in the culturally salient relationships discussed above are also alienably possessed, as is *ḡorotati* 'family'. Alienable kin terms include:

(5.37) a. *ido*   'mother'   d. *vave*   'in-law'
b. *mama* 'father'   e. *ḡorotati* 'family'
c. *kaka*   'grandparent'

Possession of these kin terms can only be expressed by means of the general indirect possession host, and cannot take direct suffixing.

(5.38) a. *nafu=na*   **no-ḡu**   *mama*   b. **no-na**   **ḡorotati**   *zemesi*
       base=3SGP   GENP-1SGP father   GENP-3SGP family   PN
       'because of my father'   'James's family'

5.5.2.2 Other alienably possessed items

The general possessor-indexing host *no-* marks possession of ordinary physical objects:

(5.39) a. *ara a*   *fa-kraño=ri*   *fea* **no-ḡu**   *pohe*   *ide*
       I   1EXCS CS-be.dry=3PLO   INIT GENP-1SGP clothing   theseR
       'I will dry my clothes first.'

      b. *a*   *friñhe ara ka*   **no-ḡu**   *tesenine*
          1EXCS   work   I   LOC   GENP-1SGP plantation
          'I will work in my plantation.'

This applies equally to non-physical alienably possessed items:

(5.40)   *tana n-e-ke*   *toke*   *ira*   **no-na**   *naitu manei*
       then   RL-3S-PFV   arrive   thePL   GENP-3SGP devil   he
       'Then this man's devil arrived.'

The general host is used with any other possessed item including intangible items that are not actually owned:

(5.41)   *hae*   *bo*   *palu*   *wiki*   *e*   *toke=i*
       where   CNT   two   week   3S   arrive=3SGO
       'I think that we return two weeks before

       ia   **no-mai**   *nare*   *mala friñhe tañano*
       theSG   GENP-1EXCP   day   PURP   work   food
       the day for making food.'

5.6 Semantic bases of possessive categories

Aside from the handful of obligatorily inalienably possessed nouns discused in §5.4.2, the three possessor indexing strategies do not correspond to syntactic categories of nouns. Instead, coding strategy choice is dependent on the semantics of the relationship between possessor and possessum.

5.6.1 Variability in possessor-indexing choice

Nouns normally treated as in an alienable relationship with a possessor may in certain contexts be marked with direct possessor-indexing. In (5.27) and (5.28) above, normally alienable nouns like *mane* 'man' and *mandatau* 'chief' may be treated as being in an inalienable possessive relationship with a location, and in that context alone marked accordingly. The corollary is equally true: nouns that typically occur with direct possessor-indexing may occur with indirect possessor-indexing in an appropriate context. For example, *nene* 'leg', being a body part, is typically inalienably possessed:

(5.42)   ***nene=g̅u=ine***
        leg=1SGP=thisR
        'my leg (of my body)'

However, if the leg is a chicken leg that the speaker intends to eat, it would be alienably possessed with the 'consumed' host *ge-*. Alternatively, if a table has been dismantled and several people will take the legs to use for timber, a speaker may refer to the leg they will take with the general indirect host *no-*:

(5.43) a. ***ge-g̅u   nene   ine***   b. ***no-g̅u   nene   ine***
        CNSM-1SGP   leg   thisR   GENP-1SGP   leg   thisR
        'my leg (to eat)'   'my leg (as a general object)'

This variation in possessor-indexing suggests that the three formal possessor-indexing strategies do not apply to syntactic classes of nouns, but represent kinds of relationships. Some nouns, because of their semantics, are normally regarded as being in an inalienable relationship with a possessor, and consequently typically occur in the direct indexing construction. The referents of others are normally regarded as being in a consumed or non-consumed alienable possessive relationship and so typically occur with the appropriate indirect possessor-indexing strategy. However, nouns with each semantically motivated tendency may occur with any of the other indexing strategies in the appropriate context. The possession in Kokota therefore does not involve *syntactic* classes of nouns. Instead the determining criteria are semantic.

5.6.2 Systematic variation between possessor-indexing strategies

The semantics of some nouns mean that they occur systematically and commonly in more than one of the possessor-indexing constructions.

5.6.2.1 Consumed and general indirect possessive variation

Enitities that are normally regarded both as an ordinary possession, and also as being edible or drinkable, routinely occur with either indirect host. For example, potentially consumed possessions such as *zora* 'pig' (both the live animal and its meat) and *koilo* 'coconut' (both the tree and its fruit) are treated as in a consumed or general alienable possessive relationship, depending on how the speaker is regarding them.

(5.44) a. ***no-ḡu***   ***zora***=*na*   *ara*   b. ***ge-ḡu***   ***zora***=*na*   *ara*
      GENP-1SGP pig=thatN   I   GENP-1SGP pig=thatN   I
      'my pig (as livestock)'   'my pork (to eat)'

    c. ***no-mi***   ***koilo***   *are*   d. ***ge-mi***   ***koilo***   *are*
      GENP-2PLP coconut thoseN   GENP-2PLP coconut thoseN
      'your coconuts (to sell)'   'your coconuts (to eat or drink)'

5.6.2.2 Direct and indirect possessive variation

5.6.2.2.1 Intrinsic characteristics possessable by others

Some items may be regarded as being an intrinsic characteristic of one entity, while at the same time may be in an alienable possessive relationship with a different entity. Such items may be possessed inalienably or alienably, depending on which possessor is being referred to. This includes physical objects such as pictures and photographs. Possession by the subject of the picture is treated as inalienable possession, regardless of who owns the picture, as in (5.45)a., because the picture is the image of the subject and therefore treated as an intrinsic characteristic. On the other hand an individual who is the owner of the picture as a physical object, but who is not necessarily the subject, as in (5.45)b. is realized as an alienable possessor. The same is true of books, where the book is inalienably possessed by the entity whose story it tells, but is alienably possessed by its physical owner ([5.45]c.–d.).

(5.45) a. *totogale*=***ḡu***   *ara*   *ine*
      picture=1SGP   I   thisR
      'this photo of me (that I may or may not own)'

    b. ***no-ḡu***   *totogale*   *ara*   *ine*
      GENP-1SGP picture   I   thisR
      'this photo I own (that may or may not be of me)'

    c. ***buka***=*na*   *tikilave*   *an-lau*   *ginai friñhe*=*di*   *bla*   *manei*
      book=3SGP   PN   thatN-SPC   FUT   work=3PLO   LMT   he
      '"Book of Tikilave", that's what he'll make.'

    d. *ide-hi*   *n-e-ke*   ***no-ḡu***   ***buka***   *ara*
      theseR-EMPH RL-3S-PFV   GENP-1SGP book   I
      'These used to be my books.'

Items that are not physical objects but are the intrinsic characteristic of the possessor, and are possessable by other individuals, demonstrate the same variability. These include *histori* 'history', *fakasai* 'history', and *tuturi* 'story':

157

(5.46) a. *ginai*   *aḡe*   *ḡonu*   *ia*   **histori=na**   *nau=ne*
       FUT   go   not.know   theSG   history=3SGP   place=thisR
       'The history of this place will be forgotten.'

     b. *a-hi-la*   **no-ḡu**   **histori=na**
         thisT-EMPH-SPC   GENP-1SGP   history=3SGP
         'This is my history [of it].'

Both refer to the history of a place. In (5.46)a. the possessor is the location, so its history is an intrinsic characteristic and the relationship is inalienable. In (5.46)b. the possessor is a person claiming custom ownership of the history.[40] This possessor is in an alienable relationship. Here *histori* is also inalienably possessed by the unstated place the history applies to. (Note also this variability with the loans *histori* and *buka* indicates the productivity of the phenomenon.)

Similarly, the spirit that causes an illness and the medicine that treats it are treated as inalienably possessed intrinsic characteristics of the illness. However, both may be possessed by individuals in an alienable relationship.

(5.47) a. *ḡ-e-la*   *are*   *e=u*   *bla*   **naitu=di**   *foḡra*
       NT-3S-go   thoseN   3S=be.thus   LMT   devil=3PLP   sick
       'That's all about sickness devils.'

     b. *tana*   *n-e-ke*   *toke*   *ira*   **no-na**   **naitu** *manei*
         then   RL-3S-PFV   reach   thePL   GENP-3SGP   devil   he
         'Then his devils came.'

     c. *tahe*   *la=ri*   *bl=ago*   *keha*   *foḡra*   *aro*
         say   go=3PLO   LMT=youSG   NSP   sick   theseT
         'Just tell some sicknesses

         mereseni   *ḡazu*   *he=ba*   **mereseni=di=re**
         medicine   wood   who=ALT   medicine=3PLP=thoseN
         and whatever medicine trees are their medicines.'

     d. *teo*   *ḡ-e-ge*   *surai*   *gato=ri*   *bla*   *gai*
         not.exist   NT-3S=CNT   ??   think=3PLO   LMT   weEXC
         'So we don't much think about

         ira   **no-mai**   *mereseni*   **kastom**   *gai*
         thePL   GENP-1EXCP   medicine   custom   weEXC
         our custom medicines.'

---

[40] Histories demonstrate knowledge of a place and are evidence of land ownership.

5.6.2.2.2 Intrinsic ways and temporary plans

Puhi 'way' usually refers to behavior characteristic of, or associated with, an entity (see §5.4.1.6), so is direct possessed.

(5.48) ***puhi=na=na***   *kastom=na*   *ka*   *gai*   *tifaro*
        way=3SGP=thatN   custom=thatN   LOC   weINC   before
        'the way of our custom before'

However, if the 'way' is a means of doing something that applies to a particular situation and is one of a number of possible ways, it may be treated as alienably possessed. In (5.49) there has been a dispute about how a game should be played. One participant in the dispute then concedes.

(5.49) *ehe* *keli* *bo* *ka=ira*   ***no-u***   ***puhi*** *ago*   *vave*
        yes   good   CNT   LOC=thePL   GENP-2SGP   way   youSG   in.law
        'Yes, alright, in your way, in-law.'

It is not known whether this applies to the other 'way' terms *zazaho* and *hana*.

5.6.2.2.3 Possession of children

The term *tu-* 'child' refers to offspring, and must be inalienably possessed by the parents. The term *suli* refers to children in general, and may be alienably or inalienably possessed. *Suli* is alienably possessed by someone other than the child's parents, as in (5.50)a., where the speaker is a teacher; but inalienably possessed by those for whom the child is an offspring, as in (5.50)b.:

(5.50) a. *are*   ***no-ḡu***   ***suli***   *ara*
           thoseN   GENP-1SGP   child   I
           'Those are my children [i.e., students].'

      b. *...e* *au...* *ka* *sikolu=ne*   *ka* ***suli=da***   *gita*
           3S   exist   LOC   school=thisR   LOC   child=1INCP   weINC
           '...they can stay in the school for our children.'

In (5.50)b. the speaker and the addressee are members of the same village community, and the inclusive 'we' refers to the whole village community, rather than the speaker and addressee specifically. Consequently, although *suli* here refers to the children of the village in general, rather than any specific children, it nonetheless focuses on them as offspring.

5.6.2.2.4 Multiple possessor-indexing

The potential for nominals to be possessed alienably or inalienably, depending on the semantics of the possessive relationship, creates the potential for dual possessor-indexing, with both the owner of an object and the entity for which the object represents an intrinsic characteristic to be expressed simultaneously:

(5.51) gu   tu~turi=na   ka ara *noḡu*   *mereseni=na* mheke
        be.thus RD~tell=thatN LOC I   GENP-1SGP medicine=3SGP dog
        'So, my story is my medicine for dogs.'

5.6.3 Indexing variation without apparent contextual variation

Some nouns are routinely treated as either alienably or inalienably possessed, with no apparent contextual difference. The basis for the choice is unclear.

5.6.3.1 Variable possession in human relationships

A number of human relationships seeem to be regarded as potentially alienable or inalienable. One such term is *nakrupe* 'wife'. This term is distinct from *nafe* 'spouse', which is inalienably possessed. Both indirect and direct possessive constructions occur involving *nakrupe* in apparent free variation. Although both possessive constructions are possible, the form is typically treated as inalienably possessed and only rarely as alienably possessed.

(5.52) a. ia   *nakrupe=ḡu* ara n-e   mai
          theSG   wife=1SGP   I   RL-3S   come
          'My wife is coming.'

       b. nakodou ana   *no-ḡu*   *nakrupe* ara
          woman   thatN GENP-1SGP   wife   I
          'That woman is my wife.'

5.6.3.2 Non-intrinsic characteristics

A number of nominals occurring in both indirect and direct constructions have a particularly close relationship with their possessor, to the extent that they may be regarded as characteristics of the possessor. However, these characteristics are temporary or non-intrinsic in some other way. These nominals are treated as either alienably or inalienably possessed, with, to varying extents, a statistical tendency towards direct indexing. These non-intrinsic characteristics include *gagato* 'thought', *foḡra* 'sickness', *nau* 'place', *suḡa* 'house', *vetula* 'law', *velepuhi* 'religion', and *kastom* 'custom'.

(5.53) a. *ara ka **ga~gato=ḡu=re*** *gita ginai korho namhari...*
I   LOC RD~think=1SGP=thoseN weINC FUT   pull   fish
'I think we will catch fish [tomorrow].'

b. *ka **no-ḡu** ga~gato ara ge ne-ke friñhe=i=ña...*
LOC GENP-1SGP RD~think I   SEQ RL-PRF work=3SGO=IMM
'I thought to do [that].'

c. *ka la au fufunu **foḡra=na** manei...*
LOC go exist begin be.sick=3SGP he
'at that starting to get sick of his...'

d. ***no-ḡu** foḡra ara n-e-ke-ge keli*
GENP-1SGP sick I   RL-3S-PFV-PRS be.good
'My sickness has got better.'

e. *kaike letasi fufunu mai=na ka **nau=ḡu***
one letter begin come=thatN LOC place=1SGP
'a letter from my home'

f. *ara=ña **no-ḡu** **nau**=ro si=aro*
I=IMM GENP-1SGP place=thoseNV FOC=theseT
'They're my home.'

g. *ka ta la mai=o*
LOC SBD go come=thatNV

*ia **vetula=na**=na ia ḡavana...*
theSG law=3SGP=thatN theSG government
'When the law of the Government came...

...ho~hogo=na blau ḡ-e=u
RD~be.true=thatN LMT NT-3S=be.thus

*ira **no-na** vetula ḡavana*
thePL GENP-3SGP law government
...the laws of the Government are true.'

There is no discernable systematicity to the distribution of indirect versus direct possession with these nominals. In (5.53)g. the two examples were produced by a single speaker only a few clauses apart in a single text. It should be noted that while these nominals are treated as inalienably possessed, far more commonly than alienably, they in fact typically occur without reference to any possessor or possessive relationship at all, especially *foḡra* 'sickness' and *nau* 'place'.

5.7 Pseudo-locative possession

So far, the discussion of possession has dealt with head-marking strategies for indexing the possessor on the possessum. However, these are not the only ways of expressing possession in Kokota. The possessive relationship may also be expressed by realizing the possessor as an adnominal locative adjunct, with no indexing on the possessum. As with adverbial locative adjuncts, there is a formal distinction between prepositional phrases and location names.

5.7.1 Pseudo-locative possession by prepositional phrase

Prepositional phrases using the general locative preposition *ka* occur widely as adjuncts and adnominal modifiers, expressing a wide range of semantic relationships. The use of a PP embedded within a NP modifies the NP in a number of ways (see §3.3.2.2.3.1). An additional function is to realize a relationship of possession. This is not strictly a possessive construction, but a locative construction in which the possessor is presented as a kind of metaphorical location of the possessum.

(5.54) a. *ara n-a   ñha=ni   ḡausa   ka maneri*
I   RL-1EXCS eat=3SGO   betel.nut LOC they
'I ate their betel nut.'

b. *manei   n-e-ke   reregi=ni=na   zuta-pamu   k=ara*
he   RL-3S-PFV look.after=3SGO=thatN lamp-pump LOC=I
'He took care of my tilly lamp.'

In indirect or direct possessive constructions the possessor is realized as a NP that is the complement of the possessor enclitic or suffixed host. With prepositional pseudo-locative possession the possessor is realized as an adjunct to the NP, as with any other non-subcategorized PP.

Prepositional pseudo-locative possession typically expresses possessive relationships that are regarded as alienable. This is evident in the alienable interpretation typically placed on relationships expressed in this way. A term such as *totogale* 'picture' may be alienably or inalienably possessed (see §5.6.2.2.1). When *totogale* is possessed inalienably the possessor is the subject of the picture (i.e., the image is an intrinsic characteristic of the possessor). When it is possessed alienably, the possessor is the owner of the physical object, and may or may not be the subject of the image. If the possessor is expressed as a PP, however, the only possible reading is that the possessor is the owner of the physical object. A prepositional possessor cannot also be the subject of the picture. This is true of all the nouns discussed in §5.6.2.2.1. Thus possession of a medicine may be expressed prepositionally but only if the possessor is the individual who owns the medicine, not the illness the medicine treats:

(5.55) *...ta aḡe no-mai koko=di n-a=u=gu*
    SBD go GENP-1EXCP leave=3PLO RL-1EXCS=be.thus=CNT
    '...that we've gone and left them behind,

    *ira mereseni **ka tagi-mai gai** **nakoni** zuzufra.*
    thePL medicine LOC REFL-1EXCP weEXC person black
    the medicines of our own, we black people'

In keeping with this alienability criterion, nominals with referents that are typically inalienably possessed, body parts, do not normally occur with prepositional possessors, while items that are typically treated as alienable occur commonly in that construction, as (5.54) illustrates. This is true of all types of typically alienably possessed items, including alienable kin:

(5.56) *ia ḡorotati **ka zemesi***
    theSG family LOC PN
    'James's family'

However, the apparent free variation with many nominals, as described in §5.6.3, means that potentially inalienably possessed nominals occur with prepositional possessors. This includes some human relationships:

(5.57) a. *mai fea nakrupe=o **k=ara**...*
     come INIT wife=thatNV LOC=I
     'First my wife will come...'

   b. *suli=re **ka dorisi** ide-hi*
     child=thoseN LOC PN theseR-EMPH
     'Doris's children are these ones.'

It also occurs commonly expressing the possession of non-intrinsic characteristics such as those discussed in §5.6.3.2.

(5.58) a. *puhi=na=na kastom=na **ka gai** tifaro*
     way−3SGP=thatN custom=thatN LOC weINC before
     'the way of that custom of ours before'

   b. *ga~gato are **ka nakoni** are*
     RD~think thoseN LOC person thoseN
     'those thoughts of those people'

While prepositional pseudo-locative possession normally gives an alienable reading, nominalized verbs may occur with prepositional pseudo-locative possession, despite their normally direct treatment (compare, for example, [5.59]b. with [5.29]a.):

(5.59) a. *ia   au   ka   gai*
       theSG exist LOC weINC
       '...our way of life

       ka=ia   fufunu   mai=na   ia   velepuhi
       LOC=theSG begin   come=3SGP theSG right.way
       when Christianity first came'

   b. *ara n-a   dia-nanafa   gu=na   ia   lehe ka   manei*
      I   RL-1EXCS be.bad-heart CNTX=3SGP theSG die LOC he
      'I am sad because of his death.'

5.7.2 Pseudo-locative possession by location name

Place names are inherently locations. When a common noun occurs as a locative adjunct it must occur within a prepositional phrase. Location names, however, function as such without the preposition. This is paralleled in pseudo-locative possession. While all other nominal types may occur as a possessor in the form of a prepositional adjunct, as discussed above, location names do so without a preposition.

(5.60) a. *e=u   mane ide   kokota n-e-ke   kulu   tarai*
      3S=be.thus man   theseR PNLOC RL-3S-PFV be.first pray
      'So these Kokota people were the first to start prayer.'

5.8 Zero marked possession within prepositional phrases

In limited circumstances possession is expressed in a way that not only does not involve possessor-indexing on the possessum, but in which the possessor is not expressed as a prepositional pseudo-locative. This only occurs when the possessor is a pronoun or a personal name, and the possessum is itself a complement of the preposition *ka*. The relationship may involve a location (other than a location name) with which the possessor is closely associated:

(5.61) a. *ara mai   ka   suḡa ine   ago   ba,*
      I   come LOC house thisR youSG   ALT
      'Will I come to your house,

      ago   mai   ka   suḡa=o   ara
      youSG   come LOC   house=thatNV I
      or will you come to my house?'

   b. *lao ka   suḡa zemesi*
      go LOC house James
      'Go to James's house.'

c.   ...*ka=ia*   *puhi boñihehe ka*   *gizu=na*   *a-hi*   **gai**
     LOC=theSG way heathen   LOC island=3SGPthisT-EMPH weINC
     '...in the heathen time on this island of ours'

d.   ...*ia*   *vetula=na*   *ḡavana*   *ka=ia*   *ḡilu=na nau*   **gai**
     theSG law=3SGP   government LOC=theSG   in=3SGP place   weEXC
     '...the Government's law inside our village'

Alternatively the possessum may be an intrinsic characteristic of the possessor:

(5.62) a. *ka=ia*   *kastom* **gai**   *tana*   *goi momoru*   *e=ni...*
          LOC=theSG custom   weINC   then   VOC turtle.net   3S=3SGO
          'In our custom, then, man!, *momoru* we call it...'

b. *tu~turi aro*   **gita**
     RD~tell   thoseN weINC
     'these stories of ours'

5.9 Possessor-indexed NP structure

5.9.1 Heads and adjuncts in possessor-indexed NPs

In NPs displaying possessor-indexing (as opposed to pseudo-locative possession) the head is the element of the phrase that carries possessor-indexing. The possessor is expressed as a NP complement of the possessor-indexing. Direct possession involves an enclitic attaching to the nominal core (see §3.3.1.4), whose head is the nominal expressing the possessum (see §3.3.1.3). In (5.63)a. possessor-indexing attaches to the phrasal head *nañha-* 'name'. In (5.63)b., where a post-head core modifier *dou* 'be big' occurs, the enclitic attaches to the modifier, but itself modifies the core head *tomoko* 'war canoe'. Phrases of this kind are ordinary, common noun NPs.

(5.63) a. **nañha**=na nau=ne   b. *tilo*   **tomoko**   *dou=di*   *wistin*
         name=3SGP place=thisR   three   war.canoe   be.big=3PLPwestern
         'the name of this village'   'three big war canoes of the westerners'

With indirect possession it is the possessor-indexing host that is the syntactic head, and the phrase is a NP$_{POSS}$ (see §3.4.2). The actual possessum nominal is an adjunct specifying the exact nature of the possessed item. Thus in (5.64) the phrasal head is the general possessor-indexing host *no-*.

(5.64)   **no-ḡu**   *suḡa*   *ara*
        GENP-1SGP   house   I
        'my house'

Possessor-indexing hosts typically occur with a specifying nominal like *suḡa* in (5.64). However, this is an adjunct and does not occur if the reference is to possessed objects whose actual nature or identity is not important. The indexed host in this context is non-referential, as in (5.65).

(5.65)　*ta　mai　au　la　gai　ade, a-ke　mai　siko　ginai*
　　　　SBD　come　exist CND　weINC　here　1EXCS-PFV　come　steal　FUT
　　　　'If we come and live here, we would come and steal

　　　　*ka=ira　**ge-di**　**no-di**　e=u*
　　　　LOC=thePL　CNSM-3PLP　GENP-3PLP　3S=be.thus
　　　　from the food and things of

　　　　mane　n-e-ke　kusu　au=de　ade
　　　　man　RL-3S-PFV　be.first　exist=theseR　here
　　　　the people who already live here.'

With both direct and indirect possessor-indexing, the possessor NP is a complement of the indexing morphology, but may be omitted if the identity of the possessor is recoverable from the discourse context:

(5.66) a.　*nene=ḡu=ine*
　　　　　leg=1SGP=thisR
　　　　　'my leg'

　　　b.　*no-ḡu　suḡa*
　　　　　GENP-1SGP　house
　　　　　'my house'

5.9.2 Possessor as complement

While the possessum is the head of the NP itself, the possessor-indexing has its own argument structure, subcategorizing for a possessor argument. The embedded possessor NP is, therefore, the complement of the possessor-indexing. However, if the discourse precludes ambiguity the possessor need not be overtly realized. This may occur where the possessor is prominent in the discourse due to a recent overt mention, as in (5.67)a., or where it is unambiguously understood from the discourse context, as in (5.67)b.:

(5.67) a.　*...aḡe=ña　**X**[41]　nogoi　n-e　aḡe　n-e　la=ni*
　　　　　go=IMM　PN　VOC　RL-3S　go　RL-3S　go=3SGO
　　　　'...X went, man! He went and he put

---

[41] This name has been omitted for cultural reasons.

    *ka   keha   hobo-ḡazu=o   keha **lholhoḡuai=na=o***
    LOC NSP   branch-wood=thatNV NSP   coil=3SGP=thatNV
    on a branch that coil of his,

    *ke la ade bo ke la nai keha **lholhoḡuai=na=o** ade...*
    PFV go here CNT PFV go put NSP   coil=3SGP=thatNV here
    [he] went here, [he] went and put a coil of his here…'

b. *n-a   hod-i=Ø   kaike letasi*
     RL-1EXCS take-TR=3SGO one   letter
     'I have received a letter

     *fufunu   mai=na   ka   **nau=ḡu***
     begin   come=CNT LOC place=1SGP
     from my home.'

The effect of the latter is that speaker and addressee possessors rarely have an overt pronominal mention.

5.9.3 Recursion

Where a possessor is realized by a nominal that itself is possessed, a nested structure of recursive possessive phrases occurs. Possessor complements occur as a NP embedded in the main NP. This complement may in turn have a possessor expressed as an embedded NP. There are no restrictions on the kind of possessive construction that may be involved, including prepositional pseudo-locative possession:

(5.68) a. *pamu=na=o   zuta-pamu=ana   **ka** ago*
        pump=3SGP=thatNV lamp-pump=thatN LOC youSG
        'the pump of that tilly lamp of yours'

     b. *ia   suga   **ka**   no-ḡu   ido*
        theSG house LOC GENP-1SGP mother
        'your mother's house'

     c. *ia   **no-na**   suga   tamo=mu*
        theSG GENP-3SGP house younger.sibling=2SGP
        'your brother's house'

5.10 Predicative possession

Possession may be expressed predicatively in two ways: by a nonverbal clause with the possessum as subject, or by a verb of possession, with the possessor as subject.

5.10.1 Nonverbal predicative possession

Ownership may be expressed by a special possessive predicative construction with the possessum as subject and a nonverbal predicate consisting of the appropriate host indexed to the possessor. The possessor itself is expressed within the predicate:

(5.69) a. *keha   pile=di=re   **no-na**   bla   tagi-na*
        NSP   side=3PLP=thoseN   GENP-3SGP   LMT   REFL-3SGP
        'Some parts simply belong to him himself.'

    b. *mala-ñhau are   **ge-ḡu**   ara*
        PURP-eat   thoseN   CNSM-1SGP   I
        'That food is mine.'

Only alienable possession is expressible in this way. Verbless clauses are discussed in detail in §8.1.

5.10.2 Verbs of possession

Possession may be expressed in a verbal construction involving verbs of possession. One verb, *kuru* 'possess' has only this function. Two further verbs express possession as one of their functions. These are the positive and negative existential verbs *au* and *teo*.

(5.70) a. *n-a   **kuru**   ga~gato=ḡu   ara*
        RL-1EXCS   possess   RD~think=1SGP   I
        'I have my ideas.'

    b. *manei   n-e   **au**   puhi   ta   dia*
        he   RL-3S   exist   way   SBD   be.bad
        'He has bad ways.'

    c. *manei   n-e   **teo**   nehu   dou*
        he   RL-3S   not.exist   nose   be.big
        'He does not have a big nose.'

These verbs of possession distinguish alienable and inalienable possessive relationships. The examples in (5.70) all express inalienable relationships.

Alienable relationships are expressed in the same way except that the verb occurs with an object enclitic coreferentially indexing the possessor subject:

(5.71) a. *a*   ***kuru=ḡai***   *gai*   *la bla*
     1EXCS   possess=1EXCO   weEXC   ?? LMT
     'We have

     kokolo=di   *foḡra*   *t=au=are*
     class=3PLP   sick   SBD=exist=thoseN
     all those kinds of sicknesses.'

    b. *ara n-a*   ***au=nau***   *kaike zuta-pamu*
      I   RL-1EXCS exist=1SGO   one   lamp-pump
      'I have one tilly lamp.'

    c. *gita*   *da*   ***teo=gita***   *faiba*
      weINC 1INCS not.exist=1INCO   boat
      'We haven't got a boat.'

This middle voice construction is discussed in §6.1.3.2.

5.11 Possessive marking in the verb complex

The general possessor-indexing host occurs inside the verb complex with adverbial functions. It may occur preverbally as a desiderative. Only the general host is permissible in this construction, even where the action involves consumption by mouth:

(5.72) a. *mane=aro*   *n-e*   ***no-di***   *faroho=ḡai gai*
     man=thoseN RL-3S GENP-3PLP smite=1INCO weINC
     'Those men want to hit us.'

    b. *ara n-a*   *papara gu=na*   *n-a*   ***no-ḡu***   *ñhau*
      I   RL-1EXCS suffer   CNTX=3SGP RL-1EXCS GENP-1SGP eat
      'I'm suffering because I want to eat.'

The indexed host also occurs postverbally giving a sense of immediacy to the predication. In this construction both the general and 'consumed' hosts occur:

(5.73) a. *n-e-ge*   *kusu*   *la toga* ***no-di=u***   *bagovu*
     RL-3S-PRS be.first go arrive GENP-3PLP=CNT PNLOC
     'They were the first to arrive at Bagovu.'

b. *manei*   *n-e*   *ñhau*   **ge-na**
     he   RL-3S   eat   CNSM-3SGP
     'He is eating.'

Adverbial modification by possessor-indexing host is discussed in more detail in §7.5.4.3 and §7.6.1.

CHAPTER 6: ARGUMENT STRUCTURE

6.1 Argument-indexing

6.1.1 Argument role hierarchy

The assignment of argument-indexing in the verb complex is driven by a hierarchy of semantic roles. At the extremes of this hierarchy are the prototypical actor and the prototypical undergoer.

At the bottom of the hierarchy is the macro-role 'undergoer'. This role reflects participants that undergo the event, i.e., they are acted upon in some way. As a result of the event they are affected by the action, they change in some way. This may involve a change of activity (theme) or of state (patient). To use the 'primitive operator' terminology of Role and Reference Grammar (Foley and Van Valin [1984]; Van Valin [1993]), undergoer covers the roles of all arguments that are CAUSE DO and CAUSE BE by the situation coded by the predication. These are [-A] arguments.

The other end of the hierarchy is the macro-role 'actor', reflecting participants that carry out the event. These participants perform the action, either volitionally (agent) or non-volitionally (active theme); or cause it to happen, either volitionally (agent) or non-volitionally (force). In other words, actor covers the roles of all arguments that DO or CAUSE the situation coded by the predication. These are [+A] arguments.

A further category of argument, statives, are treated in Kokota in the same way as prototypical actors. Statives are participants that are in a state, but are not acted upon, and therefore do not undergo the predication (corresponding to unaccusative subjects). These arguments are not acted upon, so are not undergoers, and are therefore not [-A] arguments. Instead they are arguments that BE the situation coded by the predication.

Such arguments behave in the same way as actors. The highest position in the semantic hierarchy thus encompasses the semantic roles of all arguments that DO, CAUSE, or BE the situation coded by the predication. For the purposes of representing the fact that actors and statives behave in the same way, both will be referred to as [+A] arguments. It should be kept in mind, however, that this umbrella term covers statives as well as actual actors.

In between are a number of argument roles that neither DO, CAUSE, nor BE anything, nor do they have anything done to them that causes them to DO or BE anything. These are experiencers, instruments, and locatives.

In experiencing an event no volition is involved, and a participant does not DO anything, or CAUSE anything to be done, or BE anything. Equally, however, that participant is not acted upon by another participant. Consequently experiencers are neither actors nor undergoers. However, the requirement that an experiencer has a sentient quality makes experiencer the most actor-like of the non-actor roles, and consequently the highest in the hierarchy below actor.

The role instrument applies to participants that are in a way the opposite of experiencers. While experiencers are not included in actor or undergoer because they neither carry out nor undergo an event, so don't have key characteristics of either, an instrument is not included in actor or undergoer because it has some defining characteristics of *both*: it acts upon another participant to cause it to do or be something (so has the characteristics of an actor), while at the same time is acted upon by another participant that causes it to do something (so has the characteristics of an undergoer). Having some characteristics of both, it is grouped with neither. However, since it does not have the sentience requirement of experiencers, it falls below experiencer in the hierarchy. The location of instrument below experiencer in the hierarchy is demonstrated by the fact that experiencers may be subjects, while instruments may not, as discussed below.

Like the terms 'actor' and 'undergoer', 'locative' here is an umbrella term, in this case covering semantic roles including temporal and spatial locative, goal, and source, which all behave in a similar way, and involve arguments that are the location associated with the primitive operators BE AT, CAUSE BE AT, and CAUSE NOT BE AT. Locatives do not do anything, or cause anything to be done, or be anything. Equally, they are not acted upon and caused to do or be anything by any other participant. Consequently locative also falls into neither the [+A] category of actor/stative nor the [-A] category of undergoer.

The semantic role hierarchy may be characterized as follows:

(6.1)   ACTOR/ → EXP → INSTR → LOC → UNDERGOER
         STATIVE

Verbs do not subcategorize for the grammatical roles of their arguments. Instead the subcategorization frame dictates the semantic roles of arguments. In addition, verb subcategorizations dictate whether the arguments subcategorized are core arguments or obliques. In some instances an argument may be realized by a core *or* an oblique argument. In addition the optionality of arguments is represented in verbal subcategorization. This is all exemplified in §6.1.3.

6.1.2 Argument agreement indexing

Argument agreement is assigned on the basis of the semantic role hierarchy. Two forms of agreement exist: preverbal agreement in the form of an argument-indexed modal/subject particle, and postverbal agreement. These superficially resemble subject and object-indexing respectively.

6.1.2.1 Preverbal agreement

Preverbal modal/subject particles occur in two competing systems. In the standard system the modal/subject particle is indexed for the subcategorized argument with the semantic role highest on the semantic hierarchy given in (6.1). This system recognizes the categories of first person exclusive, first person inclusive, second person, and third person, but does not distinguish number. The forms (repeating Table 3.1) are:

TABLE 6.1. PREVERBAL ARGUMENT AGREEMENT

1 EXC	1 INC	2	3
a	*da*	*o*	*e*

With the exception of the first inclusive category, these preverbal particles are immediately preceded by one of a set of modal markers (one of which is realized as zero). First inclusive particles typically make no modal distinctions.

In the competing modal particle system, discussed in detail in §7.5.2.5, person categories are not distinguished. As no arguments are indexed in this system, it does not form part of the agreement system.

6.1.2.2 Postverbal agreement

Postverbal agreement recognizes the same person categories as preverbal indexing: first exclusive, first inclusive, second, and third persons. In addition it also distinguishes between singular and plural in all but the first inclusive category (where no singular exists). This agreement takes the form of a series of indexed enclitics on the verb complex. The forms (repeating Table 3.2) are:

TABLE 6.2. POSTVERBAL ARGUMENT-INDEXING

	1 EXC	1 INC	2	3
SG	=au ~ =nau	-	=igo ~ =nigo	=i ~ =ni ~ Ø
PL	=ḡai	=gita	=ḡau	=di ~ =ri

6.1.2.2.1 Postverbal agreement allomorphy

The third singular category includes a zero allomorph. This occurs solely in conjunction with the transitivizing suffix -*i*, and is discussed further in §6.3.2.

The remaining third singular forms, along with the first and second singular enclitics, involve an allomorph with the initial consonant /n/, and an allomorph without the consonant. The distribution of these allomorphs is partially systematic and phonologically motivated: the /n/ initial forms occur when the host has a final vowel identical to the initial vowel of the enclitic (/i/ for 2SG and 3SG, /a/ for 1SG). Verbs with other final vowels may occur with either allomorph; however, there is a tendency towards the non-/n/ forms. The free variation of the allomorphs is demonstrated by the following two clauses, both produced by the same elderly speaker:

(6.2) a. *ara-hi   a   turi tufa=nigo   kaike tu~turi...*
       I-EMPH 1EXCS tell affect=2SGO one RD~tell
       'I'm going to tell you a story...'

   b. *ara a-ke   turi tufa=igo   ago   kaike tu~turi...*
      I   1EXCS-PFV tell affect=2SGO youSG   one RD~tell
      'I'm going to tell you a story...'

Tables 6.3, 6.4, and 6.5 illustrate the third singular enclitic allomorphy in action.

The third plural allomorphy also appears to be partly phonologically motivated, or derived from a previous system that was phonologically motivated. Many verbs occur with either allomorph; however, verbs that are /i/ final tend to occur with the =*ri* form, as do /e/ final verbs to a lesser extent. Verbs with other final vowels freely occur with either form. One speaker expressed the view that =*di* was the true Kokota form, while =*ri* was a borrowing from the neighboring Zabana language. Possible supporting evidence for this is that there is an apparent tendency for speakers to give =*di* in elicitation. Whatever the origins, aside from the partial phonological motivation, synchronic distribution is in free variation. The following two examples were produced by the same speaker only a few clauses apart:

(6.3) a. *ḡ-e   la   naboto-u ba,   varedake-u ba,   tulufulu teḡe*
       NT-3S go ten-NMLZ ALT twenty-NMLZ ALT   thirty   turtle
       '(It) might be ten, might be twenty, thirty turtles

       ta   la hod-i=di=re   gai
       SBD go take-TR=3PLO=thoseN weEXC
       that we take.'

   b. *kaike hod-i=ri   gudu   bla...*
      one   take-TR=3PLO EXHST LMT
      'We take them all...'

6.1.2.2.2 Postverbal agreement as clitic

The postverbal agreement markers cliticize to the core of the verb complex. Verbal predicates may consist of a single verb or a number of verbs in a serial construction (see §6.5.) Where a single verb is present any postverbal agreement marker present is cliticized to that verb. Where a serial construction is marked for agreement postverbally, it is the final element that carries the agreement marker, whether or not that is the root the marking applies to. No agreement marking is possible within the verb complex core.

It is a feature of serial verb constructions that certain verbs may occur series-finally modifying the head verb. In the following example, the verb *mai* 'come' is modifying the verb *hoda* 'take' to give the meaning 'bring':

(6.4) *o la hoda **mai**=ni=u*   *ia   raro ta   dou*
       2S go take   come=3SGO=CNT theSG pot SBD be.big
       'Go [and] bring the big pot.'

The directional verb *mai* does not itself subcategorize for an argument other than agent or active theme. The undergoer in the clause is subcategorized by *hoda* 'take'. However, it is the final element of the verb complex, *mai*, that carries the postverbal agreement indexing, not the verb that subcategorizes for the indexed argument. Furthermore, the non-final element occurs in its intransitive form (*hoda*, instead of its transitivized counterpart *hod-i*).

When more than one bivalent verb occurs in a series, and all subcategorize for the same complement, the complex predication subcategorizes for that one complement. Agreement indexing cliticizes to only the final verb, but indexes an argument subcategorized by each of the verbs. In (6.5) both *zikra* 'pour out' and *koko* 'leave' subcategorize for a theme. The participant filling this role is identical for each. The complex predication subcategorizes for only that undergoer, and that argument is indexed only on the final of the two verbs:

(6.5)   *ta   moita   la   raisi   ana,*
        SBD be.cooked CND rice   thatN
        'If the rice is cooked,

        zikra   koko=ni   bakru=na=na
        pour.out leave=3SGO liquid=3SGP=thatN
        pour away its liquid.'

However, when several bivalent verbs subcategorize for different complements the complex predication subcategorizes for all the arguments. The complement of the final verb in the series is indexed by the enclitic, complements of non-final verbs occurring as subsequent, unindexed, complements:

(6.6)   *toka   fa-nhigo   tufa=nau   ḡazu   ine*
         chop   CS-be.finished   affect=1SGO   wood   thisR
         'Finish chopping this wood for me.'

The first and second verbs subcategorize for a patient, and the clause contains an overt patient. However, the final verb, *tufa* 'affect', subcategorizes for a goal (in this instance as a benefactive). The argument that is indexed postverbally is not the patient subcategorized by the head and overtly realized in the clause, but the goal subcategorized by *tufa*.

The clitic status of the postverbal agreement forms can be most clearly seen when postverbal adverbial forms are also present. In (6.7)a. possessor-indexing host (*no-ḡu* 'my') occurs with an adverbial function (the adverbial functions of possessor forms are discussed in §7.5.4.3 and §7.6.1). With its adverbial function this modifier occurs within the verb complex core. As this modifier is therefore the final element of the verb complex core in (6.7)a., postverbal agreement indexing is cliticized to that form, and not to the verb itself. In (6.7)b. the modifier *fakamo* 'always' occurs, again finally in the verb complex core. Again the agreement enclitic attaches to that core-final element, not the verb. In (6.7)b., however, a further postverbal modifier occurs—the continuous aspect marker =*u*. As this is a non-core modifier, it follows the agreement enclitic:

(6.7) a. *ara n-a   dupa   **no-ḡu=ni**   mane   ine*
           I   RL-1EXCS punch   GENP-1SGP=3SGO   man   thisR
           'I'm hitting this man.'

       b. *ge   e   teo   ḡe lao ge   hoda **fakamo=i=u**   gai...*
           SEQ 3S not.exist   NT go   SEQ take   always=3SGO=CNT   weEXC
           'We don't always go and take turtles...'

6.1.3 The assignment of agreement

The agreement indexed by both the preverbal and postverbal agreement markers is assigned in a unified manner following the semantic role hierarchy discussed above. This assignment is driven by an interface between the semantic role hierarchy and the subcategorization frames of individual verbs, with three constraints:

(6.8) a. Agreement may only index a core argument.
       b. Preverbal agreement is indexed to the subcategorized argument with the semantic role that is highest in the hierarchy.
       c. Postverbal agreement is indexed to the subcategorized argument with the semantic role that is highest in the hierarchy **below** [+A] (i.e., below actor/stative).

This drives the assignment of agreement in the following way. If a verb subcategorizes for a single argument, preverbal agreement looks for the argument with the highest semantic role, finds the sole subcategorized argument, and maps on to that. Postverbal agreement looks for the argument with the highest role lower than actor. If the sole argument subcategorized conforms to that constraint, then it is also indexed by the postverbal agreement, giving coreferential agreement. If that argument is an actor, then postverbal agreement is blocked from mapping on to it. Postverbal agreement then looks for the next highest argument, but with no other arguments being subcategorized, postverbal agreement then exhausts (i.e., is not assigned and thus not realized in the clause).

If a verb subcategorizes for more than one argument, preverbal agreement looks for the subcategorized argument with the highest semantic role, and maps on to that. Postverbal agreement looks for the argument with the highest role below actor, and maps on to it. If that argument is realized as an oblique, then the agreement is blocked from mapping on to it, and looks for the subcategorized argument with the next highest role. If no further argument is present then that agreement exhausts. If a further argument is subcategorized, postverbal agreement maps on to that, unless it too is an oblique. This process is carried out until the agreement is assigned, or no further arguments are available to be mapped on to and the agreement exhausts. If on the other hand postverbal agreement is assigned, and there is a further argument lower in the hierarchy, then that argument is realized without any agreement being marked, no agreement being left unassigned and free to index that argument.

6.1.3.1 Agreement assignment mapping

To expand on the discussion of the assignment of argument agreement above, we can consider initially the interface of the semantic role hierarchy with the verbal subcategorization frames of stative verbs.

6.1.3.1.1 Monovalent verbs

A stative verb such as *dou* 'be big' is monovalent, subcategorizing for a single argument with the semantic role stative, subcategorized as a core argument. The subcategorization frame is < ST_{CR} >. The production of a clause with only this verb involves preverbal agreement looking for the subcategorized argument with the highest semantic role in the hierarchy. This agreement finds the argument subcategorized as stative, and maps on to that. Postverbal agreement looks for the subcategorized argument that is highest in the role hierarchy below [+A] (i.e., actor/stative). No such argument exists in the subcategorization frame, so postverbal agreement finds no argument to map on to and consequently exhausts. In other words the absence of a suitable argument on which to map prevents any postverbal agreement from being realized. This generates a clause such as the following:

(6.9)   *su̱ga ine   n-e   dou*
          house thisR RL-3S be.big
          'This house is big.'

Here preverbal agreement is indexed to the stative, while no postverbal agreement is present. A similar result is reached with monovalent active verbs. A verb such as *kota* 'go ashore' subcategorizes for a single argument that is an agent and is a core argument. The subcategorization frame is < AG$_{CR}$ >. Preverbal agreement looks for the subcategorized argument with the highest semantic role, and finds and maps on to the agent. Postverbal agreement looks for the argument with the highest semantic role below [+A], finds no such argument, is unable to map on to anything, and so exhausts, giving a clause such as the following:

(6.10)   *ara n-a   kota*
          I   RL-1EXCS go.ashore
          'I am going ashore.'

6.1.3.1.2 Bivalent verbs

Many bivalent verbs subcategorize for two core arguments, one of which is agent and the other patient. For such verbs, both preverbal and postverbal agreement are realized. *Dupa* 'punch' has the subcategorization frame < AG$_{CR}$ PAT$_{CR}$ >. Here preverbal agreement looks for the subcategorized argument with the highest semantic role, and finds and maps on to the agent. Postverbal agreement looks for the subcategorized argument with the highest semantic role below [+A], finds patient, and maps on to that. Both preverbal and postverbal agreement are satisfied and thus realized, generating a clause such as the following:

(6.11)   *ara n-a   dupa=i   manei*
          I   RL-1EXCS punch=3SGO he
          'I hit him.'

Not all verbs that subcategorize for two arguments will generate clauses in which both preverbal and postverbal agreement are present. It may be that one of the arguments is optional. The verb *ñhau* 'eat', for example, subcategorizes for an agent and a patient; however, the patient is optional. The subcategorization frame is < AG$_{CR}$ (PAT$_{CR}$) >. This is identical to the subcategorization for *dupa*, except that the patient is coded as optional. With this verb preverbal agreement will look for the subcategorized argument with the highest semantic role and find and map on to agent. Where the patient is realized, postverbal agreement looks for the argument with the highest role lower than [+A], and finds and maps on to patient, giving a clause such as:

(6.12) *ara n-a*   *ñha=ni*   *ḡausa*   *ka*   *maneri*
        I   RL-1EXCS eat=3SGO betel.nut LOC they
        'I ate their betel nut.'

Where the patient is not realized, postverbal agreement looks for the argument with the highest role below [+A], and finding no such argument, exhausts:

(6.13) *ge*   *da*   *turi=ña*   *gita,* *gita* ***da*** *kusu*   *ñhau* *fea*
        SEQ 1INCS tell=IMM   weINC weINC 1INCS be.first eat   INIT
        'Before we talk we should eat.'

For the verbs discussed above the only core argument below [+A] is patient. However, many bivalent verbs subcategorize for arguments with other semantic roles. The verb *mhok-i* 'sit on' is bivalent (derived by the transitivizing suffix from the intransitive root *mhoko* 'sit'). This verb subcategorizes for an agent and a spatial locative, both core arguments, and both obligatory. The subcategorization for *mhok-i* is < AG$_{CR}$ SLOC$_{CR}$ >. Here the preverbal agreement looks for the subcategorized argument with the highest semantic role, and finds and maps on to agent. Postverbal agreement looks for the subcategorized argument with the highest role below [+A], finds spatial locative, and maps on to that. This generates clauses such as:

(6.14) *n-a*   *mhok-i=Ø*   *ara* *kaike* *ifra*
        RL-1EXCS sit-TR=3SGO I   one   mat
        'I sit on one mat.'

Most verbs can cooccur with a spatial locative; however, few subcategorize for a participatory inner locative as *mhok-i* does. Clauses may include a locative, either temporal or spatial, but where that is not subcategorized, it is a circumstantial outer locative, and is realized by an oblique adjunct. As an adjunct, it may not be indexed. However, where a verb subcategorizes for an argument that may be an oblique, adjunct status does not block the assignment of agreement. Instead, it is the argument's oblique status that precludes indexing. Some verbs subcategorize for an argument as either core or oblique. In this situation several different constructions may be generated, as the basic emotion verbs *fahega* and *dia-nanafa* exemplify. These two stative verbs code the presence of an emotional state. *Fahega* codes the presence of a positive emotional state, and may be interpreted as 'be happy', 'be grateful', or any other positive emotional state. *Dia-nanafa* is a compound, literally 'be.bad-heart', which codes the presence of a negative emotional state. This verb may be interpreted as meaning 'be sad' or 'be sorry', but not 'be sorry for' (as in 'to pity'). It also does not realize the notion of 'anger' that, while treated as a negative emotion in English, is treated as an experienced sensation in Kokota (using the verb *bula* 'be angry', see §6.1.3.2.3).

These two basic emotion verbs subcategorize for a stative (the person in the emotional state), and the source of the emotion. They both have the subcategorization frame < ST_{CR} ($SC_{CR/OBL}$)>. In this frame not only is source optional, but it may be realized either by a core argument, or by an oblique. The preverbal agreement looks for the highest subcategorized argument role and finds and maps on to the stative. The postverbal agreement looks for the highest subcategorized argument role below [+A]. Where no source is realized that agreement exhausts:

(6.15)   *heve   n-e=u   ge   n-o   dia-nanafa=ña   ago*
         what   RL-3S=be.thus   SEQ   RL-2S   be.bad-heart=IMM   youSG
         'Why are you sad?'

Where a source is present and is realized as an oblique, postverbal agreement finds the source but is blocked from mapping on to it by the constraint on non-core agreement, so exhausts:

(6.16)   *ara   n-a   fahega   ka   ago*
         I   RL-1EXCS   be.happy   LOC   youSG
         'I'm happy with you.'

Where a source is present but is realized by a core argument, postverbal agreement finds that and maps on to it:

(6.17)   *ara   n-a   fahega=nigo   ago*
         I   RL-1EXCS   be.happy=2SGO   youSG
         'I'm happy with you.'

6.1.3.1.3 Trivalent verbs

Several trivalent verbs exist. For example, *tore* 'request' has the subcategorization frame < AG_{CR} (THM_{CR}) ($GL_{CR/OBL}$) >

This verb is maximally trivalent, subcategorizing for an agent (the requester), a theme (the item that is requested), and a goal (the person to whom the request is directed). Both the theme and goal are optional. Consequently *tore* may occur in an intransitive predication:

(6.18)   *ara   n-a   tore*
         I   RL-1EXCS   ask
         'I asked.'

Here preverbal agreement looks for the highest argument present, finds the agent, and maps on to that. Postverbal agreement looks for the highest argument below [+A]. No such argument exists so no postverbal agreement occurs. With this verb both agent and theme must be realized by a core argument, while the goal may be realized by a core argument or an oblique. As both the theme and goal are optional, *tore* may occur in a transitive predication, with either as core argument complement. In (6.19)a. the theme is complement, in (6.19)b. the goal is. In both examples preverbal agreement maps on to the agent. Postverbal agreement looks for the highest argument below [+A], and finds and maps on to the theme in (6.19)a., and the goal in (6.19)b.

(6.19) a. *n-a*   *tore=i*   *kaike* *bia*
       RL-1EXCS ask=3SGO one   beer
       'I asked for one beer.'

     b. *n-a*   *tore=i*   *mane* *ana*
       RL-1EXCS ask=3SGO man   thatN
       'I asked that man.'

However, all three arguments may occur. When the goal is expressed as a core argument the semantic hierarchy dictates argument order. In pragmatically unmarked clauses arguments are expressed in the order in which they occur in the hierarchy. As goal falls under the LOC umbrella, it is higher than theme and must be expressed before it, ([6.20]a.). The reverse is ungrammatical ([6.20]b.).

(6.20) a. *n-a*   *tore=i*   *mane* *ana*   *kaike* *bia*
       RL-1EXCS ask=3SGO   man   thatN   one   beer
       'I asked that man for a beer.'

     b. **n-a tore=i kaike bia mane ana*   'I asked that man for a beer.'

However, when the goal is expressed as an oblique different criteria apply. As discussed in §8.2.2, core arguments precede obliques in pragmatically unmarked clauses. Consequently, the grammaticality of the two argument order possibilities is the opposite of that in (6.20):

(6.21) a. *n-a*   *tore=i*   *kaike* *bia* *ka*   *mane* *ana*
       RL 1EXCS ask=3SGO one   beer LOC man   thatN
       'I asked for a beer from that man.'

     b. **n-a tore=i mane ana ka kaike bia* 'I asked that man for a beer.'

As only one complement may be indexed postverbally, when all three arguments are present one complement must remain unindexed. Goal is higher in the hierarchy than theme. Consequently in (6.20)a., where goal is realized as a core argument, postverbal agreement looks for the highest argument below [+A], finds goal, and maps on to it. Although a core argument theme is also present, it is not indexed, as no indexing remains unassigned and available to map on to it.

However, where the goal is realized as an oblique, as in (6.21)a., the indexing is assigned differently. Postverbal agreement looks for the highest argument below [+A], and finds goal but is blocked from mapping on to it by the constraint on indexing non-core arguments. It then looks for the next highest argument, and finding theme, maps on to that.

6.1.3.2 Middle voice: coreferential indexing

A number of classes of verbs have subcategorization frames that interact with the hierarchical assignment of agreement to generate clauses with coreferential indexing. These consist primarily of verbs that subcategorize for an experiencer. These include verbs that code negative sensations, involuntary bodily actions, pleasure or displeasure, and ownership. It does not, however, include basic emotion verbs (as discussed above). In addition to experiencer verbs, one verb assigns agreement coreferentially to temporal locatives.

Coreferential assignment is a predictable result of the interface between the subcategorization frames of the verbs and the hierarchical process of agreement assignment. As discussed above, preverbal assignment is assigned to the argument subcategorized which has the highest semantic role in the hierarchy. As most verbs subcategorize for a stative or an actor of some kind, preverbal agreement will be assigned to that argument for those verbs. Postverbal agreement is assigned to the subcategorized argument with the highest role in the hierarchy below [+A]. Consequently that agreement will be assigned to any further core arguments, such as patient, that are present in the subcategorization frame. If no other arguments are present, the postverbal agreement finds nothing to map on to and exhausts.

However, where a verb has no [+A] argument, i.e., where its highest subcategorized argument is an argument lower in the hierarchy than [+A], that argument attracts both preverbal and postverbal agreement. If, for example, a verb has an experiencer as its highest subcategorized argument, that argument, being the highest in the hierarchy present, attracts preverbal agreement. Since that argument is also the highest argument present below [+A], it also attracts postverbal agreement. Any further arguments subcategorized by the verb, being still lower in the hierarchy, attract no agreement, because all possible agreement has already been assigned.

6.1.3.2.1 Involuntary bodily actions

A class of verbs exists that code bodily actions that may be involuntary. The members of this class are:

(6.22) a. *sune* 'sniff'   e. *sihe* 'sneeze'
     b. *hekna* 'hiccup'[42]   f. *hohoa* 'yawn'
     c. *knaha* 'cough'   g. *kala-hohoa* 'burp' (lit. 'hair/leaf-yawn')
     d. *ḡloña* 'choke'

Verbs in this class assign argument roles in two different ways, reflecting two separate perspectives on the nature of the event, and reflected in parallel subcategorization frames. The events coded by verbs in this class may be regarded as actions that the participant has control over. In this perspective the verb subcategorizes for an agent. Alternatively, and more typically, the events may be regarded as sensations experienced by the participant, in which case the verb subcategorizes for an experiencer.

Where verbs in this class are treated as an action, they have the subcategorization frame $< AG_{CR} >$. With this subcategorization the resulting clause structure resembles that of most verbs with only one core argument. Preverbal agreement looks for the subcategorized argument with the highest semantic role and finds and maps on to the agent. Postverbal agreement looks for the highest argument below [+A], and finding no such argument, exhausts. This generates clauses such as:

(6.23) a. *ago*   *n-o*   *hekna*
       youSG RL-2S hiccup
       'You hiccup.'

      b. *n-e*   *knaha*   *manei*
        RL-3S cough   he
        'He's coughing.'

If these verbs are treated as an experienced sensation, they subcategorize for an experiencer, and an optional source of the experience: $< EXP_{CR} (SC_{CR}) >$. With this subcategorization preverbal agreement looks for the highest argument, finds experiencer, and maps on to that. Postverbal agreement looks for the highest subcategorized argument below [+A], also finds experiencer, and also maps on to that. The result is coreferential preverbal and postverbal agreement indexing:

(6.24) a. *ago*   *n-o*   *hekna=**nigo***
       youSG RL-2S hiccup=2SGO
       'You hiccup.'

      b. *ara*   *n-a*   *sihe=**nau***
        I   RL-1EXCS sneeze=1SGO
        'I am sneezing.'

---

[42] This is a reduced form of the now archaic *hehekna*.

When a source is also present the same coreferential indexing occurs. Preverbal agreement looks for the subcategorized argument with the highest role, and finds and maps on to experiencer. Postverbal agreement looks for the highest argument below [+A], and also finds and maps on to experiencer, experiencer being higher in the hierarchy than source. The source, being a core argument, could potentially attract agreement, but does not because all possible agreement has already been assigned. The result is a clause with two core arguments, and both preverbal and postverbal agreement, but where both forms of agreement coreferentially index one argument, while the other remains unindexed:

(6.25) a. *ara n-a   sihe=**nau**   karipauda   ana*
   I RL-1EXCS sneeze=1SGO curry.powder thatN
   'I am sneezing from that curry powder.'

  b. *manei   n-e   knaha=**i**   kufu   ine*
   he RL-3S cough=3SGO smoke thisR
   'He is coughing from this smoke.'

6.1.3.2.2 Verbs of illness

A similar situation applies to verbs expressing degrees of illness:

(6.26) a. *foḡra* 'be/feel unwell'
  b. *fo~foḡra* 'be/feel a little bit unwell'

As the glosses suggest, the derived reduplicated form has a sense of a lesser degree of illness—not really sick, just a little unwell. As with the involuntary bodily action verbs, each has two argument structures. However, here the difference is between an experienced sensation and a state, rather than a volitional act. Both have one possible argument structure in which the participant is treated as being in a state of being unwell. With this sense the verbs have the subcategorization frame $< AG_{CR} >$. This gives clauses such as:

(6.27) a. *ara n-a   foḡra*
   I RL-1EXCS sick
   'I am sick.'

  b. *ara n-a   fo~foḡra*
   I RL-1EXCS RD~sick
   'I am a little bit sick.'

However, both verbs have an alternative subcategorization frame in which the verbs are treated as experienced sensations, rather than states: $< EXP_{CR}$ $(SC_{CR/OBL}) >$. As with the involuntary bodily action verbs, preverbal agreement looks for the highest argument present, and finds and maps on to the experiencer. Postverbal agreement looks for the highest subcategorized argument below [+A], and also finds and so maps on to experiencer. Again the result is coreferential preverbal and postverbal agreement indexing:

(6.28) a. *ara n-a*   *foḡra=nau*
            I   RL-1EXCS   sick=1SGO
            'I feel sick.'

       b. *ara n-a*   *fo~foḡra=nau*
            I   RL-1EXCS   RD~sick=1SGO
            'I feel a little bit sick.'

The semantic distinction between the examples in (6.27) and the corresponding examples in (6.28) is captured by the use of *am* and *feel* in the free translations. As the subcategorization frame indicates, the source of the feeling of illness may be realized as an oblique argument. Such an argument does not attract agreement indexing due to the constraint on indexing non-core arguments:

(6.29)   *ara n-a*   *(fo)-foḡra=nau*   *ka*   *mala-ñhau*   *are*
           I   RL-1EXCS   RD~sick=1SGO   LOC   PURP-eat   thoseN
           'I feel (a little bit) sick from that food.'

However, as with both the involuntary bodily action verbs, where the source is expressed as a core argument, the same coreferential indexing occurs, leaving the source unindexed. Preverbal agreement looks for the subcategorized argument with the highest role, and finds and maps on to experiencer. Postverbal agreement looks for the highest argument below [+A], and also finds and maps on to experiencer. The resulting clauses again have two core arguments, and both preverbal and postverbal agreement, but again both forms of agreement coreferentially index one argument, leaving the other unindexed:

(6.30)   *ara n-a*   *(fo)~foḡra=nau*   *mala-ñhau*   *are*
           I   RL-1EXCS   RD~sick=1SGO   PURP-eat   thoseN
           'I feel (a little bit) sick from that food.'

6.1.3.2.3 Negative sensory states

A similar situation applies to a class of verbs that code certain negative sensory states, including:

(6.31) a. *marhi-*   'feel pain'
       b. *bula-*   'feel angry'
       c. *huñu-/humu-*   'have heartburn'

While the verbs in (6.22) are treated as potentially intentional acts, pain, anger, and heartburn are not treated as anything other than experienced sensations. Verbs in this class have the subcategorization frame < EXP_{CR} ($\text{SC}_{\text{CR/OBL}}$) >. When only the experiencer is present, preverbal agreement looks for the subcategorized argument with the highest role in the hierarchy, finds experiencer, and maps on to that. Postverbal agreement looks for the subcategorized argument with the highest role lower than actor, also finds experiencer, and also maps on to that. This gives clauses such as the following:

(6.32) a. *ara n-a   marhi=nau*
        I   RL-1EXCS feel.pain=1SGO
        'I am in pain.'

    b. *ḡ-e   bula=i=ña   manei*
        NT-3S feel.angry=3SGO=IMM he
        'He was angry.'

    c. *ara n-a   huñu=nau*
        I   RL-1EXCS have.heartburn=1SGO
        'I have heartburn.'

Here the coreferential indexing is the only possible outcome of the interface between the semantic role hierarchy and the subcategorization frames of these verbs. It is impossible for this interface to generate a clause without postverbal agreement, and such a clause would be ungrammatical:

(6.33)   **ara na **marhi***   'I am in pain.'

Coreferentially indexing clauses do not represent reflexive constructions. Reflexive constructions require a subcategorization for patient or theme, and a realization of that argument by an overt reflexive form. To form a reflexive construction, the verbs in (6.31) require causative marking overriding the subcategorization frame of the verb, introducing an agent and requiring a patient. This patient may be realized by an overt reflexive argument, giving a reflexive construction that contrasts with the coreferential indexing in (6.32):

(6.34)   *ara n-a   fa marhi=nau   tai-ḡu*
        I   RL-1EXCS CS feel.pain=1SGO REFL-1SGP
        'I have hurt myself.'

This parallels non-reflexive causative constructions:

(6.35) a. *ara n-a   fa marhi=nigo   ago*
        I   RL-1EXCS CS feel.pain=2SGO yousG
        'I have hurt you.'

   b. *t=au=ana*   *n-e*   **fa** *bula=nigo*   *ago*
      SBD=exist=thatN RL-1EXCS CS feel.pain=2SGO   yousG
      'That is making you cross.'

As with the verbs of illness, the source of the pain, anger, or heartburn may be realized as an oblique argument that does not attract agreement indexing:

(6.36) a. *ago*   *n-o*   *marhi=nigo*   *ka*   *nene=mu=ana*
       yousG RL-2S feel.pain=2SGO LOC leg=2SGP=thatN
       'You are in pain from that leg of yours.'

     b. *ago*   *n-o*   *bula=nigo*   *ka*   *manei baiu*
       yousG RL-2S feel.angry=2SGO LOC he   maybe
       'Maybe you are angry with him.'

     c. *ara n-a*   *huñu=nau*   *ka*   *maliri=na zora ana*
       I   RL-1EXCS have.heartburn=1SGO LOC fat=3SGP   pig thatN
       'I have heartburn from that pig fat.'

However, as with both the involuntary bodily action verbs and the verbs of illness, where the source is expressed as a core argument the same coreferential indexing occurs, leaving the source unindexed:

(6.37) a. *ago*   *n-o*   *marhi=nigo*   *nene=mu=ana*
       yousG RL-2S feel.pain=2SGO   leg=2SGP=thatN
       'You are in pain from that leg of yours.'

     b. *ara n-a*   *bula=nau*   *tu~turi* *are*
       I   RL-1EXCS feel.angry=1SGO RD~tell thoseN
       'I am angry about those stories.'

     c. *ara n-a*   *huñu=nau*   *maliri=na zora ana*
       I   RL-1EXCS have.heartburn=1SGO fat=3SGP pig thatN
       'I have heartburn from that pig fat.'

6.1.3.2.4 Verbs of possession

A similar situation applies to a class of verbs of possession, but here both arguments are obligatory. This class consists of three verbs:

(6.38) a. *kuru* 'have'
     b. *au*   'exist'
     c. *teo*   'not exist'

Of these, only *kuru* occurs solely as a verb of possession. *Au* and *teo* occur primarily as existential verbs (positive and negative respectively—discussed in §6.5). With that function they are monovalent. However, they also occur with *kuru* as bivalent verbs of possession.

The realization of the relationship of possession by possessive verbs is treated in two different ways, depending on whether the possessive relationship is alienable or inalienable (see §5.10.2). Where the relationship is inalienable it is treated as a state. The possessor is a stative. Preverbal agreement looks for the highest argument, finds the stative, and maps on to that. Postverbal agreement looks for the highest argument below [+A], which excludes the stative. For reasons that are at this stage not understood, the possessum complement, whatever its role may be, is not then mapped on to by postverbal agreement. It does not attract agreement at all.[43] The result is clauses such as the following:

(6.39) a. *n-a*   *kuru*   *ga~gato=ḡu*   *ara*
RL-1EXCS own   RD~think=1SGP   I
'I have my ideas.'

    b. *manei*   *n-e*   *au*   *puhi*   *ta*   *dia*
he   RL-3S exist   way   SBD   be.bad
'He has bad ways.'

    c. *manei*   *n-e*   *teo*   *nehu*   *dou*
he   RL-3S not.exist   nose   be.big
'He doesn't have a big nose.'

By contrast, where the relationship is alienable, it is treated as a phenomenon that is experienced by the possessor, rather than one in which the owner is in some way active or stative. The corollary to the coding of the owner as the experiencer of the ownership is the treatment of the thing owned as the source of the experience. The subcategorization frame of these verbs in alienable relationships is therefore $< \mathrm{EXP_{CR}}\ \mathrm{SC_{CR}} >$.

Here preverbal agreement looks for the subcategorized argument with the highest semantic role in the hierarchy, and finds and maps on to the experiencer. Postverbal agreement looks for the argument with the highest role below [+A], and also finds and maps on to experiencer. The source does not attract agreement since both forms of agreement are already assigned. Again this is the only possible result of the interface between the hierarchy and the subcategorization frame of these verbs. The result is clauses like the following:

---

[43] This could be because the possessed argument may be incorporated (see §6.4). If so, an alternative analysis could be that NP cores expressing an inalienably possessed entity are incorporated, while those expressing alienably possessed entities cannot be.

(6.40) a. *a kuru=ḡai gai la bla kokolo=di foḡra t=au=are*
2S own=1EXCOweEXC ?? LMT class=3PLP sick SBD=exist=thoseN
'We have all those kinds of sicknesses.'

    b. *ara n-a au=nau kaike zuta-pamu*
I RL-1EXCS exist=1SGO one lamp-pump
'I have one tilly lamp.'

    c. *gita da teo=gita faiba*
weINC 1INCS not.exist=1INCO boat
'We haven't got a boat.'

Again the resulting structure involves bivalent verbs marking agreement twice, with both forms of agreement coreferential to one argument, with the second argument not indexed.

6.1.3.2.5 Verbs of pleasure and displeasure

One further class of verbs has experiencer as its highest subcategorized argument. As discussed in §6.2, one function of reduplication is to derive bivalent forms from monovalent, typically stative, verbs. This valency-augmenting derivation applies to the stative verbs *dia* 'be bad' and *keli* 'be good', generating the forms *didia-* 'be displeased by' and *kekeli-* 'be pleased by'. These subcategorize for an experiencer and an optional source, both core arguments, with the subcategorization frame $< EXP_{CR} (SC_{CR}) >$. Again preverbal agreement looks for the subcategorized argument with the highest semantic role, and finds and maps on to experiencer. Again postverbal agreement looks for the highest argument below [+A], also finds experiencer, and also maps on to that. Where the source is not present this process results in clauses resembling those in (6.24) and (6.32):

(6.41) a. *n-a ke~keli=nau*
RL-1EXCS RD~be.good=1SGO
'I am pleased.'

    b. *ara ginai a di~dia=nau*
I FUT 1EXCS RD~be.bad=1SGO
'I will be displeased.'

If a source is present the same assignment of agreement occurs, coreferentially indexing the experiencer, with the source attracting no agreement, all possible agreement indexing having already been assigned. This gives clauses resembling those in (6.37) and (6.40):

(6.42) a. *n-a*   *ke~keli=**nau***   *ara* *sote* *ine*
RL-1EXCS   RD~be.good=1SGO   I   shirt   thisR
'I am pleased by this shirt.'

b. *n-e*   *di~dia=**ni***   *t=au=ana*
RL-3S   RD~be.bad=3SGO   SBD=exist=thatN
'He is displeased by that.'

The effect on valency of reduplication with these verbs is discussed in §6.3.1.2.

6.2 Permissible subject roles

The grammatical relation 'subject' is limited to arguments with semantic roles at the top end of the semantic role hierarchy given in (6.1), the cut-off point falling between experiencer and instrument.

All argument roles encompassed by the macro-role actor (i.e., all arguments that CAUSE or DO the situation coded by the predication) are permissible subjects. This includes agents of both transitive and unergative predications (as in [6.43]a.–b.); active themes ([6.43]c.); and force ([6.43]d.):

(6.43) a. ***ara*** *n-a*   *dupa=i*   *manei*
I   RL-1EXCS   punch=3SGO   he
'I hit him.'

b. ***ara*** *n-a*   *kota*
I   RL-1EXCS   go.ashore
'I am going ashore.'

c. *ia*   ***koilo***   *n-e*   *zogu* *ka*   *kokorako*
theSG   coconut   RL-3S   drop   LOC   chicken
'The coconut fell on the chicken.'

d. *ia*   ***dihunare***   *n-e*   *fa kokopo=i*   *hore*   *ana*
theSG   rough.sea   RL-3S   CS capsize=3SGO   dugout   thatN
'The rough sea capsized that dugout canoe.'

In addition, statives (i.e., arguments that BE the situation coded by the predication) are permissible subjects:

(6.44)   ***suḡa***   *ine*   *n-e*   *dou*   *ḡlehe*
house   thisR   RL-3S   be.big   very
'This house is very big.'

The highest position in the semantic role hierarchy in Kokota is occupied by all roles that CAUSE, DO, or BE the situation coded by the predication (see §6.1.1). This encompasses all roles exemplified as subjects in (6.43) and (6.44).

The next highest role is experiencer. This is also a permissible subject, as illustrated extensively in §6.1.3.2. It is possible to hypothesize that experiencers are permissible subjects as they share certain crucial semantic features with prototypical actors. It is inherent in the notion of experiencer that the participant be sentient. It may be argued that sentience carries with it an implicit capacity for volition. Experiencers are, therefore, inherently potential agents. Experiencer is, however, the lowest semantic role permissible as subject. The next lowest role, instrument, is not a permissible subject:

(6.45) *vilai ine   n-e   fa-lehe=i   kokorako   ana
        knife thisR RL-3S   CS-die=3SGO   chicken   thatN
        'This knife killed that chicken.'

It is clear from discussion with speakers that such clauses are unacceptable purely on semantic grounds—that the knife in (6.45) cannot kill the chicken because it cannot act on its own. Inanimate objects may be transitive subjects, but only as force, not as instrument. Thus the context of (6.46) dictates the clause's acceptability. The first reading is acceptable because the coconut is an active theme—it fell without being acted upon, and in doing so killed the chicken. The second reading is unacceptable because the coconut was being used as an instrument and was therefore being acted upon.

(6.46) a. koilo   ine   n-e   fa-lehe=i   kokorako   ana
           coconut   thisR RL-3S   CS-die=3SGO   chicken   thatN
           'This coconut killed that chicken.'
           [The coconut fell onto the chicken without being acted upon.]
           *[I clubbed the chicken with the coconut.]

All argument roles lower in the hierarchy are ineligible to be subject. Locatives are ineligible. A location name or a NP coding a physical or temporal location may be subject, but not with the semantic role of locative. Locations may function with other roles, including undergoer, in which case it is object. In (6.47) a location name is a theme ([6.47]a.) and a patient ([6.47]b.).

(6.47) a. ...tabar-i=Ø=u   manei   banesokeo ana
           buy-TR=3SGO=CNT   he   PNLOC   thatN
           '...he bought that Banesokeo.'

       b. aria   d-aḡe   nhura=i   fitupoḡu
           1INC.IMP 1INCS-go   destroy=3SGO PNLOC
           'Let's go and destroy Fitupoḡu!'

At the other end of the semantic hierarchy, locations may function as statives. As discussed in §6.1.1, statives BE the situation coded by the predication and share highest position in the hierarchy. As such they are eligible to be subject:

(6.48)   *sisīga   n-e   namo   bla*
         PNLOC   RL-3S be.near LMT
         'Sisīga is simply nearby.'

Locations with a semantic role encompassed by the macro-role LOC (such as locative, goal, source, etc.) are ineligible to be subject.

Undergoers (including theme and patient) occupy the lowest position in the hierarchy, and as such are also ineligible to be subject. A significant manifestation of this constraint is the complete absence of passive constructions.

6.3 Valency alteration

Three derivational strategies exist that change the valency of a verb. One, reduplication, reduces the valency of a verb (with two partial exceptions). The other strategies, causative marking and a transitivizing suffix, augment valency.

6.3.1 Valency altering reduplication

Reduplication has a general derivational function that in some cases changes word class, and in others does not (see §2.4.1.1). Relevant to transitivity is verb reduplication, affecting the valency of the verb. In a major functional subregularity, transitive verb roots are reduplicated to derive intransitive verbs, reduplication thereby reducing valency by one argument. With two semantically related forms, reduplication idiosyncratically derives a valency-augmented, bivalent form, although not a transitive but an experiencer verb.

6.3.1.1 Valency reducing reduplication

Subregular valency altering reduplication reduces the valency of the underived form by deriving an unergative verb from a transitive root. However, a small number of forms display reduplication idiosyncratically, deriving an unaccusative form from a transitive root.

6.3.1.1.1 Unergative derivation

Unergative valency reducing reduplication appears to be productive, to the extent that if a verb root is reduplicated, it will be interpreted as an unergative intransitive verb unless some other lexically specified meaning exists.

Unergative reduplicative derivation operates by removing the lowest subcategorized argument in the semantic hierarchy from the verb's argument structure. Since transitive verbs subcategorize for a [+A] and a [-A] argument, this effectively means that the [-A] argument is removed from the subcategorization frame. For example, *dupa* 'punch', subcategorizes for an agent and a patient in the frame < AG_{CR} PAT_{CR} >. The derived verb *dudupa* 'be punching' is an unergative verb with the frame < AG_{CR} >.

(6.49) a.   *manei*   *n-e-ke*   *dupa=nau*   *ara*
          he   RL-3S-PFV   punch=1SGO   I
          'He punched me.'

     b.   *manei*   *n-e*   *du~dupa*   *bla*
          he   RL-3S   RD~punch   LMT
          'He was just punching.'

The same applies when the [-A] argument is a theme. Transitive *gato* 'think about s.th.' reduplicates to derive the unergative *gagato* 'think'. The underived frame is < AG_{CR} THM_{CR} >, while the derived verb has the frame < AG_{CR} >.

(6.50) a.   *ara*   *n-a*   *gato=igo*   *ago*
          I   RL-1EXCS   think=2SGO   yousG
          'I'm thinking about you.'

     b.   *ara*   *n-a*   *ga~gato*
          I   RL-1EXCS   RD~think
          'I'm thinking.'

6.3.1.1.2 Unaccusative derivation

A small number of transitive roots are reduplicated to derive intransitive verbs that are unaccusative. This appears to be idiosyncratic and lexically specified. As with unergative derivation, the effect of this operation is to reduce the valency of the root by removing one argument from its argument structure. However, unlike unergative derivation, it is the [+A] argument, the agent, which is removed, not the [-A] undergoer. The remaining argument also undergoes modification of its semantic role. An undergoer in the underived frame, it becomes a stative in the derived frame. For example, the root *laḡe* 'castrate' subcategorizes for an agent and a patient with the frame < AG_{CR} PAT_{CR} >. The derived *lalaḡe* 'be castrated' is an unaccusative verb with the frame < ST_{CR} >.

(6.51) a.   *manei*   *n-e*   *laḡe=i*   *zora ana*
          he   RL-3S   castrate=3SGO   pig   thatN
          'He castrated that pig.'

b. *zora   ana   n-e   la~laḡe*
   pig   thatN   RL-3S   RD~castrate
   'That pig is castrated.'

Unaccusative derivation only occurs where the underived undergoer is patient. The derived stative is then in the state resulting from the action coded by the transitive root. This state may be permanent, as in (6.51), but may equally be a temporary state. For example, *hoti* 'sting' (< AG_{CR} PAT_{CR} >) is derived as *ho~hoti* 'be very sore and tender' (< ST_{CR} >):

(6.52) a. *kaike   toi-kame   ikoa   n-e   hoti=nau   ka   kame=ḡu=ine*
          one   cook-arm   be.small   RL-3S   sting=1SGO   LOC   arm=1SGP=thisR
          'A small centipede has stung me on my hand.'

b. *kame=ḡu=ine   n-e   ho~hoti   ḡlehe*
   arm=1SGP=thisR   RL-3S   RD~sting   very
   'My hand is very sore and tender.'

6.3.1.2 Valency augmenting reduplication

Reduplicative derivation augmenting the valency of a verb occurs only with two semantically related roots: *keli* 'be good' and *dia* 'be bad'. These reduplicate to derive the bivalent verbs *ke~keli-* 'be pleased (by s.th.)' and *di~dia-* 'be displeased (by s.th.)'. Although the derived forms are bivalent, they are not transitive verbs but experiencer verbs, the second argument being the source of the experience. These experiencer verbs are discussed further in §6.1.3.2.5. Reduplication in these two cases derives a verb that subcategorizes for one more argument than the underived roots. The underived forms subcategorize only for a stative with the frame < ST_{CR} >. The derivation introduces a new argument, an experiencer, and changes the role of the existing argument from stative to source, giving the subcategorization frame < EXP_{CR} (SC_{CR}) >.

(6.53) a. *sote   ine   n-e   keli*
          shirt   thisR   RL-3S   be.good
          'This shirt is good.'

b. *n-a   ke~keli=nau   ara   sote   ine*
   RL-1EXCS   RD~be.good=1SGO   I   shirt   thisR
   'I am pleased by this shirt.'

6.3.2 Valency augmentation by the transitivizing suffix

A class of underlyingly monovalent verbs exists that derive a bivalent form by means of the replacive suffix *-i*. This suffix replaces the final vowel of the root, and is homophonous with (and historically related to) an allomorph of the 3SG postverbal agreement marker.[44] Postverbal argument-indexing for ordinary bivalent verbs is on the pattern shown in Table 6.3 (see §6.1.2.2). With /i/ final roots the 3SG postverbal agreement enclitic has the allomorph =*ni*, as shown in Table 6.4. A different pattern applies to verbs taking the transitivizing suffix. The valency of the monovalent form is augmented by the transitivizing suffix replacing the final vowel of the root. The suffixed form then takes postverbal agreement enclitics in the normal way, with the exception of the 3SG category. Instead of the normal enclitic, that category is zero marked, as in Table 6.5.

TABLE 6.3. VERB FORM AND ARGUMENT-INDEXING FOR MOST VERBS WITHOUT THE FINAL VOWEL /i/

ITR	TR [-3SGO]	TR [+3SGO]
n-o ***tore***	*n-e* ***tore=nau*** *ara*	*n-a* ***tore=i*** *manei*
SG RL-2S ask	RL-3S ask=1SGO I	RL-1EXCS ask=3SGO he
'You're asking.'	'He asked me.'	'I asked him.'

TABLE 6.4. VERB FORM AND ARGUMENT-INDEXING FOR MOST VERBS WITH THE FINAL VOWEL /i/

ITR	TR [-3SGO]	TR [+3SGO]
n-e ***piri***	*n-e* ***piri=nau*** *ara*	*n-a* ***piri=ni*** *manei*
RL-3S bind	RL-3S bind=1SGO I	RL-1EXCS bind=3SGO he
'He tied up.'	'He tied me up.'	'I tied him up.'

TABLE 6.5. VERB FORM AND ARGUMENT-INDEXING FOR VERBS THAT TAKE THE TRANSITIVIZING SUFFIX

ITR	TR [-3SGO]	TR [+3SGO]
n-e ***hoda***	*n-e* ***hod-i=ri*** *maneri*	*n-e* ***hod-i=∅*** *manei*
RL-3S take	RL-3S take-TR=3PLO they	RL-3S take-TR=3SGO he
'He took.'	'He took them.'	'He took him.'

Membership of the class of verbs that take the transitivizing suffix may be deduced from the form of the verb with 3SG postverbal agreement. If such a form has as its final vowel /i/, it is possible that it is an underlying bivalent verb with that final vowel, or that it is an underlying monovalent verb marked with the transitivizing suffix. If the verb is underlyingly bivalent and /i/ final it will index 3SG postverbally with the suffix =*ni*, following the pattern shown in Table 6.4. If on the other hand the 3SG category is realized by a zero, the verb must

---

[44] Both the replacive suffix and 3SG agreement marker reflect the Proto Oceanic transitive marker *-i*. The agreement marker appears to be a reduction of the earlier sequence *-i-a, the *-a reflecting the POc 3SG agreement marker (Malcom Ross pers. com.).

follow the pattern shown in Table 6.5. In other words if an /i/ final bivalent verb indexes 3SG with zero, the final vowel must be the transitivizing suffix.

The behavior of 3SG postverbal agreement enclitic allomorphy in relation to /i/ final roots and transitivized verbs makes it possible to identify verbs that are derived diachronically from a transitivizing suffix-marked form, but where that form has been reanalyzed as the final vowel of the root. In some instances this diachronic regularization is under way but is not yet complete.

An example of the reanalysis of the transitivizing suffix as a root final vowel occurs with the bivalent verb *nomhi* 'hear'. The form **nomho* does not occur synchronically, but existed at an earlier stage in the language. This earlier form allowed both transitivizing suffix and causative derivation, as well as causative marking of a reduplicated form. Both the causative marked forms have since undergone semantic reanalysis, giving the monovalent verbs *fanomho* 'be quiet' and *fanonomho* 'listen'. The bivalent verb has the final vowel /i/, which may be treated as the transitivizing suffix, with commensurate zero 3SG postverbal agreement, despite the absence of a synchronic underived counterpart.

(6.54) a. *n-o-ti*   *noto* ***fanomho***
RL-2S-NEG   stop   be.quiet
'You didn't stop and be quiet.'

b. *ara n-a*   ***fanonomho*** *bo,*
I   RL-1EXCS   listen   CNT
'I listened

*ge   teo   bla   ḡe   **nomh-i=Ø=u***
SEQ   not.exist   LMT   NT   hear-TR=3SGO=CNT
but I didn't hear it.'

The bivalent form in (6.54)b. line 2 has zero 3SG agreement, demonstrating the presence of the transitivizing suffix. However, *nomhi* may also be treated as monomorphemic, attracting the 3SG indexing appropriate to /i/ final roots:

(6.55)   *ara n-a   **nomhi=ni** ia   mheke*
I   RL-1EXCS hear=3SGO theSG   dog
'I heard the dog.'

The two postverbally indexed 3SG forms *nomh-i* and *nomhi=ni* occur in free variation, and speakers are aware of this fact. It is, however, noteworthy that the reanalyzed monomorphemic version only occurs in my corpus in direct elicitations.

6.3.2.1 Arguments introduced by the transitivizing suffix

The presence of the transitivizing suffix has the effect of raising the valency of underlyingly monovalent verbs by introducing an additional core argument to the verb's subcategorization. Almost all verbs taking the transitivizing suffix are unergative, with the introduced argument an undergoer, or in some instances a locative. A very small number of unaccusative verbs also take the transitivizer. With these, the introduced argument is an agent.

6.3.2.1.1 Augmentation of unergative verbs

The presence of transitivizing suffix marking on an unergative monovalent verb has the effect of introducing a second argument. Whether the introduced argument is an undergoer or a locative depends on the semantics of the underived root. In their underived monovalent forms all of the transitivizer-taking roots have an implicit additional argument that is not subcategorized. With some roots that implicit second argument is an undergoer, either patient or theme. It is implicit in the semantics of a verb like *hoda* 'take' or *korho* 'pull' that there something is taken or pulled. However, in their monovalent forms, these verbs have the subcategorization frame $< AG_{CR} >$:

(6.56) *n-e-ge* *ʃa-ḡo-no-di=ña* *ago* *ge* **hoda** *bla*
RL-3S-PRS CS-forget-GENP-3PLP=IMM youSG SEQ take LMT
'You [can] make a mistake and [it] will simply take [record].'

These verbs occur rarely without an overt undergoer. The undergoer is typically expressed, cooccurring with the monovalent form because it is incorporated ([6.57]a.), or because the root is non-final in a serial construction ([6.57]b.):

(6.57) a. *ḡ-a-ke* **hoda** *neti*
NT-1EXCS-PFV take net
'We took nets.'

b. *n-e* **hoda** *mai=di=ña* *no-ḡu* *letasi iao* *ara*
RL-3S take come=3PLO=IMM GENP-1SGP letter thatPV I
'He brought my mail.'

When this class of verbs have their valency augmented by the transitivizing suffix, the introduced argument is an undergoer, giving subcategorization frames $< AG_{CR} PAT_{CR} >$ or $< AG_{CR} THM_{CR} >$. This generates clauses such as:

(6.58) ...*ḡ-e* **hod-i=Ø=u** *ooe* *t=au=ao* *tikilave*
NT-3S take-TR=3SGO=CNT word SBD=be-thisT PN
'...Tikilave got that story.'

With at least one transitivizer-taking root the implicit second argument of the monovalent form is locative. A verb such as *mhoko* 'sit' is monovalent, but has implicit in its semantics a location where the sitting takes place. This locative is often not overtly realized:

(6.59)   **mhoko**   *lao*   *ago*
        sit   go   youSG
        'You go and sit.'

When overtly realized, a locative is typically realized by a prepositional adjunct:

(6.60)   *n-a*   **mhoko**   *ara*   *ka*   *palu*   *ifra*
        RL-1EXCS sit   I   LOC   two   mat
        'I sat on two mats.'

Transitivizing suffix marking of verbs in this class has the effect of introducing a core argument that is locative, giving the subcategorization frame $< \text{AG}_{CR}$ $\text{LOC}_{CR} >$. This generates clauses such as:

(6.61)   *n-a*   **mhok-i=Ø**   *ara*   *kaike*   *ifra*
        RL-1EXCS sit-TR=3SGO   I   one   mat
        'I sat on one mat.'

Unergative verb roots that take the transitivizing suffix include:

(6.62) a.   *faroho*   'be smiting'   *faroh-i*   'smite s.th.'
      b.   *hoda*   'be taking'   *hod-i*   'take s.th.'
      c.   *huhu*   'be asking (questions)'   *huh-i*   'ask s.th.'
      d.   *korho*   'be pulling'   *korh-i*   'pull s.th.'
      e.   *maḡra*   'be fighting'   *maḡr-i*   'fight s.th.'
      f.   *mhoko*   'sit'   *mhok-i*   'sit on s.th.'
      g.   *puḡra*   'be severing'   *puḡr-i*   'sever s.th.'
      h.   *ruma*   'be entering'   *rum-i*   'enter s.th.'
      i.   *safra*   'be missing'   *safr-i*   'miss s.th.'
      j.   *sofo*   'be catching'   *sof-i*   'catch s.th.'
      k.   *tabara*   'be buying'   *tabar-i*   'buy s.th.'
      l.   *ufu*   'be blowing'   *uf-i*   'blow on s.th.'

6.3.2.1.2 Augmentation of unaccusative verbs

With unaccusative verbs the presence of the transitivizing suffix has a more complex effect on argument structure. In its monovalent form, a stative verb has as its sole core argument a participant that is in the state coded by the verb, i.e., a stative. The subcategorization frame for such verbs is $< \text{ST}_{CR} >$. The presence of the transitivizing suffix changes the argument structure by introducing an additional argument. With unergative verbs the additional argument is either undergoer or locative, and the existing argument, the agent, remains unchanged. When the valency of an unaccusative verb is augmented by the transitivizing suffix, the argument that is in the state coded remains the argument that state applies to; however, it is no longer simply in that state, but rather is undergoing an event that causes it to change state, i.e., it becomes a patient. The introduced argument is then the agent that brings about the change in state of the patient. For example, with *tora* 'be open' the sole subcategorized argument is stative, with the subcategorization frame $< ST_{CR} >$:

(6.63) *n-e*   ***tora***   *bla kokopa ine*
         RL-3S be.open LMT door   thisR
         'The door is open.'

When this root is derived by the transitivizing suffix the stative of the underived root is demoted to patient. The introduced argument is agent, i.e., the participant that is causing the change of state in the patient. The augmented subcategorization frame is thus $< AG_{CR}\ PAT_{CR} >$, generating clauses such as:

(6.64) *ara n-a-ke*   ***tor-i=Ø=na***   *kokopa=na*
         I   RL-1EXCS-PFV   open-TR=3SGO=thatN door=thatN
         'I opened that door.'

6.3.3 Valency augmentation by causative marking

In addition to transitivizing suffix marking, valency augmentation may occur by means of the preposed causative particle *fa*. The formal characteristics of the causative particle are discussed in §2.5.6.2. Functionally, causative marking introduces a new argument, an agent, force, into the subcategorization, and demotes to undergoer (patient or theme) the existing argument. In addition, causativized verbs have exactly two arguments. Causative derivation of a monovalent verb increases the argument structure from one to two arguments. Bivalent verbs may not be causativized. All verbs that may occur in transitive predications have monovalent and bivalent variants. This is illustrated by many of the transitivizer-taking verbs in (6.62), where there is a formal distinction between the monovalent and bivalent variants. Causative derivation of such verbs applies only to the monovalent form.

The effects of causative derivation may be characterized in the following way:

(6.65) a. a new argument is introduced that is an agent or force;
       b. the existing argument is demoted to undergoer;
       c. only monovalent verb forms may be causativized.

6.3.3.1 Causative marking of monovalent stative verbs

A class of monovalent verbs exists that subcategorize for a single argument, where that argument has the semantic role stative (i.e., the argument that is in the state coded by the predication). Causative marking of these verbs introduces a new argument that is an agent or cause. This argument affects another participant by changing that participant's state from a state that is not that coded by the underived verb into a state that is that coded by the underived verb. The existing argument of the monovalent verb is demoted from stative to patient. The semantic relations of the uncausativized monovalent verb may be characterized as: 'participant X is in state Z' (X BE Z); while the semantic relations of the causative marked bivalent verb may be characterized as 'participant Y affects participant X and as a result participant X is in state Z' (Y CAUSE X BE Z).

The subcategorization frame for these monovalent verbs is $< ST_{CR} >$, and for the causative marked forms $< AG/CS_{CR} \ PAT_{CR} >$.

The verb *fodu* 'be full', for example, subcategorizes for a single argument with the semantic role of stative. The causative marked form involves an agent that is acting upon the drum in some way to change its state from 'not full' to 'full':

(6.66) *daramu ine   n-e   fodu*
        drum   thisR RL-3S be.full
        'This drum is full.'

(6.67) *gita   da-ke   fa fodu=i   daramu ine*
        weINC 1INCS-PFV CS be.full=3SGO drum   thisR
        'We filled this drum.'

This causative marking occurs productively with any unaccusative verb. The example above involves a physical state, but the process applies equally to non-physical states:

(6.68) a. *goinode gita   da   nhigo*
          todayRL   weINC 1INCS be.finished
          'Now we're finished.'

    b. *a   fa-nhigo=ri=u*
       1EXCS CS-be.finished=3PLO=CNT
       'I will finish them.'

The introduced argument may be either an agent or a force; however, some verbs tend to occur with agent actors and others with force actors. Causative marking of verbs such as *nhigo* 'be finished' above typically introduce an agent.

Causative marking of a verb such as *lehe-ñhau* 'be hungry' typically introduces a participant (often expressed as a subordinated clause) that is force:

(6.69) a. *ginai*   *o*   **lehe-ñhau**   *gau-palu*
          todayIRR 2S die-eat   youPL-two
          'You two will get hungry.'

     b. *birho ravata*   *n-e*   **fa lehe-ñhau=nigo** *ago*
        sleep afternoon   RL-3S CS die-eat=2SGO   youSG
        'Sleeping in the afternoon is making you hungry.'

6.3.3.2 Causative marking of monovalent active verbs

Where a monovalent verb has as its argument an actor, causativization again introduces a new actor (an agent or force), and the existing argument is demoted, this time from agent or active theme to patient or theme. The existing argument is demoted from being the participant carrying out the action, to being caused to carry out that action. The semantic relations of the unergative monovalent verb may be characterized as: 'participant X is carrying out action Z' (X DO Z), while the semantic relations of the causativized verb may be characterized as 'participant Y affects participant X and as a result participant X is carrying out action Z' (Y CAUSE X DO Z). So, for example, *ñhau* 'eat' subcategorizes for an agent with the frame $< AG_{CR} >$ ([6.70]a.). Causativization introduces a new agent or force that causes the existing participant to eat. That participant, the agent of the underived form, is therefore demoted to patient, being the undergoer of the causing. The derived frame is therefore $< AG/CS_{CR} \ PAT_{CR} >$ ([6.70]b.).

(6.70) a. *ara n-a*   **ñhau**   *no-g̃u*
          I   RL-1EXCS eat   GENP-1SGP
          'I am eating.'

     b. *ara n-a-ke*   **fa ñhau=nigo** *ago*
        I   RL-1EXCS-PFV CS eat=2SGO   youSG
        'I made you eat.'

With active verbs, causative marking demotes the existing argument from actor to undergoer. Most active verbs are unergative, and for these causativization involves the former agent taking the role patient. However, some active monovalent verbs are nonagentive, with an active theme rather than an agent as the subcategorized argument. With a verb such as *zogu* 'drop', for example, the actor is non-volitional. The subcategorization frame for this verb is $< A.THM_{CR} >$ (as in [6.71]a.). Causativization introduces a new agent, force, and demotes the existing active theme actor to undergoer theme, with the causative derived frame $< AG/CS_{CR} \ THM_{CR} >$ (as in [6.71]b.).

(6.71) a. *koilo   ana   n-e   zogu=ña*
        coconut thatN RL-3S drop=IMM
        'That coconut just dropped.'

    b. *manei   n-e   la   fa zogu=i   koilo   ine   k=ara*
        he   RL-3S go CS drop=3SGO coconut thisR LOC=I
        'He went and threw down this coconut to me.'

6.3.3.3 Causative marking restriction to monovalent verbs

Verbs that may occur in transitive predications have monovalent and bivalent forms. Causativization in Kokota only occurs with monovalent verbs. Many verbs have no formal distinction between their monovalent and bivalent variants, only the subcategorization frames differing. However, some, such as the transitivizer taking verbs discussed in §6.3.2.1, do differ. With these, the constraint on causativizing bivalent verbs is most visible. A verb such as *sofo* 'be catching' is monovalent, subcategorizing only for an agent with the subcategorization frame < AG_{CR} > (as in [6.72]a.). Its transitivized counterpart, *sof-i* 'catch s.th.', is bivalent, subcategorizing for an agent and a patient with the frame < AG_{CR} PAT_{CR} > (as in [6.72]b.).

(6.72) a. *pusi ana   n-e   sofo   bla*
        cat thatN RL-3S catch LMT
        'That cat was simply catching.'

    b. *pusi ana   n-e   sof-i=di   palu   kubiliki   are*
        cat thatN RL-3S catch-TR=3PLO two   rat   thoseN
        'That cat caught those two rats.'

When causativized, the untransitivized, not the transitivized, form is marked:

(6.73)   *manei n-e   fa sofo=i   pusi ana*
        he   RL-3S CS catch=3SGO cat thatN
        'He made that cat catch.'

As with any monovalent active verb, causativization introduces a new agent or force, and demotes the actor of the underived root to undergoer. *Fa sofo* has the derived subcategorization frame < AG_{CR} PAT_{CR} >. A participant that would occur as the core argument undergoer of the transitive form (such as the rats in [6.72]b.) may be expressed with a causative verb, but only as an oblique adjunct ([6.74]a.), not as a second core argument complement ([6.74]b.):

(6.74) a. *manei n-e   fa sofo=i   pusi ana   ka   palu kubiliki are*
        he   RL-3S CS catch=3SGO cat thatN LOC two rat   thoseN
        'He made that cat catch those two rats.'

b. *manei n-e fa sofo=i pusi ana **palu kubiliki are***

The constraint on causativizing bivalent verbs is less readily observed with roots that do not distinguish formally between monovalent and bivalent variants. The effect of the constraint is visible, however, in the behavior of the undergoer of the bivalent variant. The verb ñhau 'eat', may be monovalent or bivalent, with no formal distinction between the forms. Compare (6.70)a. with (6.75):

(6.75)   ara n-a   ñhau **tañano are**
         I   RL-1EXCS eat   food   thoseN
         'I ate that food.'

The undergoer of a causativized verb is the participant that occurs as the agent of the underived root. The undergoer of the underived verb is expressible, but only as an oblique, paralleling the behavior of *fa sofo* in (6.74):

(6.76) a. ara n-a   fa ñhau=nigo ago   **ka tañano are**
           I   RL-1EXCS CS eat=2SGO youSG LOC food   thoseN
           'I made you eat that food.'

b. *ara n-a fa ñhau=nigo ago **tañano are***

6.4 Incorporation

A process of incorporation exists in the language that allows any non-specific undergoer to be incorporated into the verb complex. Incorporation applies to not merely a nominal root, but to the NP core (see §3.3.1).

6.4.1 Incorporating verb forms

Any verb that subcategorizes for an undergoer may have an incorporated undergoer. However, the verb must be in its intransitive form. Where a verb's intransitive and transitive variants are formally identical, incorporation is distinguished only by the presence or absence of postverbal agreement. In (6.77) postverbal agreement occurs, indexing the undergoers. In (6.78) no postverbal agreement is present, despite the presence in the clause of an overt undergoer, the undergoer being incorporated:

(6.77) a. n-a   manahagi=di gudu   ara namhari gudu
          RL-1EXCS want=3PLO   EXHST I   fish   EXHST
          'I want all the fish.'

b. ara n-a   flalo=i   vaka-flalo ine
       I   RL-1EXCS fly=3SGO ship-fly   thisR
       'I'm flying this plane.'

(6.78) a. *n-a* *manahagi* **namhari** *gudu* *ara*
    RL-1EXCS want fish   EXHST I
    'I want all the fish.'

  b. *ara* *mala* *flalo* **vaka-flalo**
    I RL-1EXCS fly ship-fly
    'I fly planes.'

Where a formal distinction exists between intransitive and transitive variants of a verb, it is the intransitive form that occurs with an incorporated undergoer. The intransitive verb *korho* 'be pulling', for example, is transitivized by the suffix *-i* discussed in §6.3.2.1, giving the transitive form *korh-i* 'pull s.th.'. In a normal transitive clause the transitivized form occurs with postverbal agreement indexing an undergoer:

(6.79) *ara* *n-a*   **korh-i=ri** *palu* *namhari* *are*
   I RL-1EXCS pull-TR=3PLO two fish   thoseN
   'I caught those two fish.'

When the undergoer is incorporated the underived intransitive form occurs:

(6.80) *ara* *n-a*   **korho** **namhari**
   I RL-1EXCS pull fish
   'I caught fish.'

6.4.2 Incorporated nominals

Incorporated undergoers are not limited to a nominal root alone. Instead, the entire NP core is incorporated. In (6.78), (6.80), and (6.85) the incorporated cores consist only of a nominal root. However, other elements may modify the incorporated root. In addition to the nominal head, the core may contain one of the pre-head multitude markers *tehi* 'many' and *toga-tehi* 'very many' (see §6.3.2.1). Being within the core, these may occur with incorporated nominals:

(6.81) a. *ago* *n-o* *hoda* **tehi** **kaku**
    youSG RL-2S take many banana
    'You took many bananas.'

  b. *ara* *n-a*   *korho* **toga-tehi**   **namhari**
    I RL-1EXCS pull thousand-many fish
    'I caught very many fish.'

Both verbs in (6.81) belong to the class that takes the transitivizing suffix *-i*. The presence of the intransitive verb forms demonstrates the incorporated status of the undergoers.

In addition, the core contains one post-head modifier position. that may contain one member of a number of word classes including adjectives, nouns, stative verbs, personal and location names, and spatial locatives (see §3.3.1.2). In (6.82), for example, an incorporated nominal is modified by another noun:

(6.82)   *n-a-ke*   *friñhe **suḡa** tetena*
        RL-1EXCS-PFV work house sago
        'We built sago-thatch houses.'

Incorporation is not limited to nouns plus one core modifier. NP cores of any size can participate in incorporation. In (6.83) direct possessor-indexing and an adjective modify the head:

(6.83)   *ara manahagi no-ḡu*   ***gorha foforu=na***
        I   want   GENP-1SGP paddle be.new=3SGP
        'I need a new paddle.'

Incorporated undergoers may not be a definite or specifically identified member of the class of entities they belong to. No articles or demonstratives may modify incorporated nominals, these falling outside the NP core. Incorporated nominals may also not be specified for number, the numerals being a NP outer modifier.

In addition to the core of a common noun NP, the core of a NP with an indirect possessor-indexing host as head (a NP$_{POSS}$; see §3.4.2) may be incorporated:

(6.84)   *ara n-a*   *hoda **ge-ḡu***   ***kaku***
        I   RL-1EXCS take CNSM-1SGP banana
        'I'm taking my bananas.'

6.4.3 Structure of incorporating verb complexes

No constituents may intervene between the root component(s) of the verb complex and the incorporated nominal. It is not, for example, possible for another argument to intervene. In non-incorporating clauses the pragmatically unmarked constituent order places the argument with the semantic role highest in the hierarchy in the immediate postverbal position, with the next highest following, and so on. This generates transitive clauses in which the actor precedes the undergoer, intervening between the verb and the undergoer:

(6.85)   *n-e* *korh-i=ri*   ***manei*** *palu namhari are*
        RL-3S pull-TR=3PLO he   two   fish   thoseN
        'He caught those two fish.'

However, with incorporated undergoers the order reflected in (6.85) is impossible, as the actor would intervene between the verb and the incorporated nominal (as in [6.86]b.). Instead the reverse order occurs ([6.86]a.):

(6.86) a.   *n-e*   *korho*   *namhari*   ***manei***
        RL-3S   pull   fish   he
        'He caught fish.'

      b.   **n-e korho **manei** namhari*

This applies equally to postverbal outer modifiers, which follow the verb complex core. In non-incorporating clauses these precede any arguments (as in [6.87]). In incorporating clauses they follow the incorporated nominal ([6.88]):

(6.87) a.   *ḡ-a*   *fa-lehe=ri*   ***gudu***   *ña*   *gai*   *teḡe*   *are-lau*
        NT-1EXCS CS-die=3PLO   EXHST   IMM   weEXC   turtle   thoseN-SPC
        '...we kill every one of those turtles'

      b.   *n-e-ge*   *mai*   *fakae=ni=u*   *mane*   *ine*
          RL-3S-PRS come   see=3SGO=CNT   man   thisR
          'He is coming and seeing this man.'

(6.88) a.   *n-a*   *manahagi*   *namhari*   ***gudu***   *ara*
        RL-1EXCS want   fish   EXHST   I
        'I want all the fish.'

      b.   *manei teo*   *ḡ-e*   *korho*   *namhari=u*
         he   not.exist   NT-3S   pull   fish=CNT
         'He wasn't catching fish.'

This constraint does not apply to verbs such as directionals occurring finally in a serial construction. In incorporating clauses these occur in their normal position preceding the incorporated nominal:

(6.89)   *gai*   *n-a*   *hoda*   ***mai***   *mala-ñhau*
        weEXC   RL-1EXCS   take   come   PURP-eat
        'We bring food.'

6.4.4 Object-indexing on incorporating verb complexes

The incorporation of an undergoer generates a complex predicate consisting of the verb(s) plus the undergoer. These complex predicates are typically intransitive in the sense that the entire predication does not subcategorize for a second argument indexed by a postverbal enclitic. All examples of incorporation above show this. However, transitive incorporating predications are possible.

This involves a complex predication with an incorporated undergoer, where the entire predication itself has a complement that is indexed postverbally. As postverbal indexing involves an enclitic attached to the verb complex core, and an incorporated nominal is the final element in the core, the enclitic attaches to the incorporated nominal. In (6.90)a. *hoda faña* 'take give.food' has the incorporated theme *kaku* 'banana'. The resulting complex predication, *hoda faña kaku* 'take bananas to' itself has a goal complement indexed by the enclitic on the verb complex. Similarly, in (6.90)b. the verb series *turi tufa* 'tell affect' has the incorporated nominal *tu~turi* 'story'. The entire complex predication *turi tufa tu~turi* 'tell stories to' itself has a goal complement indexed by an enclitic.

(6.90) a. *nakodou   ana   n-e   hoda faña   kaku=i   hei*
         woman   thatN RL-3S take give.food banana=3SGO who
         'Who did that woman give bananas to?'

       b. *mane=ne   n-e-ke   turi tufa   tu~turi=di   ira   suli*
          man=thisR RL-3S-PFV   tell affect RD~tell=3PLO thePL child
          'This man told stories to the children.'

6.5 Verb serialization

The verb complex core may contain a single verb root. However, up to three roots may be serialized to form a single complex predicate. Any verb may occur in first and second position. Third position is limited to a small set of verbs. Verb series have the structure in (6.91). This means that a verb series may comprise V_1+V_2, or V_2+V_3, or $V_1+V_2+V_3$.

(6.91) (V_1) V_2 (V_3)

6.5.1 $V_1 + V_2$ series

Any verb may occur in V_1 or V_2 position. However, V_1 verbs are typically verbs of general motion, commencement, or completion, or the desiderative, abilitative, or unitative verbs. Verbs commonly occurring in V_1 position include:

(6.92) a. *lao*   'go (towards)'   g. *manahagi* 'want, need'
       b. *mai*   'come'   h. *fufunu*   'begin'
       c. *aḡe*   'go'   i. *nodo/noto* 'stop'
       d. *zaho*   'go (away from)'   j. *nhigo*   'be finished'
       e. *boka*   'be able'   k. *kusu/kulu* 'be first'[45]
       f. *kaike*   'be one' (i.e., 'act in unison')[46]

---

[45] *Kusu* and *kulu* are variants of the same verb. The reason for the variation is unclear, but may result from influence from Cheke Holo, where *kulu* is an adverbial meaning 'first'.

[46] *Kaike* functions primarily as the numeral 'one', but also functions as a verb 'be one'.

When occurring with a non-motion V_2, motion verbs in V_1 position indicate a motion event preceding the V_2 event:

(6.93) a. ...ḡ-e **la au**   iaro   hurepelo keha=re...
        NT-3S go exist thosePV PNLOC   NSP=thoseN
        '...some of them went [and] lived over at Hurepelo...

        ...ade-hi   goveo ḡ-e   **mai**   **au=gu**   gai   keha ide
        here-EMPH PNLOC NT-3S come exist=CNT weEXC NSP   theseR
        ...[and] some of us came [and] are living here in Goveo.'

    b. **ka** **mai** **rum-i=Ø=na**   ia   suḡa dou...
        LOC come enter-TR=3SGO=thatN theSG house be.big
        'When [they] came [and] entered the big house...'

    c. **ka=t=au=ana**   ḡ-e   **aḡe** **tob-i=ri**...
        LOC=SBD=exist=thatN NT-3S go   kick-TR=3PLO
        'At that he went [and] kicked them...'

When a V_1 motion verb occurs with a motion V_2, the two motion events occur simultaneously:

(6.94)   n-e   **zaho** **ñhañha=na**...
        RL-3S go   run=thatN
        'He ran away...'

Two motion verbs, *lao* and *aḡe*, occur very commonly in V_1 position with the non-literal meaning 'proceed' or 'go ahead and':

(6.95) a. ta **la mai=o**   ia   vetula=na=na ia   ḡavana...
        SBD go come=thatNV theSG law=3SGP=thatN theSG government
        '[When] ...the law of the government proceeded to come...

    b. n-e-ge   **la maku=ña**   manei...
        RL-3S-PRS go be.hard=IMM it
        'It [a gas tap on a stove] becomes firm...'

(6.96) a. ...ḡ-e **aḡe sugu** ia   to~toi...
        NT-3S go hiss theSG RD~cook
        '...the fire went ahead [and] hissed...'

The verbs of commencement and completion occur as single verb predicates, but as serial V_1, indicate the start or finish of the event expressed by the V_2:

(6.97) a. *ara n-a-ge* **fufunu lase**=*i*   *ooe kokota*
      I   RL-3S-PRS begin   know=3SGO   talk   PNLOC
      'I am beginning to understand the Kokota language.'

    b. **nhigo**   **ri~riso**
      be.finished   RD~write
      'Finish writing!'

The abilitative, unitative, and desiderative verbs also occur with predictable meanings in relation to the V_1 event:

(6.98) a. *gai*   *a*   **boka**   **ñha**=*di*   *gudu...*
      weEXC   1EXCS   be.able   eat=3PLO   EXHST
      'We could eat them all...'

    b. *gita-palu*   **kaike au**   *bo*
      weINC-two   one   exist   CNT
      'We two still live together.'

    c. *ara n-a*   **manahagi tore**=*ḡau*   *gau*   *ira*   *kompanion*
      I   RL-1EXCS want   ask=2PLO   youPL   thePL   Companion
      'I want to ask you, the Companions,[47]

      ta   *friñhe*=*i*=*na*   *fea*   *kaike suḡa...*
      SBD   work=3SGO=thatN   INIT   one   house
      to build me a house...'

Although the verbs in (6.92) are a majority of verbs occurring in V_1 position, there is no restriction on other verbs occurring in this position:

(6.99) a. *manei n-e-ke*   **kumai fa knaso**=*i*   *botolo swepi*   *ine*
      he   RL-3S-PFV drink   CS be.empty=3SGObottle soft.drink thisR
      'He drank empty this bottle of soft drink.'[48]

    b. *ara n-a*   **tarai togo**=*di*   *ira*   *nakoni ta*   *foḡra*
      I   RL-1EXCS pray   help=3PLO   thePL   person   SBD   sick
      'I prayed for the sick people.'

    c. *n-a*   *babao*   *no-ḡu*
      RL-1EXCS be.tired   GENP-1SGP
      'I am tired

---

[47] The Companions of the Brotherhood of the Church of Melanesia, a local Solomon Islands organization of Anglican brothers.
[48] *Swepi*, a loan from the brand name *Schweppes*, is the generic term for any soft drink.

gu=na=na   **friñhe heta**   *jakamo*
CNTX=3SGP=thatN   work   be.strong   always
because I always work hard.'

d. *bi=mu=de*   *ago*   *n-e*   **siri**   **dia=de**
fart=2SGP=theseR   youSG   RL-3S   smell   be.bad=theseR
'These farts of yours smell bad.'

6.5.2 V₂ + V₃ series

V₃ position is confined to verbs of directional movement, including arrival and departure, the verb of completion, and the affective verb, shown in (6.100). The directional verbs *zaho* 'go (away)' and *aḡe* 'go' do not appear to occur as V₃.

(6.100)a. *mai*   'come'   g. *pulo*   'return'
     b. *lao*   'go'   h. *koko*   'leave'
     c. *hage*   'ascend'   i. *toke*   'arrive'
     d. *kave*   'descend'   j. *toga*   'arrive'
     e. *kota*   'go ashore, land'   k. *nhigo*   'be finished'
     f. *salupu*   'pass'   l. *tufa*   'affect'

As with V₁ motion verbs, where a V₃ motion verb occurs with a V₂ that itself has inherent motion, the motion events occur simultaneously, the V₃ effectively indicating the direction in which the V₂ motion occurred:

(6.101)a. *ara ginai* **pulo mai** *ka fa-palu wiki ana*
         I   FUT   return come   LOC CS-two   week   thatN
         'I will return in two weeks.' [lit. '...on the second week.']

     b. *n-e*   **korho ma=di**   *ia*   *ḡobi-lho~lhoguai=na*   *e=u*
         RL-3S pull   come=3PLO thePL   hundred-RD~coil=3SGP   3S=be.thus
         'He pulled towards him his hundred coils, like that.'

     c. *ia*   *kakau*   *n-e*   **seha kave**   *ka*   *raro=no*
         theSG crab   RL-3S climb descend   LOC pot=thatNV
         'The crab climbed out of the pot.'

     d. *kubiliki ana*   *n-e*   **ruma lao** *ka*   *ḡilu=na*   *korosa*
         rat   thatN RL-3S enter   go   LOC inside=3SGP   hole
         'That rat went inside the hole.'

     e. **fa loga mai** *katana*   *kareseni*   *ña*   *bo*
         CS pour come modicum kerosene   IMM CNT
         'Pour out a little bit more kerosene!'

f. *ḡ-e   koko   la=ni=ña*   *sara*   *rauru*
    NT-3S leave go=3SGO=IMM   thereD seaward
    'He threw him there seaward.'

The function of the V_3 to indicate the direction of the V_2 motion applies even if the V_2 motion is metaphorical, as in the telling of a story or in recollection:

(6.102)a. *are-lau   ago   ne-ge   turi salupu=di=ro   bla   ago*
          thoseN-SPC youSG RL-PRS tell pass=3PLO=thoseNV LMT youSG
          'Those ones [parts of the story] you're telling past [i.e., leaving out].'

     b. *ka   varedake palu   zulai*
        LOC twenty   two   July
        'On the twenty second of July

        ginai e gato pulo=i   ia   sekon apointed dei
        FUT 3S think return=3SGO theSG Second.Appointed.Day
        [one] will remember the Second Appointed Day.'[49]

As with V_1 motion verbs, where the V_2 does not involve directed motion a V_3 motion verb indicates a sequential, not simultaneous, event:

(6.103) *legu=na   toka kave=i=na   gita   ḡazu ana...*
         behind=3SGP chop descend=3SGO=thatN weINC wood thatN
         'After we have chopped down that tree...'

The exception to this is when the nature of the V_2 event precludes subsequent motion. In that case the reading is again of simultaneity. In this case a V_1 motion verb will give a sequential reading (as in [6.104]a.) while the same verb in V_3 position will give a simultaneous reading ([6.104]b.):

(6.104)a. *mai   mhoko*   b. *mhoko mai*
          come sit   sit   come
          'Come and sit down.'   'Sit towards me.'/'Sit over here.'

The completive verb *nhigo* 'be finished' occurs in isolation with the sense that a volitional subject has finished an unspecified but understood activity (as in [6.105]a.), or that an activity associated with a non-volitional subject has been completed ([6.105]b.), or that an event expressed by a subordinate clause subject is finished ([6.105]c.):

---

[49] The anniversary of the Second Appointed Day, on which Provincial powers were devolved to the island of Santa Isabel.

(6.105)a. ...*n-e ğrui~ğrui   la=ni=ña   ka   ğuku=na...*
         RL-3S RD~garden   go=3SGO=IMM   LOC road=3SGP
         '...they brushed the road...

         *gu   maneri **nhigo**=u...*
         be.thus they   be.finished=CNT
         so, they were finished [doing that]...'

    b. ...*ia   tu~turi=na   marha-pau=o   **nhigo**...*
         theSG RD~tell=3SGP feel.pain-head=thatNV be.finished
         '...the [telling of] story of the headache will be finished...'

    c. *friñhe=ni   ia   suğa   n-e   **nhigo**=u...*
         work=3SGO   theSG house RL-3S be.finished=CNT
         'Building the house is finished...'

As a serial V_1, *nhigo* indicates completion of the event expressed by the V_2, as illustrated in (6.97)b. As a serial V_3, *nhigo* indicates that the V_2 event has been carried to completion:

(6.106)   *manei n-e-ke   **fa-lehe nhigo**=ri   gudu kokorako are*
         he   RL-3S-PFV CS-die be.finished=3PLOEXHST chicken thoseN
         'He killed [to completion] all those chickens.'

The affective verb *tufa* in isolation is normally interpreted with a meaning similar to 'give'. When it is final in a serial construction it is benefactive or malefactive depending on the semantics of the overall predication.

(6.107)a. *fa doli   tufa=nau   zuta=na*
         CS be.alive affect=1SGO lamp=thatN
         'Light that lamp for me.'

    b. *an-lau   e   mhemhe   tufa=ğai   gai*
         thatN-SPC 3S be.difficult affect=1EXCO weEXC
         'That makes it hard for us.'

6.5.3 Three-verb series

A maximum of three verbs may occur in a serial construction. Three-verb series conform to the constraints and tendencies discussed above for each of the serial verb positions. Again there is a tendency for the verb in V_1 position to be a verb of motion, commencement, or completion, or the desiderative, abilitative, or unitative, as in (6.108) (see also [6.110]), but again this is a tendency only and other verbs may occur, as in (6.109).

6.7 Adjuncts

The formal characteristics of PPs and various types of adjuncts are discussed in chapter 4. The functional characteristics of each are discussed here.

6.7.1 The Prepositional Phrase

One preposition exists in Kokota: the general purpose locative *ka*. This acts as the head of prepositional phrases with a variety of semantic roles, including locative, goal, source, cause, instrument, and benefactive. The semantic role of a PP in any clause is determined by a combination of the semantics of the predication and the semantics of the constituent governed by the preposition.

6.7.1.1 Spatial locatives

The existential verb *au* has a broad meaning covering notions such as 'exist' 'be (somewhere)', 'stay', and 'live'. Due to the inherently location-dependant nature of the event expressed by this verb, prepositional phrases occurring with *au* are interpreted as having the semantic role of spatial locative, as in (6.124). *Au* also often occurs with a location name or spatial deictic locative (see §6.7.2).

(6.124)   *...gita-palu ḡe **au** la **ka nasona** a-hi   ḡerona keli*
          weINC-two NT exist CND LOC point   thisT-EMPH PNLOC be.good
          '...if you and I lived at the point at Gerona [that would be] good.'

In clauses where the semantics of the predication do not indicate some other kind of peripheral notion, any PP is typically interpreted as a locative (rather than, say, a goal or source). In (6.125)a. the PP is interpreted as a locative although the predicate *friñhe* does not have an implicit location built into its semantics (beyond a general requirement that all events take place somewhere). In (6.125)b. the PP is again interpreted as a locative, not a goal or source: the clause does not mean '...chase...into the garden' or '...chase...from the garden'.

(6.125)a. *e=u   friñhe n-e-ke   **friñhe**=ni=na   palu mane aro*
          3S=be.thus work RL-3S-PFV work=3SGO=thatN two man   theseT
          'That's the thing these two men did

          ka   nasona ine   ḡerona
          LOC point thisR PNLOC
          at this point at Gerona.'

       b. *ira   mheke n-e   **toḡla**=di   ia   zora **ka=ia**   ḡrui*
          thePL dog   RL-3S chase=3PLO theSG pig LOC=theSG garden
          'The dogs chased the pig in [i.e., within] the garden.'

The PP in this example refers to a physical location, so lends itself to a locative interpretation. However, the interpretation of a PP as a locative when occurring with a non-location-dependent verb is not limited to PPs referring to physical locations, such as 'the point at Gerona' in (6.125). PPs whose referents would not otherwise be regarded as locations are interpreted as such:

(6.126)a. ...*ḡ-e* *la* *uf-i=Ø*   *ia*   *to~toi*
NT-3S go blow-TR=3SGO theSG RD~cook
'...he went and blew on the fire

      ka=ia   *papaḡu*   *ḡazu*
      LOC=theSG stack   wood
      on the pile of wood.'

    b. *ḡ-e* *knusu* *bla* *ka=to~toi=ne=n-e-ke=u*
      NT-3S break LMT LOC=RD~cook=thisR=RL-3S-PFV=be.thus
      'It broke on the fire, it was like that.'

In (6.126)a. the pile of wood is given as the location of the blowing, not the location of the fire. Neither of the predications in (6.125) have an implicit location, and neither of the PPs have referents that would be interpreted as locatives in other constructions.

PPs that do not even refer to physical items, such as customs or languages, are also typically interpreted as locatives:

(6.127)a. ...*ka=ia*   *kastom gai*   *tana goi*
      LOC=theSG custom weEXC then VOC
      '...in our custom, man!,

      momoru *e=ni*   *e=u*
      momoru   3S=3SGO 3S=be.thus
      it's called *momoru*.'

    b. ...*malaria* *ta=ni=o*   *nañha=na=na*   *e=u*
      malaria SBD=3SGO=thatNV name=3SGP=thatN 3S=be.thus
      '...malaria, as it's called

      ka *ooe-vaka*
      LOC talk-ship
      in English.' [lit. '...which does that name of it in English.']

Locatives of this kind are often governed by the form *fai*, usually translated by speakers as 'side'. This may refer literally to the side of a physical object:

(6.128) *roha=i* **ka fai hage=na** **naprai** *e=u* *ba*
scrape=3SGO LOC side ascend=3SGP sun 3S=be.thus ALT
'Scrape it [the bark of a tree] on the side where the sun comes up.'

However, *fai* often occurs with a sense of 'on the part of', 'in the context of':

(6.129)a. *e=u* *e tehi* *la bla gai* *kokolo=di foḡra*
3S=be.thus 3S be.many ?? LMT weEXC class=3PLP sick
'There are many kinds of sicknesses

    ka=ia *fai dokta*
LOC=theSG side doctor
to do with doctors.'

  b. *palu* *ḡlepo bla* **ka fai kastom=de** **bla**
two thing LMT LOC side custom=theseR LMT
'two things on the part of [i.e., to do with] custom'

Locatives extend to events that take place in a person's thoughts:

(6.130) *ara ka* *ga~gato=ḡu=re* *gita* *ginai korho namhari...*
I LOC RD~think=1SGP=thoseN weINC FUT pull fish
'I think we will catch fish...'

6.7.1.2 Source and goal

Some verbs code events that inherently involve directed motion or action. PPs occurring with these verbs will be interpreted as goal or source, depending on an interaction of the semantics of the predication and the referent of the PP itself. Several verbs code motion that is inherently directional. These include *mai* 'come', *lao* 'go (towards)', *zaho* 'go (away)', and *aḡe* 'go'. PPs occurring with these verbs are interpreted as goals:

(6.131)a. *...ge* *ḡ-e* **lao=ña** **ka=ia** *suḡa...*
SEQ NT-3S go=IMM LOC=theSG house
'...then she will go to the house...'

  b. *ginai* **mai** *gudu bla* *baiu* **ka** **sikolu=ne** **bla**
FUT come EXHST LMT PSBL LOC school=thisR LMT
'I think they will all come just to this school.'

  c. *ara n-a* **aḡe ka=ia** *sitoa*
I RL-1EXCS go LOC=theSG store
'I went to the store.'

d. *zaho ka no-u   suḡa=o*
   go   LOC GENP-2SGP house=thatN
   'Go to your house!'

This applies equally to causativized forms of these verbs:

(6.132) *n-e fa mai=ni   kaike letasi k=ara*
         RL-3S CS come=3SGO one letter LOC=I
         'They have sent a letter to me.'

Several verbs code various concepts of return or arrival, including *pulo* 'return', *posa* 'emerge', *toke* 'arrive back', and *toga* 'arrive'. PPs occurring with these verbs are also interpreted as goal:

(6.133)a. *ke pulo... ka=n-e-ke   hure=ro   ira   tilo tomoko*
          PFV return LOC=RL-3S-PFV carry=thoseNV thePL three war.canoe
          'They went back...to where they had carried the three canoes.'

       b. *...n-e-ke   posa   maneri ka toa=na   e=u*
          RL-3S-PFV emerge   they   LOC fort=thatN 3S=be.thus
          '...they emerged at the fort'

       c. *ḡ-e toke ka=ia   suḡa*
          NT-3S return LOC=theSG house
          'They go back to the house.'

       d. *n-e   toga ka rarata=o*
          RL-3S arrive LOC beach=thatNV
          'He arrived at that beach.'

Kokota has two verbs translatable as 'put': *nai* and *lisa*. Both subcategorize for a theme complement, and with both, a PP is interpreted as goal:

(6.134) *...hod-i=Ø   aḡe nai=ni   ka suḡa tarai=ne*
         take-TR=3SGO go put=3SGO LOC house pray=thisR
         '...take it and put it in the church'

A number of other verbs of motion prompt goal interpretations of PPs expressing locations. These include verbs such as *flalo* 'fly', where the actors themselves change location (as in [6.135]a.), or verbs such as *korho* 'pull', where it is an acted-upon undergoer that changes location (as in [6.135]b.–c.):

(6.135)a. *ara ginai flalo ka nau=ḡu=o*
          I   FUT fly   LOC place=1SGP=thatNV
          'I will fly to my home.'

b. ...*korho=u tagi-di* **ka=nau** *fai kokota a-hi*...
   pull=CNT REFL-3PLP LOC=place side PNLOC thisT-EMPH
   '...they pulled themselves to this place Kokota...'

Some verbs that are not motion verbs prompt a goal interpretation of PPs with specific kinds of referents. For example, a verb expressing an event that brings about the existence of small objects will prompt a goal interpretation of a PP that has as its referent an item that could function as a receptacle. In (6.128) the PP with *roha* 'scrape' is interpreted as a locative. In (6.136) the resultative nature of the event interacts with the semantics of the PP to prompt a goal interpretation:

(6.136) **roha**=*i* *nhigo* **ka botolo ba ka tini**
   scrape=3SGO be.finished LOC bottle ALT LOC tin
   'Scrape it into a bottle or tin.'

PPs occurring with the directional verb *hage* 'ascend' are interpreted as goal:

(6.137)a. *n-e* **la hage**=*u=na* *manei* **ka toa**
   RL-3S go ascend=CNT=thatN he LOC fort
   'He was going up to the fort.'

   b. ...*ḡ-a* **fa hage**=*i* **ka hinage**
   NT-1EXCS CS ascend=3SGO LOC boat
   '...we lift it into the boat'

However, with its antonym, *kave* 'descend', a PP will be interpreted as source:

(6.138) *ia kakau n-e* **seha kave ka raro**=*no*
   theSG crab RL-3S climb descend LOC pot=thatNV
   'The crab climbed out of the pot.'

With some other verbs, like *fufunu* 'begin', a PP is again interpreted as source:

(6.139) *ara n-a* **fufunu ka**=*ia* **sitoa**
   I RL-1EXCS begin LOC=theSG store
   'I started from the store.'

When a serial verb construction involves both a goal-oriented directional verb such as *mai* 'come' or *lao* 'go', and a verb with which PPs have a source interpretation, such as *kave* 'descend' or *fufunu* 'begin', the source interpretation applies:

(6.140)a. *tana* **kave mai ka**=*ia* **riñata**
   then descend come LOC=theSG doorway
   '...then they come out from the doorway'

b. *manei n-e* *fufunu mai=na* *ka suḡa tarai*
he RL-3S begin come=thatN LOC house pray
'He is coming from the church.'

However, when a serial verb construction involves a goal-oriented directional verb and a verb that has no implicit direct motion or action (like those discussed in §6.7.1.1), a PP is interpreted as goal. In (6.141)a., for example, *ravi* 'hide from' occurs with a PP that is interpreted as locative. However, in (6.141)b. the presence of *lao* 'go' means that a PP occurring with the complex predication is interpreted as goal:

(6.141)a. *hei n-e* *ravi=nau* *ana ka bakla=na*
who RL-3S hide.from=1SGO thatN LOC flat.root=thatN
'Who is hiding from me behind that flat root?'

b. *manei ḡ-e-ke* *ravi lao ka=ira* *bakla*
he NT-3S-PFV hide go LOC=thePL flat.root
'He hid down among the flat roots.'

This applies equally to non-physical events:

(6.142) *mane sala ge ruruboñi n-e-ke namha mai ka suaragi*
man PN and PN RL-3S-PFV love come LOC PN
'Sala and Ruruboñi were kind to Suaragi.'

At least one verb, *fa kamo* 'go across' (lit. 'cause to cross'), often occurs with two PPs, one interpreted as a source and the other a goal, in that order (the order is presumably temporally iconic):

(6.143) *fa kamo=i* *bakru* *ta=au=ana*
CS go.across=3SGO liquid SBD=exist=thatN
'Transfer that tea

ka timosi ana ka panakini ana
LOC thermos thatN LOC cup thatN
from that thermos to that cup.'

Like locatives, sources and goals may be physical locations, physical objects, people, or non-physical items. In (6.144) a PP occurs in each of the two clauses, one a source, the other a goal. Both refer to points in a story:

(6.144) *fufunu ka keli-kava=o* *n-e la mai=u*
begin LOC be.good-earth=thatNV RL-3S go come=CNT
'Start from the peace [until it] goes ahead [and] comes

(6.108)a. *manei n-e* **fufunu toka kave=i**   *ia*   *g̃azu*
       he   RL-3S begin   chop   descend=3SGO theSG   wood
       'He started chopping down the tree.'

      b. *ara* **manahagi turi tufa**=*nigo*   *ago*   *ka*   *gu=na...*
         I   want   tell   affect=2SGO   youSG   LOC   CNTX=3SGP
         'I want to tell you about...'

      c. *tehi=di*   *mane=re*   *n-e*   **kaike isi** **hage** *ka*   *g̃uku ana*
         many=3PLP man=thoseN RL-3S one   flee   ascend LOC   road thatN
         'Many of the people ran away up the road.'

(6.109)   **toka fa nhigo**   **tufa**=*nau*   *g̃azu*   *ana*
         chop   CS   be.finished affect=1SGO   wood   thatN
         'Finish chopping that wood for me.'

6.5.4 The argument structure of serial predications

When only one verb in a serial verb construction is transitive the complex predicate subcategorizes for that complement. The postverbal agreement enclitic attaches to the final verb in the series, regardless of whether that is the transitive verb. Transitive verbs appear in their intransitive form when non-final in a series. In (6.110) only the V_2 verb is transitive. The entire predication subcategorizes for the theme complement of that verb. The postverbal agreement enclitic attaches to the final element of the verb complex core, being the final verb in the series, *mai* 'come', although that verb itself is intransitive. The V_2 verb occurs in its intransitive form *hoda*, not in its transitivized form *hod-i*:

(6.110)   *o la hoda mai=ni=u*   ***ia***   ***raro*** *ta*   ***dou***
         2S go take   come=3SGO=CNT   theSG   pot   SBD   be.big
         'Go [and] bring the big pot.'

When more than one transitive verb occurs, and the complement subcategorized by all verbs represents the same participant, the complex predication subcategorizes for that one complement. Each of the verbs may subcategorize for a complement; however, postverbal agreement is again only marked on the final verb: In (6.111) both verbs are transitive and subcategorize for a theme. The entire predication consequently subcategorizes for that one theme, and the series-final verb carries the agreement enclitic:

(6.111)   *ta*   *moita*   *la*   *raisi*   *ana,*
         SBD   be.cooked   CND   rice   thatN
         'If the rice is cooked,

zikra	*koko=ni*	**bakru=na=na**
pour.out	leave=3SGO	liquid=3SGP=thatN

pour away its liquid.'

When several transitive verbs occur, subcategorizing for complements representing different participants, the complex predication subcategorizes for all the complements, generating a ditransitive predication. In this situation it is the complement of the final verb in the series that is indexed by the postverbal enclitic. Complements of non-final verbs occur as additional, unindexed, complements. In (6.109), three verbs occur. The V_1 and V_2 verbs each subcategorize for a patient representing the same participant: *ḡazu ana* 'that wood'. The complex predication, therefore, also subcategorizes for that complement. However, the V_3 verb also subcategorizes for a complement, a benefactive (in this case the speaker). The complement that is indexed postverbally is the complement of the series-final verb. This argument is not also overtly realized by a full mention, but could be. The complement of the V_1 and V_2 verbs is overtly realized, but is a second complement and is not indexed.

Various functions that are performed by adverbials in some other languages are performed by serialized verbs in Kokota. This is discussed in §7.4.

6.6 Existential predications

Existential predications in Kokota involve the use of existential verbs. Two existential verbs exist—the positive existential *au* 'exist' and the negative *teo* 'not exist'. Both verbs have a number of other functions.

6.6.1 Positive existential verb *au*

The form *au* is fundamentally an existential verb expressing a range of closely related meanings. It frequently functions to place an entity in a location, either temporarily (as in [6.112]a.), long term ([6.112]b.), or permanently ([6.112]c.). Thus it is normally translatable as 'live at' or 'be at':

(6.112)a.   *...mane n-e-ke*   **au**=ro   *ka*   *ḡilu=na*   *tema=na*
     man   RL-3S-PFV   exist=thoseNV   LOC   inside=3SGP   hut=thatN
     '...the men who were inside the small house'

     b. *n-e-ge*   *mai*   **au**   *banesokeo*
        RL-3S-PRS   come   exist   PNLOC
        'He came and lived at Banesokeo.'

     c. *mala=na=re*   *au*   *ka*   *ḡahipa*   *sare-lau*
        footprint=3SGP=thoseN   exist   LOC   stone   thereP-SPC
        'Those footprints of his are in the stone there.'

As (6.112)c. illustrates, the located participant need not be human or even animate. In fact it need not be a physical object:

(6.113)   *...la mai=u   kilau=ne   e=u*
           go come=CNT religion=thisR 3S=be.thus
           '...this religion [Christianity] came.

           *n-e   mai   **au**   buala   e=u*
           RL-3S come exist PNLOC 3S=be.thus
           It came and was at Buala.'

Clauses like those in (6.112) and (6.113) are existential clauses with a specified location of the existence. The meanings are thus more literally "the men who existed inside the small house"; "it came and existed at Buala"; and so on. Without an overt locative adjunct, *au* simply indicates the existence of an entity. This may occur when the actual location is apparent from the context:

(6.114) *manahagi=ḡau gau   mane huhurañi kaike mai   au   gudu*
         want=2PLO   youPL man   PNLOC   one   come exist EXHST
         '[I] want you Huhurangi people to together come and all live

         *ade-hi   kokota, ge   ḡ-e   **au**=ña   velepuhi,*
         here-EMPH PNLOC SEQ NT-3S exist=IMM right.way
         here at Kokota, then there will be a Catechist,

         *ḡ-e   mala   **au**=ña   suḡa tarai*
         NT-3S PURP exist=IMM house pray
         there will be a church.'

In other instances no locative adjunct is present because the verb is used to express the existence of an entity, rather than its presence in any location:

(6.115) *n-e-ge   **au** dokta, n-e-ge   **au** ira   mereseni...*
         RL-3S-PRS exist doctor   RL-3S-PRS exist thePL medicine
         'Now there are doctors, now there are the medicines...'

The fundamentally unitary nature of the locative and purely existential functions of *au* are illustrated when an overt location adjunct is present but does not represent a physical location:

(6.116) *ka   ira   mane-vaka e   **au**   no-di   fama*
         LOC thePL man-ship   3S exist GENP-3PLP farm
         'With the white men there are their farms.'

The presence of a non-physical 'location' and the use of irrealis mood, indicating in this instance a habitual state, combine to give a simultaneously locative and existential sense in clauses of this kind.

As an extension of its existential function, *au* also functions as a verb of possession (see §5.10.2), and with middle voice (see §6.1.3.2.4).

6.6.2 Negative existential verb *teo*

The form *teo* occurs as the exclamatory 'no', opposing *ehe* 'yes'. It also functions as a negative existential verb. The positive existential verb *au*, discussed in §6.6.1, occurs with both a locative and purely existential sense. *Teo*, however, only occurs with a purely existential sense:

(6.117)a. ***teo***   *namhari*
       not.exist   fish
       'There are no fish.'

   b. ***teo***   *ihei*   *mane ta*   *torai*
       not.exist   whoeverSG   man   SBD   definitely
       'There isn't anyone who actually

       mai   reregi=ni=na   *ia*   *vetula=na*   *ḡavana...*
       come   look.after=3SGO=thatN   theSG   rule=3SGP   government
       looks after the government's law...'

Although a locative adjunct is present in (6.117)b., it is in the relative clause, and does not modify *teo*. The main clause expresses the absence of the existence of the subject, not the subject's non-presence in the village. This example would be more literally translated as 'Someone who looks after the Government's law in our village does not exist'.

The non-existence in (6.117) represents a stable state; however, *teo* may also express the result of a change of state:

(6.118)   *n-e-ge*   *la **teo***   *ira*   *nakoni*   *n-e=u*
       RL-3S-PRS   go not.exist   thePL   person   RL-3S=be.thus
       'There were no more people.'
       [lit. 'The people had gone to non-existence.']

In (6.117) and (6.118) *teo* is the antonym of *au*. However, *teo* does not also have a counterpart to the locative function of *au*. The non-presence of an entity in a location is expressed using the negative subordinating construction discussed in §8.7.2. In this construction a subordinated clause functions as the subject of the negative existential verb. To express the non-presence of an entity in a location the subordinate clause has the positive existential verb *au* as its predicate. The opposite of (6.119)a. is therefore (6.119)b. A negative locative use of *teo*, as in (6.119)c., is ungrammatical.

(6.119)a. *n-e   au   buala*
        RL-3S exist   PNLOC
        'He is in Buala.'

    b. *n-e-ge   teo   ḡ-e   au   buala*
        RL-3S-PRS not.exist NT-3S   exist   PNLOC
        'He isn't in Buala.' [Lit. 'His being in Buala is not.']

    c. **n-e-ge teo buala*

As with *au*, *teo* also functions as a verb of possession (expressing the non-possession of an entity) (see §5.10.2), and in middle voice (see §6.1.3.2.4).

6.6.3 Structure of existential clauses

Existential clauses resemble other intransitive clauses in constituent structure possibilities. The unmarked structure may occur, with the sole core argument following the predicate and any oblique occurring subsequent to that ([6.114] to [6.118]). Alternatively, topicalization may occur, with fronting of a subject ([6.112]c.) or oblique ([6.116]). Existential predications may occur as main clause predication, as in most examples above, or a subordinate clause predication, either a relative clause ([6.112]a.) or clausal argument (line 1 of [6.114]).

6.6.4 Causativized existential verbs

Existential verbs can be marked with the causative particle, encoding an effective change of state brought about by an agent or force. Thus *fa au* encodes the bringing about of the existence or presence of an entity, while *fa teo* encodes the bringing about of the cessation of existence of an entity. The entity that would be the subject of the existential verb becomes the object of the causativized forms:

(6.120)a. *n-a   fa au=i   kaike suli*
        RL-1EXCS CS exist=3SGO one   child
        'I have created a child.' [lit. 'I have caused a child to exist.']

    b. *n-e   fa au=ri   mane are*
        RL-3S CS exist=3PLO man   thoseN
        'He told those men to stay.' [lit. 'He caused those men to be present.']

c. *n-a-ke*   **fa teo=i**   *haidu*   *ana*
RL-1EXCS-PFV   CS not.exist=3SGO meeting   thatN
'I stopped that meeting.' [lit. 'I caused that meeting to not exist.']

The range of meanings of these causativized forms corresponds to those of the root verbs. While the causativized positive existential verb expresses existence or presence, the negative expresses only non-existence, and not non-presence. As (6.120)a. shows, the causativized positive existential verb can mean to cause the life of a person (by parenting it). The causativized negative existential verb alone does not have the opposite sense of 'kill'. It does, however, occur in a lexicalized collocation with *faro(go)ho* 'smite' with that meaning:

(6.121)   *ḡ-e*   **farogoho fa teo=ri**   *mane...*
         NT-3S smite   CS not.exist=3PLO man
         'He killed the men...' [50]

The causativized existential verbs are transitive. *Fa teo* also occurs as a ditransitive predication. In this construction the indirect object is a subordinate clause expressing an event that was prevented from occurring by the agent. The direct object is not an entity that would be the subject of *teo* in an uncausativized clause, but instead is the subject of the subordinate clause IO:

(6.122)   *n-e*   **fa teo=i**   *gase*   *ana*
         RL-3S CS not.exist=3SGO woman   thatN
         'He didn't allow that girl

         ta   *lao=na*   *ka*   *sikolu=na*
         SBD go=thatN   LOC school=thatN
         to go to school.'

6.6.5 *Teo* as a verb proform

The negative existential verb *teo* also functions as a verb proform 'not do':

(6.123)   *ara manahagi=nigo ago*   *ta*   *dupa=i=na*   *manei*
         I   want=2SGO   youSG   SBD punch=3SGO=thatN   he
         'I wanted you to hit him,

         ge   *ne*   **teo**   *bla*   *ago*
         SEQ RL   not.exist LMT   youSG
         but you didn't.'

---

[50] This verb is undergoing diachronic loss of the third syllable to *faroho*.

6.7 Adjuncts

The formal characteristics of PPs and various types of adjuncts are discussed in chapter 4. The functional characteristics of each are discussed here.

6.7.1 The Prepositional Phrase

One preposition exists in Kokota: the general purpose locative *ka*. This acts as the head of prepositional phrases with a variety of semantic roles, including locative, goal, source, cause, instrument, and benefactive. The semantic role of a PP in any clause is determined by a combination of the semantics of the predication and the semantics of the constituent governed by the preposition.

6.7.1.1 Spatial locatives

The existential verb *au* has a broad meaning covering notions such as 'exist' 'be (somewhere)', 'stay', and 'live'. Due to the inherently location-dependant nature of the event expressed by this verb, prepositional phrases occurring with *au* are interpreted as having the semantic role of spatial locative, as in (6.124). *Au* also often occurs with a location name or spatial deictic locative (see §6.7.2).

(6.124)   ...*gita-palu ḡe au la ka nasona a-hi ḡerona keli*
weINC-two NT exist CND LOC point thisT-EMPH PNLOC be.good
'...if you and I lived at the point at Gerona [that would be] good.'

In clauses where the semantics of the predication do not indicate some other kind of peripheral notion, any PP is typically interpreted as a locative (rather than, say, a goal or source). In (6.125)a. the PP is interpreted as a locative although the predicate *friñhe* does not have an implicit location built into its semantics (beyond a general requirement that all events take place somewhere). In (6.125)b. the PP is again interpreted as a locative, not a goal or source: the clause does not mean '...chase...into the garden' or '...chase...from the garden'.

(6.125)a.   *e=u friñhe n-e-ke friñhe=ni=na palu mane aro*
3S=be.thus work RL-3S-PFV work=3SGO=thatN two man theseT
'That's the thing these two men did

   ka nasona ine ḡerona
LOC point thisR PNLOC
at this point at Gerona.'

   b.   *ira mheke n-e toḡla=di ia zora ka=ia ḡrui*
thePL dog RL-3S chase=3PLO theSG pig LOC=theSG garden
'The dogs chased the pig in [i.e., within] the garden.'

219

The PP in this example refers to a physical location, so lends itself to a locative interpretation. However, the interpretation of a PP as a locative when occurring with a non-location-dependent verb is not limited to PPs referring to physical locations, such as 'the point at Gerona' in (6.125). PPs whose referents would not otherwise be regarded as locations are interpreted as such:

(6.126)a. ...ḡ-e **la**   **uf-i=Ø**   ia   to~toi
         NT-3S go   blow-TR=3SGO theSG RD~cook
         '...he went and blew on the fire

         ka=ia   **papaḡu**   **ḡazu**
         LOC=theSG stack   wood
         on the pile of wood.'

      b. ḡ-e   **knusu**   bla   **ka=to~toi=ne=n-e-ke=u**
         NT-3S break   LMT LOC=RD~cook=thisR=RL-3S-PFV=be.thus
         'It broke on the fire, it was like that.'

In (6.126)a. the pile of wood is given as the location of the blowing, not the location of the fire. Neither of the predications in (6.125) have an implicit location, and neither of the PPs have referents that would be interpreted as locatives in other constructions.

PPs that do not even refer to physical items, such as customs or languages, are also typically interpreted as locatives:

(6.127)a. ...**ka=ia**   **kastom gai**   tana goi
         LOC=theSG custom weEXC then VOC
         '...in our custom, man!,

         momoru   e=ni   e=u
         momoru   3S=3SGO 3S=be.thus
         it's called momoru.'

      b. ...malaria   ta=ni=o   nañha=na=na   e=u
         malaria SBD=3SGO=thatNV name=3SGP=thatN 3S=be.thus
         '...malaria, as it's called

         ka   **ooe-vaka**
         LOC talk-ship
         in English.' [lit. '...which does that name of it in English.']

Locatives of this kind are often governed by the form *fai*, usually translated by speakers as 'side'. This may refer literally to the side of a physical object:

(6.128) *roha=i   ka   fai   hage=na   naprai   e=u   ba*
        scrape=3SGO LOC side ascend=3SGP sun   3S=be.thus ALT
        'Scrape it [the bark of a tree] on the side where the sun comes up.'

However, *fai* often occurs with a sense of 'on the part of', 'in the context of':

(6.129)a. *e=u   e   tehi   la bla gai   kokolo=di   foḡra*
        3S=be.thus 3S be.many ?? LMT weEXC class=3PLP sick
        'There are many kinds of sicknesses

        ka=ia   fai   dokta
        LOC=theSG side doctor
        to do with doctors.'

    b. *palu   ḡlepo bla   ka fai kastom=de   bla*
       two   thing LMT LOC side custom=theseR LMT
       'two things on the part of [i.e., to do with] custom'

Locatives extend to events that take place in a person's thoughts:

(6.130) *ara ka   ga~gato=ḡu=re   gita   ginai korho namhari...*
        I   LOC RD~think=1SGP=thoseN weINC FUT   pull   fish
        'I think we will catch fish...'

6.7.1.2 Source and goal

Some verbs code events that inherently involve directed motion or action. PPs occurring with these verbs will be interpreted as goal or source, depending on an interaction of the semantics of the predication and the referent of the PP itself. Several verbs code motion that is inherently directional. These include *mai* 'come', *lao* 'go (towards)', *zaho* 'go (away)', and *aḡe* 'go'. PPs occurring with these verbs are interpreted as goals:

(6.131)a. *...ge   ḡ-e   lao=ña   ka=ia   suḡa...*
        SEQ NT-3S go=IMM LOC=theSG house
        '...then she will go to the house...'

    b. *ginai mai   gudu bla   baiu ka sikolu=ne   bla*
       FUT   come EXHST LMT PSBL LOC school=thisR LMT
       'I think they will all come just to this school.'

    c. *ara n-a   aḡe ka=ia   sitoa*
       I   RL-1EXCS go LOC=theSG store
       'I went to the store.'

d. *zaho ka no-u suḡa=o*
go LOC GENP-2SGP house=thatN
'Go to your house!'

This applies equally to causativized forms of these verbs:

(6.132) *n-e fa mai=ni kaike letasi k=ara*
RL-3S CS come=3SGO one letter LOC=I
'They have sent a letter to me.'

Several verbs code various concepts of return or arrival, including *pulo* 'return', *posa* 'emerge', *toke* 'arrive back', and *toga* 'arrive'. PPs occurring with these verbs are also interpreted as goal:

(6.133)a. *ke pulo... ka=n-e-ke hure=ro ira tilo tomoko*
PFV return LOC=RL-3S-PFV carry=thoseNV thePL three war.canoe
'They went back...to where they had carried the three canoes.'

b. *...n-e-ke posa maneri ka toa=na e=u*
RL-3S-PFV emerge they LOC fort=thatN 3S=be.thus
'...they emerged at the fort'

c. *ḡ-e toke ka=ia suḡa*
NT-3S return LOC=theSG house
'They go back to the house.'

d. *n-e toga ka rarata=o*
RL-3S arrive LOC beach=thatNV
'He arrived at that beach.'

Kokota has two verbs translatable as 'put': *nai* and *lisa*. Both subcategorize for a theme complement, and with both, a PP is interpreted as goal:

(6.134) *...hod-i=Ø aḡe nai=ni ka suḡa tarai=ne*
take-TR=3SGO go put=3SGO LOC house pray=thisR
'...take it and put it in the church'

A number of other verbs of motion prompt goal interpretations of PPs expressing locations. These include verbs such as *flalo* 'fly', where the actors themselves change location (as in [6.135]a.), or verbs such as *korho* 'pull', where it is an acted-upon undergoer that changes location (as in [6.135]b.–c.):

(6.135)a. *ara ginai flalo ka nau=ḡu=o*
I FUT fly LOC place=1SGP=thatNV
'I will fly to my home.'

b. ...*korho=u* *tagi-di*   *ka=nau*   *fai* *kokota* *a-hi*...
     pull=CNT REFL-3PLP LOC=place side PNLOC thisT-EMPH
     '...they pulled themselves to this place Kokota...'

Some verbs that are not motion verbs prompt a goal interpretation of PPs with specific kinds of referents. For example, a verb expressing an event that brings about the existence of small objects will prompt a goal interpretation of a PP that has as its referent an item that could function as a receptacle. In (6.128) the PP with *roha* 'scrape' is interpreted as a locative. In (6.136) the resultative nature of the event interacts with the semantics of the PP to prompt a goal interpretation:

(6.136)   *roha=i*   *nhigo*   *ka* *botolo* *ba* *ka* *tini*
          scrape=3SGO be.finished LOC bottle ALT LOC tin
          'Scrape it into a bottle or tin.'

PPs occurring with the directional verb *hage* 'ascend' are interpreted as goal:

(6.137)a. *n-e* *la* *hage=u=na*   *manei* *ka* *toa*
          RL-3S go ascend=CNT=thatN he   LOC fort
          'He was going up to the fort.'

     b. ...*ḡ-a*   *fa* *hage=i*   *ka*   *hinage*
          NT-1EXCS CS ascend=3SGO LOC boat
          '...we lift it into the boat'

However, with its antonym, *kave* 'descend', a PP will be interpreted as source:

(6.138)   *ia*   *kakau* *n-e* *seha* *kave*   *ka* *raro=no*
          theSG crab RL-3S climb descend LOC pot=thatNV
          'The crab climbed out of the pot.'

With some other verbs, like *fufunu* 'begin', a PP is again interpreted as source:

(6.139)   *ara* *n-a*   *fufunu* *ka=ia*   *sitoa*
          I   RL-1EXCS begin   LOC=theSG store
          'I started from the store.'

When a serial verb construction involves both a goal-oriented directional verb such as *mai* 'come' or *lao* 'go', and a verb with which PPs have a source interpretation, such as *kave* 'descend' or *fufunu* 'begin', the source interpretation applies:

(6.140)a. *tana* *kave*   *mai* *ka=ia*   *riñata*
          then descend come LOC=theSG doorway
          '...then they come out from the doorway'

    b. *manei n-e*   **fufunu mai=na**   *ka* *suḡa* *tarai*
       he   RL-3S begin   come=thatN LOC house pray
       'He is coming from the church.'

However, when a serial verb construction involves a goal-oriented directional verb and a verb that has no implicit direct motion or action (like those discussed in §6.7.1.1), a PP is interpreted as goal. In (6.141)a., for example, *ravi* 'hide from' occurs with a PP that is interpreted as locative. However, in (6.141)b. the presence of *lao* 'go' means that a PP occurring with the complex predication is interpreted as goal:

(6.141)a. *hei n-e*   **ravi=nau**   *ana* *ka* **bakla=na**
         who RL-3S hide.from=1SGO thatN LOC flat.root=thatN
         'Who is hiding from me behind that flat root?'

     b. *manei ḡ-e-ke*   **ravi lao ka=ira**   *bakla*
         he   NT-3S-PFV hide go LOC=thePL flat.root
         'He hid down among the flat roots.'

This applies equally to non-physical events:

(6.142) *mane sala ge ruruboñi n-e-ke*   **namha mai** *ka* *suaragi*
        man PN and PN   RL-3S-PFV love   come LOC PN
        'Sala and Ruruboñi were kind to Suaragi.'

At least one verb, *fa kamo* 'go across' (lit. 'cause to cross'), often occurs with two PPs, one interpreted as a source and the other a goal, in that order (the order is presumably temporally iconic):

(6.143) **fa kamo=i**   *bakru* *ta=au=ana*
        CS go.across=3SGO liquid SBD=exist=thatN
        'Transfer that tea

        ka *timosi* *ana*   *ka* *panakini ana*
        LOC thermos thatN LOC cup   thatN
        from that thermos to that cup.'

Like locatives, sources and goals may be physical locations, physical objects, people, or non-physical items. In (6.144) a PP occurs in each of the two clauses, one a source, the other a goal. Both refer to points in a story:

(6.144) *fufunu* *ka* *keli-kava=o*   *n-e* *la mai=u*
        begin   LOC be.good-earth=thatNV RL-3S go come=CNT
        'Start from the peace [until it] goes ahead [and] comes

ka	*ḡilu=na*	*toke=i=a*	*ta*	*dia*
LOC	inside=3SGP	arrive=3SGO=theSG	SBD	be.bad

to reaching the badness.'

6.7.1.3 Temporal locatives

The semantic interpretations discussed in §6.7.1.1 and §6.7.1.2 do not apply when the PP refers to a temporal location of some kind. Temporal expressions occurring within a PP always locate the event in time, regardless of the semantics of the verb realizing the event.

(6.145)a. *hage* ***ka saigona=na sarere ana***
ascend LOC evening=3SGP Saturday thatN
'[They] went up on that Saturday evening.'

b. ***ka nare t=au=ana bla*** *e-ke* *aḡe* *keli* *bla* *manei*
LOC day SBD=exist=thatN LMT 3S-PFV go be.good LMT he
'On that very day he recovers.'

As discussed in §4.2.3, some deictic temporal forms are inherently locative and occur as a temporal locative without being governed by a preposition. However, some temporal locative NPs may, but need not, be governed by a preposition. In (6.146) the preposition is optional:

(6.146) *niha* *fata* *lao* *ago* *buala* **(*ka*)** ***wiki*** *ta* *aḡe=o*
how.many occasion go youSG PNLOC LOC week SBD go=thatNV
'How many times did you go to Buala last week?'

6.7.1.4 Cause

In some instances the semantics of the PP referent combined with the semantics of the predication prompt an interpretation of the PP as a cause. With the verb *lehe* 'die, be dead', for example, most PPs would be interpreted as the location of the dying or being dead, as in (6.147):

(6.147) *n-e-ge* ***lehe*** *ia-hi* *kolodadara* ***ka*** *pau=na* *kumai=na*
RL-3S-PRS die thatPV PNLOC LOC head=3SGP water=thatN
'He died at Kolodadara at the headwater.'

Equally, PPs with human referents are normally interpreted as locatives, goals, or sources, depending on the verb, as in (6.148):

(6.148) *ke* ***mai*** ***ka*** ***suaragi***
PFV come LOC PN
'[They] came to Suaragi.'

However, since deaths are generally assumed by the Kokota to result from a cause of some kind, PPs with human referents in clauses with the verb *lehe* are interpreted as having the semantic role cause:[51]

(6.149)a. ***ka   sala   ge   ruruboñi   bla*** *n-a*   ***lehe**=na* *ara*
        LOC PN   and   PN   LMT RL-1EXCS die=thatN   I
        'Simply from Sala and Ruruboñi I am dying.'

     b. *n-e-ke* ***lehe hogo**=na* *bla* *ka* ***mane aro*** *si=ba=ia*
        RL-3S-PFV die   be.true=thatN LMT LOC   man   theseT FOC=ALT=PRO
        'He really did die from these men.'

This interpretation applies to several other physical or emotional responses that are seen as having an implicit cause. With the verb *mhoto* 'sweat', a heat source will be interpreted as a cause, not a locative ([6.150]a.). With a verb such as *fahega* 'be happy' a much wider range of PP referents, including humans or events, will be interpreted as having the semantic role cause ([6.150]b.).

(6.150)a. *ago* *n-o* ***mhoto ka naprai ana***
        youSG RL-2S sweat   LOC sun   thatN
        'You are sweating from that sun.'

     b. *ara* *n-a*   ***fahega ka ago***
        I   RL-1EXCS be.happy   LOC youSG
        'I'm happy with you.'

The interpretation of a PP as cause is particularly common with predications containing an experiencer verb. As discussed in §6.1.3.2, several classes of verbs subcategorize for an experiencer. With these verbs, a broad range of PPs are interpreted as the cause of the experienced sensation. In this context a PP is subcategorized for by the verb and is therefore a complement, not an adjunct:

(6.151) *ago* *n-o* ***humu**=nigo*   *ka* ***maliri**=na* *zora=na*
        youSG RL-2S be.heartburn=2SGO LOC fat=3SGP   pig=thatN
        You have heartburn from that pig fat.

The positive and negative existential verbs *au* and *teo* each have a number of closely related senses, including a general existential meaning and a sense of 'live', 'reside', or 'stay'. As discussed in §6.7.1.1, the latter senses prompt the interpretation of PPs as spatial locatives. However, in some contexts the general existential sense occurs with a PP representing an event or a participant, prompting an interpretation of that as a cause of the existence or non-existence.

---

[51] Particularly since the Kokota generally assume that human intervention, usually with the assistance of a 'devil' or spirit, plays a part in any sickness or death.

The two examples in (6.152) come from a narrative about a devil giant who was eating people and killed almost the entire population before himself being killed:

(6.152)a. *n-e-ge*   ***teo***   *sini* ***ka***   ***naitu parahaḡal=a-hi***
      RL-3S-PRS   not.exist   FOC   LOC   devil   giant=thisT-EMPH
      'We are finished because of this giant.'

    b. *n-e-ke*   ***kaike au***   *nakoni=de=ña*
        RL-3S-PFV   one   exist   person=theseR=IMM
        'These people together lived on still,

        ka   ***lehe=na=na***   ***naitu t=au=ne***
        LOC   die=3SGP=thatN   devil   SBD=exist=thisR
        because of the death of that devil.'

6.7.1.5 Instrument

With some clauses a combination of the semantics of the predication and a PP prompt an interpretation of the PP as having the semantic role instrument.

With a verb of hitting or striking, such as *faroho* 'smite', a PP will normally be interpreted as a locative, or if referring to a body part, then a goal. A verb of physical contact carries an implicit point of contact, and a body part term governed by a PP will be interpreted as that point of contact:

(6.153)   *ia*   *nakodou n-e*   ***faroho*=*ri*** *ira*   *mheke*
        theSG   woman   RL-3S   smite=3PLO thePL   dog
        'The woman hit the dogs

        ka   ***pau=di=re***
        LOC   head=3PLP=thoseN
        on their heads.'

However, the verb also involves an implicit instrument. If the PP refers to a physical object that may be wielded, it is interpreted as an instrument:

(6.154)   *ira*   *huḡru suli n-e*   ***faroho*=*ri*** *ira*   *mheke* ***ka***   ***ḡazu***
        thePL   all   child RL-3S   smite=3PLO thePL   dog   LOC   wood
        'All the children hit the dogs with sticks.'

Equally, a PP with a verb of tying, such as *piri* 'bind', will normally be interpreted as a locative. However, when the PP refers to an object that is long and flexible, it is interpreted as an instrument:

(6.155)   *n-e*   *la* **piri**=*ni*=*u*   *ka=ia*   **kolu**   *e=u*
           RL-3S go bind=3SGO=CNT LOC=theSG snake   3S=be.thus
           'He tied him up with the snake,

           ka=ia   **kolu-seku**=*na=o*   *manei*
           LOC=theSG snake-tail=3SGP=thatN he
           with his snake's tail.'

Instruments need not be physical objects. In both examples in (6.156) *fa-lehe* 'kill' (lit. 'cause-die') occurs with PPs referring to non-physical items that are interpreted as instruments. Note that in (6.156)b. the instrument is an adjunct of the negative existential verb *teo* (functioning as a verbal proform). However, it relates semantically to *falehe*, the predicate of the preceding clause.

(6.156)a. **ka** *fari-namha-i a-hi*   *da*   **fa-lehe**=*i*=*u*   *mane=ne*
          LOC RECP-love-?? thisT-EMPH 1INCS CS-die=3SGO=CNT man=thisR
          'With this mutual kindness we will kill this man.'

     b. *mala* **fa-lehe**=*i*=*u*   *n-e-ke*=*u*=*o*   *b=ara,*
          PURP CS-die=3SGO=CNT RL-3S-PFV=be.thus=thatNV ALT=I
          'I intended to kill him,

          teo   *bla si=boka=ḡu=na*   *ka* **kuiti** *aro-hi*
          not.exist LMT FOC=be.able=1SGP=thatN LOC trick   theseT-EMPH
          but I just wasn't able to [lit. my ability just was not] with these tricks.'

6.7.1.6 Benefactive

A number of verbs refer to a process of making something. With such verbs, where a PP refers to a physical location of some kind it has the role of locative. However, if the referent of the PP is a person, it is interpreted as a benefactive:

(6.157)a. *heve* *n-e* **friñhe**=*i*=*na*   *ka=man* *ta* *foḡra=u*
          what RL-3S work=3SGO=thatN LOC=man SBD sick=CNT
          'What was done for the man who is sick?'

     b. ...*ke* *la* *toi*   *mala-ñhau* *ka=manei*
          PFV go cook PURP-eat LOC=he
          '...[they] went [and] cooked food for him.'

6.7.1.7 Comitative

With a number of verbs a PP referring to a human participant is interpreted as comitative. These verbs all encode interpersonal contact of some kind: talking, shaking hands, having sex, etc. This is distinct from participants expressed by a complement of the associative noun *tareme-* (see §4.6 and §6.7.2.3). The associative gives the sense that the actor performs the event while in the company of the referent of the associative adjunct. With prepositional comitative the event is instead directed towards the participant as a co-participant.

Two general speech act verbs, *ooe* 'talk' and *turi/tu~turi* 'tell stories, chat', prompt a comitative interpretation of a PP with a human referent. *Ooe* has both ditransitive and intransitive argument structures. With the ditransitive variant the interlocutor is realized as a core argument (as is the thing said, typically expressed as a subordinate clause):

(6.158)   *ara   n-a-ke   ooe=ni   manei*
          I   RL-1EXCS-PFV   talk=3SGO   he
          'I told him

          ta   mala   tazi=ni   n-e=u   reregi=ni
          SBD   PURP   keep=3SGO   RL-3S=be.thus   look.after=3SGO
          to keep and look after

          t=au=na   no-ḡu   zuta=na
          SBD=exist=thatN   GENP-1SGP   lamp=thatN
          my lamp.'

With the intransitive form, however, the interlocutor is treated as a co-participant and is realized as a prepositional comitative adjunct:

(6.159)   *ara   manahagi   ooe ka   ago   ginai*
          I   want   talk LOC youSG todayIRR
          'I want to talk with you later.'

Turi and *tu~turi* are the transitive root and derived intransitive counterparts of a verb meaning 'tell stories, chat'. With the transitive form *turi* the thing told is expressed as a core argument theme:

(6.160)   *turi=di=re   keha   tu~turi=di   kokota*
          tell=3PLO=thoseN   NSP   RD~tell=3PLP   PNLOC
          'Tell some Kokota stories.'

However, with the intransitive *tu~turi* a PP referring to a human participant is interpreted as comitative, again expressing a co-participant interlocutor:

(6.161)   *ara   n-a   tu~turi ka   manei*
          I   RL-1EXCS   RD~tell LOC   he
          'I chatted with him.'

The verb *kubai* 'shake hands' can only be intransitive, and may occur with a PP referring to a human participant that is interpreted as a co-participant:

(6.162) *ago*   *n-o*   **kubai**   *bo*   **ka**   **nakoni=de**
         youSG RL-2S shake.hands   CNT LOC   person=theseR
         'You shook hands with these people.'

Three verbs refer to sexual intercourse: the dedicated non-respect term *ome*, along with *visi* 'play' and *friñhe-puhi* 'do bad things' (lit. 'work-way') used metaphorically for politeness or formality. With all three a PP with a human referent is interpreted as a comitative adjunct expressing a co-participant:

(6.163)a. *ara* *n-a*   **ome ka** **gase**   **ana**
          I   RL-1EXCS fuck LOC   woman   thatN
          'I fucked with that woman.'

      b. *ara* *n-a*   *no-ḡu*   **visi ka**   **ago**
          I   RL-1EXCS GENP-1SGP play LOC   youSG
          'I want to play [i.e., have sex] with you.'

      c. *ara* *n-a*   *no-ḡu*   **friñhe-puhi ka**   **ago**
          I   RL-1EXCS GENP-1SGP work-way   LOC   youSG
          'I want to do bad things [i.e., have sex] with you.'

6.7.2 Other adjunct types

The formal characteristics of these adjunct types are discussed in chapter 4.

6.7.2.1 Deictics and local nouns

Spatial deictic locative forms (see §4.2.1) and local nouns (see §4.4) have the semantic roles of spatial locative, goal, or source, depending on the semantics of the verb. Source interpretations, however, occur rarely. In (6.164) deictics and location names occur with a spatial locative role, and in (6.165) as goal:

(6.164)a. *teo*   *ḡ-a*   *manahagi=nigo* *ta*   **au=na**   **ade**
          not.exist NT-1EXCS want=2SGO   SBD exist=thatN here
          'I don't want you to stay here.'

      b. *t=au=ana*   *n-e*   **au**   **mautu** *bo*
          SBD=exist=thatN RL-3S exist   right   CNT
          'That's on the right.'

(6.165)a. *hage   mai   ade*
       ascend come here
       'Come up here!'

    b. *n-e   lao=u   fate*
       RL-3S go=CNT above
       'He's going up on top.'

Temporal deictic locative forms (see §4.2.3) function as temporal locatives. The local nouns *legu* 'behind' and *ḡilu* 'inside' occur with a temporal locative role as well as spatial locatives. This is discussed in §4.4.1, and illustrated with examples (4.22)c.–d. and (4.23).

6.7.2.2 Location names

The proper names of physical locations (see §4.4) typically function as adjuncts. They occur commonly with the existential verb *au* as a locative:

(6.166)   *ḡ-e   au=gu   buala   e=u*
        NT-3S exist=CNT PNLOC 3S=be.thus
        'He [was] living in Buala.'

When *au* occurs as the final verb in a serial construction a location name remains locative, rather than a goal or source, even when the construction also involves a directional verb:

(6.167)a. *ke   aḡe au   paloho*
       PFV go exist PNLOC
       'He went [and] stayed at Paloho.'

    b. *n-e   mai   au   buala   e=u*
       RL-3S come exist PNLOC 3S=be.thus
       'It came [and] was at Buala.'

This also applies when other non-motion verbs occur following motion verbs in serial constructions:

(6.168)a. *...ḡ-e   mai   haidu=na   selana*
       NT-3S come meet=thatN PNLOC
       '...he came and held a meeting at Selana'

    b. *ḡ-e   mai   lehe=u   bla n-e=u   are   rabaka...*
       NT-3S come die=CNT LMT RL-3S=be.thus thoseN PNLOC
       'They came [and] died, some at Rabaka...'

As with prepositional phrases, some verbs prompt a goal interpretation:

(6.169)a. *n-e-ge*   **kusu   la   toga**   *no-di=u*   **bagovu**
RL-3S-PRS be.first go arrive GENP-3PLP=CNT PNLOC
'They're the first to be going and arriving at Bagovu.'

    b. * age da*   **hage=u**   *fitupogu*
go 1INCS ascend=CNT PNLOC
'Let's go up to Fitupogu.'

    c. *ke* **pulo** *e=u*   *tana* *zelu*
PFV return 3S=be.thus then   PNLOC
'[They] returned to Zelu.'

With other verbs the adjunct is interpreted as a source:

(6.170)   *gita*   *da-ke*   **fufunu mai=da**   **hograno**
weINC 1INCS-PFV begin   come=1INCP PNLOC
'We came from Hograno.'

While physical locations typically function as a locative, goal, or source, in certain semantically or contextually dictated circumstances they may have other semantic roles. For example, in §6.7.1.4 PPs with human referents were shown to have the semantic role cause when the predication included the verb *lehe* 'die'. This also applies when a location name occurs as the oblique, the sense being that people from that location caused the death:

(6.171)   *n-e*   *la* **lehe mariñi,**   *ka*   *mane* *aro*
RL-3S go die PNLOC   LOC man   thoseN
'He is dead from Maringe, from those men.'

In addition to functioning as adjuncts, location names may function as a core argument with semantic roles including stative and theme or patient (see [6.47]).

6.7.2.3 Contextualizer and associative nouns

Contextualizer nouns, discussed in §4.5, and associative nouns, discussed in §4.6, have the semantic roles of context and associative respectively.

CHAPTER 7: THE VERB COMPLEX

7.1 Overview of verb complex

In clauses other than those with a nonverbal predicate (see §8.1) the predicate consists formally of a verb complex. The verb complex consists of two layers. The inner layer, the verb core, is opaque to the outer modifiers. The outer layer consists of various forms that modify the verb core as a whole. In addition to core and outer modifiers, a group of constituent modifiers occur at the clause level modifying the entire verb complex. These constituent modifiers also modify other constituent types, and are discussed in §8.8. Verb complex core and outer modifiers are discussed in this chapter.

7.2 Verb derivation

Verbs may be derived by compounding or reduplication, or by forming a single lexicalized verb with an accreted causative preposed particle *fa* or the preposed reciprocal particle *fari*.

7.2.1 Verb compounding

Nominal compounding is a productive and relatively common derivational strategy (see §3.1.1.1). Compounding is also employed, to a considerably lesser extent, to derive verbs. Compound verbs are left-headed and endocentric. The left-hand root must be a verb root. The right-hand form may be a verb, as in (7.1)a.–d., a noun ([7.1]e.–f.), or even a root adjective ([7.1]g.):

(7.1) a. *do~dou-ñhau*   'be a glutton' (lit. 'RD~be.big-eat')
      b. *lehe-ñhau*   'be hungry' (lit. 'die-eat')
      c. *gato-ḡonu*   'forget' (lit. 'think-be.insensible')
      d. *foḡra-dou*   'be very sick' (lit. 'be.sick-be.big')
      e. *dia-nanafa*   'feel bad' (sad, sorry, etc.) (lit. 'be.bad-heart')
      f. *dia-tini*   'be unwell' (lit. 'be.bad-body')
      g. *turi-tove*   'tell custom stories' (lit. 'narrate-old')

7.2.2 Reduplicated verbs

Reduplication derives intransitive verbs from transitive roots. In some instances a verb may also be derived from a verb root giving habitual, ongoing, or diminutive verbs, or with semantically unpredictable results. In addition a handful of verbs are derived by reduplication from noun roots. These derivations are illustrated, and the function of reduplication is discussed, in §2.4.1.1. The effects of reduplication on valency are discussed in §6.3.1.

7.2.3 Causative derivation

The preposed causative particle *fa* combines with a verb to give a complex verb with an increased valency. This regular productive process is discussed in §6.3.3. However, a number of verbs exist in which *fa* combines with the root to form a single phonological word, giving a derived verb. In some instances the semantics of the resulting verb are predictable, as in (7.2)a.–b. In others the semantics is unpredictable and lexicalized, as in (7.2)c.:

(7.2) a. *fa-lehe* 'kill' ('CS-die')
     b. *fa-nodo* 'stop (TR)' ('CS-be stopped')
     c. *fa-ku~kumai* 'give s.o. custom medicine to drink' ('CS-RD~drink')

The stress basis for determining wordhood with *fa* is discussed in §2.5.6.2.

7.2.4 Derivation with the 'reciprocal' marker *fari*

The preposed particle *fari* combines productively with verbs to indicate that the marked event applies mutually to more than one participant (see §7.3). However, the form also combines phonologically with certain verbs to form a single lexicalized derived verb. These include:

(7.3) a. *fari-dia-i* 'be bad to each other, hate each other' (*dia* 'be.bad')
     b. *fari-namha-i* 'be kind to each other, love each other' (*namha* 'love')

These derived verbs display the final vowel /i/. This may derive diachronically from third singular object marking or the transitivizing suffix. Synchronically it appears to be functionally and semantically empty, as the verbs are intransitive:

(7.4) a. *n-a-ke*   *fari-dia-i=u*
     RL-1EXCS-PFV RECP-be.bad-??=CNT
     'We were hating each other.'

     b. *ka* **fari-namha-i** *a-hi*   *da*   *fa-lehe=i=u*   *mane=ne*
     LOC RECP-love-?? thisT-EMPH 1INCS CS-die=3SGO=CNT man=thisR
     'With this mutual kindness we will kill this man.'

7.2.5 Comparative suffix *-ia ~ -a*

The suffix *-ia ~ -a* marks stative verbs with a comparative meaning:

(7.5) a. *laini ine*   *n-e*   *sodu*   *ña*   *laini ana*   *n-e*   *sodu-a*
     line thisR RL-3S be.long but line thatN RL-3S be.long-CMP
     'This washing line is long, but that washing line is longer.'

b. *mala-ñhau ide   n-e   tehi*
   PURP-eat theseR RL-3S be.many
   'These foods are many,

   ña   mala-ñhau are   n-e   tehi-a
   but   PURP-eat   thoseN RL-3S be.many-CMP
   but those foods are more plentiful.'

All stative verbs may take this suffix, including verbs such as *fafra* 'be quick' and *bnakoa* 'be slow', but color terms may not. Verbs with the final vowel /a/ take the *-ia* allomorph, while those with other vowels take *-a*. Verbs taking the comparative suffix include two forms that occur typically as local nouns: *fate* 'above, on top, be high' and *pari* 'below, be low':

(7.6) *tugle ine   n-e   fate,   ña tugle ana   n-e   fate-a*
       hill thisR RL-3S be.high but hill thatN RL-3S be.high-CMP
       'This hill is high, but that hill is higher.'

The comparative suffix does not occur with causativized stative verbs. There is, for example, no **fa puku-a* 'make it shorter [than something else]'.

The comparative suffix also marks four direction verbs, indicating movement in the direction further than some other movement in that direction:

(7.7) a. *lao*   'go (towards)'   *lao-a*   'go further (towards)'
       b. *zaho* 'go (away)'   *zaho-a* 'go further (away)'
       c. *hage* 'ascend'   *hage-a* 'go further up'
       d. *kave* 'descend'   *kave-a* 'go further down'

(7.8) *suka n-e   zaho ña belama n-e   zaho-a*
       PN   RL-3S go   but PN   RL-3S go-CMP
       'Suka went away but Belama went further away.'

In addition, the suffix may mark the four absolute locatives (see §4.4.2) when they occur postverbally, indicating direction or location of an event:

(7.9) a. *goino   ara n-a-ke   lao rhuku,*
          todayRL I   RL-1EXCS-PFV   go   landward
          'Today I went inland,

          ña fufugo   ara a-ke   lao rhuku-a
          but tomorrow I   1EXCS-PFV   go   landward-CMP
          but tomorrow I will go further inland.'

b. *no-u   suḡa   n-e   au   paka*
GENP-2SGP house RL-3S exist west
'Your house is in the west [of the village],

ña   ia   suḡa   tarai   n-e   au   paka-ia
but theSG house pray RL-3S exist west-CMP
but the church is further west.'

Two other strategies exist for marking the comparative. One involves the form *ia*, not suffixed to the verb, but following it forming a single phonological word with the immediacy particle *ña* and contrastive marker *bo*. The other involves the directional verb *la* 'go (towards)' (or possibly the constituent marker *la* [function unclear]) occurring in place of *ia* in the same construction:

(7.10) a. *manei   n-e   dou   ña   ara   n-a   dou-a*
he   RL-3S be.big but   I   RL-1EXCS be.big-CMP
'He is big, but I am bigger.'

b. *manei   n-e   dou   ña   ara   n-a   dou   ia=ña=bo*
he   RL-3S be.big but   I   RL-1EXCS be.big CMP=IMM=CNT
'He is big, but I am bigger.'

c. *manei   n-e   dou   ña   ara   n-a   dou   la=ña=bo*
he   RL-3S be.big but   I   RL-1EXCS be.big go=IMM=CNT
'He is big, but I am bigger.'

All three strategies may be used with stative verbs. The last strategy may also be used with active verbs, suggesting that it is the comparative form that is limited to occurring with statives, not the notion of comparison:

(7.11) a. *manei   n-e   ñhañha   ña   ara   n-a   ñhañha   la=ña=bo*
he   RL-3S run   but   I   RL-1EXCS run   go=IMM=CNT
'He ran, but I ran further.'

b. *manei   n-e   mhoko   ña   ara   n-a   mhoko   la=ña=bo*
he   RL-3S sit   but   I   RL-1EXCS sit   go=IMM=CNT
'He sat, but I sat for longer.'

No specific formal strategy exists for marking the superlative, the intensifier *ḡlehe* 'very' having a superlative sense in an overt comparison:

(7.12) *ḡazu   ine   n-e   dou,   ḡazu   ana   n-e   dou-a,*
wood thisR RL-3S be.big wood thatN RL-3S be.big-CMP
'This tree is big, that tree is bigger,

ña ḡazu iao n-e dou ḡlehe
but wood thatPV RL-3S be.big very
but that tree yonder is very big.'

7.3 Causative and reciprocal marking

Verbs may be modified by one of two preposed particles: the causative *fa*, and
the reciprocal *fari*. These mark individual verbs, not entire predications, and any
verb in a serial construction may be marked with either.

The causative particle is discussed in detail in §6.3.3. The preposed particle *fari*
marks verbs to indicate that the event applies mutually to more than one
participant. The particle, in fact, may be productively preposed to nouns or
verbs. With nouns it emphasizes the joint role of the marked participants:

(7.13)   ...*kotu=ña   ooe   fa ma~maḡra,   **fari**   t=au=na*
           sprout=IMM say CS RD~fight   RECP   SBD=exist=thatN
           '...fighting talk developed, between

           *ka   tagi-mai   **fari**   datau t=au=are*
           LOC REFL-1INCP   RECP   chief SBD=exist=thoseN
           ourselves, those chiefs.'

It also occurs optionally with the local noun *hotai* 'middle', giving the complex
local noun *fari hotai* 'between' (see §4.4.1):

(7.14)   *popoheo n-e   au   ka   **fari**   **hotai**=di   goveo ge buala*
           PNLOC   RL-3S exist LOC RECP   middle=3PLP PNLOC and PNLOC
           'Popoheo is between Goveo and Buala.'

With verbs the particle marks the event as applying mutually to each participant
included in a plural subject:

(7.15) a. *gita   da   **fari**   lase=i   nañha=na=na   manei*
           weINC 1INCS RECP   know=3SGO   name=3SGP=thatN he
           'We know his name.'

       b. *teo   ḡ-e-ke   **fari**   roge=u   n-e-ke=u*
           not.exist NT-3S-PFV RECP   plan=CNT RL-3S-PFV=be.thus
           'They had not been making plans between them,

           mane datau=ro...
           man   chief=thoseNV
           those chiefs...'

7.4 Adverbial-like functions of verb serialization

The verb core often consists of a single verb. However, verbs may also combine in serial constructions. The causative and reciprocal markers discussed in §7.3 modify individual verbs, regardless of whether the verb occurs in a serial construction, or where in the series it occurs. All other verb complex modifiers modify the entire predication, whether it is a single verb or a series. The internal characteristics of verb serialization are discussed in §6.5.

Many functions performed by adverbials in some languages are performed by serialized verbs in Kokota, typically verbs in V_1 or V_3 position (see §6.5). All are verbs that freely occur as the sole verb in a predication or in any position in a serial construction, but in certain positions give particular adverbial-like senses.

Verbs in V_1 position contribute notions such as commencement, initiality, rapidity, and closeness:

(7.16) a. *manei n-e* **fufunu** *toka kave=i*   *ia*   *ḡazu*
     he   RL-3S begin   chop   descend=3SGO theSG wood
     'He started chopping down the tree.'

    b. **fafra**   *mai*   *gau*
       be.quick come   youPL
       'Come quickly, you lot.'

    c. *ne*   **namo**   *nhigo*   *gita*
       RL   be.near   be.finished weINC
       'We were nearly finished [i.e., wiped out].'

In V_1 position the verb *kusu/kulu* 'be first' gives the sense that the event expressed by the rest of the predication occurred first in relation to some other event (as in [7.17]a.), or that the subject of the clause performed the event first in relation to other participants performing the event ([7.17]b.):

(7.17) a. **kulu**   *zaho ka=ia*   *kokori*   *mau*   *mala*   *ñhau*   *ka*   *toa...*
     be.first   go   LOC=theSG dig.taro taro   PURP   eat   LOC fort
     'First go to dig taro to eat in the fort...'

    b. *...mane n-e-ke*   **kusu**   *au=de*   *ade*
       man   RL-3S-PFV be.first exist=theseR here
       '...[the] people who lived here first'

In V_1 position the motion verbs *lao* 'go (towards)' and *aḡe* 'go, proceed', give a sense akin to the English 'go ahead, proceed', in the case of *lao* potentially at odds with its actual directional meaning:

(7.18) *n-e-ke*   **la mai**=*u*   *mane* *ide*   *kokota*
RL-3S-PFV go come=CNT man   theseR PNLOC
'These Kokota men used to come.' [lit '...to go ahead and come']

In V₃ position motion verbs provide directional information that is given adverbially in some other languages:

(7.19) a. *manei* *n-e*   *tao*   **mai**
he   RL-3S swim   come
'He swam towards me.'

b. *ia*   *kubiliki n-e*   *seha* **lao** *ka*   *ḡilu*=*na*   *raro*=*no*
theSG rat   RL-3S climb go   LOC inside=3SGP pot=thatNV
'The rat climbed into the pot.'

c. *manei n-e*   *fufunu toka* **kave**=**i**   *ia*   *ḡazu*
he   RL-3S begin chop   descend=3SGO   theSG wood
'He started chopping down the tree.'

The adverbial-like function of these V₃ verbs is clear in (7.19)c., where *kave* 'descend' indicates a directed motion resulting from the chopping, not a downward movement on the part of the subject of the clause.

Other common verbs in V₃ position with adverbial-like functions include *hohogo* 'be true', *ñheñhe* 'be separate', *ḡonu* 'be insensible'[52]

(7.20) a. *n-e-ke*   *lehe*   **hohogo**=*na*   *bla*
RL-3S-PFV die   be.true=thatN   LMT

ka   *mane* *aro*   *si*=*ba*=*ia*
LOC man   theseT FOC=ALT=PRO
'He really died from those men.'

b. *gai*   *manahagi* *ta*   *au*   **ñheñhe**
weEXC want   SBD   exist be.separate
'We want to be alone.'

---

[52] The verb *ḡonu* has a meaning associated with a lack of awareness or conciousness. It combines with *gato* 'think' to form the compound *gato-ḡonu* 'forget'. Independently it often has the sense 'not understand', or 'not know':

ginai aḡe **ḡonu**   *ia*   *histri-na*   *nau*=*ne*...
FUT go   be.insensible   theSG history=3SGP place=thisR
'The history of this place will become unknown...'

239

c. *n-e*   *birho*   *g̈onu*
RL-3S lie   be.insensible
'He's asleep.'[53]

7.5 Pre-head verb modifiers

Numerous modal, aspectual and tense marking forms may precede a predication's verbal head. Two, the abilitative *boka* and the desiderative *manahagi*, function both as main verbs, and as pre-head adverbials. Others are phonologically independent, but occur only as modifiers, while still others combine to form a pre-head modal/subject particle indexed to agree with the subject.

7.5.1 Modality, aspect, and tense overview

The modality, aspect, and tense system is based primarily on a modal distinction between realis and irrealis. Tense constitutes a secondary system complementing modality, with two tense categories, present and future, optionally expressed. In addition a number of aspectual categories are recognized, including perfective and continuous.

7.5.2 Modal/subject particles

7.5.2.1 Modal/subject particle forms and structure

The modal/subject particle is comprised of up to five possible functional elements: a marker of modality and a subject agreement marker, both obligatory, and optional forms marking negative, perfective aspect, and present tense. Whichever of these are represented in a clause combine to form a single phonological word, the structure being representable as:

(7.21)   MOD/SBJ →   MOD + SBJ + (NEG) + (PFV) + (PRS)

7.5.2.2 Modal and subject agreement forms

Three modal categories are recognized: realis, irrealis, and a neutral category that underspecifies realis status. Of these three categories, only the realis and neutral category are overtly expressed. Irrealis is expressed by zero marking. This is typologically unusual, as crosslinguistically it is typically the realis category that is unmarked. Realis is realized by the particle-initial morpheme *n-*, and neutral by *g̈-*. Subject agreement, discussed at more length in §6.1.2.1, recognizes four person categories but does not distinguish number.

---

[53] The verb *birho* has a meaning that encompasses both 'be lying down' and 'sleep'. *Birho g̈onu* is used to distinguish actual sleep.

TABLE 7.1. MODAL/SUBJECT PARTICLE FORMS

	1EXC	1INC	2	3
Irrealis	*a*	*da*	*o*	*e*
Realis	*n-a*	*da*	*n-o*	*n-e*
Neutral	*ḡ-a*	[*ḡe-*]*da*	*ḡ-o*	*ḡ-e*

The single C of the modal forms combines with the single V of the first exclusive, second, and third person subject agreement markers, giving monosyllabic modal/subject forms in those person categories. However, the modal forms do not combine readily with the first inclusive agreement marker *da*, itself having a CV structure. Typically, no overt modal forms occur, and the modal distinctions are neutralized. However, occasionally a neutral modal form does occur with first inclusive agreement in a disyllabic particle (as in [7.22]). This only occurs with the neutral modal, and does not also occur with the realis.

(7.22) *ḡ-e   la heve e=u   ge   **ḡe-da**   fa-lehe=i=ña*
        NT-3S go what 3S=be.thus SEQ NT-1INC CS-die =3SGO=IMM
        'How are we going to kill him?'

7.5.2.3 Modal categories

7.5.2.3.1 Irrealis

Irrealis particles occur in clauses that code either future events, or habitual actions, or past or present events that are not taking place (counterfactuals). Where an event is located in the future irrealis, marking typically conveys this without any tense marking, as in (7.23)a. However, the future tense marker *ginai* may cooccur with irrealis marking ([7.23]b.):

(7.23) a. ***Ø-o***   *la   ka=ni=ña   tagi-mi*[54]
           IRR-2S go   see=3SGO=IMM REFL-2PLP
           'Go and look at him yourselves.'

       b. ***ginai Ø-o***   *lehe-ñhau gau-palu*
           FUT   IRR-2S   die-eat   youPL-two
           'You two will get hungry.'

Future irrealis events may also be marked for perfective aspect:

(7.24) *gai   **Ø-a-ke***   *pulo*
        weEXC IRR-1EXCS-PFV   return
        'We will go back.'

---

[54] In this section irrealis will be represented by an overt Ø.

The irrealis category also marks habituality. This applies whether the action is habitual at the time of speaking, as in (7.25)a., or was habitual at some point in the past, as in (7.25)b.:

(7.25) a. *manei* ***Ø-e*** *keha ñheñhe,*
he IRR-3S NSP be.separate
'He is different,

Ø-e-ti fari fata ka gita ira nakoni
IRR-3S-NEG RECP ?? LOC weINC thePL person
he is not the same as we humans.'

b. *ara* ***Ø-a*** *lao tarai e=u tifaro ka sade ide*
I IRR-1EXCSgo pray 3S=be.thus before LOC Sunday theseR
'I used to go to church every Sunday.'

Counterfactual events are coded as irrealis. In (7.26) the main clause predicate consists of the negative existential verb *teo*, and is marked irrealis:

(7.26) ***Ø-e*** *teo kaike ihei*
IRR-3S not.exist one someone
'There is not anyone

ta aḡe boka fa-lehe=i=na ia to~toi
SBD go be.able CS-die=3SGO=thatN theSG RD~cook
who can kill the fire.'

Irrealis may also occur with present tense marking, giving a sense of immediacy to the futurity. In this construction continuous aspect marking is also obligatory:

(7.27) ***Ø-e-ge*** *fufunu=gu bla tu~turi=ana*
IRR-3S-PRS begin=CNT LMT RD~tell=thatN
'That story is starting straight away.'

7.5.2.3.2 Realis

The realis particles mark real, specific events that are actually happening at the time of speaking, as in (7.28)a., or have actually happened at some previous time, as in (7.28)b.:

(7.28) a. *maneri* ***n-e*** *ḡauai*
they RL-3S be.distant
'They are far away.'

b. ***n-e***   *hage=ña*   *belama*
   RL-3S ascend=IMM PN
   'Belama went up.'

Realis particles freely cooccur with the perfective aspect marker *ke* and present tense *ge*, but do not cooccur with the future tense marker *ginai*.

7.5.2.3.3 Neutral

Particles coding the neutral category occur in clauses that conform to the criteria for realis or irrealis: events located in the past ([7.29]a.) or present ([7.29]b.) (here the historical present); or future ([7.29]c.) or habitual events ([7.29]d.).

(7.29) a. *manei*   **ḡ-e-ke**   *ravi lao ka=ira*   *bakla*
         he   NT-3S-PFV hide go LOC=thePL flat.root
         'He hid down in the roots.'

    b. *sofo n-e-ge=ni*   *bla*   *ia*   *sebele, ka sala bla nogoi,*
         grab RL-3S-PRS=3SGO LMT theSG axe   LOC PN   LMT VOC
         'He grabs the axe [and uses it] on Sala, man!,

         ḡ-e-ge   *faroh-i=Ø*   *manei* *sala=n-e-ke=u*
         NT-3S-PRS smite-TR=3SGO he   PN=RL-3S-PFV=be.thus
         and he kills Sala, that's how it was.'

    c. *ginai*   *saigona*   *si=ge*
         todayIRR evening FOC=SEQ
         'This evening

         ḡ-o   *tahe=i=ña*   *t=au=ana*   *ba*
         NT-2S tell=3SGO=IMM SBD=exist=thatN ALT
         you tell them that.'

    d. *ge* *ḡ-e*   *hod-i=Ø*   *ḡ-e=u=ña*   *ia*   *suli,*
         SEQ NT-3S take-TR=3SGO NT-3S=be.thus=IMM theSG child
         'Then they take the baby

         ḡ-e   *puḡri=ña* *ia*   *buklo=na*
         NT-3S cut=IMM   theSG umbilical.cord=3SGP
         and they cut its umbilical cord.'

Neutral particles may occur with perfective aspect and present tense markers, as (7.29)a.–b. illustrate, but do not appear to cooccur with the future tense particle.

The neutral category is used to maintain a modal status (realis or irrealis) that has already been established. This can involve maintaining in a subordinate clause of a modal status established in its main clause; or it can involve a main clause maintaining a modal status established in the preceding discourse.

(7.30)   *ka   tema=na la bla   **n-e**   faroh-i-=Ø=na*   *sala manei.*
        LOC hut=thatN ?? LMT RL-3S smite-TR=3SGO=thatN PN he
        'At that small house he killed Sala.

        tana   nogoi age ḡ-e   tetu=ña   *manei ge*
        then   VOC SEQ NT-3S stand=IMM   he   SEQ
        Then, man!, he stood up and,

        nogoi ḡ-e   kaike maḡra
        VOC NT-3S one   fight
        man!, he fought everyone.

        nogoi ḡ-e   farogoho fa-teo=ri   *mane*
        VOC NT-3S smite   CS-not.exist=3PLO man
        Man!, he killed all the men

        n-e-ke   au=ro   ka   ḡilu=na   tema=na e=u
        RL-3S-PFV exist=thoseNV LOC inside=3SGP hut=thatN 3S=be.thus
        who were inside that hut.'

Typically in a narrative the modal status of the events is established, and this remains the status of most of the discourse, except for a few specific clause types such as reported speech, relative clauses, and so on. As a consequence, the neutral particles occur much more frequently in narratives than in conversation or exposition. This means that even when clauses that have another modal status intervene (for example, with reported speech), the neutral signifies a return to the established discourse modal status. In other words that status has taken on a default status for that discourse, and the neutral signifies a reversion to the discourse default modal status.

The use of neutral particles in a narrative as opposed to modally marked forms is a stylistic choice. In narrative some speakers use the neutral forms extensively, establishing the modal status of the events early in the discourse, and reverting to realis or irrealis forms only occasionally, typically to prevent ambiguity. Other speakers use the neutral forms infrequently, maintaining the use of realis or irrealis particles throughout the discourse. The most common use of neutral particles is not, however, in the main clauses of separate sentences, but in subordinate and coordinate clauses of various kinds. These include clauses coordinated to a sentence-final 'be thus' clause; as well as the formulaic uses with negation and in irrealis 'why' questions.

'Be thus' tag clauses, discussed in §10.4.1, may mark modal status, with the host clause taking its modal status from the tag:

(7.31) *ḡ-e   fa-hage=u   ka   kame=na=re   n-e-ke=u*
        NT-3S CS-ascend=CNT   LOC   arm=3SGP=thoseN RL-3S-PFV=be.thus
        'He put [them] up on his arms, he was like that.'

In one negative construction a main clause with the negative existential verb *teo* governs a subordinate clause realizing the negated event (see §8.7.2). In this construction this subordinate clause is always marked with a neutral particle:

(7.32) *n-e   teo=ña   ḡ-e   mai=u   mane huhurañi are*
        RL-3S not.exist=IMM NT-3S come=CNT man PNLOC   thoseN
        'Those Huhurangi people aren't coming.'

Cause interrogatives (see §9.2.3.2) are expressed by two coordinated clauses— an interrogative and a declarative. The first clause is a 'be thus' clause with *heve* 'what' as subject. The second clause realizes the event the cause of which is being questioned. Where the reasons for a realis event are questioned the interrogative clause and the declarative clause are both marked realis:

(7.33) *heve n-e=u   ge   n-e   lao=ña   manei buala*
        what RL-3S=be.thus SEQ RL-3S go=IMM   he   PNLOC
        'Why did he go to Buala?'

Where the event is irrealis, the interrogative clause is irrealis, while the declarative clause has a neutral particle:

(7.34) *heve e=u   ge   ḡ-e   lao=ña   buala*
        what 3S=be.thus SEQ NT-3S go=IMM   PNLOC
        'Why will he go to Buala?'

7.5.2.4 Competing particles unmarked for subject

An alternative and competing modal particle system exists, probably reflecting a shift from the system described in §7.5.2.1–2, realizing both subject agreement and modal categories, to one distinguishing modality but not subject agreement. The subject agreement function appears to be being lost. In the competing system, the third person agreement forms, the *e* forms, have expanded to cover the other person categories, forming a part of the modal marker:

TABLE 7.2. SUBJECT-UNMARKED MODAL PARTICLES

Realis	Irrealis	Neutral
ne	*e*	*ḡe*

In (7.35)a., for example, the subject is second person, so the equivalent subject-indexed particle would be *o-ge*. In (7.35)b. the subject is first inclusive, so the subject-indexed equivalent form would be *da*.

(7.35) a. *e-ge   lao bla ago...*
        IRR-PRS go   LMT youSG
        'You just go ahead now...'

    b. *gita-palu   ña   ne   au   fa-g̃onu...*
        weINC-two IMM   RL   exist CS-be.insensible
        'We two are living wrong...'

The replacement of preverbal subject-indexed particles by invariant forms is occurring with apparently all speakers using the subject-unmarked forms occasionally, particularly when subject-indexing using postverbal possessive marking is present (see §7.6.1), making the preverbal subject-indexing function redundant. It appears that younger speakers use the subject-unmarked forms more commonly than older speakers. This suggests that the language is in the process of losing its preverbal agreement in favor of a non-indexing particle.

There also appears to be a hierarchy of person categories most frequently replaced. The third person-indexed particles are homophonous with the subject-unmarked forms. Of the other person categories, first person exclusive particles are the most commonly replaced with the subject-unmarked forms, with second person forms less commonly replaced, and first person inclusive by far the least commonly replaced. This hierarchy may be explained by a convergence of two unrelated factors. The first is that the hierarchy corresponds roughly to a frequency of use hierarchy. Clauses with third person subjects are the most common, with first person exclusive (typically singular) subjects the next most common. It is not clear without further analysis whether second person or first inclusive subjects are the least common, but the rough correspondence of third, first exclusive, and the rest, indicates that the most commonly used categories are the most likely to be replaced. The second factor is phonetic. Of the forms realizing the three non-third person categories, the first exclusive and second person forms are the most similar to the third person forms, consisting of a single vowel that combines with the modal consonant, while the first inclusive form (*da* in every modal category) is much more distinct. The likelihood of the replacement of subject-indexed forms with forms unindexed for subject corresponds to the frequency of use of the categories replaced and the phonetic distinctiveness of the forms realizing those categories in relation to the replacement form. In addition, it appears that unindexed particles are more likely to occur where the clause has an overt subject that occurs post-verbally, and less common where there is no overt subject (in which case the agreement may be more crucial), or where the subject is overtly realized pre-verbally (with the particle immediately following the nominal it indexes).

7.5.2.5 Modal/subject particle deletion

As discussed in §7.5.2.2, irrealis is the unmarked modal category in Kokota. The weakness of subject-indexing reflected in the loss of subject distinctions described in §7.5.2.4 is also reflected in a tendency for particles with no overt form marking the modal category—irrealis—to be omitted. Where context allows no ambiguity, irrealis particles are frequently omitted in casual speech. This occurs commonly in imperatives, as in (7.36)a.; or in clauses with the desiderative *manahagi*, where the subject is assumed to be the speaker unless otherwise specified, as in (7.36)b. It also occurs where the subject (particularly a first person subject) is overtly realized preverbally, rendering the subject-indexing of the particle redundant, as in (7.36)c.

(7.36) a. *hage   mai   ade*
        ascend   come   here
        'Come up here!'

    b. *manahagi=nigo   nariha   ta   mai...*
       want=2SGO   day.after.tomorrow   SBD   come
       'I want you, the day after tomorrow, to come [here]...'

    c. *ara   ke   nhogi   visi   a-hi   ka   gita-palu*
       I   PFV   payback   game   thisT-EMPH   LOC   weINC-two
       'I will reverse this game of ours.'

7.5.2.6 Negative marker *ti*

In one of the two negation strategies in the language (see §8.7) the negative marker *ti* is suffixed to the modal/subject particle:

(7.37)   *buka are-lau   e-ti-ke   mala fa za~zaho hae   ge   hae*
        bookthoseN-EMPH   3S-NEG-PFV PURP   CS RD~go where and where
        'These books will not be for sending just anywhere.'

7.5.2.7 Perfective aspect marker *ke*

Perfective aspect is marked by the form *ke*, which is suffixed to the modal/subject particle. The perfective occurs freely with particles of any of the three modal categories: irrealis, realis, and neutral, as in (7.38), or either overt tense marker—future or present—as in (7.39):

(7.38) a. *gai   a-ke   pulo*
        weEXC   1EXCS-PFV return
        'We will go back.'

    b. *n-e-**ke***   *birho sara*   *mogare*   *maneri*
        RL-3S-PFV   sleep   thereD   PNLOC   they
        'They slept there at Mogare.'

    c. *manei*   *ḡ-e-**ke***   *ravi lao ka=ira*   *bakla*
        he   NT-3S-PFV   hide go   LOC=thePL   flat.root
        'He hid down in the roots.'

(7.39) a. ***ginai ke***   *tore=igo=ña*   *bo*   *ago*
          FUT   PFV   ask=2SGO=IMM   CNT   youSG
          'He will ask you to tell more later.'

    b. *n-e-**ke**-ge*   *aḡe*
        RL-3S-PFV-PRS   go
        'He has gone.' [Response to question 'Where is X?']

The combination of the perfective and the present tense marker give a sense corresponding roughly to the English *already*. The example in (7.39)b. has a sense of "now he has completed going". However, the combination of present with perfective often has the implication of the event having taken place on a previous occasion:

(7.40)   *manei*   *nañha=ḡu*   *n-e-**ke**-ge*   *riso=i*   *e=u*
           he   name=1SGP   RL-3S-PFV-PRS   write=3SGO   3S=be.thus
           'He has already written my name (on a previous occasion).'

The implication of a previous occasion on which a similar event had taken place may be present in future tense marked clauses containing the perfective. The following example would be said by someone who had traveled to Buala already on the day of speaking, and was planning to travel there again that day:

(7.41)   *ara* ***ginai** a-**ke***   *lao buala*
           I   FUT   1EXCS-PFV   go   PNLOC
           'I will go to Buala.'

This perfective particle usually forms a single phonological word with the modal/subject particle. However, when the particle is deleted the perfective may still be realized, as in (7.36)c. When the particle is overtly realized, the only particle that can intervene between the particle and *ke* is the abilitative *boka*:

(7.42)   *a*   ***boka***   ***ke***   *fa-keli=ni*   *bo*
           1EXCS be.able   PFV   CS-be.good=3SGO   CNT
           'We can make well

ihei	*ia*	*ta*	*toke=i=na*	*ia*	*malaria*
whoeverSG	theSG	SBD	arrive=3SGO=thatN	theSG	malaria

whoever [it is] who catches malaria.'

7.5.2.8 Present tense marker *ge*

The present tense marker *ge* typically occurs with the realis particles, indicating that the event referred to is actually happening at the time of speaking:

(7.43)	***ne-ge***	*aḡe*	*fa-ho~hogo=na*		*gai*
	RL-PRS	go	CS-RD~be.true=thatN		weEXC

'Now we believe in

ka=ia	*mereseni*	*mane-vaka*
LOC=theSG	medicine	man-ship

the white man's medicine.'

The present tense marker may also occur with irrealis particles, indicating that the event, while in the future and so not yet real, will occur immediately:

(7.44)	*e-**ge***	*fufunu=gu*	*bla*	*tu~turi=ana*
	3S-PRS	begin=CNT	LMT	RD~tell=thatN

'That story is starting straight away.'

The particle also occasionally occurs with neutral particles, particularly in the historical present. Kokota speakers make frequent use of the historical present in storytelling, typically to bring immediacy to an important or exciting moment. The following example comes from a story about a payback killing. The narrative consists of about two hundred clauses, the first two thirds of which deal with planning the raid, the build up to the killing, and tricking the main victim into presenting an easy target. This all involves realis particles with no present tense marking. The narrative then switches to present tense:

(7.45)	*sofo*	*n-e-**ge**=ni*	*bla*	*ia*	*sebele,*	*ka*	*sala*	*bla*	*nogoi,*
	grab	RL-3S-PRS=3SGO	LMT	theSG	axe	LOC	PN	LMT	VOC

'He grabs the axe [and uses it on] Sala, man!,

*ḡ-e-**ge***	*faroh-i=∅*	*manei*	*sala=n-e-ke=u*
NT-3S-PRS	smite-TR=3SGO	he	PN=RL-3S-PFV=be.thus

and he kills Sala, that's how it was.

"lehe	*ne=u*	*gita,*	*ira*	*tara*	*nogoi"*
die	RL=be.thus	weINC	thePL	enemy	VOC

"You and I are dead, enemy!"

ḡ-e-**ge**=ni=ña   *manei nogoi*
NT-3S-PRS=3SGO=IMM   he   VOC
he says to him!'

The speaker then reverts to realis modality with no tense marking for the remainder of the narrative.

The present tense marker cooccurs with the perfective marker, apparently only along with a realis particle, giving the sense that the event is, at the time of speaking, concluded:

(7.46)   *ia   foḡra=ḡu   ara   **n-e-ke-ge**   keli*
          theSG sick=1SGP   I   RL-3S-PFV-PRS be.good
          'My sickness has got better.'

7.5.3 Abilitative *boka* 'be able to'

The abilitative *boka* has two functions: as a main verb, and as a pre-head modal modifier. In its verbal root function *boka* has the meaning 'be able':

(7.47)   *...ḡ-e fa-lehe=i=u,*   *ḡ-e-la   **boka**   bo*
          NT-3S CS-be.dead=3SGO=CNT NT-3S-go be.able CNT
          '[Tell them to] kill it, if they are able to.'

It is potentially transitive, the ability relating to an event that is expressed by a complement clause, represented in square brackets in (7.48)a., or that is established within the preceding discourse, as in (7.48)b.:

(7.48) a. *a   **boka**=i   bo   gai*
          1EXCS be.able=3SGO   CNT weEXC
          'We are able

          [ke   fa-doli=ni=na   ia   nakoni]...
          PFV CS-be.alive=3SGO=thatN   theSG person
          to make the person live on...'

      b. *ña   e-ke   keha   foḡra   ñheñhe   bo...*
         but 3S-PFV NSP   sick   be.separate   CNT
         'But if there is a different sickness

         *teo=ña   gai   **boka**=i=na   e=u*
         not.exist=IMM weEXC be.able=3SGO=thatN   3S=be.thus
         we aren't able to do [i.e., cure] it.'

Example (7.48)b. is from a discussion of custom medicines. The abilitative verb in this instance is understood to refer to the curing of the sickness. In its pre-core modifier role, *boka* indicates that the actor or subject is able to carry out the event coded by the predicate:

(7.49) e   teo   kaike ihei
        3S   not.exist one   whoeverSG
        'There is not anyone

        ta   ḡ-e   **boka**   fa-lehe=i=na   ia   to~toi
        SBD NT-3S be.able   CS-be.dead=3SGO=thatN   theSG   RD~cook
        who can kill the fire.'

With this function *boka* is a true modifier rather than a verb in a serial construction. This is evident by the fact that other pre-head aspectual particles, such as the frequency marker *fani*, may intervene between *boka* and other verbs.

Because *boka* codes the ability of a participant to do something, this is treated as habitual and can only occur in irrealis or modally neutral clauses. Consequently it doesn't cooccur with a realis marked particle. The habitual-like sense of *boka* also precludes it from occurring in a clause marked for temporal specificity. So while it can occur in clauses marked with the form *ginai* with its future tense marking function, it does not occur in clauses marked by *ginai* with its temporal meaning of 'today (irrealis)'.

The abilitative cannot cooccur with the desiderative *manahagi*.

7.5.4 Desideratives

Three ways exist in Kokota for expressing a desire on the part of an actor to carry out an action, or to have an action performed by others. Of these, one, the pre-head desiderative modifier *ḡroi*, occurs rarely. The two common means of performing this function are with the desiderative verb *manahagi*, and by the use of the general possessor-indexing host as a pre-head adverbial modifier.

7.5.4.1 Desiderative verb *manahagi*

The desiderative *manahagi* has two functions: that of a main verb, and that of a pre-head adverbial modifier. As a verb it is a general desiderative, with a combined sense of liking and wanting. A feature of the cultural context of this language community is that it is implicit that if someone likes something they also want it. It is possible to express liking for an object without the implicit wanting of *manahagi* by using the verb *ke~keli-* 'please', in a construction translatable as "it pleases me". However, this is much less commonly used than constructions involving *manahagi*.

As a transitive main verb *manahagi* can have as its direct object a NP realizing the object that is wanted or liked, as in (7.50)a., or a complement clause realizing an event that the speaker wants to happen, as in (7.50)b.:

(7.50) a. *ara   manahagi=di   **tupe**   **ide-hi***
        I   want=3PLO   coconut.crab theseR-EMPH
        'I want these coconut crabs.'

     b. *teo*   *ḡ-e   manahagi=ni=u gai*   ***ta=hage=na***   ***ade***
        not.exist NT   want=3SGO=CNT weEXC SBD=ascend=thatN here
        'We don't want to come up here.'

Alternatively, the verb may be ditransitive, with a NP direct object and an indirect object complement clause. The direct object realizes the participant whom the speaker wants to carry out the action expressed by the indirect object:

(7.51)   *manahagi=ḡau*   [*gau   mane   huhurañi*]
        want=2PLO   youPL man   PNLOC
        'I want you Huhurangi people

        [*kaike   mai   au   gudu   ade-hi   kokota*]
        one   come exist EXHST here-EMPH PNLOC
        to all come up together and live here at Kokota.'

With these transitive functions *manahagi* carries a postverbal agreement enclitic, though occasionally this seems to be omitted. Like any transitive verb *manahagi* can display an incorporated nominal object, and no postverbal agreement:

(7.52)   *ara   **manahagi**   sileni*
        I   want   money
        'I want money.'

However, as a preverbal modifier *manahagi* indicates a desire on the part of the actor to carry out the action realized by a main verb present in the same clause:

(7.53)   *ara   **manahagi**   turi-tufa=nigo   ago   kaike   tu~turi...*
        I   want   tell-give=2SGO youSG one   RD~tell
        'I want to tell you a story...'

This is not a serial verb construction, as *manahagi* may precede the future tense marker *ginai*, itself only a pre-head modifier. These two particles may occur in either order, with commensurate meaning variation. If the desiderative occurs first it indicates that the actor currently wants to carry out the action, but at some point in the future, as in (7.54)a., while if the future marker precedes *manahagi* it is read as indicating that the wanting itself will be in the future, as in (7.54)b.

(7.54) a. *ago* ***manahagi*** *ginai lao buala*
      youSG want   FUT go PNLOC
      'You want to go to Buala (at some time in the future).'

    b. *ago*   *ginai* ***manahagi*** *lao buala*
      youSG FUT   want   go PNLOC
      'You will want to go to Buala.'

Manahagi and the abilitative *boka* do not cooccur.

7.5.4.2 Desiderative marker *ḡroi*

The form *manahagi* is a desiderative verb that can be used as a preverbal modifier. The form *ḡroi*, on the other hand, appears to have the sole function of marking desiderative mood:

(7.55) a. *ara n-a*   ***ḡroi*** *dupa=i*   *manei*
      I   RL-1EXCS DSDR punch=3SGO he
      'I want to hit him.'

    b. *ara a*   ***ḡroi*** *ñhau*
      I   1EXCS   DSDR eat
      'I am going to want to eat.'

This desiderative may occur in realis or irrealis clauses, as (7.55) illustrates. In realis clauses the subject at the moment of speaking wants to act. In irrealis clauses the subject will want to act at some point in the very near future.

This form cannot function as a verb (and there is, for example, no plural object form *ḡro=ri*). It is used interchangeably with *manahagi* in its modifier role and with the pre-verbal possessor-indexing host in its adverbial desiderative function (see §7.5.4.3), and cannot cooccur with either.

7.5.4.3 General possessor-indexing host as preverbal desiderative modifier

A typologically unusual feature of some Northwest Solomonic languages is the use of possessive marking with verb-marking functions. As touched on in §5.11, in Kokota, forms that function as possessives in noun phrases also occur as verbal modifiers in two ways, one involving a preverbal location in the clause, the other involving a postverbal location. Postverbal possessives are discussed in §7.6.1. Preverbal possessive forms mark desiderative mood.

Pre-head adverbial possessive modifiers consist of the general possessor-indexing host *no-* (see §5.5), with a suffix agreeing with the person and number of the actor or subject of the clause, the suffix forms being identical to those indexing the host for possessor in NPs. (The paradigm is presented in Table 5.2.) With its adverbial function this indexed host indicates a desire on the part of the actor or subject to carry out the action coded by the predication:

(7.56)   *mane aro   n-e   **no-di**   faroho=ḡai   gai*
        man   theseT RL-3S GENP-3PLP smite=1INCO   weINC
        'These men want to hit us.'

Only the general possessor-indexing host is permissible in this construction. The 'consumed' host (see §5.5.1) does not occur, even when the action involves consumption by mouth:

(7.57) a. *maneri n-e   papara gu=na   n-e   **no-di**   ñhau*
          they   RL-3S suffer CNTX=3SGP RL-3S GENP-3PLP eat
          'They are suffering because they want to eat.'

     b. **n-e ge-di   ñhau*
        RL-3S CNSM-3PLP   eat
        'They want to eat.'

With this desiderative function the host is volitional: it may only mark events the subject has control over. Consequently it only occurs with unergative and transitive agent subjects. It cannot mark stative or experiencer verbs, as in (7.58)a. It can mark the bodily action verbs discussed in §6.1.3.2.1, which may be interpreted as volitional or non-volitional, but only with their volitional (and thus not middle voice) reading ([7.58]b.–c.). It can also mark the existential verb *au*, with its sense of being, staying, or living somewhere ([7.58]d.):

(7.58) a. **ara n-a   no-ḡu   bula=nau/heta*
         I   RL-1EXCS GENP-1SGP feel.angry=1SGO/be.strong
         'I want to be angry/be strong.'

     b. *ara n-a   no-ḡu   knaha*
        I   RL-1EXCS GENP-1SGP cough
        'I want to cough.' [on purpose]

     c. **ara n-a   no-ḡu   knaha=nau*
         I   RL-1EXCS GENP-1SGP cough=1SGP
         'I want to cough.' [as an involuntary experience]

     d. *ara n-a   no-ḡu   au   bla*
        I   RL-1EXCS GENP-1SGP exist LMT
        'I want to just stay [here].'

As with *ḡroi*, the desiderative possessor-indexing host may occur in realis or irrealis clauses, with the same semantic distinction between wanting to act at the moment of speaking, and the anticipation of wanting to act at some point in the very near future:

(7.59)   *ara a*   ***no-ḡu***   *soso*
        I   1EXCS GENP-1SGP piss
        'I am going to want to piss [soon].'

Pre-head possessive adverbial modification differs from all other pre-head adverbial modifiers in that it may itself be modified by the preposed causative particle *fa*, indicating that the actor of the clause causes another participant to want to perform the action coded by the main verb. In (7.60) the actor is a nominalized clause functioning as a force argument:

(7.60)   *kumai bia ine*   *n-e* ***fa no-ḡu***   *soso=nau* *ḡlehe ara*
        drink beer thisR RL-3S CS GENP-1SGP piss=1SGO very I
        'This drinking beer is really making me want to piss.'

The possessor-indexing host also occurs in restricted exclamations of desire consisting of a first person indexed host and a single lexical item, either a noun, as in (7.61)a., or a verb, as in (7.61)b.:

(7.61) a. *no-ḡu*   *sileni*
           GENP-1SGP money
           'I want money!' [in this context <u>not</u> 'My money!']

      b. *no-ḡu*   *zaho*
           GENP-1SGP go
           'I want to leave!'

In this exclamatory construction both the general and the 'consumed' possessor-indexing hosts occur. Indeed, both may occur with verbs of consumption. Both of the following are grammatical:

(7.62) a. *ge-ḡu*   *ñhau*
           CNSM-1SGP eat
           'I want to eat!'

      b. *no-ḡu*   *ñhau*
           GENP-1SGP eat
           'I want to eat!'

CHAPTER 7

This prompts the hypothesis that the source of the adverbial desiderative use of a possessor-indexed host lies in these kinds of exclamations. It is possible to hypothesize that first person possessor-indexed nouns were used as desiderative exclamations (as in [7.61]a.). Once the desiderative exclamatory function became entrenched it was extended to verbs (desired events) ([7.61]b.) as well as nouns (desired objects). The use of the forms as preverbal desideratives was then generalizable to other syntactic structures including full clauses ([7.56]). The fact that most verbs do not express an act of consumption may have meant that only the general host was generalized to full clauses, leading to the situation illustrated in (7.57). This may, as a result, be flowing back to the exclamatory construction leading to the introduction of forms like (7.62)b. in competition with (7.62)a.. This is, however, speculative.

7.5.5 Unitative *kaike*

The form *kaike* has a root function as the numeral 'one'. It also has a secondary function as a pre-head adverbial with a sense of the action applying to a number of participants in unison or as one. This operates in an absolutive manner, with the unitary nature of the participants applying to the undergoer of verbs that have an undergoer as part of their semantic structure, and to the actor or subject of verbs that do not.

When it occurs in intransitive clauses *kaike* indicates that the action is carried out by a group of participants acting together or in the same way:

(7.63) *tehi=di   mane=re   n-e   kaike isi   hage...*
        many=3PLP man=thoseN RL-3S one   flee   ascend
        'Many of the people ran away together...'

In transitive clauses *kaike* gives the sense that the action is performed on several undergoers as a group or in the same way to each. In transitive clauses *kaike* appears to always cooccur with the exhaustive marker *gudu*:

(7.64) *...ḡ-a   kaike fa-lehe=ri   gudu ña   gai   teḡe are-lau*
        NT-1EXCS one   CS-die=3PLO EXHST IMM weEXC turtlethoseN-SPC
        '...we kill every one of those turtles.'

Kaike follows any other pre-head adverbial modifiers.

7.5.6 Purposive *mala*

The effect of the purposive marker *mala* differs between volitional and non-volitional subjects. With a volitional subject it indicates that the event is the *intention* of the actor/subject, as in (7.65). With non-volitional subjects it indicates that the event is the *purpose* of the subject, as in (7.66):

(7.65) **mala** *fa-lehe=i=u*   *n-e-ke=u=o*   *b=ara...*
        PURP CS-die=3SGO=CNT   RL-3S-PFV=be.thus=thatNV ALT=I
        'I intended to kill him...'

(7.66) *...e-ti-ke*   **mala** *fa za~zaho hae   ge   hae*
        3S-NEG-PFV   PURP CS RD~go   where and   where
        '...they will not be for sending just anywhere.'

Mala occurs in two possible positions. It may occur as a pre-head modifier within the verb core, modifying the verbal head. In this position it follows the modal/subject particle, as in (7.66) Alternatively, it may occur as an immediate pre-core modifier, preceding the particle and modifying the entire core:

(7.67) *fa puku~puku=ri*   *bla*   *ago*   *e=u*   *bla goi*
        CS RD~be.short=3PLO LMT   yousG 3S=be.thus LMT VOC
        'You make it short, man,

        mala *n-e-ge*   *au*   *bo*   *turi=di=re...*
        PURP RL-3S-PRS   exist CNT tell=3PLP=thoseN
        so that these stories fit [on the tape].'

Purposive subordinate clauses are discussed in detail in §10.2.7.

7.5.7 *Torai* 'definitely'

The particle *torai* indicates that the event realized by the clause has definitely happened or will definitely happen:

(7.68) *n-e-ge*   **torai**   *nhigo*   *teteḡu*   *manei*
        RL-3S-PRS   definitely be.finished fish(V)   he
        'He has definitely finished fishing now.'

With stative verbs this often has the effect of an intensifier:

(7.69) *nakodouine*   *n-e*   **torai**   *foḡra-dou.* *ginai* *e*   *lehe=u*
        woman thisR RL-3S definitely sick-be.big FUT   3S die=be.thus
        'The old woman is very sick. She will die.'

When *torai* marks a future event with a volitional subject it indicates obligation:

(7.70) a. *manei*   *ginai* **torai**   *zaho*   *lao* *fufugo*
          he   FUT   definitely go   go   tomorrow
          'He must leave tomorrow.'

b. ... *teo*   *ihei*   *mane ta*   ***torai***
not.exist whoeverSG man   SBD definitely
'...there isn't anyone who has to

mai reregi=ni=na   *ia*   *vetula=na ǧavana...*
come look.after=3SGO=thatN theSG law=3SGP government
look after the government's law...'

Torai typically occurs within the verb core as a pre-head modifier, following the modal/subject particle and modifying the verbal head of the predication, as in (7.68) and (7.69). Alternatively, it may occur as an immediate pre-core modifier, preceding the particle and modifying the entire core:

(7.71)   *ara **torai**   a   lao buala*
         I   definitely 1EXCS go PNLOC
         'I have to go to Buala.'

Torai cannot cooccur with the abilitative *boka*.

7.5.8 Future tense marker *ginai*

The form *ginai* occurs as a temporal locative with the meaning 'today (irrealis)' (i.e., 'later today') (see §4.2.3):

(7.72)   *ai*   *lehe=ña gita*   ***ginai***
         EXCLM die=IMM weINC todayIRR
         'Oh! We're about to die.'

The form *ginai* also has the grammaticalized function of marking future tense. As such it marks futurity of any temporal distance, and is not limited to later within the same day corresponding to the temporal locative function:

(7.73)   *ara **ginai** pulo   mai   ka   fa palu wiki=ana*
         I   FUT   return come LOC CS two   week=thatN
         'I will come back in two weeks.'

The time coded by the future marker may be distant. In (7.74) the event referred to is anticipated to occur at some unknown and unspecified time certainly later than the year after the time of speaking:

(7.74)   ***ginai** mai   gudu   bla   baiu ka   sikolu=ne   bla*
         FUT   come EXHST LMT PSBL LOC school=thisR LMT
         'I think they will all come to this school.'

As future events are inherently irrealis, *ginai* cannot occur with a realis or neutral particle. It may occur with irrealis particles, which are often omitted in future tense marked clauses. Futurity is often not overtly marked. In irrealis marked clauses the context frequently clarifies that a future rather than habitual sense is intended. Equally, clauses containing an overt future temporal often do not also carry future tense marking. The future marker *ginai* is used optionally to clarify or emphasize the futurity of the event. As a temporal locative *ginai* occurs on the clause periphery. As the grammaticalized future tense marker it occurs within the verb complex as a preverbal modifier in one of two positions. It may occur as an immediate pre-core modifier, preceding the particle and modifying the entire core, as in (7.75)a. Alternatively, it may occur within the verb core as a pre-head modifier, following the particle and modifying the verbal head ([7.75]b.):

(7.75) a. *ka   varedake palu   zulai*
        LOC twenty   two   July
        'On the twenty second of July

        ginai *e   gato   pulo=i   ia   sekon apointed dei*
        FUT   3S think return=3SGO theSG second.appointed.day
        [one] will remember the Second Appointed Day.'[55]

    b. *manei   e   **ginai** au   ka   nau   ine*
        he   3S FUT   exist LOC place thisR
        'He will live in this village.'

7.5.9 Frequency markers *fani* and *tuma*

The particles *fani* and *tuma* both indicate that the event coded by the predicate they modify occurs regularly. The difference is one of frequency. With *tuma* the modified event occurs very frequently. The exact inference of frequency depends on the nature of the modified event. With normal domestic activities, for example, the inference is that the event occurs every day, or close to it, as in (7.76)a. With events requiring more time and effort, as in (7.76)b., the implicit frequency is not necessarily daily, but nonetheless more frequently than is usual.

(7.76) a. *manei e **tuma**   teteg̃u*
        he   3S very.often fish(V)
        'He goes fishing very often.'

    b. *suka e **tuma**   lao buala*
        PN   3S very.often go   PNLOC
        'Suka goes to Buala very often.'

---

[55] The anniversary of the day when Provincial powers were devolved to Santa Isabel.

Events expressed by clauses marked with *fani* also occur frequently, but less so than those marked with *tuma*.

(7.77) *ara a* **fani** *korho namhari e=u*
I 1EXCS often pull fish be.thus
'I often catch fish.'

Actions that are performed often are normally thought of as habitual. As habitual actions are treated as irrealis in Kokota, clauses containing *fani* and *tuma* are typically irrealis. Realis particles usually only occur with *fani* or *tuma* when the clause refers to events that formerly, but no longer, occurred frequently. In this case the clause is obligatorily also marked with the perfective aspect marker *ke*.

(7.78) *tifaro ara* **n-a-ke** **fani** *lao buala*
before I RL-1EXCS-PFV often go PNLOC
'Before, I used to often go to Buala.'

7.6 Post-head modifiers and agreement markers

A small number of particles and clitics occur within the verb complex, following the actual verbs. Of these, the possessor-indexing host, argument agreement forms, and incorporated arguments occur within the verb complex core. Others occur outside the verb core as outer modifiers, or may occur either inside or outside the core.

7.6.1 Possessor-indexing host as post-head immediacy marker

In many Northwest Solomonic languages possessive marking occurs within the verb complex with adverbial functions (see §7.5.4.3). This typologically unusual phenomenon occurs in Kokota. A possessor-indexed host (see §5.5) occurs as a pre-head desiderative adverbial marker (see §7.5.4.3). In addition, Kokota shares with many NWS languages a clausal construction in which a possessor-indexed host occurs post-verbally.[56] This construction appears to be historically derived from a nominalization structure. In Kokota it is optional, and marks the event as having high saliency or immediacy. It often occurs as a response to a question such as 'what are you doing?' or 'how are you feeling?', and typically carries a sense of the event occurring 'right now':

(7.79) a. *ara n-a* *babao* **no-ḡu**
I RL-1EXCS be.tired GENP-1SGP
'I'm tired.'

---

[56] Ross (1982) discusses the occurrence of this phenomenon in several Bougainville languages, and later (1988:247–251) in Roviana and Cheke Holo (as Maringe).

b. *ḡe   aḡe   mhemhe   **no-mai**   *n-e=u*
   NT   go   be.difficult GENP-1EXCP   RL-3S=be.thus
   'We find [that] difficult.'

While the construction typically indicates an event or state applying at the moment of speaking, it can refer to past or future events. Past events marked in this way usually have a sense of the event having just occurred, right before the moment of speaking, as in (7.80)a.. However, if another temporal frame has been established, it may indicate that the event had high saliency at the moment indicated, as in (7.80)b.

(7.80) a. *ara n-a-ke*   *toga*   **no-ḡu**
         I   RL-1EXCS-PFV arrived   GENP-1SGP
         'I have just arrived [right now].'

      b. *ka=t=au=ana*   *ḡe la lehe **no-ḡu***   *bo=sini*
         LOC=SBD=exist=thatN   NT go die   GENP-1SGP   CNT=FOC
         'At that I nearly died.'

With irrealis marking the postverbal possessive marking indicates that the event is about to occur, immediately after the moment of speaking:

(7.81)   *maneri e   zaho   **no-di***
          they   3S   go   GENP-3SGP
          'They are about to go [right now].'

In imperatives the form gives a sense that the event should occur immediately. Example (7.82)b. is particularly interesting as the marking applies only to the second of the two serialized verbs, as the first inclusive indexing demonstrates.

(7.82) a. *zaho **no-u***
          go   GENP-2SGP
          'Go away!'

      b. *mai   ome   **no-da***
         come fuck GENP-1INCP
         'Come and let's fuck!'

Unlike preverbal possessive marking, both the general and 'consumed' possessor-indexing hosts occur postverbally. The 'consumed' host occurs with the same function as the general host, but marks events of consumption:

(7.83)   *manei n-e   pipiala **ge-na***
          he   RL-3S smoke   CNSM-3SGP
          'He is smoking.'

The postverbal indexed host occurs as a modifier within the verb core. Consequently in transitive clauses it precedes realization of the object, either in the form of an object agreement enclitic (in which case it hosts the enclitic), as in (7.84)a.–b., or an incorporated noun, as in (7.84)c.:

(7.84) a. *manahagi* *ta* *aḡe* *kae* ***no-ḡu=ni***
        want   SBD go   see GENP-1SGP=3SGO
        'I want to go and see this.'

    b. *ara* *n-a*   *hoda* ***no-ḡu=di***   ***palu kokorako*** *ide*
       I   RL-1EXCS take GENP-1SGP=3PLO two chicken   theseR
       'I'm taking these two chickens.'

    c. *manei* *n-e-ke*   *ñhau* ***ge-na***   ***namhari*** *nhigo*
       he   RL-3S-PFV eat CNSM-3SGP fish   be.finished
       'He has just eaten fish.'

Note that in (7.84)b. the verb itself is in its intransitive form, not its transitivized form *hod-i*. Verbs that take the transitivizing suffix only do so when no constituents intervene between the verb and object enclitic. When the possessor-indexing host is present it intervenes, blocking the presence of the suffix.

The indexed host also precedes the continuous aspect enclitic:

(7.85) *n-e-ge*   *kusu*   *la* *toga* ***no-di=u***   *bagovu*
       RL-3S-PRS be.first go arrive GENP-3PLP=CNT PNLOC
       'They are going to Bagovu.'

The immediacy indicated by the possessor-indexing host may be emphasized by its cooccurrence with the immediacy particle *ña* (see §8.8.5):

(7.86) *ara* *n-a*   *babao* ***no-ḡu=ña***
       I   RL-1EXCS be.tired GENP-1SGP=IMM
       'I'm tired [right now].'

For three verbs, *mhagu* 'be afraid', *dogoho* 'be lazy, be unwilling', and *ḡonu* 'be insensible, not know', the verb root frequently occurs in a reduced form compounded with the post-verbal possessor-indexing host. In this compounding the root is reduced to its initial syllable, the host replacing the non-initial syllables. The semantics of these verbs mean they are likely to have frequently cooccurred with the host in exclamations meaning 'I'm afraid', 'I don't want to', and 'I don't know/understand', the frequency of collocation presumably leading to concatenation and reduction of the forms.

The verbs *mhagu* and *ḡonu* typically occur in intransitive clauses, though both subcategorize for an optional object—the source of fear in the case of *mhagu*, the subject matter of the lack of understanding or knowledge with *ḡonu*:

(7.87) a. *ara n-a **mhagu***
       I   RL-1EXCS be.afraid
       'I'm afraid.'

    b. *ara n-a **ḡonu***
         I   RL-1EXCS be.insensible
         'I don't understand.'

    c. *ara n-a **mhagu=ni** ia lehe=ḡu*
         I   RL-1EXCS be.afraid=3SGO theSG be.dead=1SGP
         'I am afraid of my death.'

    d. *hei n-e **ḡonu=nau=na** ara*
         who RL-3S be.insensible=1SGO=thatN   I
         'Who doesn't know about me?'

These combine with the possessor-indexing host to form the compounds *mha-no-* and *ḡo-no-*, with meanings identical to a combination of the meaning of the root and the immediacy given by the modifier. The compound *mha-no-* may be intransitive; however, it typically occurs as a transitive verb. The compound *ḡo-no-* is only transitive:

(7.88) a. *n-a **mha-no-ḡu***
       RL-1EXCS be.afraid-GENP-1SGP
       'I'm afraid.'

    b. *n-a **mha-no-ḡu=di** kakafre are*
         RL-1EXCS be.afraid-GENP-1SGP=3PLO spider thoseN
         'I am afraid of those spiders.'

    c. *n-a **ḡo-no-ḡu=ni** nañha=na=na manei*
         RL-1EXCS be.insensible-GENP-1SGP=3SGO name=3SGP=thatN he
         'I don't know his name.'

The corresponding uncompounded collocations **mhagu no-* and **ḡonu no-* do not occur. With *dogoho* the uncompounded and compound forms both occur and are semantically identical and intransitive only:

(7.89) a. *ara   n-a   **dogoho no-ḡu**   si=ñ̄=ara   nogoi*
I   RL-1EXCS be.lazy GENP-1SGP FOC=IMM=I   VOC
'I can't be bothered, man!'

b. *ne **do-no-ḡu=ña**   ara*
RL be.lazy-GENP-1SGP=IMM   I
'I don't want to

o-ti   huhuru=nau e=u   goi
2S-NEG   force=1SGO 3S=be.thus VOC
so don't force me, man!'

c. *n-e-ke   **do-no-di**=ro   keha   mane=ro*
RL-3S-PFV be.lazy-GENP-3PLP=thoseNV NSP   man=thoseNV
'Some people just are lazy

ka=t=au=are   bla
LOC=SBD=exist=thoseN LMT
for those [tasks].'

7.6.2 Transitivizing suffix

The replacive transitivizing suffix *-i* is discussed in §6.3.2. It occurs with a specific class of verb roots, but only occurs when the root is the final constituent before an object enclitic. It does not occur on non-final verbs in a series, or to final verbs where an adverbial constituent such as *fakamo* 'always' or the postverbal possessor-indexing host intervenes as (7.100) and (7.84)b. show.

7.6.3 Postverbal argument-indexing

A postverbal agreement enclitic occurs in all transitive clauses (see §6.1.2.2).

7.6.4 Demonstrative agreement enclitics

The penultimate position in the verb complex core is occupied by a cliticized demonstrative form. The behavior of these cliticized demonstratives in subordinate clauses is discussed in various relevant sections of 10.2. In main clauses they are optional, and agree with the absolutive argument. When occurring in an intransitive clause a cliticized demonstrative agrees with the number and deictic features of the sole core argument. This applies whether the subject is unergative, as in (7.90), or unaccusative, as in (7.91).

(7.90) a. *mane mariñi ge   mane ḡao,   **mane** n-e-ke   aḡe=ro=u...*
man   PNLOC and man   PNLOC man   RL-3S-PFV go=thoseNV=CNT
'The Maringe people and the Gao people, those people went...'

b. ...*zaho ḡ-e*   *la*   *au*   *iaro*   *hurepelo keha=re,*
        go   NT-3S   go   exist   thosePV   PNLOC   NSP=thoseN
        '...some went and lived over at Hurepelo,

        mai   *au=de-hi*   *ade-hi*   *goveo*
        come   exist=theseR-EMPH   here-EMPH   PNLOC
        and these came and lived here at Goveo,

        ḡ-e   *mai*   *au=gu*   **gai**   **keha=ide**
        NT-3S   come   exist=CNT   weEXC   NSP=theseR
        these of us came and are living at Goveo.'

(7.91) a. **dadara**   *e=u*   *blau*   *n-e-ke*   *zikra=ro*
        blood   3S=be.thus   LMT   RL-3S-PFV pour=thoseNV
        'Blood was pouring out.'[57]

     b. *maḡra*   *t=au=la*   *manei*
        fight   SBD=exist=CND   he
        'If there is a fight,

        kame=ḡu   *n-e*   *au=de*   *bla*   *la*   *bo...*
        hand=1SGP   RL-3S   exist=theseR   LMT   ??   CNT
        my hands are here...'

A demonstrative cliticized to a transitive predicate agrees with the object:

(7.92) a. *a*   *fa*   *nhigo=**ri**=ro=u*
        1EXCS   CS   be.finished=3PLO=thoseNV=CNT
        'I will finish those [stories].'

     b. *e=u*   *n-amhagu-mhagu=**di**=re*   *ara*
        3S=be.thus   RL-1EXCS be.afraid-be.afraid=3PLO=thoseN   I
        'So I'm a bit afraid of those [things happening].'

7.6.5 Incorporated arguments

The position in the verb complex that is occupied by an object-indexing enclitic in a formally transitive clause may be occupied instead by an incorporated NP core (with the proviso that the agreement indexing forms cliticize to the preceding word, while incorporated nominals do not). All formally transitive clauses must have either an object-indexing enclitic or an incorporated nominal, and cannot have both. Incorporation is discussed in detail in §6.4.

---

[57] *Dadara* 'blood' is plural in Kokota.

7.6.6 Continuous marker =*gu* ~ =*u*

Continuous aspect is marked by the enclitic =*gu* ~ =*u*, and indicates that the situation coded by the predication is ongoing at a point in time established within the temporal frame of the clause. The allomorphic variation in the marker is phonologically motivated. The underlying form =*gu* surfaces following any /u/ final form, including those ending with the diphthongs /au/ and /ou/. Where /ɣ/ is not needed to separate the marker from the preceding vowel it is omitted:

(7.93) a. *ḡ-e au=**gu** ḡerona*
   NT-3S exist=CNT PNLOC
   'They were living at Gerona.'

  b. *...n-e kota=**u**   manei...*
   RL-3S go.ashore=CNT he
   '...he is going ashore...'

This accords with /ɣ/ deletion occurring elsewhere in Kokota (see §2.1.1.2.3.3).

The continuous marker can occur in clauses with any modal/subject particle. However, continuous with an irrealis particle indicates that the event is not taking place at the moment of speaking, but is about to take place immediately:

(7.94) a. *ara a aḡe=**u***
   I 1EXCS go=CNT
   'I am going now.'

  b. *mala lase=ri=**u** gau*
   PURP know=3PLO=CNT youPL
   'So you will [be] know[ing] them [the stories].'

Continuous marking is not limited to active verbs. It can also occur with stative verbs, as in (7.95)a. or experiencer verbs ([7.95]b.):

(7.95) a. *...ḡ-e aḡe keli=**u** bla nakoni ana*
   NT-3S go be.good=CNT LMT person thatN
   '...that man goes good [i.e., gets well] [again].'

  b. *n-a bula=nau=**gu** ara*
   RL-1EXCS feel.angry=1SGO=CNT I
   'I am (very) cross.'

The continuous marker is an enclitic occurring verb-core finally. It attaches to whatever constituent occurs in penultimate position in the core. In most intransitive clauses this is a verb (as in [7.94]a.). In most transitive clauses it is the postverbal agreement enclitic (as in [7.94]b.) When an incorporated nominal is present the marker is cliticized to that, as the following comparison reveals:

(7.96) *manei teo   ḡ-e   korho namhari=u*
       he   not.exist NT-3S pull fish=CNT
       'He wasn't catching fish.'

7.6.7 Completive aspect marker *nhigo*

As discussed in §6.5.2, the verb *nhigo* 'be finished' can occur as V₃ in a serial verb construction, modifying the rest of the verbs in the series, and indicating that the event expressed by those verbs is carried to completion. The form also occurs as a post-core modifier, modifying the entire verb complex core, and indicating that the entire predication is completed at the time of speaking, a sense akin to the English *already*. The example in (7.97)a. illustrates the serial V₃, (7.97)b. the post-core modifier. The formal distinction is revealed by the position of the form in relation to the postverbal agreement indexing enclitic:

(7.97) a. *ara n-a   dupa **nhigo=i**   manei*
        I   RL-1EXCS punch be.finished=3SGO he
        'I have finished hitting him.'

     b. *ara n-a   dupa=i   **nhigo**   manei*
        I   RL-1EXCS punch=3SGO be.finished he
        'I have already hit him.'

As with any post-core modifier, this follows not only object agreement, but also incorporated nominals (in this example the NP core *ge-na namhari* 'his fish'):

(7.98) *manei n-e-ke   ñhau ge-na   namhari **nhigo***
       he   RL-3S-PFV eat CNSM-3SGP fish be.finished
       'He has already eaten his fish.'

As a serial verb, *nhigo* freely occurs in irrealis clauses, indicating that at some point in the future an event will be carried to completion. As a post-core modifier it cannot occur in an irrealis clause, the notion of an event already having occurred clashing with the unrealized nature of irrealis events. *Nhigo* may cooccur with perfective aspect *ke*, indicating that the event had already been completed at some point in the past, as in (7.99)a. With the present tense marker *ge* it indicates that the event is complete at the time of speaking, as in (7.99)b.:

(7.99) a. *manei n-e-**ke** toga **nhigo***
        he   RL-3S-PFV arrive be.finished
        'He had already arrived.'

b. *manei*   *n-e-ge*   *toga*   **nhigo**
he   RL-3S-PRS arrive be.finished
'He has already arrived.'

7.6.8 *Fakamo* 'always'

The adverb *fakamo* indicates that the event expressed by the predication always occurs. It occurs in two possible positions. It may occur within the verb core modifying the verb or verbs present in the core:

(7.100) *e* *teo*   *ḡe lao* *ge* *hoda* **fakamo=i=u**   *gai*
         3S not.exist   NT go   and   take   always=3SGO=CNT   weEXC
         '...we don't always go and take it

         le~legu   *nare...*
         RD~behind   day
         every day...'

More typically the form occurs in the immediate post-core modifier position, modifying the entire verb complex. The semantic result is effectively identical. The formal distinction is revealed by the relative positions of the adverb and the postverbal agreement indexing enclitic:

(7.101) *fakae=ni*   **fakamo** *bla* *gai*
         see=3SGO   always LMT weEXC
         'We always see

         au=gu   *mala=na=re*   *naitu* *t=au=ana*
         exist=CNT footprint=3SGP=thoseN devil   SBD=exist=thatN
         those footprints of that devil existing [there].'

As an outer modifier *fakamo* follows any incorporated nominal:

(7.102) *ara* *a*   *korho namhari* **fakamo**
         I   1EXCS pull   fish   always
         'I always catch fish.'

Fakamo cannot cooccur with the post-head possessor-indexing host saliency modifier, or with *nhigo* 'be finished'.

7.6.9 Exhaustive marker *gudu*

The form *gudu* is an exhaustive marker able to modify verbs or nominals. Its use with nominals is discussed in §3.2.2.4. As an adverb it occurs in the immediate post-core modifier position, modifying the entire predication and indicating that the action was carried out exhaustively. This is effectively absolutive: in transitive clauses it indicates that the event was performed on every possible undergoer, while in intransitive clauses it indicates that the event was performed by every possible actor/subject:

(7.103)a. *ḡ-a   kaikefa-lehe=ri* **gudu** *ña gai   teḡe are-lau*
NT-1EXCS one CS-die=3PLO EXHST IMM weEXC turtlethoseN-SPC
'...we kill every one of those turtles.'

    b. *ginai mai* **gudu** *bla baiu   ka   sikolu=ne   bla*
FUT   come EXHST LMT PSBL LOC school=thisR LMT
'[I think] maybe they will all come to this school.'

The adverbial *gudu* may only occur with active predications, and not with statives. This places it in complementary distribution with the post-core intensifier *ḡlehe*, which only occurs with stative predications.

7.6.10 Intensifier *ḡlehe*

The form *ḡlehe* occurs in immediate post-core modifier position. It occurs with stative predications intensifying the state coded by the verb:

(7.104)a. *ḡrugu=o   n-e-ke   **ḡlaba**   **ḡlehe***
night=thatNV RL-3S-PFV be.moonbright very
'Last night was very moonbright.'

    b. *n-e* **dia** **ḡlehe**
RL-3S be.bad very
'[That] is very bad.'

It also marks experiencer verbs (see §6.1.3.2). However, for bodily action verbs, which may be experiencer or active verbs, only the middle voice experiencer version may be modified by *ḡlehe*:

(7.105)a. *n-a*   **sihe=nau**   **ḡlehe**
RL-1EXCS sneeze=1SGO very
'I'm really sneezing.'

    b. **n-a sihe ḡlehe*

Interestingly, *ḡlehe* also marks transitive predications consisting of a causativized stative or experiencer verb. In this construction it does not intensify the causing by the actor, but the state or experience applying to the patient resulting from the causation:

269

(7.106)a. *naprai ana   n-e   **fa babao**=nau   **ḡlehe***
      sun   thatN RL-3S CS be.tired=1SGO very
      'That sun is making me very tired.'

   b. *kumai ana   n-e   **fa boe**=ni   **ḡlehe** ḡazu ine*
      water thatN   RL-3S CS be.rotten=3SGO very wood thisR
      'The water has really rotted this wood.'

   c. *karipauda=na   n-e   **fa sihe**=nau   **ḡlehe** ara*
      curry.powder=thatN RL-3S CS sneeze=1SGO very I
      'That curry powder is really making me sneeze.'

This applies even when a causativized stative occurs within an active serial construction. In (7.107) *ḡlehe* is modifying the causativized *heta* 'be strong':

(7.107)   *ago   n-o   gorha **fa heta**   **ḡlehe***
       youSG RL-2S paddle CS be.strong very
       'You are paddling very strongly.'

Glehe also occurs with a small group of active verbs that code an event resulting in a state applying to a patient. These verbs include:

(7.108)a. *tazi* 'keep, retain'   c. *namha* 'love, be kind to'
   b. *faña* 'feed, give food to' d. *ohai* 'keep' (as a domestic animal)

(7.109)   *manei n-e   **tazi**=nau   **ḡlehe***
       he   RL-3S keep=1SGO   very
       'He really looked after me.'

In addition, the desiderative verb *manahagi* may be modified by *ḡlehe*, suggesting that wanting is treated conceptually as a state, although the verb itself is not stative:

(7.110)   *ara **manahagi**=ni **ḡlehe** ta   lao=na   buala*
       I   want=3SGO   very SBD go=thatN PNLOC
       'I want very much to go to Buala.'

Other than the effective verbs shown in (7.108), *ḡlehe* may not modify an active verb or entire active predication, only that part of an active predication that is stative. It is in complementary distribution with the post-core exhaustive marker *gudu*, which only occurs with active predications. Two exceptions exist to the restriction on *ḡlehe* marking active predications. One is limited to *hage* 'ascend' and *kave* 'descend', and to clauses referring to the escape of caged animals:

(7.111)a. *zora   ana   n-e   **kave**   **ḡlehe***
       pig   thatN RL-3S descend very
       'That pig always gets out [of its pen].'

    b. *memeha   ana   n-e   **hage**   **ḡlehe***
       bird   thatN RL-3S ascend very
       'That bird always gets out [of its cage].'

Again, one can speculate that a conceptual state applies to the referent animals in these instances—a state of being that predisposes the animals to escape.

The other exception applies to the pre-head frequency modifiers *fani* 'often' and *tuma* 'very often' (see §7.5.9). Any active clause marked with either of these modifiers may also be marked with *ḡlehe*:

(7.112)   *ago   n-o   **tuma**   ñhau   ḡausa   **ḡlehe***
         yousG RL-2S very.often eat   betel.nut very
         'You really chew betel nut all the time.'

In this instance it may be that the modifiers ascribe a characteristic to the subject that is conceptually somewhat akin to a state of being.

7.7 Verb complex structure

7.7.1 Verb complex core structure

Within the verb complex, the verb complex core (representable as V') contains all lexical verbs along with several pre-head and post-head inner modifiers.

The pre-head core modifiers consist of the modal/subject particle, and four pre-head core modifier positions. The first of these is the particle position. The internal structure of the modal/subject particle is represented in (7.21). The second position is a tense position that may be filled only by the future tense marker *ginai*. The third position is a mood position that may contain the abilitative *boka*, the purposive *mala*, the definite marker *torai*, or one of the three desiderative markers: *manahagi*, *ḡroi*, or the pre-head possessor-indexing. The fourth position may be filled by one of the frequency markers *fani* 'often' and *tuma* 'very often'. Position five allows only the unitative marker *kaike*. These pre-head modifiers are followed by a verb or up to three verbs in a serial construction. The verbs are followed by post-head inner modifiers, comprising a post-head aspect modifier position, which may be filled by either *fakamo* 'always' or the post-head possessor-indexing host immediacy/saliency marker. This is followed by an agreement/object position comprising an argument-indexing enclitic plus a demonstrative enclitic, or an incorporated nominal. The final core modifier position is a second aspect position that may be filled only by the continuous aspect marker $=gu \sim =u$. This may be summarized as:

(7.113)   V' → (MOD/SBJ) + (TNS) + (MOOD) + (FRQ) + (UNIT)

$$+ \text{V*} + (\text{ASP1}) + \left\{ \begin{array}{l} (\text{OBJ}) + (\text{DEM}) \\ (\text{INCORP}) \end{array} \right\} + (\text{ASP2})$$

With forms displayed (other than modal/subject particle forms) this schema represents the following for pre-head modifiers:

$$(7.114) \quad \text{V'} \rightarrow (\text{MOD/SBJ}) + (ginai) + \left\{ \begin{array}{l} (boka) \\ (mala) \\ (torai) \\ (manahagi) \\ (\bar{g}roi) \\ (no\text{-}) \end{array} \right\} + \left\{ \begin{array}{l} (fani) \\ (tuma) \end{array} \right\} + (kaike)$$

With forms displayed (other than object-indexing, demonstrative agreement, and incorporated nominals) the schema represents the following post-head modifiers:

$$(7.115) \quad \text{V'} \rightarrow \left\{ \begin{array}{l} (fakamo) \\ (no\text{-} \sim ge\text{-}) \end{array} \right\} + \left\{ \begin{array}{l} (\text{OBJ}) + (\text{DEM}) \\ (\text{INCORP}) \end{array} \right\} + \quad (=gu \sim =u)$$

7.7.2 Verb complex outer modifier structure

The overall verb complex (representable as V") comprises the verb core, with one pre-core and one post-core outer modifier position.

The pre-head modifier position may contain the purposive marker *mala*, the future tense marker *ginai*, or the definite marker *torai*, all of which may alternatively occur within the core. The same form may not occur both within the core and in the pre-core position. The post-core outer modifier position may contain either the completive aspect marker *nhigo* (which also occurs within the core as a verb), the aspect marker *fakamo* 'always' (which may also occur within the core in ASP1 position), the exhaustive marker *gudu*, or the intensifier *ḡlehe*. The overall verb complex structure may be summarized as:

$$(7.116) \quad \text{V''} \rightarrow \begin{array}{l} (mala) \\ (ginai) \\ (torai) \end{array} + \text{V'} + \begin{array}{l} (nhigo) \\ (fakamo) \\ (gudu) \\ (\bar{g}lehe) \end{array}$$

CHAPTER 8: CLAUSE STRUCTURE

This chapter describes nonverbal clauses and the structure of verbal clauses, including pragmatically unmarked clause structure, as well as overt topicalization and argument focusing, the clause position of adjuncts, negation, and the function of constituent level modifiers.

8.1 Verbless clauses

Two kinds of verbless predications exist in Kokota: equative predicates and possessive predicates. The structure of main clauses with verbless predicates is discussed here. Negation of these predications is discussed in §8.7.

8.1.1 Equative predicates

8.1.1.1 Basic equative clauses

Equative clauses equate the subject to a nominal that specifies a characteristic of the subject. The equated characteristic tends to be habitual or a permanent state. As with verbal clauses, equative predications of this type are coded as irrealis. Irrealis in Kokota is unmarked, and in verbal clauses the remaining subject agreement component of the particle is typically omitted (see §7.5.2.5). This is also true of equatives, as a comparison of (8.1) and (8.2) shows. (In examples in this section the predication is enclosed in square brackets.)

(8.1) a. *abrose varigutu*   [*datau=na*   *goveo*]
           PN   chief=3SGP   PNLOC
           'Ambrose Varigutu is the chief of Goveo.'

       b. *nakoni* [*kaike* *ḡlepo*   *ta*   *doli*]
           person   one   thing   SBD   live
           'People are one [kind of] living thing.'

(8.2)   *taio* [*e*   *pusi*   *ga~gase=na*]
           PN   3S   cat   RD~woman=3SGP
           'Taiyo is a female cat.'

Where the equated characteristic applied at a particular time in the past but no longer applies, or applies at the time of speaking but did not always apply, a realis particle may occur, typically with the perfective aspect or present tense marker present:

(8.3) a. *ḡetu*   [*n-e-ke*   *mane*   *datau*]
           PN   RL-3S-PFV   man   chief
           'Getu was the chief [at that time].'

    b. *manei*   [***n-e-ge***   *nakodou*]
       she   RL-3S-PRS old.woman
       'She is an old woman.'

Other pre-head predicate modifiers occur, including the future tense marker *ginai* (in either pre- or post-modal/subject particle position), the frequency marker *fani*, and the purposive *mala*:

(8.4) a. *belama*   [***ginai*** *e*   *mane polisi*]
        PN   FUT   3S   man   police
        'Belama will be a policeman.'

    b. *ia*   *mane n-e-ke*   *lehe* [*e **fani*** *mane premie*] *e=u*
       theSG man RL-3S-PFV die 3S often man Premier 3S=be.thus
       'The man who died used to be Premier.'

    c. *totogale* *mala* ***no-na***   *belama*
       picture   PURP GENP-3SGP PN
       'a photo that is intended to belong to Belama'

Not all pre-head modifiers may occur. None of the desiderative particles may occur. The frequency marker *tuma* 'very often' and the intensifier *torai* do not occur in equatives in the present corpus. It is not clear whether this reflects a restriction or a gap.

8.1.1.2 Possession of predicate by subject

A predicate nominal may be inalienably possessor-indexed to the subject:

(8.5) a. *gita*   [*nakoni*   *posa=**da***]
        1INC   person   emerge=1INCP
        'We were visitors.'

    b. *ara* [*mane=ḡu* *ka*   *nohi=ne*]
       I   man=1SGP LOC district=thisR
       'I am a man of this district.'

8.1.1.3 Subject-predicate constituent order in equative clauses

The pragmatically unmarked constituent order (see §8.2.1) does not occur in equative clauses. The sole core argument of an equative clause typically occurs before the predicate in topic position (as in examples [8.1] to [8.5]). This construction is only departed from when the subject occurs in clause-final focus position. When this occurs the subject must be marked with the focus particle *si*:

(8.6)   a.   [*mane   gabili*]   *si=n̄a=ro*
             man   be.aggressive   FOC=IMM=thoseNV
             'These are fighting men.'

        b.   [*e-ti   nan̄ha=di   nakoni*]   *si=la=re*
             3S-NEG   name=3PLP   person   FOC=??=thoseN
             'Those aren't the names of people.'

The structure of equative clauses is therefore:

(8.7)   S → $\begin{cases} \text{NP}_{\text{TOP}} & + & \text{PRED} \\ \text{PRED} & + & \text{NP}_{\text{FOC}} \end{cases}$

8.1.1.4 Equative clause information weighting

The subject of an equative clause is typically a previously established or known participant, about whom new information is given. Consequently, the subject typically requires a less detailed mention for identification than the predicate. Often it is realized only by a demonstrative or pronoun. Occasionally discourse information structure leads to an atypical weighting of information, as in (8.8). Information weightings like this occur but are uncommon in normal discourse.

(8.8)   *suli ta   fani   fa dia   puhi   t=au=re*   [*suli   ide*]
         childSBD often CS be.bad way   SBD=exist=thoseN child theseR
         'The children who make trouble are these children.'

8.1.1.5 Telling the time

Linguistic divisions of time smaller than periods such as morning and afternoon are a recent introduction. Expressing time in terms of these divisions is performed using an equative construction in which the nominal *tanhi* 'time' occurs as subject. Hour divisions are expressed as cardinal nominals functioning as an equative predicate. Temporal interrogatives have the same construction, with the quantitative interrogative functioning as the predicate, as in (8.9). Divisions of time smaller than an hour are expressed with the same construction, with a predicative NP expressing numerically quantified minutes, inalienably indexed to a possessor expressing the relevant hour, as in (8.10).

(8.9)   A. *tanhi* [*nihau*]   B. *tanhi* [*fitu-gu*]
            time   how.much   time   seven-CRD
            'What's the time?'   'The time is seven o'clock.'

(8.10)   *tanhi* [*naboto-ai   ḡaha miniti   kenu/legu=na   fitu-gu*]
          time   ten-plus   five   minute   front/behind=3SGP seven-CRD
          'The time is fifteen minutes to/past seven.'

Periods of fifteen and thirty minutes cannot be expressed using terms equating to 'half past', 'a quarter to', etc. Only full-minute enumeration is possible.

8.1.1.6 Equative naming predication

8.1.1.6.1 Main clause naming equatives

Equative clauses that associate a name with an entity may have the basic equative clause structure discussed above:

(8.11) *nañha=di=re*   [*belama, kodere, ihebohebohebo*] *e=u*
        name=3PLP=thoseN PN   PN   whoeverSG   3S=be.thus
        'Their names are Belama, Kodere, whoever, it's like that.'

However, names are more usually assigned to entities by a predication where the irrealis particle is directly marked with an object enclitic, with the meaning 'does it/them', whose complement is a NP with *nañha-* 'name' as its head:

(8.12) a. *varigutu* [*e=ni*   *nañha=na=na*]
          PN   3S=3SGO   name=3SGP=thatN
          'Varigutu is his name.' [lit. '...does that name of his.']

      b. *ğuanha* [*e=ni*   *bla*   *nañha=na=na*   *ğazu*   *t=au=ao*]
         inhale   3S=3SGO   LMT   name=3SGP=thatN   wood   SBD=exist-thisT
         '*Guanha* simply is the name of this tree.' [i.e., '...does that name...']

As with objects of lexical verbs, the complement is often not overtly realized if context prevents ambiguity:

(8.13) *ḡ-a-ke*   *hoda neti* *e=ni*   *ka*   *mane-vaka ide,*
        NT-1EXCS-PFV   take   net 3S=3SGO   LOC   man-ship   theseR
        'We take a net, as it's called with these white men,

        ka   gai...   momoru *e=ni*   *e=u*
        LOC weEXC turtle.net 3S=3SGO   3S=be.thus
        with us... it's called *momoru*, it's like that.'

Names formerly used are indicated by use of the perfective aspect marker *ke*, in which case the irrealis zero-marked subject particle is omitted:

(8.14) *...naitu tahi* *ke=ni*   *nañha=na=na*   *e=u*
        devil   sea   PFV=3SGO name=3SGP=thatN   3S=be.thus
        '..."sea devil" did that name of it, like that.' [i.e., '...was its name']

As with basic equative clauses the sole argument of a naming predicate occurs in pre-head topic position. It is unclear whether the subject of a naming predicate can be focused.

8.1.1.6.2 Naming equatives as relative clauses

Two types of relative clauses are formed from naming equatives. The naming equative in line 1 of (8.13) exemplifies one type, with the same structure as a main clause except for the omission of the controlled argument. A second type has the subordinator *ta*. With equatives using this second construction, as with all *ta* subordinate clauses, no modal/subject particle is present. Instead the object enclitic attaches directly to the subordinating particle itself, and an obligatory demonstrative references whichever main clause argument is the relative head:

(8.15) a. ...*fadalao* ***ta=ni=na***   *naitu* *t=au=ne*
PN   SBD=3SGO=thatN   devil SBD=exist=thisR
'...Fadalao, which does this devil.' [i.e., '...as this devil's called.']

b. ...*malaria* ***ta=ni=o***   *nañha=na=na*   *e=u*
malaria   SBD=3SGO=thatNV   name=3SGP=thatN   3S=be.thus
'...malaria, which does [names] that name of it

ka   *ooe-vaka*
LOC   talk-ship
in English' [i.e., '...as it's called in English']

8.1.2 Possessive predicates

A possessive relationship may be expressed by use of a verbless possessive predication in which the ownership of an entity is assigned to a possessor. The possessum subject always occurs in pre-predicate topic position. The predication itself consists of a possessor-indexed host with its possessor NP complement (see §5.5). Both the general and 'consumed' hosts may occur:

(8.16) a. *keha* *pile=di=re*   [***no-na***   *bla*   *tagi-na*]
NSP   side=3PLP=thoseN   GENP-3SGP   LMT   REFL-3SGP
'Some parts will simply belong to him himself.'

b. *mala-ñhau*   *are*   [***ge-ḡu***   *ara*]
PURP-eat   thoseN   CNSM-1SGP   I
'That food is mine.'

As with equative clauses, modal/subject particles and other pre-head modifiers may occur:

(8.17) a. *ide-hi*   [***n-e-ke***   *no-ḡu*   *buka* *ara*]
      theseR-EMPH RL-3S-PFV GENP-1SGP book I
      'These used to be my books.'

    b. *a-hi*   [***ginai*** *no-ḡu*   *vilai* *ara*]
      thisT-EMPH FUT   GENP-1SGP knife I
      'This will be my knife.'

    c. *tazi=ri*   *boboke=mu=are*   [***mala*** *no-ḡu*   *ara*]
      keep=3PLO inner.thigh=2SGP=thoseN PURP   GENP-1SGP I
      'Keep your inner thighs for me,

      n-o-ke=u=o
      RL-2S-PFV=be.thus=thatNV
      you said you would.'

Only alienable relationships are expressible using possessive predications. Verbless predicates expressing inalienable relationships involve an ordinary equative construction in which the topicalized subject is equated with an inalienably possessed entity, as in (8.18)a. In such constructions the subject is typically not overtly realized, as in (8.18)b.

(8.18) a. *are=bla*   *ira*   *doli=mai* *gai*
      thoseN=LMT thePL live=1EXCP weEXC
      'Just those [things] are our lives.'

    b. *totogale=ḡu* *ara*
      picture=1SGP I
      '(It's) a photo of me.'

8.2 Declarative verbal main clauses—pragmatically unmarked structure

8.2.1 Pragmatically unmarked core argument structure

A number of pragmatically marked clause structures exist, (see §8.3 and §8.4). An unmarked structure also exists. Kokota is fundamentally verb-initial, with all pragmatically unmarked arguments occurring after the verb complex. With intransitive verbs the sole core argument immediately follows the verb complex, whether it is an unergative ([8.19]a.) or an unaccusative ([8.19]b.) subject.

(8.19) a. *n-o-ge*   *mai* *bl=**ago**,*   *vave*
      RL-2S-PRS come LMT=youSG in.law
      'So you've come, in-law.'

b. *ginai lehe bla **gita***
   FUT   die LMT weEXC
   'We're going to die.'

In transitive clauses the unmarked order is actor followed by object:

(8.20)   *n-o   fa-lehe=ri*   [*ago*] [*kokorako **are***]
         RL-3S CS-die=3PLO youSG chicken   thoseN
         'You are killing those chickens.'

In clauses with ditransitive verbs the object that is indexed by the postverbal agreement enclitic precedes the unindexed object:

(8.21)   *ara   a   tu~turi   tufa=nigo   [*ago*]*
         I   1EXCS RD~tell   affect=2SGO youSG
         'I am going to tell you

         [*keha mereseni ka   gai   ade kokota*]
         NSP   medicine LOC weEXC here PNLOC
         some medicines of us here in Kokota.'

The pragmatically unmarked constituent order for core arguments is therefore VS/VAO. This does not mean, however, that such clauses are typical in normal discourse, particularly transitive clauses with more than one overt argument. The notion of markedness used here relates to information structure, not frequency. In pragmatic terms the unmarked structure is that which has no special function in information structure, such as the foregrounding, or backgrounding, of an argument. As with most Oceanic languages, agreement marking in the verb complex means that participants, once established in the discourse, typically do not receive an overt mention again unless pragmatic factors such as backgrounding or foregrounding of arguments, emphasis (contrastive or otherwise), and the prevention of ambiguity (see §8.3 to 8.5) motivate a fresh mention. The frequency of zero anaphora and overt topicalization in Kokota means that the full pragmatically unmarked structure occurs in a minority of clauses in discourse. Nonetheless, since varying clause structures in Kokota have varying pragmatic affects, it is more meaningful to use the terms 'marked' and 'unmarked' in their pragmatic sense when discussing clause structure.

8.2.2 Pragmatically unmarked adjunct structure

Pragmatically unmarked adjuncts follow any postverbal core arguments present:

(8.22) a. *ḡ-e   lao=ña   tikani **ka   bili***
          NT-3S go=IMM PN   LOC PN
          'Tikani went to Billy.'

279

b. *ḡ-e   la   uf-i=Ø   ia   to~toi*
  NT-3S go blow-TR=3SGO theSG RD~cook
  'He went and blew on the fire

  ka=ia   papaḡu   ḡazu
  LOC=theSG stack   wood
  on the wood stack.'

Note that in (8.22)b. the transitivized *uf-i* 'blow' subcategorizes for a patient, *ia totoi* 'the fire' therefore being a direct object.

Where several obliques occur in the same clause no syntactic order restrictions apply. In some clauses with more than one *ka* prepositional phrase the semantics of the verb will dictate the order of the arguments. In (8.23) the semantics of *fa kamo* 'cause to cross' require a source and a goal, which participate in the process temporally in that order. The order of the obliques realizing these participants is then iconic, with the source preceding the goal:

(8.23)   *fa kamo=i   bakru t=au=ana*
        CS go.across=3SGO liquid SBD=exist=thatN
        'Transfer that tea

        [ka timosi ana] [ka panakini ana]
        LOC thermos thatN LOC cup   thatN
        from that thermos to that cup.'

In other clauses the semantics of the verb does not have this effect and any order is possible. In (8.24) the two PPs could occur in either order.

(8.24) a. *zemesi e   au   [ka nau   ine   goveo]*
         PN   3S exist LOC place thisR PNLOC
         'James lives in this village of Goveo

         [ka nohi=ne   kokota]
         LOC district=thisR PNLOC
         in this Kokota district.'

   b. *e   au   no-di   fama [ka=ira   buluka], [ka=ira   zora]*
     3S exist GENP-3PLP farm LOC=thePL cow   LOC=thePL pig
     'They have their farms with cows, with pigs.'

Where a prepositional phrase occurs with another adjunct such as an associative oblique or a temporal locative, either order is possible, as (8.25) and (8.26) show. However, there is a strong tendency for the PP to precede the other oblique—the constructions in (8.25)b. and (8.26)b. occur less commonly.

(8.25) a. *ara n-a lao* [*ka=ia sitoa*] [*tareme=na kodere*]
     I   RL-1EXCS go   LOC=theSG store   with=3SGP   PN
     'I went to the store with Kodere.'

   b. *ara n-a lao* [*tareme=na kodere*]   [*ka=ia sitoa*]
     I   RL-1EXCS go   with=3SGP   PN   LOC=theSG store
     'I went to the store with Kodere.'

(8.26) a. *ara n-a lao* [*ka sitoa*] [*le~legu nare*]
     I   RL-1EXCS go   LOC=theSG store   RD~behind day
     'I go to the store every day.'

   b. *ara n-a lao* [*le~legu nare*] [*ka=ia sitoa*]
     I   RL-1EXCS go   RD~behind day   LOC=theSG store
     'I go to the store every day.'

8.3 Zero mentions

Participants that have been established in the discourse are typically not overtly mentioned in subsequent clauses as long as they are not topicalized or focused, unless an overt mention is necessary to prevent ambiguity (including where an established argument occurs with a new grammatical relation). This applies as much to first and second person as to third person referents. As long as a participant maintains the same grammatical relation it is not overtly mentioned after the initial reference, unless a clause intervenes in which a different participant is in that relation.

The fragment of text in (8.27) illustrates the maintenance of participants in established grammatical relations with zero mentions. A participant overtly mentioned in clause 1 as an intransitive subject occurs again in clause 2, this time as a transitive actor. Being the subject of the preceding clause, no overt mention is necessary for the listener to interpret that participant as the actor of this clause. In the same clause a further participant is overtly mentioned as the object of the predication. Clause 3 is outside the events of the narrative. The subject is an anaphoric reference to the events of the preceding clauses. Apart from emphatic observations like this on the part of the narrator, all subsequent core arguments represent the subject/actor and object established in clauses 1 and 2. Once established in their roles, neither participant receives an overt core argument mention again, being maintained in their grammatical relations by a series of zero mentions. No further overt mentions are needed for the listener to be able to follow the narrative, despite the fact that both participants are 3SG and thus subject and object agreement markers could both potentially refer to either.

The only further overt mention of either participant in (8.27) is in the second part of clause 5, where the subject is mentioned overtly as the possessor of the snake-tail. The only other overt mention is of an instrument in clause 5. This participant, once established is also not mentioned overtly in the subsequent clause where it is assumed to be the instrument of the same predicate.

(8.27) 1. *...n-e hage* **X**[58]
RL-3S ascend PN
'...X went up,

    2. *kai gilai n-e la toke=i bla*
LOC until RL-3S go arrive=3SGO LMT
until [he] reached

    2.–3. ***mane n-e-ke seha=n-lau.*** *e=u si=la=na*
man RL-3S-PFV climb=thatN-SPC 3S=be.thus FOC=??=thatN
that man who was climbing. That's how it was,

    4. *lao sini ge age n-e lao=ña*
go FOC SEQ and RL-3S go=IMM
Go, and then [he] went.

    5. *n-e la piri=ni=u* ***ka=ia*** ***kolu*** *e=u,*
RL-3S go tie=3SGO=CNT LOC=theSG snake 3S=be.thus
[He] went and was tying [him] up with the snake, like that,

    ka=ia ***kolu-seku=na=o*** ***manei,***
LOC=theSG snake-tail=3SGO=thatNV him
with that snake-tail of his,

    6.–7. *la piri fa-lehe=i=u sini-ge age ḡ-e hure=i=ña*
go tie CS-die=3SGO=CNT FOC=SEQ and NT-3S carry=3SGO=IMM
went and was tying up and killing [him], and then [he] carried [him].

    8.–10. *n-e hage=u ḡ-e hage=u ḡ-e hage=u*
RL-3S ascend=CNT NT-3S ascend=CNT NT-3S ascend=CNT
[He] was going up, [he] was going up, [he] was going up,

    11. *ḡ-e toke=u sara fate sini ge*
NT-3S reach=CNT thereD high FOC SEQ
[he] was arriving there on top and then

    12. *n-e la de~deke=u sini ge*
NT-3S go RD~step=CNT FOC SEQ
[he] went and stepped [with his tail on the ground],

---

[58] This name has been omitted for cultural reasons.

13. *age ḡ-e   koko-la=ni=ña   sara   rauru*
    SEQ NT-3S leave-go=3SGO=IMM   thereD seaward
    and then [he] threw [him] there seaward.'

Where a different participant intervenes, an established participant may receive
an overt mention to clarify that the relevant relation has switched back to it. In
(8.28) clause 2 the subject and object both receive an overt mention. In clause 3
a new subject occurs, and receives an overt mention. As this participant, the
turtle, received an overt mention only two clauses earlier, a proform mention is
sufficient. However, an overt mention of some kind is made because the subject
of clause 3 is not the same as the subject of the preceding clause 2. This occurs
despite the fact that the subject-indexing in clause 3 makes it clear that the
subject must be a different participant. In clause 4 the subject is the same as in
clause 3 so no overt mention is necessary. In 5, however, subject has switched
back to the subject of clause 2. Now an overt mention re-establishes that
participant as subject, although again subject-indexing also indicates that. Once
established, that participant again receives a zero mention in the next clause 6.

(8.28) 1. *...n-a   la fakae=ni=u   ka   tahi are   teḡe ine e=u*
          RL-1EXCS go see=3SGO=CNT LOC sea thoseN turtlethisR 3S=be.thus
          '...we go and see in the sea this turtle, like that.

   2. *ḡ-a   koko=ni=ña   **gai**   momoru   ana*
      NT-1EXCS leave=3SGO=IMM   weEXC   turtle.net thatN
      We throw out that turtle net.

   3. *ḡ-e   mai   kale=u   **manei** ka   momoru   ana   e=u*
      NT-3S come   snag=CNT it   LOC turtle.net thatN 3S=be.thus
      It comes and gets caught in that turtle net, like that,

   4. *mai   kale=u   ka   momoru   ana   si=ge*
      come   snag=CNT LOC turtle.net thatN FOC=SEQ
      comes and gets caught in that turtle net and then

   5. *ḡ-a   zogu=ña **gai***
      NT-1EXCS fall=IMM weEXC
      we drop [into the water],

   6. *ḡ-a   fa hage=i   ka   hinage*
      NT-1EXCS CS ascend=3SGO LOC boat
      [we] lift it into the boat.'

An established participant may also receive an overt mention if it occurs in a
new grammatical relation, typically when an established subject becomes an

object. In (8.29) a subject participant receives an overt mention in clause 1. and a zero mention as subject in clauses 2. and 3. In 5. the subject is assumed to be the participant newly introduced with an overt mention in 4. Typically a newly introduced overtly mentioned subject supplants a previously established subject. When this occurs, if the relevant clause is transitive, the most recently mentioned subject is assumed to be the actor, and the next most recently mentioned argument is assumed to be the object, even if that argument was itself subject. However, the change in relation of the former subject often motivates a further overt mention of the argument in its new role, as in clause 5. This is particularly common where ambiguity is possible. As both participants in clause 5 are 3SG, neither subject nor object-indexing maps a participant to a relation.

(8.29) 1. *'mane ine   n-e-ge   mai   mhoko*
         man   thisR RL-3S-PRS   come sit
         This man comes and sits.

    2.–3. *n-e-ge   au=gu   ka   nafu-ḡazu ine.   n-e-ge   au=gu*
          RL-3S-PRS   exist=CNT   LOC   base-wood thisR   RL-3S-PRS exist=CNT
          He stays at this tree base. He stays.

    4. *posa   mai=na=o   bla X*[59]
       emerge   come=3SGP=thatNV   LMT PN
       That emergence of X.

    5. *n-e-ge mai   fakae=ni=u   mane ine,   nakoni ine*
       RL-3S   come see=3SGO=CNT   man   thisR   person thisR
       He's coming and seeing this man, this person'

A switch in relations does not require overt mentions, as long as no ambiguity is possible. A participant established as subject in one clause may participate as an object with a zero mention in a subsequent clause if a further subject has been established and no ambiguity is possible. In (8.30) the semantics of the clauses make the roles of the participants clear, as does the object-indexing in clause 3.

(8.30) 1. *n-e-ke   la zaho   ia   naitu*
         RL-3S-PFV   go go   theSG devil
         'The devil went away.

    2. *tetu=ña   ira   naitu toke   nogoi*
       stand=IMM   thePL devil arrive VOC
       The arriving devils stood up, man!

---

[59] This name has been omitted for cultural reasons.

3. *ḡ-e   toḡla=ni   n-e-ke=u*
NT-3S chase=3SGO RL-3S-PFV=be.thus
and chased [him].'

In (8.30) clause 1 a devil (whose identity was established much earlier in the narrative) receives an overt mention as subject. In the next clause a group of other devils receive an overt mention as subject. In the transitive clause 3 both actor and object receive zero mentions without ambiguity. The most recently mentioned subject (the group of 'arriving devils' mentioned in the preceding clause) is assumed to remain subject of the new clause. This is reinforced by the fact that the clause involves an event of chasing. As the preceding two clauses involved one participant going away (*zaho* involves movement away from a location), and the other participants then standing up, it is clear who is likely to be doing the chasing. The potential for ambiguity is also removed by the object-indexing in 3, which indicates that it is the singular previously mentioned participant that is the object. (The subject-indexing does not contribute to the prevention of ambiguity since it marks only person, not number.)

In normal discourse zero mentions occur with high frequency. In a typical narrative text, for example, the proportion of overt mentions to zero mentions in main clauses was:

TABLE 8.1. PROPORTION OF OVERT TO ZERO MENTIONS IN A TYPICAL NARRATIVE TEXT

	Overt pragmatically unmarked mentions	Overtly mentioned topicalized arguments	Zero mentions
A	1	3	4
S	18	4	23
O	7	0	0
OBL	11	2	0

Zero mentions account for half of all subject arguments, transitive and intransitive. However, all object and oblique arguments receive overt mentions. While both do receive zero mentions in discourse, most mentions are overt. Both these findings accord with the crosslinguistic tendency for subjects, particularly A arguments, to be already established participants, and for objects and obliques to be new information. These crosslinguistic tendencies are reflected in the information structure of Kokota. Since only established participants may occur as zero mentions, it is to be expected that a high proportion of A and S arguments will receive a zero mention. Conversely, it is to be expected that objects and obliques, tending to represent new information, will overwhelmingly receive overt mentions. The result is that a majority of intransitive clauses have no overtly mentioned core arguments, while a majority of transitive clauses have only one overt core argument, usually the object. The occurrence of a transitive clause with two overt arguments is unusual in normal discourse.

8.4 Topicalization

In overt topicalization the topicalized argument is realized in preverbal position. An argument in any grammatical relation may be fronted in this way. Subjects of any kind may be topicalized, including transitive actors ([8.31]a.), and unergative ([8.31]b.) and unaccusative ([8.31]c.–d.) intransitive subjects:

(8.31) a. *ago*   *n-o*   *fa-lehe=au*   *ara*
       yousG   RL-2S CS-die=1SGO I
       'You are killing me.'

    b. *ia*   *tara=ña*   *n-e*   *mai=ne*
       theSG enemy=IMM RL-3S come=thisR
       'The enemy has come.'

    c. *tilo*   *tomoko*   *n-e*   *au=re*   *zelu*
       three war.canoe RL-3S exist=thoseN PNLOC
       'Three war canoes are at Zelu.'

    d. *manei* *e* *keha* *ñheñhe*
       he   3S NSP be.separate
       'He is different.'

Objects also occur as preverbal topics:

(8.32) a. *ia*   *pike mau=ḡu*   *n-e-ke*   *hod-i=Ø=o*
       theSG piecetaro=1SGP RL-3S-PFV take-TR=3SGO=thatNV

       sala ge *ruruboñi bla*
       PN and PN   LMT
       'My piece of taro just Sala and Ruruboñi brought.'

    b. *are-lau*   *tahe=di*   *ago*
       thoseN-SPC tell=3PLO yousG
       'Those ones [parts of a story] you will tell.'

Although objects may be topicalized, this occurs rarely in natural discourse. Subjects, both transitive and intransitive, occur much more commonly. In the first 100 verbal main clauses of a typical narrative text, the following breakdown of argument position occurrence applied:

TABLE 8.2. PROPORTION OF ARGUMENTS IN PREVERBAL, FOCUSED, AND PRAGMATICALLY UNMARKED POSITION

	Preverbal topicalized arguments	Focused arguments	Arguments in unmarked position	Total
A	2 (28.5%)	0	5 (71.5%)	7 (100%)
S	8 (15.5%)	2 (4.0%)	41 (80.5%)	51 (100%)
O	1 (5.5%)	0	17 (94.5%)	18 (100%)

Table 8.2 shows that overtly realized arguments of all types overwhelmingly occur in their pragmatically unmarked positions. However, a cline exists from A arguments, which are most likely to be overtly topicalized, to O arguments, which are the least likely. Slightly more than half the proportion of S arguments are topicalized as A arguments, and only a third as many O arguments as S arguments. Only one sixth the proportion of Os are topicalized as As.

Topicalization occurs when the speaker assumes that the referent participant is prominent in the listener's mind, typically because the participant has recently been mentioned in the discourse. In most instances such a participant will receive a zero mention (see §8.3). However, there are some instances when a zero mention is not sufficient to identify the argument. In such instances an overtly realized topicalized mention occurs. This occurs for a number of reasons. It may be that a participant has been recently mentioned, but another participant has received a subsequent mention. Attention may switch back to the previously mentioned participant, but without an overt mention this will not be clear. Consequently the participant receives an overt mention to preclude ambiguity, but due to the recent mention and consequent assumed prominence of the participant in the listener's mind, the argument is backgrounded. In (8.33) a text fragment of three clauses illustrates this. In clause 1 the subject occurs in its unmarked position. In clause 2 a new subject occurs (itself topicalized as a result of prominence arising from a recent overt mention). In clause 3 the subject of clause 1 is again subject. Due to its prominence this participant would receive a zero mention if it were not for the intervening subject of clause 2. The switching back of the subject in clause 3 requires an overt mention. Without it the subject would be assumed to remain the subject of the preceding clause (clause 2). However, due to the very recent mention of the relevant participant, the subject of this clause is backgrounded through topicalization:

(8.33) 1. *n-e-ke*   *la mai=u*   **mane ide**   **kokota**
           RL-3S-PFV   go come=CNT   man   theseR   PNLOC
           'These Kokota men used to come [to pray].'

2. **huhurañi** *tana   teo   e=u*
   PNLOC   then   not.exist   3S=be.thus
   [The] Huhurangi [people] didn't.

3. *e=u   **mane ide**   **kokota** n-e-ke   kulu   tarai...*
   3S=be.thus man   theseR   PNLOC   RL-3S-PFV   be.first   pray
   So these Kokota men were the first to start praying....'

Overt topicalization also occurs when a participant that has already been established and is assumed to be prominent in the listener's mind occurs with a new grammatical relation. Often no overt mention is needed in this situation because the subject and object-indexing make clear the new relations, or the semantics of the clause as a whole allows only one reading. However, in some instances an overt mention is needed to indicate the participant's new relation. In (8.34) two participants are introduced in clause 1 as an adjunct. In the next clause they occur as subject with an anaphoric reference. Although they have only just been mentioned and are assumed to be prominent in the listener's mind, they receive an overt mention to clarify their shift from adjunct to subject. However, their prominence allows a topicalized mention.

(8.34) 1. *ara-hi   a   turi tufa=nigo kaike tu~turi fakasai=di*
      I-EMPH   1EXCS tell   affect=2SGOone   RD~tell   history=3PLP
      'I will tell you a history story of

      *nau=de   gu=di   **ḡetu   ge   hugo hebala**...*
      place=theseR   CNTX=3PLP PN   and   PN
      these places, about Getu and Hugo Hebala....

2. *ka   au=di=re   **palu mane aro**   n-e-ke   au   buala*
   LOC   exist=3PLP=thoseN two   man   theseT RL-3S-PFV exist PNLOC
   In their living these two men were at Buala.'

Overt topicalization also occurs when an argument refers to a participant that is assumed to be prominent in the listener's mind as the result of a recent overt reference, but is being referred to in a different way. In (8.35) clause 3 has a topicalized subject. The subject is the event expressed in clause 1. This event is assumed to be prominent in the listener's mind, as it has just been mentioned, but it has not previously been referred to in the way it is in clause 3. As it has just been mentioned and is prominent it receives a proform mention, and is backgrounded through topicalization. However, the new nature of the reference to it means it must receive an overt mention.

(8.35) 1. *n-e   teo   ña*
      RL-3S not.exist   IMM
      '[If] it is not so

> *ḡe aḡe mhoko fa-lehe=i ago to~toi=ne ge*
> NT go sit CS-die=3SGO youSG RD~cook=thisR SEQ
> that you go and sit on and kill this fire, then

2. ***ago*** *teo bla ḡe heta=u e=u*
   youSG not.exist LMT NT be.strong=CNT 3S=be.thus
   you are not strong.

3. ***a-hi*** *bla fa-gilagila=na k=ara*
   thisT-EMPH LMT CS-test=3SGP LOC=I
   This alone will be the sign of it to me.'

The text fragment in (8.35) illustrates a further use of overt topicalization. This fragment is taken from a discussion between two participants, one of whom, the speaker, hopes to kill the addressee by tricking him to sit on the fire. In clause 2 the subject is the same participant as the subject of the preceding clause. Here the topicalization is contrastive—the implication of the overt topicalization in clause 2 is that the addressee will reveal himself to not be strong in contrast with the speaker. The participant receives an overt mention to create that contrast, but the mention is topicalized to background it, so that the lack of strength can represent a comment on the addressee.

It is not always the case that the topicalized referent is previously mentioned in the discourse. Certain participants are typically assumed to be prominent in the listener's mind simply because of their relationship to the speech event. First and second pronouns are frequently topicalized on this basis. Even if a speaker or addressee has not been overtly mentioned in the discourse, they are assumed to be prominent in the listener's mind and are topicalized accordingly. In the 100 verbal main clauses analyzed in Table 8.2, of the 11 preverbal topics 5 were first inclusive, first exclusive, or second person pronouns. All but one were in reported speech. The exception was the narrator introducing the story. This was the first occasion in the text when the speaker referred to himself, but that reference was topicalized, as was the first use of the 1SG pronoun in reported speech. The first use of the first inclusive pronoun was also topicalized. In each case the speaker was assuming that he himself and the interlocutors together were already prominent in the listener's mind. Table 8.3 shows the numbers of first and second person core argument pronouns that were topicalized in the 100 verbal main clauses.

A number of special clause types typically have a topicalized subject. As discussed in §8.1, the subjects of nonverbal predicates always occur in a pragmatically marked position. Very occasionally, this is the clause-final focused position. Typically the subject of a nonverbal predicate occurs clause-initially in topic position.

TABLE 8.3. NUMBER OF FIRST AND SECOND PERSON PRONOUNS TOPICALIZED

	Preverbal topicalized arguments	Focused arguments	Arguments in unmarked position	Total
1SG	2 (40.0%)	0	3 (60.0%)	5 (100%)
2SG	1 (14.5%)	2 (28.5%)	4 (57.0%)	7 (100%)
1INC	2 (100%)	0	0	2 (100%)
1EXC	1 (100%)	0	0	1 (100%)

A further clause type typically occurring with topicalization is the sequencer clause. Sequencer clauses, a form of recapping, are common in exposition, and indicating completion of the event of the preceding clause as a prelude to the next clause. In (8.36) the subjects of clauses 2 and 4 repeat the event expressed in the preceding clauses.

(8.36) 1. *o   la   roh-i=Ø*   *ia*   *ḡuanha...*
       2S go scrape-TR=3SGO theSG inhale
       'You go and scrape [the bark of] the 'inhale' [tree]....[60]

    2. ***la roh-i=Ø***   *n-e*   *nhigo*
       go scrape   RL-3S be.finished
       Going and scraping is finished,

    3. *toke=na*   *fa blahi*
       arrive=thatN CS be.tabu
       go back and bless it.

    4. ***fa blahi***   *n-e*   *nhigo*   *ara ge*
       CS be.tabu RL-3S be.finished I   SEQ
       The blessing is finished and

    5. *age ḡ-e*   *ḡuanha=n̄a*   *nakoni*
       SEQ NT-3S inhale=IMM   person

      ta   kuru=i=ne   *foḡra   e=u*
      SBD have=3SGO=thisR sick   3S=be.thus
      then the person who has this sickness inhales.'

---

[60] *Guanha* 'inhale something' is also the name of a tree whose bark is used as an infusion for inhaling.

8.5 Focused constructions

Focus is a formal means of foregrounding information. Kokota has two focusing strategies. One focus marks a particular argument, by locating the argument in clause-final position and marking it with the focal particle *si=*. The other foregrounds the content of the entire clause using the focal particles *sini* and *si=*.

8.5.1 Clause foregrounding

8.5.1.1 Clauses foregrounded with *si*

When it occurs without marking an argument, the particle *si* marks the entire main clause as being focused. It is procliticized to the final constituent of the clause. This effectively means that it forms a part of the clause-final constituent, and cannot occur alone. A sequence of the focus particle and the clause-final sequencer *ge* occurs very commonly in discourse:

(8.37) *ke broza lao putuo, toke putuo sare **si=ge***
PFV pack go PNLOC arrive PNLOC thereP FOC=SEQ
'[We] packed up and went to Putuo, arrived there at Putuo and then

ğ-e tetu=ña man-dou mare
NT-3S stand=IMM man-be.big PN
old man Mare stood up.'

This combination of particles often marks a clause preceding reported speech:

(8.38) *n-e-ge mai fa nhigo=i=u*
RL-3S-PRS come CS be.finished=3SGO=CNT
'He came

*lao tabar-i=Ø=na banesokeo **si=ge***
go buy-TR=3SGO=thatN PNLOC FOC=SEQ
[and] bought Banesokeo and then

'teo, isa=ni ge au=i=na putuo...'
not.exist flee=3SGO PRS exist=3SGO=CNT PNLOC
"No, leave where you are at Putuo..."'"

The cooccurrence of the focal particle and the sequencer is entirely optional, and clauses with this collocation are equally grammatical without *si*.

Si combines with the clause-level modifier *ba*. As discussed in §8.8.1, this particle marks alternatives, performing in part the function served by the English conjunction *or*. The resulting form, *si=ba*, places the clause in contrastive focus.

Thus in (8.39) in the second clause of speaker B's response he is telling speaker A to follow his suggestion instead of his own idea.

(8.39) A. *ka   la   au   fufunu   fogra=na   manei,*
       LOC   go   exist   begin   sick=3SGP   he
       'When his sickness began,

       ta=ke   fufunu=na   ara
       SBD=PFV   begin=thatN   I
       that's where I'll start [the story].'

    B. *fufunu ke   la keli-kava   [e=u   lao bla si=ba]*
       begin PFV   go be.good-land   3S=be.thus go   LMT FOC=ALT
       'Start when there was peace, just go like that instead.'

Again, *si* may be omitted. The presence of *ba* alone marks the clause as contrastive, but the clause is not focused.

Si also cooccurs with the clause-level markers *ña* 'immediate' and *la* (function unclear), but only when combined with an argument. Thus **si=la* and **si=ña* alone are ungrammatical. Their occurrence with arguments is discussed below.

8.5.1.2 *Si* marking constituents other than main clauses

The focal proclitic *si* also marks constituents other than an entire main clause, when the constituent is a context for the event expressed in the following clause. The marked constituent may be a temporal locative, as in (8.40). More typically *si* marks a recapping or sequencing constituent, either a sequencing demonstrative, as in (8.41)a., or a sequencing clause, as in (8.41)b.

(8.40) A. **ginai saigona   si=ge**
       later   evening   FOC=SEQ
       'This evening then

       g-o   tahe=i=ña   t=au=ana   ba
       NT-2S   tell=3SGO=IMM   SBD=exist=thatN   ALT
       you tell them to do that instead [of now].'

    B. *ehe* **ginai saigona   si=ba**
       yes   later   evening   FOC=ALT
       'Yes, this evening instead.'

(8.41) a. *ke   fa noto   la=i   manei*
       PFV   CS stop   go=3SGO   he
       'He will stop it.

an-lau   si=ge   fa la=i=ña   tu~turi=na   a-hi
thatN-SP FOC=SEQ CS go=3SGO=IMM RD~tell=3SGP thisT-EMPH
That, then you give this story.'

b. *...ḡ-e mai   kale=u   manei ka   momoru=ana   e=u*
NT-3S come snag=CNT he   LOC turtle.net=thatN 3S=be.thus
'...it comes and gets caught in that net,

mai   kale=u   ka   momoru=ana   si=ge
come snag=CNT LOC turtle.net=thatN FOC=SEQ
comes and gets caught in that net and then

ḡ-a   zogu=i=ña   gai
NT-1EXCS drop=3SGO=IMM   weEXC
we jump in

ḡ-a   fa hage=i   ka   hinage
NT-1EXCS CS ascend=3SGO LOC boat
and lift it into the boat.'

The marking of a nonverbal constituent as a focused clause indicates that the constituent is an existential clause of the kind where no existential verb is overtly present. This is the case with the sequencing demonstrative in (8.41)a. This is not limited to sequencers, however. In (8.42) the nominal marked with a focused sequencer is functioning as a nonverbal existential predication.

(8.42)   *n-a   la   lisa=di   t=au=are*
RL-1EXCS go   put=3PLO SBD=exist=thoseN
'We go and put down those [the food],

age n-a-ke   zaho koko=ni=ña   e=u
SEQ RL-1EXCS-PFV go   leave=3SGO=IMM 3S=be.thus
and then we go away and leave it [the shrine].

ḡlepo t=au=o   si=ge
thing SBD=exist=thatNV FOC=SEQ
That thing [the devil] [is there] and then

age ḡ-e   mai=ña   ḡ-e   ñhau=gu e=u
SEQ NT-3S come=IMM NT-3S eat=CNT 3S=be.thus
then it comes and it is eating, it's like that.'

8.5.1.3 Clause-final focus marker *sini*

Si attaches to the final constituent of a clause, and cannot occur clause-finally alone. However, the variant form *sini* does occur clause-finally:

(8.43) *ka=t=au=ana*   *ḡe-la lehe no-ḡu*   *bo* **sini**
        LOC=SBD=exist=thatN NT-go die GENP-1SGP CNT FOC
        'At that I was nearly dead!'

Like *si=*, *sini* foregrounds the entire clause. However, unlike *si=* it does not also focus mark clause-final focused arguments. *Sini* only focuses entire clauses.

As with *si=*, *sini* may mark a sequencing or recapping constituent. Like *si=* it may mark a recapping demonstrative, as in (8.44)a. *Sini* also marks the recapping prepositional phrase *katau-* ([8.44]b.), which *si=* does not appear to do.

(8.44) a. *ḡ-a*   *kaike fa-lehe=ri*   *gudu*   *ña*   *gai*
          NT-1EXCS one   CS-die=3PLO EXHST   IMM   weEXC
          'We kill every one of

          teḡe   *are-lau,*   *ḡe*   *vahe=ri=u*
          turtle   thoseN-SP   NT   carve.up=3PLO=CNT
          those turtles and cut them up.

          ***an-lau* *sini* *ge* *ḡe tufa=ña*   *ka=ira*   *nakoni   mavitu...*
          thatN-SPC FOC SEQ NT affect=IMM LOC=thePL person   community
          That, and then we distribute them among the community....'

     b. *...la au*   *kuru*   *mai=di=re*   *n-e-ke=u*
          go exist   own   come=3PLO=thoseN RL-3S-PFV=be.thus
          '...and stopped them from coming.

          ka=t=au=ana   *sini* *ge* *ḡ-e*   *tetu=ña*   *solomoni*
          LOC=SBD=exist=thatN FOC SEQ NT-3S stand=IMM PN
          At that, then, Solomon stood up.'

8.5.1.4 Sentence-initial extra-clausal occurrence of *sini*

Sini also occurs in an extra-clausal sentence-initial position. Here *sini* always occurs with the sequencing conjunction *ge* between two sequenced constituents, to emphasize the sequential relationship between the preceding constituent and the following clause. The preceding constituent may be an entire clause:

(8.45)   *ke   pulo=u   ḡoḡomo*
         PFV return=CNT PN
         'Goḡomo went back.

sini *ge   age   ḡ-e   tetu=ña   ira   man-dou   kutai   kava*
FOC SEQ and NT-3S stand=IMM thePL man-be.big own.land land
Then the old men landowners stood up [i.e., spoke out]...'

Here *sini* is not occurring finally in the first clause. Admissible pauses indicate clearly that *sini ge* opens the second sentence in the example. Its pre-clausal position is clearly demonstrated by its occurrence with reported speech:

(8.46)   *'teo,   le~legu   k=ago.'   **sini**   ge   ke   hage=ña*
         not.exist RD~behind LOC=youSG FOC SEQ PFV ascend=IMM
         '"No. It's up to you" [he said]. Then [he] went up.'

8.5.2 Foregrounding of arguments

Arguments are foregrounded by occurring in clause-final focus position, marked with the focal proclitic *si=*.

8.5.2.1 Focused forms

Any core argument may be focus marked, including transitive actors, objects, and unergative, unaccusative, and middle voice subjects:

(8.47) a. *o-ti   dupa=i   manei   **si=ago***
          2S-NEG punch=3SGO he   FOC=youSG
          'Don't you hit him!'

      b. *ara n-a   toka fizi=ni   **si=ḡazu**   **ana**   ba*
         I   RL-1EXCS chop cut.up=3SGO FOC=wood thatN ALT
         'I chopped up that wood.'

      c. *n-o-ke   mai   **si=ago***
         RL-2S-PFV come FOC=youSG
         'You've come.'

      d. *n-e   keha   ñheñhe   **si=za~zaho=na=na***
         RL-3S NSP be.separate FOC=RD~go =3SGP=thatN
         'That way of it is different.'

   e. *n-o*   *bula=nigo*   **si=ago**
      RL-2S   be.angry=2SGO   FOC=youSG
      'You're angry.'

Focus is not limited to core arguments: prepositional adjuncts may be focused:

(8.48)   *e la puku*   *bai*   **si=ka**   *tepi=ana*   *n-a=u*
          3S go be.short   PSBL   FOC=LOC   tape=thatN   RL-1EXCS=be.thus
          'It might go short on that tape, I think.'

The focal particle may mark any kind of argument, including nominalized clauses:

(8.49)   *mala*   *fa-lehe=i=u*   *n-e-ke=u=o*   *b=ara,*
          PURP   CS-die=3SGO=CNT   RL-3S-PFV=be.thus=thatNV   ALT=I
          'I intended to kill him,

          teo   *bla*   **si=boka=ḡu=na**   *ka*   *kuiti*   *aro-hi*
          not.exist   LMT   FOC=be.able=1SGP=thatN   LOC   trick   theseT-EMPH
          but that ability of mine with these tricks was not [able to do it].'

The vocative *goi* may also be focused:

(8.50)   *ago*   *n-o*   *tore*   *ḡlehe*   **si=goi**
          youSG   RL-2S   ask   very   FOC=VOC
          'You're asking a lot, man!'

When the focal particle cliticizes to a vowel-initial form, a reduced form occasionally occurs. So *si + ana* may have the surface form /sana/ and *si + ide* the form /side/:

(8.51) a.   *mai*   **s=ago**
          come   FOC=youSG
          'You come!'

8.5.2.2 Focus and constituent modifiers

Foregrounded arguments may be marked with the constituent modifiers *ba* 'alternative', *ña* 'immediate', or *la* (function unclear). The 'alternative' particle may occur clause-finally as it otherwise does in non-focus clauses:

(8.52)   *puku=na*   *bla*   *bai*   **s=ana**   **ba**
          be.short=thatN   LMT   PSBL   FOC=thatN   ALT
          'I think that's short.'

However, it may also occur between the focal particle and the argument, forming a single word:

(8.53) *nogoi, ge lehe si=**b**=**ara***
         VOC   PRS die FOC=ALT=I
         'Man! I'm going to die now.'

The immediacy particle also occurs in this construction:

(8.54) *n-a   bakora si=**n̄**=**ara***   *goi*
         RL-1EXCS be.cut   FOC=IMM=I   VOC
         'I've been cut, man!'

The dubitative *bai(u)*, contrastive *bo*, and limiter *bla(u)* do not occur in this construction. However, the particle *la* does occur.

(8.55) a. *fafra   si=gau-palu   ba, ginai ḡrugu   si=**la**=**ine***
           be.quick   FOC=youPL-two   ALT FUT   be.dark FOC=??=thisR
           'Hurry up, you two, or this [day] will get dark.'

    b. *keli   blau   si=**l**=**are***
        be.good   LMT   FOC=??=thoseN
        'Those are alright.'

The function of this particle is not clear (see §8.8.7).

8.5.2.3 Focused dummy argument =ia

The focus particle occasionally occurs attached to the host *=ia*. This requires the presence of one of the clause-level modifiers discussed in §8.5.2.2 (so the form *sia* does not occur in Kokota as it does in Cheke Holo and Blablanga). The form *=ia* appears to be a dummy argument, in the sense that the resulting focused form functions as a proform in itself, without any overt argument form present:

(8.56) a. *hei si=**ba**=**ia***
           who FOC=ALT=PRO
           'Who is it?'

    b. *n-e-ke   lehe hogo=na   bla*
        RL-3S-PFV   die   be.true=thatN LMT
        'He truly died

        *ka   mane iaro   si=**ba**=**ia***
        LOC   man   thosePV FOC=ALT=PRO
        from those men [i.e., ...because of the actions of those men].'

c. *'aria,   oloue sara=ña   gita.'*
1INC.IMP ??   thereD=IMM weINC
"'Let's move. We'll go straight there."

ḡe=u=di=ña   *si=la=ia*
NT=be.thus=3PLO=IMM   FOC=??=PRO
Say [those things].'

8.5.2.4 Focus politeness in imperatives

The *si* marked focus construction occurs very commonly in imperatives where it is regarded as the respectful or polite way of forming an imperative. In imperatives it is regarded as impolite to refer to the addressee without using *si*. Both examples in (8.57) are grammatical, but (8.57)b. is not respectful and would normally only be used for addressing young people.

(8.57) a. *fafra   si=gau-palu   ba*
be.quick FOC=youPL-two ALT
'Hurry up, you two!'

b. *fafra   gau-palu ba*
be.quick youPL-two ALT
'Hurry up, you two!'

8.5.2.5 Focus marking in equative and possessive predicates

Not only the verbal predicate arguments may be foregrounded with the focal particle. The subjects of nonverbal predicates may also be marked in this way, typically with a clause-level modifier present. This construction occurs with all nonverbal predicate types, including simple equatives ([8.58]a.–b.), naming equatives ([8.58]), *ḡela* 'resemble' equatives ([8.58]d.), and possessive predicates ([8.58]e.):

(8.58) a. *n-e   ooe-vaka **bla=s=ide***
RL-3S talk-ship LMT=FOC=theseR
'These [words] are Pijin.'

b. *mane gabili   si=ñ̄=aro   mane faaknu **sini***
man be aggressive FOC=IMM=theseT man smite FOC
'Those are men who want to fight. [They are] killers.'

c. *e-ti   nañha=di   nakoni si=l=are*
3S-NEG name=3PLP person FOC=??=thoseN
'They're not the names of people.'

d. *ḡ-e-la*   *turi=di*   *nau=de*   *si=**l=are***
   NT-3S-go   tell=3PLP   place=theseR   FOC=??=thoseN
   'Those are like stories of these places.'

e. *ara=ña,*   *no-ḡu*   *nau=ro*   *s=**aro***
   I=IMM   GENP-1SGP place=thoseNV FOC=theseT
   'Me, those are my places.'

Nonverbal predicate subject focusing also occurs with equative interrogatives, where, as with imperatives, the forms are regarded as being more polite than questions without the focal particle:

(8.59) a. *hei*   *si=**ba=ia***
       who   FOC=ALT=PRO
       'Who is it?'

b. *heve* *si=**ba=na***
    who   FOC=ALT=thatN
    'What's that?'

8.6 Adjuncts

The form and function of adjuncts are discussed in chapter 4. Their behavior within clause structure is discussed here.

8.6.1 Contextual adjuncts

The form and function of contextual adjuncts are discussed in §4.5. While the contextual nouns *gu-* and *nafu-* may have a nominal complement, they typically govern a subordinate clause. Contextual adjuncts only occur clause-initially or clause-finally. In (8.60) the contextual adjuncts are clause-initial:

(8.60) a. ***gu=na***   *'ia*   *visi*   *ka*   *to~toi'*
       CNTX=3SGP theSG play LOC RD~cook
       'Because "a game with fire"

       n-o-ke=u=o   *bla* *ago* *da*   *visi* *ka* *to~toi*
       RL-2S-PFV=be.thus=thatNV LMT youSG 1INC play LOC RD~cook
       you said, [so] we will play with fire.'

b. ***nafu=na*** *n-e-ke-ge*   *no-mai*   *tañano*
    base=3SGP RL.3S-PFV-PRS GENP-1EXCP food
    'Because it's our food

> *ne* *aḡe* *mhemhe*   *no-mai=ni=u*   *gai*   *faete=na*
> RL go   be.difficult   GENP-1EXCP=3SGO=CNT   weEXC   choose=thatN
> we find it hard to choose.'

Clause-final contextual adjuncts follow any arguments and/or adjuncts present. In (8.61)a. a contextual adjunct follows an actor and subordinate clause object, in (8.61)b. a subject and deictic locative, in (8.61)c. a subject and PP, and in (8.61)d. a local noun.

(8.61) a.   *n-a*   *no-mai*   *aḡe*   *mhemhe=ni=u*   *gai*
          RL-1EXCS   GENP-1EXCP   go   be.difficult=3SGO=CNT   weEXC
          'We find it hard

          ta=ke   *fa*   *nodo=i*   *fea*
          SBD=PFV   CS   stop=3SGO   INIT
          to stop

          t=au=na   *za~zaho=na=na*   *teḡe*   *ine*
          SBD=exist=thatN   RD~go=3SGP=thatN   turtle   thisR
          this way of hunting of turtles,

          nafu=na   **are**   **bla**   **ira**   **doli=mai**   **gai**
          base=3SGP   thoseN   LMT   thePL   live=1EXCP   weEXC
          because they are our life.'

    b.   *teo*   *boka*   *mai*   *au=na*   *gai*   *ade*
          not.exist   be.able   come   exist=thatN   weEXC   here
          'We can't come and live here,

          nafu=na   **n-a-ge**   **zaho**   **koko=di**
          base=3SGP   RL-1EXCS-PRS   go   leave=3PLO
          because we would leave behind

          ira   **ge-mai**   **no-mai**...
          thePL   CNSM-1EXCP   GENP-1EXCP
          our food and our things...'

    c.   ...*a*   *boka*   *ñha=di*   *gudu*   *gai*   *ira*   *nakoni*
          1EXCS   be.able   eat=3PLO   EXHST   weEXC   theSG   person
          '...we people could eat them all

          ka=ia   *fufunu=na*   *ia*   *kastom*   *ka*   *gai*
          LOC=theSG   begin=3SGP   theSG   custom   LOC   weEXC
          in the origins of our custom

nafu=na   are   bla   ḡ-e-la   ge-mai   mitia...
base=3SGP thoseN LMT NT-3S-go CNSM-1EXCP meat
because those were our meat...'

d. *n-e-ke   kave   mai=ña   fate*
RL-3S-PFV descend come=IMM above
'He came down from heaven,

gu=da   gita   ira   huḡru   nakoni
CNTX=1INCP weINC thePL all   person
for us people.'

8.6.2 Locative and associative adjuncts

Locative and associative adjuncts have similar behavior in clause structure.
Locative adjuncts include spatial and temporal deictics (see §4.2.1 and §4.2.3),
prepositional phrases (see §4.1), and place names (see §4.4). Associative
adjuncts have the associative noun *tareme-* as head (see §4.6).

8.6.2.1 Locatives and associatives as outermost adjuncts

There is a very strong tendency for these adjuncts to occur as the outermost
adjuncts in a clause. This means that such adjuncts typically occur clause-
initially, as in (8.62), or clause-finally (8.63).

(8.62) a. *ḡ-e   lao ia-hi   la kamo   ia-hi   lego*
NT-3S go   thatPV-EMPH go go.across thatPV-EMPH PNLOC
'So he went there and crossed over there to Lego,

n-e-ke=u
RL-3S-PFV=be.thus
it was like that.

sare   n-e   la koko   kamo=u
thereP RL-3S go leave go.across=CNT
There he was going across further.'

b. *tifaro   ara   a   lao tarai fakamo le~legu   sade*
before   I   1EXCS go   pray always RD~behind Sunday
'I used to always go to prayer every Sunday

ña   goinode   teo
but todayRL   not.exist
but now I don't.'

    c. ...***huhurañi*** *au=re*   *keha=re*   *n-e-ke=u*   *gai*
        PNLOC   exist=thoseN NSP=thoseN RL-3S-PFV=be.thus   weEXC
        '...[and] some lived at Huhurangi. We were like that.'

    d. ***ka***   ***nare***   ***sade***   *ḡ-e*   *lao=u*   *ḡ-e*   *la*   *tarai=u...*
        LOC day   Sunday NT-3S go=CNT   NT-3S go   pray=CNT
        'On Sundays they were going, they were going and praying...'

    e. ***tareme=na kodere*** *n-a*   *toḡla=ni*   *ara*   *ia*   *zora*
        with=3SGP PN   RL-1EXCS chase=3SGO I   theSG pig
        'With Kodere I chased the pig.'

(8.63) a. *mhoko* *bla* *fea* *au=gu*   *ago*   ***sare***
        sit   LMT INIT exist=CNT youSG thereP
        'You sit down first there.'

    b. *n-a-ke*   *fakae=ni kaike baesu ta*   *dou*   *ḡlehe* ***nhorao***
        RL-1EXCS-PFV see=3SGO one   shark SBD be.big very   yesterday
        'I saw a shark that was very big yesterday.'

    c. *ḡ-e*   *mai*   *haidu maneri* ***kokota***
        NT-3S come meet they   PNLOC
        'They came and held a meeting at Kokota.'

    d. *e=u*   *friñhe* *n-e-ke*   *friñhe=ni=na*
        3S=be.thus work RL-3S-PFV   work=3SGO=thatN

        palu *mane* *aro*   ***ka***   ***nasona*** *ine*   *ḡerona*
        two   man theseT   LOC point   thisR   PNLOC
        'That's what those two men did at the point of Gerona.'

    e. *manei* *n-e*   *za~zaho* ***tareme=na mhagu***
        he   RL-3S RD~go   with=3SGP be.afraid
        'He walked with fear.'

These adjunct types are not all distributed equally commonly in initial and final position. Temporal and spatial deictics and prepositional phrases occur with similar frequency in either position. However, place names and associative nouns typically occur in clause-final position. While these adjuncts do occur in clause-initial position, they do so rarely.

Adjuncts may occur clause-initially when a preverbal topicalized argument is also present, as (8.62)b. and the examples in (8.64) illustrate.

(8.64) a. **sara   hae**   *manei n-e   lisa=i=na   no-ḡu   vilai ana*
thereD where he   RL-3S put=3SGO=thatN GENP-1SGP knifethatN
'Where did he put that knife of mine?'

b. **ka   pau=na   kumai t=au=ana**
LOC head=3SGP water   SBD=exist=thatN
'At the head of that river

dadara e=u   blau   n-e-ke   zikra=ro
blood   3S=be.thus LMT   RL-3S-PFV   pour=thoseNV
blood was pouring out.'

c. **ka   au=di=re**   *palu mane aro   n-e-ke   au   ḡerona*
LOC exist=3PLP=thoseN two   man   theseT RL-3S-PFV exist PNLOC
'In their living those two men were at Gerona.'

Temporal and spatial deictics and prepositional phrases follow this pattern. It is not clear whether place names and associative adjuncts also occur clause-initially with a preverbal core argument.

8.6.2.2 Non-outermost locatives and associatives

While adjuncts typically occur as the outermost elements in a clause, they infrequently intervene between the predicate and a following core argument.

Temporal and spatial deictics, location names, and prepositional phrases and associative nouns all may intervene between the verb complex and a core argument in its pragmatically unmarked postverbal position, as (8.65) illustrates. An adjunct occurs before an intransitive subject in (8.65)a.–c., a transitive actor in (8.65)d., a direct object in (8.65)e., and a (clausal) indirect object in (8.65)f.

(8.65) a. *boro bla   au   **sare** manei*
boro LMT   exist thereP she
'She just stays *boro* there.'

b. *n-e-ke   aḡe **tareme=na** keha **foḡra** ñheñhe=o   bo*
RL-3S-PFV go   with=3SGP NSP   sick   be.separate=thatNV CNT

ia   naitu tahi...
theSG devil sea
'The sea devil goes with that other different sickness...'

c. *n-a-ke   lao **buala** ara*
RL-1EXCS-PFV go   PNLOC I
'I went to Buala.'

    d. *t=au=ne*   *e tore=i*   **ka**   **hei**   *manei*
        SBD=exist=thisR   3S ask=3SGO LOC who he
        'Who will he ask this [question] to?'

    e. *n-e*   *aḡe=na*   *la=ni*   **ka**   **keha**   **hobo-ḡazu=o**
        RL-3S go=thatN   go=3SGO LOC NSP   branch-wood=thatNV
        'He went and put on a tree branch

        keha   *lholhoai=na=o*
        NSP   coil=3SGP=thatNV
        one of those coils of his.'

    f. *manahagi=nigo* **nariha**   *ta*   *mai...*
        want=2SGO   day.after.tomorrow   SBD come
        '[I] want you the day after tomorrow to come...'

In addition, temporal locatives also occasionally intervene between a preverbal topicalized argument and the predicate:

(8.66)   *ara* **fufugo**   *ginai a*   *fakae=ni*   *vaka*   *ana*
        I   tomorrow FUT   1EXCS   see=3SGO   ship   thatN
        'I tomorrow will see that ship.'

No other adjuncts are attested between a topicalized argument and the predicate.

8.6.2.3 Order of multiple adjuncts

More than one adjunct may occur in a single clause. One adjunct may occur clause-initially and one clause-finally. However, multiple adjuncts are also possible in either position.

In some instances apparent multiple adjuncts actually represent a single adjunct. This occurs where the head of an adjunct governs its own adjunct. In (8.67)a.–b. the second PP is embedded within the first, the two representing a single adjunct at the clause level. In (8.67)c. the local noun *fate* 'above' is governed by the locative head *ade* 'here', together representing a single complex spatial locative adjunct.

(8.67) a. [**ka gai**   [**ka=ia**   **kastom gai**]]
        LOC weEXC   LOC=theSG custom weEXC
        'With us in our custom

        tana   *goi momoru*   *e=ni*   *e=u*
        then   VOC *momoru*   3S=3SGO   3S=be.thus
        momoru does [i.e., names] it...'

b. *a   boka   ñha=di   gudu   gai   ira   nakoni*
1EXCS   be.able eat=3PLO EXHST   weEXC thePL   person
'...we people could eat them all

  [*ka=ia   fufunu=na   ia   kastom   [ka   gai]*]...
LOC=theSG begin=3SGP   theSG   custom   LOC   weEXC
at the beginning of our custom...'

c. *e   la fufunu   ka   n-e-ke   au=o   rei-palu   [ade [fate]]*
3S go begin   LOC   RL-3S-PFV exist=thatNV they-two here above
'It [the story] starts where they two stayed here on top.'

True multiple adjuncts do occur, however. Clause-initial multiple adjuncts are uncommon and appear to be limited to two adjuncts:

(8.68) a. [*ka=ia   kokolo=di   t=au=are   bla*]
LOC=theSG class=3PLP SBD=exist=thoseN LMT
'With those kinds of things,

  [*ka=ia   fai   dokta*]   *e   au=i   la   bla*
LOC=theSG side doctor   3S exist=3SGO   ??   LMT
on the part of doctors they have something

keha   ta   fakilo=ni   tritmenti   ka=ia   ooe-vaka
NSP   SBD   name(V)=3SGO   treatment   LOC=theSG talk-ship
that [they] call treatment in Pijin.'

b. [*ka=ia   ti   mai=na=o=ña   velepuhi*]
LOC=theSG NEG   come=3SGP=thatNV=IMM   right.way
'At the [time when] there was not yet that coming of Christianity,

  [*kokota*]   *n-e-ke   au=re   keha=re*
PNLOC   RL-3S-PFV exist=thoseN   NSP=thoseN
at Kokota some lived.'

c. [*ka=ia   ḡrui*]   [*tareme=na   kodere*]
LOC=theSG garden   with=3SGP   PN
'In the garden with Kodere

ara n-a   toḡla=ni   ia   zora
I   RL-1EXCS chase=3SGO   theSG   pig
I chased the pig.'

d. *[goinode]*   *tana*   *[ka=ia*   *heta=na*   *ia*   *mereseni*
   todayRL   then   LOC=theSG   be.strong=3SGP   theSG   medicine
   'Now, with the strength of the medicine

ka=ia   *fai   dokta]*   *tana*   *nogoi   ke*   *age*
LOC=theSG   side   doctor   then   VOC   PFV   go
on the part of doctors, man!, it's gone,

ke   age   no-mai   *fa   mana=ri=u*
PFV   go   GENP-1EXCP   CS   be.powerful=3PLO=CNT

oilagi=ri=u   *gai*
be.powerful=3PLO=CNT   weEXC
our great power is gone.'

As (8.68)c. shows, two clause-initial peripherals can occur when a preverbal topicalized core argument is also present, though this occurs very infrequently.

Much more commonly two or more adjuncts occur clause-finally. Where two PPs occur, in some instances their order is dictated by the semantics of the predicate. In (8.69)a. the locative nature of the existential predicate determines that the first PP will be interpreted as the location of the staying, the second being interpretable in whatever way is meaningful in the context. In (8.69)b. the verb of transference determines that the two PPs will be interpreted iconically in correspondence with the order of the locations: the liquid is located at the source before it is located at the goal, so the PPs are interpreted as source, then goal:

(8.69) a. *...mala   e   au*   *histri*   *are-lau*   *[ka*   *sikolu=ne]*
           PURP   3S   exist   history   thoseN-SPC   LOC   school=thisR
       '...so those histories can stay in the school

       [ka   suli=da   *gita]*
       LOC   child=1INCP   weINC
       for our children.'

   b. *fa   kamo=i*   *bakru*   *t=au=ana*
      CS   go.across=3SGO   liquid   SBD=exist=thatN
      'Transfer that tea

      [ka   timosi   ana]   *[ka   panakini   ana]*
      LOC   thermos   thatN   LOC   cup   thatN
      from that thermos to that cup.'

In other instances no semantic basis of PP order exists and the PPs can occur in either order. In (8.70) two PPs occur, one a temporal locative, one a spatial locative. These could occur in either order.

(8.70) *turi gabili* *faaknu n-e-ke* *au=re*
    tell be.aggressive smite RL-3S-PFV exist=thoseN
    '...the story of the killers who lived

    [*ka=ia puhi boñihehe*] [*ka gizu=na a-hi   gai*]
    LOC=theSG way heathen   LOC island=3SGPthisT-EMPH weEXC
    in the heathen time on this island of ours'

Where a PP cooccurs with another type of adjunct either order in possible. A PP coccurs with an associative noun in (8.71) and a temporal adverbial in (8.72).

(8.71) a. *sogemarava n-e-ke*   *aḡe=re=u*
    PN   RL-3S-PFV go=thoseN=CNT
    'Sogemarava was going

    [*ka hinage=ne*] [*tareme=di tilo mane*]=*u*
    LOC boat=thisR with=3PLP three man=be.thus
    in the boat with three men.'

   b. *ara n-a-ke*   *turi* [*tareme=na gase ana*]
     I RL-1EXCS-PFV tell with=3SGP woman thatN
     'I have talked to that woman

     [*ka kaike fata bla*]
     LOC one occasion LMT
     only once.'

(8.72) a. *ara a*   *lao tarai* [*tifaro*] [*ka sade ide*]
    I 1EXCS go pray before LOC Sunday theseR
    'I used to go and pray before on Sundays.'

   b. *ara ginai manahagi lao* [*ka sitoa*] [*fufugo*]
     I FUT want go LOC store tomorrow
     'I will need to go to the store tomorrow.'

Similar possibilities apply to combinations of other locative adjunct types.

8.7 Negation

Negation in Kokota is expressed in two ways: by use of the negative particle *ti*; and by a subordinating construction involving the negative existential verb *teo* 'not.exist'. Overall the subordinating construction is by far the more frequently employed strategy. However, in a number of environments the particle is the standard means of marking negative.

8.7.1 Negation by the negative particle *ti*

The negative particle *ti* is suffixed to the modal/subject particle, joining with other tense and aspect particles to form a single complex particle. In some clause types the particle is the only means of expressing negation, the subordinating construction not occurring. In some clause types both *ti* and the subordinating construction are possible but the *ti* construction typically occurs, while in others the preference is reversed.

The particle *ti* is the only means of expressing negation in 'be thus' clauses, in nominalized clauses, and with equative predicates.

In 'be thus' clauses the verb complex always forms a single word consisting of the verb =*u* 'be thus', the modal/subject particle, and any other tense or aspect particles that are present. Because it forms a single word, the subordinating construction does not occur. Instead *ti* is employed:

(8.73) a. *ka gau* ***e-ti=u.*** *n-e=u* *are-lau*
LOC youPL 3S-NEG=be.thus RL-3S=be.thus thoseN-SPC
'With you they're not like that [i.e., not correct]. That's how they are,

        za~zaho=di=re *friñhe=di=re* *ka maneri*
        RD~go=3PLP=thoseN work=3PLO=thoseN LOC they
        those ways of making them with them.'

   b. ***o-ti*** *ḡela* *an-lau* ***o-ti=u*** *ago*
        2S-NEG resemble thatN-SPC 2S-NEG=be.thus youSG
        'Don't be like that. Don't be like that, you.'

The particle is also the only means of marking negation in nominalized clauses:

(8.74) *ka=ia* ***ti*** *mai=na=o=ña* *velepuhi*
LOC=theSG NEG come=3SGP=thatNV=IMM right.way
'At that non-coming of Christianity [i.e., When Christianity had not yet come]

        kokota n-e-ke *au=re* *keha=re...*
        PNLOC RL-3S-PFV exist=thoseN NSP=thoseN
        some lived at Kokota...'

It will be noted that in (8.74) the negative particle occurs without the presence of an overt modal/subject particle. As discussed in §7.5.2.5 irrealis particles are omissible. This applies when *ti* is present, as (8.74) illustrates.

The particle is also the only way of expressing negation in nonverbal predications.

(8.75) a. **n-e-ti**   *ḡazu hogo=na*
         RL-3S-NEG wood be.true=3SGP
         'They're not true sticks.'

    b. **e-ti**   *nañha=di nakoni si=la=re*
       3S-NEG name=3PLP person FOC=??=thoseN
       'They aren't the names of people.'

As discussed in §8.7, negation may be expressed in imperative clauses by either *ti* or the subordinating construction:

(8.76) a. **o-ti**   *fa doli=ni   gilai au   batari foforu ago*
         2S-NEG CS live=3SGO until exist battery be.new 2SG
         'Don't turn it on until you have new batteries.'

    b. **teo**   *ḡ-o mai ago*
       not.exist NT-2S come youSG
       'Don't you come!'

However, there is a very strong preference for using the negative particle in imperative clauses, the subordinating construction occurring rarely. The same is true in relative clauses:

(8.77)   *ge e   teo   ḡe faete gai   ḡ-e-la   teḡe heve bo*
        SEQ IRR not.exist NT choose weEXC NT-3S-go turtle what CNT
        'So we didn't choose what kind of turtles

        *ta   hod-i=Ø=na   **ta=ti**   hod-i=Ø=na...*
        SBD take-TR=3SGO=thatN SBD=NEG take-TR=3SGO=thatN
        to take or to not take...'

In declarative main clauses the opposite preference exists—the tendency is strongly towards the subordinating construction (see §8.7.2). However, it is possible to use the negative particle instead:

(8.78) a. *ara-hi* **a-ti-ke**   *fufunu=di=bo   t=au=de*
         I-EMPH 1EXCS-NEG-PFV begin=3PLO=CNT SBD=exist=theseR
         'I didn't start these [arguments].'

b. ***n-o-ti*** *noto*   *fa-nomho*
RL-2S-NEG stop   CS-hear
'You didn't stop and be quiet.'

c. *buka* *are-lau*   ***e-ti-ke***   *mala* *fa* *za~zaho*
book thoseN-EMPH 3S-NEG-PFV PURP CS RD~go
'These books will not be for sending

   hae   *ge*   *hae*
   where and where
   wherever and wherever [i.e., just anywhere].'

Such clauses occur less commonly than the subordinating construction.

8.7.2 Subordinating negation

The standard means of expressing negation in declarative main clauses involves a subordinating construction in which the negative existential verb *teo* occurs with a subordinated positive declarative clause as its complement.

The negative existential verb is the negative counterpart of the positive existential verb *au*. As such it occurs without a complement, with a straightforward negative existential function:

(8.79) a. *n-e-ge*   *la* ***teo***   *ira*   *nakoni* *n-e=u*
RL-3S-PRS go not.exist thePL person RL-3S=be.thus
'The people have gone to nothing [i.e., have all died out].'

b. *e* ***teo***   *kaike* *ihei*
3S not.exist one   someone
'There is not anyone

   ta   *ḡ-e*   *boka*   *fa-lehe=i=na*   *ia*   *to~toi*
   SBD NT-3S be.able CS-die=3SGO=thatN theSG RD~cook
   who can kill the fire.' [lit. Someone who can kill the fire does not exist.]

It also functions as a negative verb of possession:

(8.80)   *ara* *n-a*   ***teo=nau***   *sileni*
    I   RL-1EXCS not.exist=1SGO money
    'I've got no money.'

Existential verbs including *teo* are discussed in detail in §6.6.

As a strategy for expressing negation, *teo* occurs as the verb of a main clause, with the negated event expressed as a positive declarative clause functioning as a sentential complement:

(8.81)   *gai*   ***teo***   [*ḡ-a*   *mai=u*   *k=ago*]
          weEXC not.exist NT-1EXCS come=CNT LOC=youSG
          'We will not be coming to you.'

Here the positive complement clause is bracketed. The subject of the main clause is also the controlled subject of the complement clause. A more literal translation would be something like 'We are not that we are coming to you'.

The subject of the main clause is always the controlled argument of the complement clause in these constructions. However, while there is a strong tendency for the controlled argument to also be the subject (or actor) of the complement clause, the controlled argument may represent a different grammatical role. In (8.82), for example, the controlled argument is the complement clause object.

(8.82)   *mane* *t=au=ana*   ***teo***   [*ḡ-a*   *lase=i*   *ara*]
          man SBD=exist=thatN not.exist NT-1EXCS know=3SGO I
          'That man I don't know.'

The literal meaning of this sentence is something like 'That man is not that I know him.'

The subject of the main clause may occur in preverbal topic position, as in (8.81) and (8.82). However, the subject may also occur after the complement clause:

(8.83)   ***teo***   [*ḡ-e* *sodu=gu*   *are*]
          not.exist NT-3S be.long=CNT thoseN
          'Those aren't long.'

When this occurs, the overt argument is, in fact, the subject of the complement clause, not the main clause. Consequently, if the complement clause is transitive, the subject and object of that clause occur in their pragmatically unmarked order:

(8.84)   ***teo***   [*ḡ-a*   *manahagi=ni=u ara*
          not.exist NT-1EXCS want=3SGO=CNT I
          'I don't want

          ta   *hoda* *kave=i=na*]
          SBD take descend=3SGO=thatN
          that [it] be taken down.'

In sentences such as these the main clause subject is semantically as well as formally empty. This is somewhat similar to English cleft constructions, except that no overt dummy subject occurs. The more literal translations of (8.83) and (8.84) would be 'it is not so that those are long' and 'it is not so that I want that [it] be taken down' (but without the pragmatic emphasis of the English sentences).

The main clause is almost always in irrealis modality. As discussed in §7.5.2.5, irrealis particles are frequently omitted, and this is the case in examples (8.81) to (8.84). Rarely, the main clause may be treated as realis:

(8.85) *n-e teo=ña*   [*ḡ-e mai=u   mane huhurañi are*]
RL-3S not.exist=IMM NT-3S come=CNT man   PNLOC   thoseN
'Those Huhurangi people aren't coming.'
(lit. It is not so that those Huhurangi people are coming.)

Equally rarely, the main clause may contain a neutral modal/subject particle:

(8.86) *ḡ-e   teo   [boka=i=na*]
NT-3S not.exist   be.able=3SGO=thatN
'They couldn't do it... '

Within the complement clause itself, in this negative construction, only a neutral particle may occur, as (8.81) to (8.85) illustrate. However, when the verb of the complement clause is the abilitative *boka*, the modal/subject particle is typically deleted, as (8.86) illustrates. This is optional, however. Complement clauses with *boka* may have a neutral particle:

(8.87) *...teo   [ḡ-e   boka   turi=di   manei*
not.exist NT-3S be.able tell=3PLO he
'...he can't tell [about]

heve ḡlepo n-e-ke   torai dia=re]
what thing RL-3S-PFV very   be.bad=thoseN
whatever things were very wrong.'

The complement clause in the subordinating negative construction is typically marked with continuous aspect, as (8.81) and (8.83) to (8.85) illustrate. However, this is not obligatory, as (8.82) illustrates. Complement clauses involving *boka*, however, cannot be marked with continuous aspect.

In subordinating negation the main clause verb *teo* is often marked with the immediacy particle *ña*, the limiter *bla*, or the possibilitative *bai(u)*:

(8.88) a. *n-e*   **teo=ña**   *ḡe aḡe mhoko*
        RL-3S not.exist=IMM   NT go   sit
        'If you don't go and sit

        fa-lehe=i   *ago*   *to~toi=ne*   *ge*
        CS-die=3SGO youSG RD~cook=thisR   SEQ
        and kill this fire,

        ago   **teo**   **bla** *ḡe*   *heta=u*   *e=u*
        youSG not.exist   LMT NT   be.strong=CNT 3S=be.thus
        you are simply not strong.'

   b. *gita*   **teo**   **baiu** *aḡe=na*   *buala*
       weINC   not.exist PSBL   go=thatN PNLOC
       'We won't go to Buala; Let's not go to Buala.'

None of the other modifiers discussed in §8.8 can modify *teo* in this construction.

8.7.3 Negation and modality

There is a very strong tendency in Kokota to treat negatives as irrealis. Realis is typically reserved for specific events that have actually occurred or are actually occurring at the time of speaking. Consequently, irrealis marks not only future events but habituals, where the events are real but no specific individual event is being referred to; and negatives, where the events are not real by virtue of not having occurred. Negative clauses, with either the particle or the subordinating construction, typically have an irrealis particle (or no overt particle as the result of irrealis particle deletion). However, it is possible to mark negative clauses as realis. In (8.75) and (8.78)b. realis particles occur with the negative particle, and in (8.85) the negative existential verb is marked with a realis particle. This use of realis occurs when the speaker is emphasizing that he or she has a particular specific non-occurrence in mind, rather than simply that an event has not occurred, for example, because someone has not done something they were supposed to do at a particular time.

8.8 Constituent modifiers

A number of modifiers exist that mark constituents at a range of levels in the syntax, from individual words to entire clauses. These include:

(8.89) a. *ba*   Alternative   e. *ña*   Immediacy
      b. *bo*   Contrastive   f. *fea*   Initiality
      c. *bla(u)*   Limiter   g. *la*   (function unclear)
      d. *bai(u)*   Possibilitative

8.8.1 *Ba* Alternative marker

The particle *ba* marks constituents of all kinds, indicating they are one of two or more alternatives or possibilities. The particle may immediately follow or immediately precede the marked constituent, with a very strong tendency towards occurring after the constituent. In (8.90)a. *ba* marks several possibilities, preceding the relevant constituent in each case. In (8.90)b. it follows two of the three possibilities.

(8.90) a.   *ke   toke=ri   bo   ira   no-mai   friñhe tañano,*
            PFV arrive=3PLO CNT thePL GENP-1EXCP work food
            '[The times] arrive for our making food,

            ***ba*   *ira   nare=di suḡa,*
            ALT thePL day=3PLP house
            like festival days

            ***ba*   *ira   krismas,* ***ba*   *ira   esta*
            ALT thePL Christmas ALT thePL Easter
            or Christmas, or Easter.'

     b.   *...ḡ-e-la   naboto-u **ba**, varedake-u   **ba**, tulufulu teḡe*
            NT-3S-go ten-CRD   ALT twenty-CRD ALT thirty   turtle
            '...it might be ten, or twenty, or thirty turtles

            ta   la hod-i=di=re   gai
            SBD go take-TR=3PLO=thoseN weEXC
            that we take.'

When several alternative constituents are overtly expressed, the particle may mark each constituent, as in (8.90)a. Alternatively it may mark all but the final constituent when postposed, as in (8.90)b., or all but the initial constituent when preposed, as in (8.91)b. Once the presentation of alternatives is established by the marking of one or more constituents with *ba*, the final constituent in the series is interpretable as a further alternative without the particle's presence. This lack of marking of the final alternative occurs commonly, and gives the particle the appearance of a conjunction functionally akin to *or* in English. However, in any such instance the final alternative may also be marked. Moreover, where the particle precedes each alternative, as in (8.90)a., the first occurrence of *ba* is not between two alternative constituents, so is clearly not functioning as a conjunction. When *ba* follows the alternatives and the final relevant constituent is marked, the same is true. Clearly *ba* marks individual constituents, rather than conjoins several constituents. The preference for a postposed realization of *ba*, and the commonness of a lack of marking of the final constituent may suggest the particle is in the process of being reanalyzed as a conjunction. However, counter evidence for this lies in the fact that in a majority of occurrences only one alternative is expressed, as discussed below.

The alternative particle marks a wide range of constituent types. But only constituents of the same syntactic type may be presented as alternatives. In (8.91) *ba* marks single words, in one instance adnominal numerals, in the other, stative verbs:

(8.91) a. *e=u*   *ge*   *ḡ-e*   *turi=ña* *gita*
       3S=be.thus SEQ NT-3S tell=IMM weINC
       'Before we talk

       da   *koze=i*   *kaike* **ba** *tilo* *koze*
       1INCS sing=3SGO one   ALT three sing
       we'll sing one or three songs.'

    b. *...ḡ-e* *ta* *ikoa,*   **ba**   *dou,* **ba** *midiam...*
       NT-3S SBD be.small ALT be.big ALT medium
       '...whether small or big, or medium...

       kaike *hod-i=ri*   *gudu*   *bla*
       one   take-TR=3PLO EXHST LMT
       we just take them all...'

Ba also marks phrasal constituents. In (8.92) it marks alternative NPs in one example, PPs in the other:

(8.92) a. *ia*   *puka* **ba**, *ia*   *do*   **ba**,
       theSG fly   ALT theSG mosquito ALT
       'A fly or a mosquito

       e=u   *n-e* *kati=nau=na*   *ara*
       3S=be.thus RL-3S bite=1SGO=thatN I
       bit me.'

    b. *...roha=i*   *nhigo*   *ka* *botolo* **ba** *ka* *tini...*
       scrape=3SGO be.finished LOC bottle   ALT LOC tin
       '...finish scraping it into a bottle or tin...'

In addition *ba* may occur with a focused pronoun or demonstrative in the construction discussed in §8.5.2.2:

(8.93)   *nogoi, ge* *lehe* *si=**b=ara***
       VOC PRS die FOC=ALT=I
       'Man! I'm going to die now.'

The particle also marks complete clauses, both main clauses, as in (8.94)a.–b., or subordinate clauses. In (8.94)c. two relative clauses are presented as alternative possibilities:

(8.94) a. *fafra*   *si=gau-palu*   **ba,**   *ginai*   *ḡrugu*   *si=la=ine*
       be.quick   FOC=youPL-two   ALT   FUT   be.dark   FOC=??=thisR
       'Hurry up, you two, or it will get dark.'

    b. *ara*   *mai*   *ka*   *suḡa*   *ine*   *ago*   **ba,**
       I   come   LOC   house   thisR   youSG   ALT
       'Will I come to your house,

       ago   *mai*   *ka*   *suḡa=o*   *ara*
       youSG   come   LOC   house=thatNV   I
       or will you come to my house?'

    c. *ta*   *la*   *hod-i=Ø*   *la*   *gai*   *ḡazu*   *t=au=o*
       SBD   go   take-TR=3SGO   CND   weEXC   wood   SBD=exist=thatNV
       'If we go and take that tree

       ta   *fa*   *ku~kumai=ni=u*   **ba**   *ta*   *fa*   *siri*   *la=i=u*
       SBD   CS   RD~drink=3SGO=CNT   ALT   SBD   CS   smell   go=3SGO=CNT
       that [one] drinks or that [one] smells

       ka   *nakoni*   *t=au=o*   *ta*   *toke=i*
       LOC   person   SBD=exist-thatNV   SBD   arrive=3SGO
       to that person who has caught

       t=au=o   *maleria boka*   *ke*   *aḡe keli*   *bo*   *bla*
       SBD=exist=thatNV malaria be.able   PFV   go   be.good   CNT   LMT
       malaria, [they] are able to just get well again.'

As indicated above, *ba* occurs most frequently with only one overt alternative. In the text corpus, out of 45 occurrences of the particle, in 34 instances (75.5%) only one alternative is expressed. Typically the marked constituent represents an alternative to a previously established possibility. In this very common use of *ba* it equates more to the English *instead* than to *or*. In the discourse preceding the exchange in (8.95) speaker B has been eager to leave in order to tell something to others, but speaker A, his chief, does not want him to leave:

(8.95) A. *ginai*   *saigona si=ge*   *ḡ-o*   *tahe=i=ña*
       todayIRR   evening   FOC=SEQ   NT-2S   tell=3SGO=IMM
       'This evening then you tell [them]

```
t=au=ana          ba
SBD=exist=thatN   ALT
that, instead [of now].'
```

B. *ehe, ginai   saigona   si=ba*
   yes todayIRR evening   FOC=ALT
   'Yes, this evening instead.'

With speaker A, in this exchange *ba* marks the entire clause. With speaker B it marks a temporal locative. In both, the marked constituent is presented as an alternative to the previously established possibility of speaker B leaving immediately.

In (8.96) *ba* marks a NP that is being presented as an alternative group to those mentioned in the preceding clause:

(8.96) *gaha mane n-e-ge   fa kenu=ri   ka=ia   hinage...*
        five man   RL-3S-PRS   CS front=3PLO LOC=theSG   boat
        'Five men were sent ahead in a boat....

        tehi=na   mane=o   ba   n-e   age rhuku   .
        many=3SGP   man=thatNV   ALT   RL-3S go   landward
        Many other people went by land...'

The sentence in (8.97) is taken from a discussion about which story a speaker should tell. A number of possibilities have been discussed. The speaker then raises the possibility of a further alternative:

(8.97) *ba   heve, naitu ine-hi*
        ALT   what   devil thisR-EMPH
        'Or what [else]? [The story of] this devil?' [speaker pointing to location of devil's home]

In other instances *ba* is used when no other alternative has previously been established, but when it is apparent from the marked constituent what alternative the speaker has in mind. In (8.98) the clause has the form of a declarative, but the intonation of interrogative. The possibility of 'that' having been opened is presented as an alternative, the other alternative being that 'that' is not open:

(8.98) *n-e-ge   tor-i=Ø   b=ana   manei*
        RL-3S-PRS   open-TR=3SGO   ALT=thatN   he
        'Has he opened that?'

Note that in this example it is not the entire clause that is marked with *ba* and presented as an alternative. Instead only the verb complex is marked.

Constructions like this are common. However, it is not clear whether in this kind of construction *ba* marks only the verb itself, or the entire verb complex. Although *ba* forms a single phonological word with *ana*, it marks the verb complex and not the demonstrative. Collapsing vowel-initial words with preceding words that have the same vowel as their final segment occurs frequently in casual speech (see §2.6.1.2). In careful speech *ba* and *ana* would be separated in (8.98).

In (8.98) *ba* marks a clause that has the structure of a declarative but the intonation of an interrogative, to seek confirmation or otherwise of the veracity of the statement. Similarly, *ba* may occur extraclausally after a statement, to seek confirmation of the statement. In (8.99) the clause itself is not a question. The *ba* then occurs separately seeking confirmation.

(8.99)   *...ge pulo mai gau-palu fufugo* **ba**
          SEQ return come youPL-two tomorrow ALT
          '...then you two are coming back tomorrow. Or [not]?'

Ba occurs frequently in interrogatives, particularly in interrogatives like that in (8.98), where a statement is presented and its veracity questioned, and in interrogatives with *heve* 'what'. In 'what' interrogatives, again, no other alternatives are presented. Instead *ba* invokes all possible alternatives:

(8.100)a. *u   heve* **ba** *n-e   fa fo~fōgra=di=re...*
        be.thus what ALT RL-3S CS RD~be.sick=3PLO=thoseN
        'What is making them sick...?'

     b. *visi ḡ-e-la   heve la* **ba**...
        play NT-3S-go what ?? ALT
        'A game that goes how...?'

In (8.100)a. the addressee is asked to say what, out of all possible causes of sickness, applies in that instance. In (8.100)b. the range of alternatives implicit in *ba* is all possible ways of making games.

Ba also occurs in self-corrections, marking the corrected constituent:

(8.101)   *...n-e=u   ana tikani. e,   mane riva*   **ba**
         RL-3S=be.thus thatN PN   EXCLM man PN   ALT
         '...said Tikani. Oh! [I mean] the man Riva.'

8.8.2 *Bo* Contrastive

The particle *bo* indicates that the marked constituent is being contrasted with another entity or event. The form is postposed and may mark constituents at various levels of the syntax, including an entire clause, as in (8.102)a., or a verb complex only ([8.102]b.):

(8.102)a. *fufugo   ara ginai a   kuru=nau hore   **bo***
        tomorrow   I   FUT   1EXCS have=1SGO dugout   CNT
        'Tomorrow I will have a canoe.'

    b. *manei n-e   au   **bo** sara   buala*
       he   RL-3S exist CNT thereD PNLOC
       'He is staying in Buala.'

When marking a clause or verb complex the event or state is contrasted with some other event or state. In (8.102)a. the speaker had intended to go fishing that day but did not have access to a canoe. The statement contrasts the availability of a canoe the following day with that day's situation. In (8.102)b. the speaker is correcting the addressee's assumption that the subject referent was in Goveo.

Bo also marks nominals and obliques of various types, including full NPs, pronouns, personal names and location names:

(8.103)a. *man-t=au=ana   teo   ḡ-a   lase=i   ara*
        man-SBD=exist=thatN not.exist NT-1EXCS know=3SGO I
        'That man I don't know his name,

        *ña   ira   naitu toke   aro   **bo***
        but   thePL devil arrive theseT CNT
        but the arriving devils

        ta   au   kuru   nañha=di=re
        SBD   exist have   name=3PLP=thoseN
        have names.'

    b. *ara **bo** n-a   lao=na   ña   zemesi teo   ḡ-e   zaho*
       I   CNT RL-1EXCS go=thatN but PN   not.exist NT-3S   go
       'I went, but James didn't go.'

    c. *ara n-a   maḡoho   bla,*
       I   RL-1EXCS be.unlucky LMT
       'I had bad luck,

        *tikani **bo** n-e   korho namhari=na*
        PN   CNT RL-3S pull fish=thatN
        but Tikani caught fish.'

d. *ara manahagi au   goveo **bo**, ña buala   teo*
   I   want   exist PNLOC CNT but PNLOC not.exist
   'I like being in Goveo, but not in Buala.'

In (8.103) each of the contrasted entities is overtly expressed. However, as (8.102) illustrates, the contrasted state, event, or entity need not be expressed. It may be understood due to having been previously established in the discourse. This applies to the contextual background for the examples in (8.102). Alternatively, nonlinguistic elements of the discourse may be contrasted despite being verbally unexpressed. In (8.104) speaker B has asked speaker A to pass one of a group of mugs on a table:

(8.104)A. *hei **bo***
       who CNT
       'Which one?'

      B. *ana-hi=bo*
        thatN-EMPH=CNT
        'That one.' [pointing]

In other instances it is apparent from the marked constituent what the contrasted state, event, or entity is:

(8.105)   *ara za~zaho pile mairi **bo***
         I   RD~go side left CNT
         'I will walk at the left side.'

This principle applies to the very commonly used expression in (8.106), the Kokota equivalent of something like *OK* in English.

(8.106)   *(n-e) keli   **bo***
         RL-3S be.good CNT
         '(It's) good.'

Bo often occurs in polar interrogatives. These have the form of a declarative, but with clause-final rising intonation. The presence of the contrastive particle reinforces that confirmation is sought as to whether the state or event expressed in the clause is true, as opposed to not true.

(8.107)   *boka   hoda aǧe=nau **bo** ago*
         be.able take   go=1SGO CNT youSG
         'Can you take me there?'

In all the examples given so far, where both contrasted states, events, or entities are overtly expressed, only one is marked with *bo*. However, this is preference, not a restriction—both may be marked:

(8.108) *ara ginai aḡe **bo**, **ba** teo **bo** e=u*
I   FUT   go   CNT ALT not.exist CNT 3S=be.thus
'I will go or not, it's like that.'

The contrast expressed by *bo* is functionally close to the presentation of alternatives performed by the alternative marker *ba*. Indeed, the two may cooccur, with *ba* in its clause-initial or clause-final position, as in (8.108) and (8.109).

(8.109) *liḡomo n-e salupu **bo** **ba**, n-e toga*
PN   RL-3S pass   CNT ALT RL-3S arrive
'Did the Ligomo go past or did it stop?'

8.8.3 *Bla(u)* Limiter

The particle *blau*, and its common reduced form *bla* mark constituents at a range of levels in the syntax, and function to constrain the marked constituent in some way. The effect is similar to that of forms such as *just*, *only*, and *simply* in English. The functional and syntactic characteristics of *bla(u)* are more akin to those of *nomo* in Pijin. *Bla(u)* constrains states and events by marking either the verb complex, as in (8.110)a.–b., or the entire clause ([8.110]c.):

(8.110)a. *ginai lehe **bla** gita*
FUT   die   LMT weINC
'We are just going to die.'

b. *ḡ-e mai tafr-i=Ø **bla** ia rereo*
NT-3S come defend-TR=3SGO LMT theSG shield
'He simply came and defended with the shield

ka sebele ka sagali...
LOC axe   LOC PN
against the axe of Sagali...'

c. *ia pike mau=ḡu n-e-ke hod-i=Ø=o*
theSG piece taro=1SGP RL-3S-PFV take-TR=3SGO=thatNV

*sala ge ruruboñi **bla**...*
PN   and PN   LMT
'My piece of taro just Sala and Ruruboñi brought...'

As well as verbal clauses, *bla* also limits equative and possessive predicates:

(8.111)a. *n-e   ooe-vaka **bla**   s=ide*
  RL-3S talk-ship LMT FOC=theseR
  'These [words] are only Pijin.'

  b. *keha   pile=di=re   no-na   **bla** tagi-na*
  NSP   part=3PLP=thoseN GENP-3SGP LMT REFL-3SGP
  'Some copies will just belong to himself.'

Nominals and other arguments of any kind may also be marked with *bla*. In (8.112) *bla* marks a full NP, a pronoun, a demonstrative, and a cardinal numeral:

(8.112)a. *teo   mereseni tehi-u   ara,*
  not.exist medicine many-CRD I
  'I don't have [i.e., know] many medicines,

  *marha-pau=ana **bla** ta   tahe aḡe=i=na*
  pain-head=thatN LMT SBD tell go=3SGO=thatN
  just that headache that [I] will tell.'

  b. *gai   **bla** n-a   hage   tarai*
  weEXC LMT RL-1EXCS ascend pray
  'Only we go up to pray

  n-e=u   nau   logahaza
  RL-3S=be.thus place PNLOC
  at the place Logahaza.'

  c. *a-hi   **bla**   fa-gilagila=na k=ara*
  thisT-EMPH LMT   CS-test=3SGP   LOC=I
  'This alone will be the sign of it to me.'

  d. *kaike-u   **bla***
  one-CRD   LMT
  'Just one.'

Adjuncts may also be marked with *bla*. In (8.113)a. a prepositional phrase is marked, in (8.113)b. a contextual adjunct:

(8.113)a. *ka   sala ge   ruruboñi **bla** n-a   lehe=na ara*
  LOC PN   and PN   LMT RL-1EXCS die=thatN I
  'Just from Sala and Ruruboñi I will die.'

b. *...teo   boka=di=ña,*
not.exist be.able=3PLO=IMM
'...[they] couldn't do those [things],

*n-e=u   nafu=na   ia   parahaḡala **blau***
RL-3S=be.thus base=3SGP theSG giant   LMT
it was like that simply because [it was] a giant.'

8.8.4 *Bai(u)* Possibilitative

The particle *baiu* is postposed to constituents at various levels of the syntax, and
marks constituents as being possible, rather than fact, corresponding roughly
with the English *might, perhaps,* or *maybe*:

(8.114)a. *fufugo   a   ginai korho namhari **baiu***
tomorrow 1EXCS FUT   pull fish   PSBL
'Tomorrow I might catch fish.'

b. *...teo   ña=bla   ooe=ḡau=na   **baiu** manei e=u*
not.exist IMM=LMT talk=2PLO=thatN PSBL   he   3S=be.thus
'...maybe he hasn't told you all'

c. *...gai   a   la au   ḡilu=na   kaike-u   fata=na*
weEXC 1EXCS go exist inside=3SGP one-CRD occasion=3SGP
'We go and stay [there] for one time,

*kaike-u wiki   **bai**...*
one-CRD week PSBL
one [whole] week maybe.'

By marking something as a possibility rather than a fact the speaker is implicitly
expressing an opinion, and possibilitative marking is in fact the way opinions are
expressed in Kokota. Opinions may be expressed using the possibilitative, with a
first person subject 'be thus' clause explicitly indicating that the statement is the
view of the speaker, as in (8.115)a.. However, often no 'be thus' clause is
present. Instead, the possibilitative alone indicates that the statement is not a fact
but the opinion of the speaker, as in (8.115)b.:

(8.115)a. *e la puku   **bai**   si=ka   tepi ana   n-a=u*
3S go be.short PSBL FOC=LOC tape thatN RL-1EXCS=be.thus
'It might go short on the tape, I'm like that [i.e., ...I think].'

b. *ginai mai gudu   bla   **baiu** ka sikolu=ne   bla*
FUT   come EXHST LMT   PSBL LOC school=thisR LMT
'I think they will simply all come just to this school.'

While the opinions expressed in this way are usually those of the speaker, opinions can be attributed to others using the same construction:

(8.116)   ...ga~gato=mu=na   ago
           RD~think=2SGP=thatN   youSG
           '...that thought of yours

           n-e-ge   nhigo   tarai   baiu   n-e=u
           RL-3S-PRS   be.finished   pray   PSBL   RL-3S=be.thus
           was that prayer is finished, like that?'
           [i.e., ...did you think prayer was finished?]

This use of the possibilitative to express opinions is mirrored in the Pijin and Solomons' English used by Kokota speakers, where opinions are typically expressed as a statement introduced by *might be*....

As the above examples illustrate, *bai(u)* most commonly modifies the verb complex. However, it may also mark a complete clause:

(8.117)   ginai a   korh-i=ri   ara palu ba tilo   namhari   baiu
          FUT   1EXCS   pull-TR=3PLO   I   two ALT three   fish   PSBL
          'I might catch two or three fish.'

Bai(u) also may mark nominal or other peripheral constituents, as (8.114)c. and the first clause in (8.118) illustrate.

(8.118)   an-lau   bla baiu puku=na   bla bai   s=ana=ba
          thatN-SPC LMT PSBL be.short=thatN   LMT PSBL FOC=thatN=ALT
          'Maybe that one. I think that's short.'

8.8.5 *Ña* Immediacy particle

The particle *ña* is postposed to the constituent it marks, and assigns to a state, event or argument an immediacy in relation to either the moment of speaking, or some other specified or established moment, or some particular salience in relation to the specified or established situation. In conversational discourse the immediacy or salience is typically in relation to the moment of speaking.

(8.119)   lehe=ña gita   ia   tara=ña   n-e   mai=ne
          die=IMM weINC theSG   enemy=IMM   RL-3S come=thisR
          'We are going to die. The enemy has come.'

The immediacy may be in relation to an already established moment in the past or future, or some established moment the exact location in time of which is irrelevant:

(8.120)a. *ge   n-e   la   fa   zogu=i=ña   man-t=au=ao*
SEQ   RL-3S   go   CS   drop=3SGO=IMM   man-SBD=exist-thisT
'Then he threw down that man.

n-e-ke=u   manei kota   mai=na   t=au=ao   ge
RL-3S-PFV=be.thus   he   go.ashore   come=thatN SBD=exist-thisT   SEQ
He did that, came down,

ḡ-e-ke   mai=ña,   ḡ-e-ke   mai   ñhau...
NT-3S-PFV   come=IMM   NT-3S-PFV   come   eat
he came, he came and ate...,

b. *...fafra   mai   gu=na*
be.quick   come   CNTX=3SGP
'...come quickly, because

nhigo   n-e=u   pati   ao-hi
be.finished   RL-3S=be.thus   feast   thisT-EMPH
...come quickly, because when this feast is finished

ke   baibel stadi=ña   bo   e=u
PFV   Bible.Study=IMM   CNT   3S=be.thus
there will be Bible Study.'

c. *n-a   la fakae=ni=u   ka   tahi   are*
RL-1EXCS   go see=3SGO=CNT   LOC   sea   thoseN
'We go and see in the sea

teḡe   ine   e=u,   tana   nogoi
turtle   thisR   3S=be.thus   then   VOC
this turtle, then, man!,

age   ḡ-a   koko=ni=ña   gai   momoru   ana
SEQ   NT-1EXCS   leave=3SGO=IMM   weEXC   turtle.net   thatN
we throw down that turtle net.'

The immediacy assigned by *ña* often gives a sense equivalent to the English *still* or *yet*. Marking a preexisting state or event with *ña* indicates that the state or event still applies at the time of speaking. With the negative existential verb, *ña* indicates that the state or event has not yet happened:

(8.121) *manei teo=ña   ḡ-e   mai=u*
he   not.exist=IMM   NT-3S   come=CNT
'He hasn't come yet./He still hasn't come.'

(8.122)A. *lao   si=ago*
     go   FOC=youSG
     'You go ahead!'

B. *teo=ña*
   not.exist=IMM
   'Not yet!'

Typically *ña* marks the verb complex, as the above examples illustrate. However, it does not appear to mark entire clauses. A series of clauses in a clause chain may all be marked to indicate that the chained events occur simultaneously, as shown in the second line of (8.123):

(8.123)   *an-lau   si=ge   ḡ-a   raragoso=ña ira   hinage*
         thatN-SPC FOC=SEQ NT-1EXCS decorate=IMM thePL boat
         'That, then we decorate the boat,

         age ḡ-a   koze=ña   tavuli=ña   rehai=ña
         SEQ NT-1EXCS sing=IMM blow.conch=IMM shout=IMM
         then we sing and blow the conch and call out.

         ḡ-a=u=ña   ḡ-a   la mai=u
         NT-1EXCS=be.thus=IMM   NT-1EXCS go come=CNT
         We're like that as we are coming [home].'

As the second clause in (8.119) illustrates, *ña* may also mark an argument. This assigns a particular immediacy or saliency to the argument in relation to the moment of speaking or a previously established situation or event. This may function to assert the saliency of a participant to an event. For example, the clause in (8.124) is a typical response to exclusion of a potential participant:

(8.124)   *ara=ña*
         I=IMM
         'Me too!'

In other instances a speaker emphasizes an asserted relationship with an event or entity using *ña*. In (8.125) the speaker is claiming ownership of disputed land:

(8.125)   *ara=ña no-ḡu   nau=ro   s=aro*
         I=IMM GENP-1SGP place=theseT FOC=theseT
         'Me! These are my places.'

In addition, the immediacy particle may occur with a focused pronoun or demonstrative in the construction discussed in §8.5.2.2:

(8.126)   *n-a   bakora si=ñ̄=ara   goi*
         RL-1EXCS be.cut FOC=IMM=I VOC
         'I've been cut, man!'

In other instances the immediacy or saliency of the marked argument is in relation to the time or place of speaking. In (8.127), for example, the relationship between the temporal location marked with *ña* and the moment of speaking is emphasized as a way of expressing a desire for the event to occur soon:

(8.127) *ginai   saigona=ña, kaike saigona=ña*
         todayIRR evening=IMM one   evening=IMM
         'This evening, one evening,

         ta=ke   hoda toke=ḡai=na   gai-palu   tati
         SBD=PFV   take   arrive=1EXCO=thatN weEXC-two mother&baby
         that [you] will take back we two, mother and baby.'

8.8.6 *Fea* 'initiality'

The particle *fea* indicates that the referent of the marked constituent must hold initially in relation to some other entity or event. The form typically marks the verb complex, and may indicate that the event will occur before any other events:

(8.128)a. *ke   pulo **fea** ara*
          PFV return INIT I
          'I'll go back first.'

       b. *ara fa kraño=ri   **fea** no-ḡu   pohe   ide*
          I   CS be.dry=3PLO INIT GENP-1SGP clothes theseR
          'I am drying my clothes first.'

In this sense it may cooccur with the verb *kulu/kusu* 'be first':

(8.129) *...ge kulu   friñhe=ni   **fea** ia   suḡa*
         SEQ be.first work=3SGO INIT theSG house
         '...then first they build the house'

The form occurs very commonly with individual verbs in imperative clauses, emphasizing that the speaker wants the action to occur immediately:

(8.130)a. *tuku   **fea***
          wait   INIT
          '[Just] wait [here]!'

       b. *zaho **fea***
          go   INIT
          'Out of the way!'

Fea also may indicate that the marked event will occur before a specified subsequent event:

(8.131) *au* *fea* *gau* *da* *zuke=ri*
exist INIT youPL 1INCS seek=3PLO
'Stay [here] first, [then] we will go and look for them.'

In this sense it frequently cooccurs with the sequencer *ge*:

(8.132) *gita* *da-ke* *turi* *fea,* *ge* *da* *lao* *friñhe=ña*
weINC 1INCS-PFV tell INIT SEQ 1INCS go work=IMM
'We talked first, then worked.'

The fact that the form typically marks the verb complex suggests that it is a post-core adverbial modifier. However, it is not limited to marking verb complexes, but may also mark other constituent types, such as a temporal locative:

(8.133) *ginai* *fea* *da* *toi=ña*
todayIRR INIT 1INCS cook=IMM
'[Later] today first [and then] we will cook.'

When marking a verb complex *fea* typically follows other constituent modifiers:

(8.134)a. *fa* *gigila=ni* *bla* *fea*
CS test=3SGO LMT INIT
'[Let's] just try it first.'

b. *ara* *lao* *bo* *fea*
I go CNT INIT
'I'll go first instead.'

8.8.7 The particle *la*

Like the limiter *bla(u)*, the particle *la* appears to mark the verb complex (as in [8.135]a.–b.) and other predicate types (for example, [8.135]c.), as well as various kinds of arguments and adjuncts (for example, [8.135]d.).

(8.135)a. *maḡra* *t=au=la* *manei*
fight SBD=exist=CND he
'If there is a fight,

kame=ḡu *n-e* *au=de* *bla* *la* *bo...*
hand=1SGP RL-3S exist=theseR LMT ?? CNT
my hands are here...'

b. ...*e*   *au=i*   ***la bla***   *keha*
   3S   exist=3SGO ?? LMT   NSP
   '...they have something

   ta   *fakilo=ni*   *tritmenti   ka=ia*   *ooe-vaka*
   SBD   name(V)=3SGO   treatment LOC=theSG talk-ship
   that [they] call treatment in Pijin.'

c. *visi   ḡ-e-la*   *heve*   ***la ba...***
   play NT-3S-go   what   ?? ALT
   'A game that goes how...?'

d. *ka*   *tema=na* ***la bla***   *n-e*   *faroh-i=Ø=na*   *sala   manei.*
   LOC   hut=thatN ?? LMT RL-3S smite-TR=3SGO=thatN PN   he
   'At that small house he killed Sala.'

In addition, the particle occurs in the focus construction discussed in §8.5.2.2:

(8.136)   *fafra*   *si=gau-palu*   *ba,*   *ginai   ḡrugu*   *si=**la**=ine*
     be.quick   FOC=youPL-two   ALT FUT   be.dark   FOC=??=thisR
     'Hurry up, you two, or this [day] will get dark.'

Apart from this focus construction, *la* appears to normally cooccur with other constituent modifiers, as (8.135) illustrates.

This particle occurs infrequently, and its function is not clear. The form *la* also functions as a conditional marker; however, the constituent modifying behavior illustrated in (8.135) and (8.136) does not seem to have any conditional sense, suggesting that the relationship between the conditional marker and constituent modifier is simple homophony. It seems more plausible that a relationship exists between this constituent modifier and the deictic specifying suffix *-lau* discussed in §3.1.4.2, paralleling the frequent use of the limiter *bla(u)* with pronouns and determiners. This too, however, remains unclear.

8.9 Vocative particle *nogoi ~ goi*

The particle *nogoi ~ goi* occurs with an emphatic vocative function. It is not vocative in the sense of being a term of address, although speakers regard it as "meaning" 'you' (and it is derived from an earlier form of the 2SG pronoun, and thus cognate with synchronic *ago*). However, its synchronic function is to strongly engage the listener in what the speaker is saying. In narratives and discourse declarative clauses it occurs when the speaker is excited or agitated by what he or she saying, and occurs with increasing frequency commensurate with the level of excitement or agitation. In narratives this typically occurs at the most exciting parts of the story, when a text may become littered with the particle.

(8.137)   *ka   tema=na la bla n-e   faroh-i=Ø=na*   *sala manei*
             LOC hut=thatN ?? LMT RL-3S smite-TR=3SGO=thatN PN   he
             'At that small house he killed Sala.

             *tana **nogoi** age ḡ-e   tetu=ña   manei ge*
             then   VOC SEQ NT-3S stand=IMM he   SEQ
             Then, man!, he stood up and

             ***nogoi** ḡ-e   kaike maḡra*
             VOC NT-3S one   fight
             he fought everyone [and],

             ***nogoi** ḡ-e   fa-rogoho fa teo=ri   mane*
             VOC NT-3S CS-smite CS not.exist=3PLO man
             man!, he killed all [the men]

             n-e-ke   au=ro   ka ḡilu=na   tema=na e=u
             RL-3S-PFV exist=thoseNV LOC inside=3SGP hut=thatN 3S=be.thus
             who were inside the small house.'

The particle also occurs commonly in imperatives.

(8.138)   *fa puku~puku=ri   bla   ago   e=u   bla **goi**...*
             CS RD~be.short=3PLO LMT   yousG 3s=be.thus LMT VOC
             'You make it short, man!...'

Although the shorter form of the particle shown in (8.138) occurs in an imperative and the longer form in (8.137) in declarative clauses, there is, in fact, no functional distinction between the two. Most individual speakers use both, although it appears that younger speakers display a higher proportionate use of the shorter form than older speakers.

The particle normally occurs at clause boundaries. The collocation of the particle with the temporal marker *tana*, shown in line 2 of (8.137), is particularly common. Although it occurs at the beginning or end of clauses, it may follow extraclausal material, such as recapping constituents:

(8.139)   *an=bla   **nogoi***
             thatN=LMT VOC
             'That, man!,

             n-e-ge   fa-roho   fa teo=ri   are   bla
             RL-3S-PRS CS-smite CS not.exist=3PLO thoseN LMT
             [and] he killed them all.'

CHAPTER 9: IMPERATIVES AND INTERROGATION

9.1 Imperative clauses

Imperative clauses are employed for commands, exhortations, and requests. No formal marker of second person imperative clauses exists. The imperative clause has normal declarative clause structure, with the restrictions that the clause must be in irrealis mood, no preverbal topicalized argument may occur, and only second person or first inclusive subjects are possible. Imperatives are typically distinguishable from declaratives by clause-final rising-falling intonation.

9.1.1 Positive imperatives

As with positive irrealis declaratives, the subject-indexed particle may occur in positive imperatives (as in [9.1]a.), but is typically omitted ([9.1]b.):

(9.1) a. *o la ka=ni=n̄a*   *tagi-mi*
           2S go look=3SGO=IMM   REFL-2PLP
           'Go and look at him yourselves!'

       b. *ke   mai   ago*
          PFV   come   youSG
          'You come here!'

The subject may be overtly expressed, as in (9.1), but is often unstated:

(9.2)   *zaho   fea*
         go   INIT
         'Go away!'

First inclusive imperatives also have the form of an irrealis declarative clause:

(9.3)   *da   āge kae=di=u*
         1INCS   go   see=3PLO=CNT
         'Let's go and see

         hae   ta   au=re   n-e   hure=ri   hinage=re   maneri
         where SBD   exist=thoseN RL-3S   carry=3PLO   boat=thoseN   they
         where they carried the boats!'

However, first inclusive imperatives usually open with the special particle *aria*:

(9.4)   ***aria***   *d-āge   nhura=i   fitupoḡu*
         1INC.IMP   1INCS-go   destroy=3SGO   PNLOC
         'Let's go and destroy Fitupoḡu!'

As with second person, first inclusive imperative subjects may be overtly stated.

Some aspect and tense modifiers may occur in imperative clauses. The continuous aspect enclitic occurs commonly with first inclusive imperatives, as (9.3) illustrates, though it is not obligatory. The perfective marker and present tense marker also occur:

(9.5) a. *t=au*   *la*   *aria*   *da-ke*   *pulo*
              SBD=exist CND 1INC.IMP 1INCS-PFV return
              'If that's so then let's go back!'

      b. *o-ge*   *lao* *ge* *tahe* *la=ri*   *bla*
          2S-PRS go   and tell   go=3PLO LMT
          'Just tell some more [stories] [now]!'

The use of present tense with irrealis modality, discussed in §7.5.2.8, gives the sense that the event will happen immediately. In (9.5)b. the use of present tense occurs because the speaker wants the addressee to tell further stories straight away. The future tense marker *ginai* appears not to occur in imperative clauses.

9.1.2 Negative imperatives

Kokota has two negative constructions (see §8.7). One employs the negative particle *ti*, the other is a subordinating construction with the negative existential verb *teo*. Both constructions occur in second person negative imperatives:

(9.6) a. *o-ti*   *lao* *sare*   *ḡilu*
          2S-NEG go   thereP inside
          'Don't go in there!'

      b. *teo*   *ḡ-o*   *mai* *ago*
          not.exist NT-2S come youSG
          'Don't you come!'

First inclusive irrealis negative imperatives appear to allow only the subordinating construction, as in (9.7)a. Clauses with the negative particle, as in (9.7)b., appear not to permit an imperative interpretation:

(9.7) a. *teo*   *ḡe-da*   *aḡe=u*
          not.exist NT-1INCS go=CNT
          'Let's not go!'

      b. *da-ti*   *teteḡu=ña*   *gita* *goinode*
          1INCS-NEG go.fishing=IMM weINC today
          'We won't go fishing today.'

9.1.3 Politeness in imperatives

No specific politeness or respect marker exists comparable to English *please*. However, where a second person pronoun subject is overtly realized it may be marked with the focus marker *si*. The absence of the focus marker in this situation, as in (9.6)b., is not regarded as respectful (see discussion in §8.5.2.4.).

9.2 Interrogation

Interrogative clauses in Kokota fall into three distinct types, on both formal and functional grounds:

(9.8)   a. Polar and option interrogatives—morphologically and syntactically identical to declarative clauses.
       b. Constituent interrogatives—seek details of an event or its participants using interrogative proforms.
       c. Contextual interrogatives—'how' and 'why' questions, involving the event expressed as a clause separate to the interrogative form.

9.2.1 Polar and option interrogatives

Polar interrogatives have the structure of a declarative clause, but are distinguished from declaratives by clause-final rising intonation, in contrast with the falling intonation of declarative clauses. Thus the clauses in (9.9) are syntactically identical to declaratives:

(9.9) a. *n-e   fa mai=ni*   ***bo***   *kodere maneko ine*
         RL-3S CS come=3SGO CNT PN   pawpaw thisR
         'Did Kodere bring this pawpaw?'

      b. *boka   hoda age=nau **bo**   ago*
         be.able take   go=1SGO CNT yousG
         'Can you take me there?'

No particles exist that mark only interrogation. However, both the contrastive marker *bo* and the alternative marker *ba* (see §8.8.1 and §8.8.2), occur commonly in polar interrogatives, as illustrated in (9.9) and (9.10) respectively.

(9.10)   *n-e-ge*   *tor-i=Ø*   ***b=ana***   *manei*
           RL-3S-PRS be.open-TR=3SGO ALT=thatN he
           'Has he opened that?'

Both the contrastive and alternative markers make explicit the existence of states or events other than that expressed by the marked clause, and emphasize the potential for polarity, and thus the interrogative nature of these clauses.

However, both also occur in declaratives, and are not obligatory in polar interrogatives:

(9.11)   *n-e-ge*   *fa* *tor-i=Ø*   *manei a-hi*
        RL-3S-PRS CS be.open-TR=3SGO he   thisT-EMPH
        'Has he opened this?'

This illustrates that it is crucially the intonation pattern that marks polar interrogatives, not any morphosyntactic phenomena. All the examples in (9.9) to (9.11) could be declarative clauses with only an intonational change.

Not only full clauses may function as polar interrogatives. Any constituent may be presented for confirmation using rising intonation. In (9.12) a personal name alone is given rising intonation, thereby giving it an interrogative sense—the identity of the individual is presented for confirmation:

(9.12)   *...ḡ-e* *triki=ña*   *mane* *n-e=u,*   *he=ba=ia,*   ***tikilave***
        NT-3S trick=IMM man RL-3S=be.thus who=ALT=PRO PN
        '...a man played a trick. Who [was it]? [Was it] Tikilave?'

Option interrogatives resemble polar interrogatives in that they also have the syntactic structure of a declarative clause. Functional similarities also exist. Neither elicit greater detail about the nature of a state or event or its participants, or the state or event's context. Polar interrogatives present a state or event, in a sense a single alternative, and seek confirmation of the veracity of the presented state or event. Option interrogatives present more than one alternative and seek identification of which alternative applies:

(9.13)   *sisiḡa* *e* *ḡauai* ***ba*** *namo*
        PNLOC 3S be.far ALT be.near
        'Is Sisiḡa near or far?'

As with polar interrogatives, intonation alone distinguishes an interrogative from a declarative reading. With falling intonation (9.13) would be declarative.

In option interrogatives at least the first option, sometimes both, are marked with the alternative marker *ba*, as in (9.13). The contrastive marker may also be present, although this is uncommon:

(9.14)   *liḡomo* *n-e* *salupu* ***bo*** ***ba,*** *n-e*   *toga*
        PN   RL-3S pass   CNT ALT   RL-3S arrive
        'Did the Ligomo [a ship] go past or did it stop?'

The alternatives presented in an option clause may be expressed as two predicates within a single clause, as in (9.13), or as separate clauses, as in (9.14).

9.2.2 Constituent interrogatives

Constituent interrogatives seek information about an event or state or its participants beyond confirming a proposition or selecting an option. These are of two functional types: those seeking the identity of a participant or nature of a state or event; and those seeking more information about an established participant, state, or event. They involve the following interrogative proforms:[61]

(9.15) a. *heve*   'what'
     b. *hei*   'who'
     c. *hae*   'where'
     d. *niha=o*   'when? (realis)'
     e. *niha=na* 'when? (irrealis)'
     f. *niha*   'how many/much?'

9.2.2.1 Identity interrogation

The locative interrogatives *niha-* 'when?' and *hae* 'where' function to inquire about the identity of spatial and temporal locations. All other participants are referred to by the interrogative proforms, *hei* 'who' and *heve* 'what'.

9.2.2.1.1 *Hei* 'who'

The proform *hei* has as its referent a participant whose identity is in question. Crucially, the participant referred to must be human. The participant in question may function as any core argument—actor, intransitive subject, or object:

(9.16) a. **hei** *n-e*   *ravi=nau=na*   *ka* *bakla=na*
       who RL-3S hide.from=1SGO=thatN LOC flat.root=thatN
       'Who is hiding from me in the roots?'

     b. *n-e=u*   **hei**
       RL-3S=be.thus who
       'Who was thus?' [i.e., 'Who said that?']

     c. **hei** *bili* *n-e*   *fakae=ni=na*
       who PN   RL-3S see=3SGO=thatN
       'Who did Billy see?'

It is not clear whether *hei* may function as an incorporated interrogative object (as *heve* 'what' may). Possibly because human objects are rarely generic, no examples of *hei* incorporation occur in the corpus.

---

[61] *Hae* 'where', *hei* 'who', and *heve* 'what' are not glossed with question marks as they also have non-interrogative functions, meaning 'wherever', 'whoever', and 'whatever'.

The participant in question may also function clausally as an adjunct, as the complement of the preposition *ka* or the associative noun *tareme-* 'with':

(9.17) a. *t=au=ne*   *e*   *tore=i*   ***ka***   ***hei***   *manei*
       SBD=exist=thisR 3S ask=3SGO   LOC who   he
       'This [question] he will ask to whom?'

     b. ***ka***   ***hei***   *n-o-ke*   *hod-i=ri=re*   *ago*   *sileni*   *are*
        LOC who   RL-2S-PFV take-TR=3PLO=thoseN   youSG money   thoseN
        'Who did you get that money from?'

     c. *manei*   *n-e*   *lao*   *buala*   ***tareme=na hei***
        he   RL-3S go   PNLOC   with=3SGP who
        'Who did he go to Buala with?'

The interrogative proform may occur in two possible positions in the clause. It may occur clause-initially, as in (9.16)a. and c., and (9.17)b. It may occur in this position even when a topicalized preverbal argument is also present, as (9.16)c. shows. When the interrogative proform occurs clause-initially, the verb complex obligatorily carries a demonstrative enclitic from the 'nearby' category. The proform may also occur in the unmarked clause position of the referent argument, as in (9.16)b. and (9.17)a. and c. When in this position no demonstrative enclitic occurs.

Realis interrogative clauses always have the main clause structure outlined above. Irrealis interrogatives may also have this structure, as (9.17)a. shows. However, irrealis interrogatives may also be expressed as an equative construction in which the interrogative proform is the subject, with a subordinate clause as predicate. This gives a pragmatically marked construction functionally somewhat akin to an English pseudo-cleft construction:

(9.18)   ***hei***   *ta*   *kulu*   *mhoko=na*   *ka*   *gita-palu*
         who   SBD   be.first   sit=thatN   LOC   weINC-two
         'Who [is it] that will sit first out of us two?'

In this construction the predicate has the formal characteristics dictated by its status as a subordinate clause, rather than those otherwise required in an interrogative main clause predicate.

The proform may also function as subject of an ordinary equative construction with a nominal predicate:

(9.19)   ***hei***   *nañha=mu=na*   *ago*
         who   name=2SGP=thatN   youSG
         'What is your name?'

9.2.2.1.2 *Heve* 'what' (referring to participants)

One function of *heve* 'what' is to act as interrogative proform for nonhuman participants. In this function *heve* parallels *hei*, differing only in the nonhuman status of the referent. As with *hei*, *heve* can stand for any core argument:

(9.20) a. **heve**   *n-e-ke*   *kati=nigo=na*   *ago*
          what   RL-3S-PFV   bite=2SGO=thatN   youSG
          'What bit you?'

     b. **heve**   *n-e*   *zogu=na*
          what   RL-3S   drop=thatN
          'What fell?'

     c. **heve**   *manei*   *n-e-ke*   *toḡla=i=na*
          what   he   RL-3S-PFV   chase=3SGO=thatN
          'What did he chase?'

Heve may occur as an incorporated interrogative object. In (9.21) the verb is in its intransitive form, with no object-indexing present. The interrogative proform is located in the incorporated object position:

(9.21)   *maneri*   *n-e*   *gorha*   **heve**
          they   RL-3S   paddle   what
          'What did they paddle?'

Because specific temporal and spatial locative interrogatives exist, *heve* occurs infrequently as an adjunct. However, such occurrences are possible, with *heve* functioning as the complement of the preposition *ka*. Often *heve* obliques are interpreted as non-locative adjuncts such as instruments:

(9.22)   *ka*   **heve**   *n-o-ke*   *fad-i=Ø=na*   *ago*   *memeha=na*
          LOC   what   RL-2S-PFV   shoot-TR=3SGO=thatN   youSG   bird=thatN
          'What did you shoot the bird with?'

If a spatial locative is intended, it is often a marked kind of location. In (9.23), for example, it is not the location in the village where the hitting happened, but the location on the dog's body:

(9.23)   *ka*   **heve=na**   *n-e*   *faroh-i=Ø=na*
          LOC   what=thatN   RL-3S   strike-TR=3SGO=thatN

          suli=na   *mheke=na*
          child=thatN   dog=thatN
          'Where [on its body] did that child hit that dog?'

Alternatively, a specific kind of location may be intended. In (9.24), for example, the anticipated answer is not a broad kind of a location (such as 'in Goveo'), but something like 'on the table' or 'in that room', responses that will involve a prepositional phrase:

(9.24)　　*ka　heve=o*　　　*n-e　　lisa=i=na*　　　　*manei*
　　　　　　LOC　what=thatNV　RL-3S　put=3SGO=thatN　he
　　　　　　'Where did he put

　　　　　　no-ḡu　　　　*vilai　ana*
　　　　　　GENP-1SGP　knife　thatN
　　　　　　that knife of mine?'

The more literal translation of (9.24) would be something like 'on/in that what, did he put...'. When *heve* is used with this spatial locative sense it typically carries a cliticized demonstrative, as in these examples.

Like *hei*, *heve* may occur clause-initially (including before a preverbal argument), or it may occur in the referent argument's unmarked clause position. Also as with *hei*, when the proform occurs clause-initially the verb complex is marked with a demonstrative enclitic, but when the proform occurs in its unmarked position there is no verb complex enclitic.

Again, irrealis interrogatives may be expressed by an equative construction in which the interrogative proform is the subject of a subordinate clause:

(9.25)　　*heve　ta　friñhe=i=na*　　　*ago*
　　　　　　what　SBD　work=3SGO=thatN　youSG
　　　　　　'What [is it] that you will be doing?'

Heve also occurs as the subject of an equative clause with a nominal predicate:

(9.26)　　*heve　b=ana*
　　　　　　what　ALT=thatN
　　　　　　'What's that?'

9.2.2.1.3 *Niha-* 'when'

The form *niha-* is used to form questions about the temporal location of the event expressed in the clause. Formally and conceptually this interrogative proform is interesting in that it must occur with one of two cliticized demonstratives: =na 'that (nearby)', and =o 'that (non-visible)', which assign irrealis and realis status respectively to the temporal location inquired about.

In an interrogative verbal main clause the irrealis 'when' must be followed by the sequencing particle *ge*. In addition, the verb complex must be marked with the immediacy particle *ña*:

(9.27) a. ***niha=na   ge   da   lao=ña   buala***
       when=thatN SEQ 1INCS go=IMM PNLOC
       'When will we go to Buala?'

    b. ***niha=na   ge   ḡ-e   fa-lehe=i=ña   manei   zora   ana***
        when=thatN SEQ NT-3S CS-die=3SGO=IMM he   pig   thatN
        'When will he kill the pig?'

The cliticization of the demonstrative =*na* is obligatory—the independent demonstrative marking *niha ana is impossible.

The realis interrogative occurs without the sequencer. The verb does not carry the immediacy particle, but is obligatorily marked with a 'nearby' category demonstrative enclitic (following the pattern discussed in §9.2.2.1.1):

(9.28) a. ***niha=o   manei n-e-ke   fad-i=Ø=na   memeha=na***
       when=thatNV he   RL-3S-PFV shoot-TR=3SGO=thatN bird=thatN
       'When did he shoot that bird?'

    b. ***niha=o   n-e-ke   posa=re   ḡlepo are***
        when=thatNV RL-3S-PFV emerge=thoseN thing thoseN
        'When did those things occur?'

The temporal interrogative proform always occurs clause-initially. As with *hei* and *heve*, there is no restriction on another argument occurring in topicalized preverbal position, as (9.28)a. illustrates.

Temporal interrogatives may be the subject of an equative construction in which the event inquired about is expressed as a subordinate clause. This construction does not occur commonly, and is a way of foregrounding the time inquired about.

(9.29)   ***niha=na   ta   mai=na   liḡomo***
        when=thatN SBD come=thatN PN
        'When [is it] that the Ligomo will come?'

In this equative construction the irrealis interrogative does not require the sequencer, and the predicate is marked in ways determined by its status within a subordinate clause, rather than in keeping with the interrogative clause predicate restrictions discussed above.

The interrogative particle itself functions as a nonverbal predicate in the standard form of asking the time, a construction involving an equative clause:

(9.30)　　*tanhi*　**niha=o**
　　　　　time　when=thatNV
　　　　　'The time [is] when?' [i.e., 'What's the time?']

The interrogative form used in this construction requires the demonstrative *=o*. Since the question relates to the moment of speaking it illustrates that the interrogative *nihao* is realis, and does not simply refer to past locations in time.

9.2.2.1.4 *Hae* 'where'

Spatial locative interrogation is expressed by *hae* 'where', which typically occurs clause-initially:

(9.31)　　**hae**　*n-o-ke*　　*doli=na*　　　*ago*
　　　　　where　RL-2S-PFV　be.alive=thatN　youSG
　　　　　'Where were you born?'

When the spatial interrogative *hae* is clause-initial, the verb complex must be marked with a 'nearby' category demonstrative enclitic, as in (9.31). Less commonly, *hae* may occur in the unmarked clause position of the locative adjunct it replaces. In that construction the demonstrative enclitic is not present:

(9.32)　　*mane=na*　*n-e*　*gorha*　*la*　**hae**
　　　　　man=thatN　RL-3S　paddle　go　where
　　　　　'Where is that man paddling to?'

Hae occurs in this unmarked position in the standard Kokota greeting:

(9.33)　　*lao*　**hae**　*(ago)*
　　　　　go　where　youSG
　　　　　'Where are you going?'

The proform replaces an entire locative adjunct, including prepositional phrases. Consequently it does not function as the complement of the preposition, as in (9.34)a. However, spatial locative interrogation may be performed by a PP with *heve* 'what' as the prepositional complement, as in (9.34)b.

(9.34) a.　***ka hae n-o-ke doli=na ago***　　　'At where were you born?'

　　　　b.　**ka**　**heve=o**　　*n-e*　*lisa=i=na*　　　*manei ia*　　*vilai*
　　　　　　LOC　what=thatNV　RL-3S　put=3SGO=thatN　he　　theSG　knife
　　　　　　'At what [location] [i.e., where] did he put the knife?'

In this construction it is the preposition that expresses the locative component of the interrogation.

In addition to its simple form, *hae* also forms a single complex interrogative proform with the deictic locative *sara* 'there (distal)':

(9.35)   ***sara***   ***hae***   *manei n-e-ke*   *toḡla=i=na*   *ia*   *zora*
          thereD   where he   RL-3S-PFV   chase=3SGO=thatN theSG   pig
          'Where did he chase the pig?'

The example in (9.35) also illustrates that the spatial locative interrogative proform may occur in clause-initial position when a topicalized preverbal argument is also present.

Hae is used to inquire about spatial locations with any function in the clause. Thus in (9.31) *hae* refers to the location at which an event took place. In (9.32) it refers to a goal. The clause in (9.35) is ambiguous as to whether it refers to a location or a goal (i.e., 'in what location did he chase the pig' versus 'where did he chase the pig to'). The form may equally be used to refer to sources:

(9.36)   ***hae***   *n-o-ke*   *klisu*   *mai=na*   *gau*
          where RL-2S-PFV   start   come=thatN   youPL
          'Where did you start [i.e., come] from?'

With irrealis events, questions of spatial location are typically formed using an equative construction in which the interrogative proform is the subject of a clause, the predicate of which is a subordinated clause. This applies equally to events that are irrealis because they have yet to occur, and those that are irrealis because they are habitual:

(9.37) a.   ***hae***   *ta*   *lao-n=ago*
           where   SBD   go=thatN=youSG
           'Where [is it] that you will go?'

       b.   ***hae***   *ta*   *uu=na*   *ago*
           where   SBD   exist=thatN   youSG
           'Where [is it] that you live?'

An equative construction also occurs with nominal predicates identifying the participant whose location is sought:

(9.38)   ***hae***   *belama*
          where   PN
          'Where [is] Belama?'

9.2.2.2 Event identification

In addition to interrogatives questioning the identity of participants in a predication, there are others that inquire about the identity of the state or event itself. Just as participant interrogation involves replacing the relevant argument with a proform, in event interrogation the predicate itself is replaced with an interrogative. However, the entire predicate is not replaced, as the modal/subject particle remains expressed:

(9.39) a. **n-e   heve   ia   zora**
      RL-3S   what   theSG pig
      'What did the pig do?'/'What happened to the pig?'

   b. **n-e   heve   ia   ḡrui**
      RL-3S   what   theSG garden
      'What happened to/in the garden?'

As *heve* has no predicate argument structure, no grammatical relation or semantic role is assigned to an overtly expressed argument in this construction. Thus in (9.39)a. the sole argument is animate and therefore may be an actor or an unergative subject. Consequently the question is interpretable as an inquiry about the actions of the pig, as well as about what may have happened to it (in which it is potentially the undergoer of the event). As most states and qualities are expressed by stative verbs in Kokota, the question is also interpretable as an inquiry about the pig's state or what qualities may be ascribed to it (in which case the overt argument would be an unaccusative subject). In (9.39)b. the overt argument is one that most commonly occurs as a location, or less commonly as an object. Consequently those are the argument relations that would normally inform the interpretation of the question, with the state or quality of the participant a further possible reading. The crucial point is that the absence of a predicate argument structure leaves entirely open the relations and roles of any overt argument.

No argument need be expressed, however. This construction occurs commonly with no argument as a general event inquiry:

(9.40)   *n-e   heve*
       RL-3S   what
       'What happened?'

As well as a general event inquiry, this commonly occurs as a generalized response to any approach, functionally equivalent to English questions like *what do you want?*. (The use of *ehe* 'yes' is not an appropriate response to an approach, in the way that *yes?* is in English.) The use of this construction as a response to a conversational opening often involves a reduction of the clause to the interrogative alone, as in (9.41)a. An equally common alternative involves *heve* as the subject of *=u* 'be thus', as in (9.41)b.

(9.41) a. *heve*
what
'What [is it]?'

b. *heve=u*
what=be.thus
'What is it?'/'How is it?'

The use of *heve* as a proform replacing the predicate occurs in another common conversational opener:

(9.42)   *n-o   heve   bo   ago*
RL-2S what   CNT   youSG
'How are you?'

Not all event interrogation involves an interrogative proform replacing the predicate, however. The function is often performed instead by what is formally participant interrogation. In this strategy the event in question is expressed as an argument, typically the complement of the verb *friñhe* 'work':

(9.43)   *heve   n-o-ke   friñhe=i=na   ago*
what   RL-2S-PFV   work=3SGO-thaN   youSG
'What were you doing?'

9.2.2.3 Supplementary detail interrogation

Certain interrogative constructions are used to seek further information about a participant or state or event, the general identity or nature of which is already established. There are three kinds of such questions: those seeking to identify the specific relevant member or subclass of an established class of entities ('which' questions, with the interrogative proform *heve*); those seeking to identify the manner in which an established event takes place (also with *heve*); and those seeking to identify the number or quantity of an established entity (using *niha* 'how many/much').

9.2.2.3.1 *Heve* 'which' questions

Questions that seek to identify the specific identity of a member or subclass of a class of entities have the interrogative proform *heve* 'what' in post-head core modifier position in a NP with the relevant nominal as head, as in speaker B's question in (9.44).

(9.44) A. *...marha-pau   ine,   a   iusi=ni   gai   ḡazu*
            pain-head   thisR   1EXCS   use=3SGO   weEXC   wood
            '...this headache, we use a tree.'

      B. **ḡazu heve** *ba=ia*
         wood what ALT=PRO
         'Which tree?'

The presence of the alternative marker *ba* in (9.44) is typical in questions of this kind, but not obligatory. Participants of any kind may be questioned in this way, including adjuncts:

(9.45)   ***ka nare heve*** *ta   lao=na   buala*
         LOC day   what SBD go=thatN PNLOC
         'On which day [is it] that [you] will go to Buala?'

Questions of this kind may be used to identify specific class-members, as in (9.45), where a unique date is sought. They are also used to identify a subclass, as in (9.44), where the information sought is the species of tree used, not the specific instantiation of that species.

Heve is used most commonly to specify participants. However, it may also be used to seek specification of a predicate. With this function it occurs in immediate post-head adverbial modifier position. Here it is the specific illness that is in question:

(9.46) A. *ara n-a   foḡra=nau*
         I   RL-1EXCS be.sick=1SGO
         'I'm sick.'

      B. *n-o   foḡra **heve***
         RL-2S be.sick what
         'What are you sick with?'

9.2.2.3.2 *Gela heve* 'in what manner/to what extent' questions

Questions of manner and extent may be formed using a construction in which a clause-initial verb is modified by a subordinate clause with the predicate *ḡ-e-la* (the neutral modal particle plus 'go') and *heve* as its complement. When the verb modified is stative the clause questions the extent to which the state applies:

(9.47) a. *dou   **ḡ-e-la**   **heve**   are   e=u*
         be.big NT-3S-go what thoseN 3S=be.thus
         'How big were they?'[lit. 'Those are/were big like what?']

b. *mañava*   *ḡ-e-la*   **heve**
   be.hot   NT-3S-go   what
   'How hot?' [lit. 'Hot like what?']

When it occurs with a dynamic verb it is the manner in which the event takes place that is in question:

(9.48) a. *lao*   *ḡ-e-la*   **heve**   *sara*   *buala*
   go   NT-3S-go   what   thereD   PNLOC
   'How [i.e., by what means of travel] will you get to Buala?'

b. *tetēḡu*   *ḡ-e-la*   **heve**
   fish(V)   NT-3S-go   what
   'How [i.e., by what fishing method] did you fish?'

In the *ḡ-e-la heve* construction the verb itself is the subject of the *ḡ-e-la* predicate. The verb alone fulfills this function and not a verb complex, so no modal/subject particle precedes the verb and no other verb complex elements occur. Nor can the verb by accompanied by a complement or adjunct.

This is not the only strategy available for manner interrogation, however. Two constructions with the 'be thus' verb *=u* also occur (discussed in §9.2.3.1).

9.2.2.3.3 *Niha* 'how many/much' questions

In inquiries about the quantity of a participant the interrogative proform *niha* 'how many/much' occurs in pre-head quantifier position:

(9.49) a. *niha*   *mane* *n-e-ke*   *toḡla=i=na*   *zora ine*
   how.many   man   RL-3S-PFV   chase=3SGO=thatN   pig   thisR
   'How many men chased the pig?'

b. *niha*   *maneko*   *n-e*   *hod-i=ri=re*   *manei*
   how.many   pawpaw   RL-3S   take-TR=3PLO=thoseN   he
   'How many pawpaw has he brought?'

Any participant type may be modified in this way. Typically the interrogative is located clause-initially, and as with participant interrogation (discussed above), this requires a postverbal demonstrative enclitic. The exception to this is where the quantity in question is not of a participant, but of the event itself. In this case the construction is formally identical to that for questions of participant quantity, except that the nominal modified by *niha* must be *fata* 'occasion', and that there is no postverbal demonstrative enclitic:

CHAPTER 9

(9.50) **niha**   **fata**   *lao   ago   buala*
        how.many   occasion go   youSG PNLOC
        'How many times did you go to Buala?'

With participant quantity, although the relevant interrogative is typically located clause-initially, it may occur in the unmarked clause position for that argument or adjunct. Again, as with participant interrogation, this does not require a postverbal demonstrative enclitic:

(9.51) a. *mane-dou   ana   n-e   turi-tufa   turi=ri*   **niha**   **suli**
          man-be.big   thatN RL-3S tell-affect tell=3PLO how.many children
          'That chief told stories [to] how many children?'

      b. *n-e   faroh-i=Ø   mheke=na ka=niha*   *ḡazu*
         RL-3S strike-TR=3SGO dog=thatN LOC=how.many   wood
         'They hit the dog with how many sticks?'

As with other interrogative types, the interrogative form, in this case with its nominal head, may function as the subject of an equative clause. In (9.52) the predicate is *ago* 'youSG':

(9.52) **niha**   *komhu=mu=na   ago*
        how.many   year=2SGP=thatN youSG
        'How old are you?' [lit. 'How many years [are] you?']

9.2.3 Contextual interrogation

Functionally, two types of context interrogatives exist: manner ('how') questions and cause ('why') questions. Both involve subordinating constructions.

9.2.3.1 Manner questions

Three strategies exist in the language for forming questions regarding the manner in which an event took place. One, also an interrogative of extent, is discussed in §9.2.2.2.2. The remaining two strategies require the verb *=u* 'be thus'. In one of these the interrogative proform *heve* 'what' occurs as the subject of *=u*, with the event in question expressed as a subordinate clause:

(9.53) **heve** *n-e=u*   [*meri tarai=na*
        what   RL-3S=be.thus PN   pray=thatN
        'How did Mary pray

        ka=man   ta   foḡra=na=o]
        LOC=man   SBD   be.sick=3SGP=thatNV
        for the man who is sick?' [lit. 'What was so, that Mary prayed...']

In this construction the 'be thus' main clause always occurs sentence-initially. The subordinate clause is of the type that has no modal/subject particle and no subordinating particle. (The *ta* subordinator in [9.53] heads a relative clause on the adjunct of a subordinate event clause.) The structure of the subordinate clause is dictated by the constraints on a subordinate clause of this type.

In the second manner interrogative constructions, two clauses are coordinated, and the sequencer *ge* is present. The form *ḡ-e-la heve* 'in what manner' (lit. 'go what') occurs in an initial clause that is relatively bleached semantically, typically with *=u* 'be thus' or modal/subject particle alone as predicate. The second clause expresses the event in question:

(9.54) a. *ḡ-e-la   heve   e=u   ge,   ḡ-a   fa-lehe=i=ña*
NT-3S-go what   3S=be.thus   SEQ   NT-1EXCS   CS-die=3SGO=IMM
'How will I kill him?' [lit. 'Go what that will be then I kill him?']

b. *ḡ-e-la   heve   e=ni   ara   an-lau   ge   ḡ-e   bnakoa=ña*
NT-3S-go what   IRR-SGO I   thatN-SPC SEQ NT-3S be slow=IMM
'How will I do that so he slowly

fa ka~kave=i   manei   e=u   ba=ine
CS RD~descend=3SGO   he   3S=be.thus   ALT=thisR
takes it down?' [lit. 'Go what [that] I will do that so...']

In this construction the clause expressing the main event has a neutral particle, and the predicate is marked with the immediacy particle *ña*.

In both constructions, order of the elements is iconic, as is the use of the sequencer in the second construction. Both constructions involve an expression of some action or event that is the manner by which the main event will be brought to realization. The Kokota concept equivalent to the English *how* is one in which an action is performed or state exists that provides the means by which the main event occurs, and is the context in which it occurs.

9.2.3.2 Cause questions

Questions of cause have a similar structure to those of manner, with two clauses conjoined and the sequencer *ge* present. The second clause expresses the main event in question and is marked with the immediacy particle *ña*. The first clause consists of *heve* 'what' and a 'be thus' clause:

(9.55) a. *heve   n-e=u   ge   n-o   si~siko=ña   ago*
what   RL-3S=be.thus   SEQ   RL-2S   RD~steal=IMM   youSG
'Why are you stealing?' [lit. 'What is thus so you are stealing?']

b. *heve* *e=u*   *ge* *ḡ-e* *lao=ña* *buala*
what 3s=be.thus SEQ NT-3S go=IMM PNLOC
'Why will he go to Buala?'

In this construction the clause expressing the main event has a realis particle if the event is realis, and a neutral particle if it is irrealis. In the first of the conjoined clauses the modal/subject particle plus 'be thus' is optional. Or to be more precise, the first element of this construction need not be a 'be thus' clause, it may be the interrogative proform alone:

(9.56)   *heve* *bla*   *ge* *ḡ-a*   *lehe-ñ=ara*
what LMT   SEQ NT-1EXCS die=IMM=I
'Why will I die?' [lit. 'Just what so I die?']

As with manner interrogatives, the order of the components is iconic, reflecting the order of events in which an action takes place or state exists that causes the event of the second clause to take place. Notions of 'why' and 'how' in Kokota are closer than in English,[62] with, in effect, three constructions available to inquire about an event or state that provides the context for a further event or state.

In addition to constructions in which the resultant event is expressed, it is possible to make a 'why' inquiry with a single clause in which *heve* 'what', marked with the immediacy particle *ña*, is the predicate. The resultant event is unexpressed:

(9.57)   *n-e*   *heve=ña*
RL-3S what=IMM
'Why?'

---

[62] Although as Pawley (pers. comm.) points out, English has *how come* as a 'why?' interrogation strategy.

CHAPTER 10: COMPLEX SENTENCES

This chapter is concerned with sentences containing more than one clause, or with major extra-clausal constituents. Multi-clausal sentences are of primarily two types: coordinated structures with more than one complete clause occuring at the same level in the syntax; and subordinating structures, in which one clause is embedded inside another. Kokota subordinate clauses have a range of functions, including modifying nominals (relative clauses) or entire main clauses (adverbial clauses), or acting as a main clause argument or adjunct. The chapter also examines a number of minor constituent types that occur outside the main clause but are not themselves coordinated main clauses, includes recapping constituents (demonstratives and reduced clauses), and 'be thus' clauses based on the verb =u 'be thus'.

10.1 Coordination

10.1.1 Particles *ge* and *age*

10.1.1.1 *Ge* and *age* as clause sequencing particles

The particle *ge* occurs clause-initially or clause-finally, coding a sequential relationship between the marked clause and another constituent. When clause-final it marks the event as occurring before the event coded by the next clause:

(10.1) a. *friñhe=ni   n-e   nhigo=u   ia   tañano si=ge,*
      work=3SGO RL-3S be.finished=CNT   theSG   food   FOC=SEQ
      'Making the food was finished and then

      n-e-ge   mai   toke=ña   kaike mane=na   koromata
      RL-3S-PRS come arrive=IMM one   maN=3SGP PNLOC
      a man from Koromata arrives.'

    b. *...ḡ-e   tetu=ña   manei ge,   nogoi ḡ-e   kaike maḡra...*
      NT-3S stand=IMM he   SEQ VOC NT-3S one   fight
      '...he stood up and then, man! he fought everyone...'

More commonly, *ge* occurs clause-initially. In this position it indicates that the event coded by the clause follows the event coded by the preceding clause:

(10.2) a. *manahagi=ḡau gau   mane huhurañi kaike mai   au   gudu*
      want=2PLO   youPL man PNLOC   one   come exist EXHST
      'I want you people from Huhurangi to all come up together [and] live

> ade-hi   kokota,   **ge**   ḡ-e   au=ña   velepuhi
> here-EMPH PNLOC   SEQ NT-3S exist=IMM right.way
> here at Kokota, then there will be catechists.'

b.   "..."   ḡ-e=u=ña   suaragi,
               NT-3S=be.thus=IMM PN
"'..."' said Suaragi,

     ge   ḡ-e   aḡe lehe=ña n-e-ke=u
     SEQ NT-3S go die=IMM RL-3S-PFV=be.thus
     and then he died, that's how it was.'

The relationship between *ge* and the marked clause is iconic: it follows clauses marked as preceding and precedes clauses marked as following. The order of the two clauses is also typically iconic, as the examples in (10.1) and (10.2) illustrate. However, while the iconic relationship between the particle and the clause it marks is obligatorily reflected in their structural relationship, the ordering of the two clauses themselves only tends to be iconic—the reverse order is also possible. In (10.3) the clause representing the event that occurred second in time actually precedes the clause representing the event that occurred first. However, the clause representing the second event is still marked with *ge* in its iconic clause-initial position:

(10.3)   **ge**   ḡe   zaho=ña gita   buala
          SEQ NT   go=IMM weINC PNLOC
          'Before we go to Buala

          gita   da   kusu   zuke faiba fea
          weINC 1INCS be.first seek dinghy INIT
          we must look for a boat.'

The fact that the sequencing particle *ge* occurs sentence-initially in (10.3), not between the coordinated clauses, demonstrates two facts. First, that the two clauses are coordinated in a single sentence, since the semantic relationship between the clauses cannot result from their order alone. Second, it demonstrates that *ge* is not a conjunction at this clausal level. The particle does not occur between the clauses so cannot be conjoining them. The particle marks individual clauses to convey information about the temporal relationship between the marked clause event and other events. No conjunction exists in these coordinated structures. In all the examples in (10.1) to (10.3) both coordinated clauses are positive. However, one of the sequenced events can be negative:

(10.4)   ara n-a   fa-no~nomho bo,
          I   RL-1EXCS CS-RD~hear CNT
          'I listened,

ge	*teo*	*bla*	*ḡe*	*nomh-i=Ø=u*
SEQ	not.exist	LMT	NT	hear-TR=3SGO=CNT

but I didn't hear it.'

Constituents related at the clausal level are not limited to pairs of clauses. Other sentence level constituents may be related sequentially to a clause. Temporal constituents may be related to a clause in this way. In (10.5)a. a temporal locative occurs with a *ge*-marked clause, indicating that the time coded by the temporal locative will precede the event coded by the clause. In (10.5)b. a temporal interrogative occurs. In (10.5)c. a local noun phrase occurs with *legu* 'behind' with its temporal meaning. This sentence level adverbial phrase is related sequentially to the clause by *ge*.

(10.5) a.

ginai	*ge*	*ḡe*	*toi=ña*
todayIRR	SEQ	NT	cook=IMM

'Later today (must come) before [we] cook.'

b.

niha=na	*ge*	*da*	*lao=ña buala*
when=thatN	SEQ	1INCS	go=IMM PNLOC

'When will we go to Buala?'

c.

legu=na	*toka*	*kave*	*ana*	*gita*	*ḡazu*	*ana*
behind=3SGP	chop	descend	thatN	weINC	wood	thatN

'After we have cut down that tree

ge	*ḡe*	*fike*	*noña*	*ago*
SEQ	NT	chop.wood	firewood	youSG

then you will make firewood.'

As discussed in §10.3, Kokota discourse style employs frequent recapping, often with a demonstrative referring to the event coded by the previous clause, or a prepositional phrase consisting of a clausal demonstrative (*ka=t=au=*), also referring to the event coded by the previous clause. With both of these recapping strategies *ge* commonly occurs marking the main clause:

(10.6) a.

friñhe=ni	*ia*	*suḡa*	*n-e*	*nhigo=u*
work=3SGO	theSG	house	RL-3S	be.finished=CNT

'Making the house is finished.

an-lau	*ge*	*kata*	*n-e=u*	*suli*	*ana*
thatN-SPC	SEQ	bite	RL-3S=be.thus	child	thatN

That, and then the child starts biting [i.e., labor pains begin].'

> **an-lau**   **ge**   ḡ-e   lao=ña   ka=ia   suḡa
> thatN-SPC   SEQ   NT-3S   go=IMM   LOC=theSG   house
> That, and then she goes to the house
>
> ḡ-e   fa   doli=ni=a   suli   e=u
> NT-3S   CS   live=3SGO=theSG   child   3S=be.thus
> [and] gives birth to the baby.'

b. *n-e-ke*   aḡe=ro=u   ḡ-e   hure   ḡ-e   aḡe=u
> RL-3S-PFV   go=thoseNV=CNT   NT-3S   carry   NT-3S   go=CNT
> 'They went (and) they carried (and) they went. .
>
> **ka=t̄=au=ana**   **ge**   tafe   ia   ñehe...
> LOC=SBD=exist=thatN   SEQ   spring.open   theSG   umbrella
> At that, the umbrella sprang open...'

Ge also occurs introducing the second clause in periphrastic manner and cause interrogatives. This is discussed in §9.2.3.

Ge has a variant form *age*, which occurs in clause-initial position only. *Age* primarily occurs when the preceding clause itself has a clause-final *ge*. This dual sequencer marking occurs often. The first of the sequentially related clauses has *ge* in final position, marking the event as preceding a subsequent event. The second clause has *age* in initial position, marking the event coded by the clause as following a preceding event. When dual sequencer marking occurs, the clause-initial second clause sequencer must have the form *age*.

(10.7) a. ḡ-e-ke=u=gu   mare   **ge**
> NT-3S-PFV=be.thus=CNT   PN   SEQ
> 'Mare was saying that, then
>
> **age** ke   broza   koko=ni=ña   putuo
> SEQ PFV   pack   leave=3SGO=IMM   PNLOC
> they packed up and left Putuo.'

b. *n-e*   la   de~deke=u   sini   **ge**
> RL-3S   go   RD~step=CNT   FOC   SEQ
> 'He stepped and then
>
> **age** ḡ-e   koko   la=ni=ña   sara   rauru
> SEQ NT-3S   leave   go=3SGO=IMM   thereD   seaward
> he threw him there seaward.'

This dual sequencer marking occasionally occurs with other sentence-initial constituents such as recapping PPs:

(10.8) *ka=t=au=ao* **ge** **age** *kuru nakoni=ña*
LOC=SBD=exist-thisT SEQ SEQ have person=IMM

n-e-ke=u=ña *aro-hi* *ade-hi*
RL-3S-PFV=be.thus=IMM theseT-EMPH here-EMPH
'From that there are people here.'

Occasionally *age* occurs clause-initially in place of *ge* in clauses where the preceding clause does not have a final *ge*:

(10.9) "..." *ḡ-e=u=ña* *tikilave,*
NT-3S=be.thus=IMM PN
'"..." said Tikilave,

age *ḡ-e* *lao=ña* *mane kokota ide* *n-e-ke=u*
SEQ NT-3S go=IMM man PNLOC theseR RL-3S-PFV=be.thus
and then these Kokota people went, it was like that.'

10.1.1.2 *Ge* as a sub-clause level conjunction

In addition to its clause marking sequencer function, *ge* occurs below the level of the clause as a conjunction. With this function there is no sequential sense, the particle simply conjoining phrasal and word level constituents. Only constituents of the same lexical or phrasal category may be conjoined in this way. In (10.10)a. two adnominal post-head core modifiers (in this case personal names) are conjoined within a single NP core and modify a single nominal head (*mane* 'man'). In (10.10)b. two verbs are conjoined in a single predication. Phrasal constituents are also conjoined by *ge*. In (10.11) a number of different NP types are conjoined. In (10.12) two locative obliques are conjoined.

(10.10)a. *mane* **sala ge ruruboñi** *n-e-ke* *namha mai* *ka* *suaragi*
man PN and PN RL-3S-PFV love come LOC PN
'Sala and Ruruboñi were kind to Suaragi.'

b. *au* *bo* *n-e* *au=gu,* **zaho ge** **zaho=u,** *ke* *pulo mai...*
exist CNT RL-3S exist=CNT go and go=CNT PFV return come
'They were staying, going and going, and would come back...'

(10.11)a. *...n-e-ge* *knusu* *ia* **papari=na,**
RL-3S-PRS break theSG wood.stack=thatN
'...they broke, that wood stack,

> *ia   hipi   ḡazu=ne   ge,   sisibe   are-lau...*
> theSG heap   wood=thisR   and   embers thoseN-SPC
> this wood heap, those embers...'

b. *la hure   kota=i   n-e=u   hinage*
   go carry go.ashore=3SGO RL-3S=be.thus boat
   'They carried their canoes ashore,

> *mane mariñi ge   mane ḡao*
> man   PNLOC and man   PNLOC
> the people from Maringe and the people from Gao.'

(10.12) *buka are-lau   e-ti-ke   mala fa-za~zaho **hae** **ge** **hae***
         book thoseN-SPC 3S-NEG-PFV PURP CS-RD~go   where and where
         'Those books won't be for sending wherever and wherever.'

10.1.2 Contrastive conjunction *ña*

The conjunction *ña* 'but, instead' conjoins clauses only. It occurs clause-initially in the second of the two conjoined clauses:

(10.13) *da   la au=gu   rhuku,   **ña** gita-palu ḡe au la*
         1INCS go exist=CNT landward but   weINC-two NT exist CND
         'We are living on the shore side [i.e., in the bush], but if we two live

> *ka   nasona a-hi   ḡerona   keli*
> LOC point thisT-EMPH PNLOC   be.good
> at the point at Gerona [that would] be good.'

The *ña*-marked clause may occur as the first clause in an utterance, but only if the situation for which the clause is an alternative has just been established in the discourse, as with speaker B's response in (10.14):

(10.14)A. *'...ḡ-e puku=ña=bla'   g-e=u=ña   ago*
          NT-3S be.short=IMM=LMT NT-3S=be.thus=IMM youSG
          '"...they are short," you said.'

B. ***ña** heve=u   sini*
   but what=be.thus FOC
   'But so what?'

Although *ña* may be sensibly glossed as 'but', it does not correspond exactly to the English conjunction. Instead, the form introduces a clause coding a situation that is presented in contrast to the situation coded by the preceding clause. This contrastive function often gives the conjunction a sense more akin to English *instead*. In the fragment of text in (10.15) the conjunction opening clause 2 relates that clause to the preceding clause with the sense that despite the situation coded in the preceding clause, the situation coded in clause 2 pertains. Specifically, despite the fact that the piece of taro was brought by the participants mentioned, and contrary to the positive expectations implicit in that, the speaker is dying from that piece of taro. The conjunction introducing clause 3 then contrasts the situation coded in that clause with that coded in clause 2.

(10.15) *ia   pike   mau=ḡu n-e-ke   hod-i=Ø=o*
theSG piece taro=1SGP RL-3S-PFV take-TR=3SGO=thatNV
'The piece of taro

sala ge   ruruboñi bla,   ña   ne   lehe=ni   a-hi   ara
PN   and PN   LMT but RL   die=3SGO thisT-EMPH I
Sala and Ruruboñi simply brought, but I'm dying from it.

ña teo   ḡ-a   lehe hae,   ḡ-o   ḡonu   la   gau
butnot.existNT-1EXCS die   where NT-2S be.insensible CND youPL
But I'm not dying from [people] just anywhere, if you are confused.

ka   sala ge   ruruboñi bla n-a   lehe=na   ara
LOC PN   and PN   LMT RL-1EXCS die=thatN I
Simply from Sala and Ruruboñi I am dying.'

The situation coded in the *ña*-marked second clause may be contrasted with a situation not overtly expressed but implicit in the preceding clause. In (10.16) the addressees live at Putuo. The situation in the second clause is contrasted with the addressees' living in Putuo, not the opinion that Putuo is not much good:

(10.16) *putuo   t=au=na   teo   ḡ-e   surai keli=u*
PNLOC SBD=exist=thatN not.exist NT-3S ??   be.good=CNT
'That Putuo is not really much good,

ña   ke   la mai   ade   bo...
but PFV go come here CNT
so instead [of living there] go ahead [and] come here [to live]...'

10.1.3 Zero conjunction

Closely related events are often expressed by clauses that are not coordinated, but are merely separate sentences juxtaposed in the discourse:

(10.17) *ara n-a   lao tetēǧu. n-a   korh-i=ri   tehi namhari*
  I RL-1EXCS go fish(v) RL-1EXCS pull-TR=3PLO many fish
  'I went fishing. I caught many fish.'

However, smaller constituents that occur within a single clause may be coordinated without an overt coordinator, especially constituents marked with a constituent marker such as *bo* 'contrastive' or *ba* 'alternative' (which are not themselves conjunctions; see §8.8). In (10.18)a. two verb complexes are coordinated, in (10.18)b. two NPs:

(10.18)a. *turi bo, frinhe bo, e=u*
   tell CNT work CNT 3S=be.thus
   '[We'll] talk and work [at the same time].'

  b. *ia puku ba, ia do ba, n-e kati=nau ara*
    theSG fly ALT theSG mosquito ALT RL-3S bite=1SGO I
    'A fly or a mosquito bit me.'

10.1.4 *N-e=u* 'it is thus' as conjunction

The form *n-e=u* consists of the verb *=u* 'be thus', preceded by the realis and 3SG subject markers *n-e*. This occurs very commonly, with a range of functions. The most common is as a tag clause (see §10.4). Another is to introduce a constituent and conjoin it to a preceding constituent. In this sense the form appears to be undergoing a process of grammaticization in which it is becoming a conjunction.

The form often occurs introducing a clause, where the situation coded by the second clause is presented as cooccurring with that coded by the first clause.

(10.19) *...ḡ-e au=gu buala e=u*
   NT-3S exist=CNT PNLOC 3S=be.thus
   '...He was living in Buala.

   n-e=u *ḡetu n-e-ke mane datau=na e=u*
   RL-3S=be.thus PN RL-3S-PFV man chief=thatN 3S=be.thus
   [At that time] Getu was the chief.'

It is not entirely clear that clauses 1 and 2 in (10.19) are even conjoined to form a single sentence. By introducing clause 2, *n-e=u* appears to mark that clause as coding a situation that is associated in some semantically close way with the situation coded by the preceding clause, in this instance, that the events occurred concurrently. In that example it is *n-e=u* alone that indicates the concurrence captured by the bracketed element of the free translation. The literal translation of *n-e=u* is something along the lines of 'it is/was thus' or 'be thus'. This meaning is readily apparent in the many instances where a clause is introduced by *n-e=u* but clearly does not form a single sentence with a preceding clause, as speaker B's response in (10.20) illustrates:

(10.20)A. *ge fufunu la=gu   e=u*
        SEQ begin   go=CNT 3S=be.thus
        'Start [telling the story] now.'

     B. **n-e=u**   *hae*
        RL-3S=be.thus where
        'Where?' [lit. 'Be thus where?']

The association with a situation coded by a preceding clause does not necessarily involve concurrence. The relationship is frequently sequential:

(10.21)   *'...da fa-lehe=i=u   mane=ne'*
        1INCS CS-die=3SGO=CNT man=thisR
        '"...we will kill this man"

        ḡ-e=u=ña   palu mane=de
        NT-3S=be.thus=IMM two   man=theseR
        said these two men,

        n-e=u   *ḡ-e fa-lehe=i=u   suaragi n-e-ke=u*
        RL-3S=be.thus NT-3S CS-die=3SGO=CNT PN   RL-3S-PFV=be.thus
        and they killed Suaragi, it was like that.'

The semantics of the clauses in (10.21) more readily give a conjunction-like appearance to *n-e=u*. However, this is more so when the form occurs between constituents smaller than a clause. In (10.22) the first instance of *n-e=u* apparently conjoins individual verbs or perhaps verb complexes. However, the presence of the limiter-marked second occurrence of *n-e=u* undermines a conjunction analysis here, suggesting as a more literal translation of the clause something like "dancing, likewise playing, they were just like that there".

(10.22) *raḡi, **n-e=u**   visi, **n-e=u**   bla maneri sare*
        dance RL-3S=be.thus play RL-3S=be.thus LMT they   thereP
        'Dance and play, that's what they did there.' [response to question]

However, in (10.23) *n-e=u* occurs between two verb complexes, apparently both marked by the same sentence-final tag clause *n-a=u* 'I am/was thus'. Here the behavior of the form is more strongly conjunction-like:

(10.23) *ne kapo   no-ḡu*
        RL feel.cold GENP-1SGP
        'I'm cold [i.e., feverish]

> *n-e=u*   *marh-i=di*   *pau=ḡu=de...*
> RL-3S=be.thus feel.pain-TR=3PLO head=1SGP=theseR
> and my head hurts...'[63]

The most conjunction-like appearance of *n-e=u*, however, is when it occurs between NPs. In (10.24)a. the form conjoins two subject NPs in a subordinate clause, in (10.24)b. it conjoins two NPs governed by a single preposition.

(10.24)a. *ka   fata   kave=ro*
          LOC occasion   descend=thoseNV

> *mane pirisi   **n-e=u***   *ira   abeabe...*
> man priest   RL-3S=be.thus   thePL   server
> 'When the priest and the servers went out...'

   b. *n-e-ge   aḡe iusi fakamo ira   mereseni*
      RL-3S-PRS go   use always thePL   medicine
      'Now we always use medicine

> *ka=ia   dokta   **n-e=u***   *mane-vaka   e=u*
> LOC=theSG   doctor   RL-3S=be.thus   man-ship   3S=be.thus
> of the doctor and white man.'

10.1.5 Presentation of alternatives

The presentation of alternatives does not involve a conjunction comparable to the English *or*. Instead, this function is performed by the marking of each alternative constituent with the constituent modifier *ba* 'alternative'. This may mark constituents of any size from individual words up to complete clauses. This particle is not a conjunction, and is discussed in detail in §8.8.1.

10.2 Subordination

Several clause types occur subordinated within a main clause. Some subordinate clauses occur immediately governed by the sentence node with the function of modifying the entire main clause, while others function adnominally. Others function as arguments of the main clause predication, or as nominal predicates in non-verbal clauses.

In general, subordinate clauses with any of these functions fall into two categories—realis and irrealis. Realis subordinate clauses have no subordinating particle. Irrealis subordinate clauses are governed by the subordinating particle *ta*. This latter category includes most conditional clauses.

---

[63] *Pau* 'head' may be plural even when referring to a single individual's head.

Several minor types of adverbial subordinate clauses also exist, each with their own formal characteristics.

10.2.1 Realis versus irrealis subordination

Most subordinate clauses fall into two types—those that code a realis event and those that code an irrealis event. The former do not involve any subordinating particle, while the latter do.

The modal characterization of events in subordinate clauses in part reflects the way those events would be treated if they were expressed by a main clause. The basis of the main clause classification of events as realis or irrealis is discussed in §7.5.2.3. However, the range of subordinate clause predications that are treated as irrealis is considerably wider than those treated as irrealis in main clauses. Any real event that actually occurred before the moment of speaking, or is actually occurring at the moment of speaking, is treated as realis. In subordinate clauses all other events are treated as irrealis. The prototypical non-real event is one that is located at a time after the moment of speaking, in other words one that has yet to occur. This prototypical distinction is neatly reflected in relative clauses in terminology for divisions of time:

(10.25)a. *ka   wiki   n-e-ke   age̅=o*
       LOC week RL-3S-PFV go=thatNV
       'last week' (lit. 'that week that went')

    b. *ka   wiki   ta   mai=ne*
       LOC week SBD come=thisR
       'next week' (lit. 'this week that will come')

In (10.25)a. the week referred to is in the past, and its going has actually occurred. As such, the relative clause coding the event is realis, with a realis particle and no subordinating particle. In (10.25)b. the coming of the week has yet to occur. As such, the event is not yet real and it is treated as irrealis and the relative clause has no modal/subject particle. Instead the subordinating particle *ta* is present. In effect, a modal/subject particle and the subordinator are in complementary distribution in subordinate clauses. The absence of a particle in irrealis subordinate clauses correlates with the omissibility of the subject-indexing particle in irrealis main clauses, and the (crosslinguistically unusual) status of irrealis as the unmarked of the two modal categories.

Any subordinated positive active predication is realis. While the examples in (10.25) are useful from a contrastive point of view, (10.25)a. does not reflect a prototypical use of a realis subordinate. The following (bracketed) relative clause is more typical:

(10.26)   ...*g-e-ke*   *mai*   *ñhau*   *ka=ira*   *tañano*
        NT-3S-PFV   come   eat   LOC=thePL   food
        '...he came and ate from the food

        [*n-e-ke*   *fafara=di*   *maneri*]   *n-e=u...*
        RL-3S-PFV   sacrifice=3PLO   they   RL-3S=be.thus
        (that) they had sacrificed...'

Irrealis subordinate clauses cover a much wider range of events. These include events that, while positive and active, have yet to occur. Such events are treated as irrealis in subordinate clauses, as they are in main clauses:

(10.27)   *mane* *ihei*   [*ta*   *mhoko* *fa-lehe=i=na*   *to~toi=ne*],
        man   whoeverSG SBD   sit   CS-die=3SGO=thatN   RD~cook=thisR
        'Whichever [is the] man who will sit [on] and kill this fire,

        an=bla   *mane=na*
        thatN=LMT   man=thatN
        that [will be] that [true] man.'

However, future events are not the only events coded as irrealis in both main and subordinate clauses. Habitual events are coded as irrealis as they are not actual specific events, as in (10.28)a. The act of referring to an entity by the word a language assigns to it is habitual so is also treated as irrealis ([10.28]b.–c.):

(10.28)a. *lao* *la*   *tehi*   *n-e=u*   *teḡe*   *ana,*
        go   CND many   RL-3S=be.thus   turtle   thatN
        'If there are many turtles,

        ḡ-e-la   *naboto-u* *ba,* *varedake-u*   *ba,* *tulufulu* *teḡe*
        NT-3S-go   ten-CRD   ALT   twenty-CRD   ALT   thirty   turtle
        then it's ten, or twenty, or thirty turtles

        [*ta*   *la*   *hod-i=di=re*   *gai*]
        SBD   go   take-TR=3PLO=thoseN   weEXC
        that we take.'

     b. *e* *au=i*   *la* *bla* *keha*
        3S exist=3SGO   ??   LMT   NSP
        'He [the doctor] has something

        [*ta*   *fakilo=ni*   *tritmenti*   *ka=ia*   *ooe-vaka*]
        SBD   name(V)=3SGO   treatment   LOC=theSG   talk-ship
        that [they] call treatment in Pijin.'

c. *ḡ-e*   *la*   *fa-lehe=i=ña*   *n-e-ke=u*   *fadalao*
   NT-3S go   CS-die=3SGO=IMM   RL-3S-PFV=be.thus PN
   'They killed Fadalao,

   [*ta=ni=na*   *naitu* *t=au=ne*]
   SBD=3SGO=thatN devil SBD=exist=thisR
   as that devil was called.'

In addition to habitual events, hypothetical events are treated as irrealis, with subordinated clauses expressing hypothetical events coded irrealis:

(10.29)   *tana* *aḡe* *toke=i*   *ia*   *nare*
           then   go   arrive=3SGO theSG day
           'Then comes the day

           [*ta*   *mala* *aḡe* *friñhe=ni*   *ia*   *mala-ñhau*]
           SBD PURP go   work=3SGO   theSG PURP-eat
           for making the food.'

Subordinate clause events located in the past or present are realis if positive. However, the non-occurrence of an event is treated as irrealis regardless of the temporal frame of the event. Thus past counterfactual ([10.30]a.) and present counterfactual ([10.30]b.) subordinated clauses are irrealis.

(10.30)a. *teo*   *ḡ-e*   *kaike* *mane*
        not.exist NT-3S one   man
        'There was not one man

        [*ta*   *kave=na*]   *ka*   *maneri* *k=au*   *toa=na*
        SBD descend=thatN LOC they   LOC=exist fort=thatN
        who came out, of those in the fort.'

   b. *e* *teo*   *kaike* *ihei*
       3S not.exist one   someone
       'There is not anyone

       [*ta* *aḡe* *boka* *fa-lehe=i=na*   *ia*   *to~toi*]
       SBD go be.able CS-die=3SGO=thatN theSG RD~cook
       who can kill the fire.'

Note that the subordinate clauses in (10.30) are not negative. Instead they express positive events. However, the wider context of the main clause indicates that these events did not occur, and thus, despite expressing positive events located in the past or present, the clauses are coded as irrealis.

Like habitual events, states have a validity that holds beyond individual temporal locations or modal status. However, in main clauses states may be coded as realis if the state actually exists or existed at a particular point in the past or present. Subordinate clauses expressing states vary in their modal coding. In relative clauses states are always coded as irrealis. This is as true of temporary states, as in (10.31)b., as it is of permanent states ([10.31]a.):

(10.31)a. *la=i*   *bla*   *kaike* *tu~turi* [*ta* *puku*]   *bl=ago*
        go=3SGO LMT one   RD~tell SBD be.short LMT=youSG
        'Just tell a story that's short.'

    b. *...ḡ-e* *tetu=ña*   *mane* [*ta* *foḡra* *marha-pau*   *a-hi*]...
       NT-3S stand=IMM man   SBD sick   be.in.pain-head thisT-EMPH
       '...[then] the man who is sick with this headache stands up...'

However, other subordinate clause types resemble main clauses in that they code real states as realis. For example, the complement clause in (10.32) is realis:

(10.32)a. *ka*   *gato* *la=i=na*   *bla* *ago*   [*n-e* *sodu=na*]...
        LOC think go=3SGO=thatN LMT youSG RL-3S be.long=thatN
        'When you think it [the story] is long....'

Like states, relationships such as knowing or possessing have a non-specific quality in reality or temporal terms. However, like states, while main clauses expressing such relationships are coded realis, subordinate clauses must be irrealis:

(10.33)a. *e=u*   *za~zaho=na=na*   *marha-pau*   *tarihi* *ḡeḡelehu*
        3S=be.thus RD~go=3SGP=thatN be.in.pain-head   pillow heavy
        'That's the way of the headache 'Heavy Pillow'

        [*ta* *lase=i=na*   *ara*]
        SBD know=3SGO=thatN I
        that I know.'

    b. *ḡ-e* *tetu=ña*   *mane* [*ta* *kuru=i=ne*   *naitu* *toke*]
       NT-3S stand=IMM man SBD have=3SGO=thisR devil arrive
       'The man who had an arriving devil stood up.'

Existential clauses are also realis as main clauses but irrealis when subordinate:

(10.34) *ge* *ḡ-e* *tufa=ña*   *ka=ira*   *nakoni* *mavitu*
        SEQ NT-3 affect=IMM LOC=thePL person community
        '...then [we] give [the food] to the people

[*ta*   *au*   *ka*   *ḡilu=na*   *no-mai*   *nau*
SBD   exist   LOC   in=3SGP   GENP-1EXCP   village
who live within our village.'

The use of the subordinator *ta* with the existential verb *au* has given rise to formulaic clausal demonstratives such as *t=au=na* 'that (nearby)' (lit. 'that which is that') and *t=au=de* 'these (within reach)' (lit. 'that which are these'). These clausal demonstratives are discussed in §3.1.3.3.

Irrealis subordinate clauses are typically marked with the subordinator *ta*, as discussed above. However, where the context makes clear the irrealis status of the subordinate clause, the subordinator is occasionally omitted. This occurs very commonly when the subordinate clause is marked with the purposive marker *mala*. The prototypically unrealized nature of intended events gives purposive subordinates a prototypical irrealis status. As discussed in §10.2.7, this licences the omission of the subordinator. However, the subordinator may occur in such clauses, as (10.35)a. illustrates. Less commonly, omission of the subordinator occurs with other irrealis subordinate clauses, typically where the event coded by the subordinate clause is located in the future within the temporal frame of the main clause. When the subordinator is omitted an irrealis particle may occur. As discussed in §7.5.2.2, irrealis is realized by zero marking, contrasting with marked realis and neutral categories. The particle thus consists only of the person-indexing vowel. This particle may occur when the subordinator is omitted, as in (10.35)b. In main clauses irrealis particles tend to be omitted when there is no ambiguity about the identity of the subject or actor. This is also true of subordinate clauses. An irrealis subordinate clause where the subordinator has been omitted may therefore have no particle, as in (10.35)c.

(10.35)a.   *manahagi=ḡau*   *gau*
        want=2PLO   youPL
        'We want you all

        [*ta*   *mala*   *fa-lehe=i=na*   *naitu*   *ao-hi*]
        SBD   PURP   CS-die=3SGO=thatN   devil   thisT-EMPH
        to kill this devil.'

   b.   *manei n-e*   *tahe=i=na*   [*ara*   *a*   *tazi=ni*   *sote ine*]
        he   RL-3S   tell=3SGO=thatN   I   1EXCS   keep=3SGO   shirt   thisR
        'He said I can keep this shirt.'

   c.   *manahagi=ḡau*   *gau*   *mane*   *huhurañi*
        want=2PLO   youPL   man   PNLOC
        'I want you Huhurangi people

[*kaike mai au gudu ade-hi kokota*]
one come exist EXHST here-EMPH PNLOC
to all come and live together here at Kokota.'

10.2.2 Constituent orders in relative and complement clauses

The pragmatically unmarked clause constituent order is VAO or VS (see §8.2). However, main clauses allow the preverbal topicalization of any argument. In addition, a clause-final focus position exists. Subordinate clauses of all types have the same pragmatically unmarked constituent structure as main clauses, but the pragmatically marked possibilities differ from those of main clauses.

10.2.2.1 Topicalization in relative and complement clauses

The topicalization possibilities for relative and complement clauses differ between zero-marked clauses and those with the subordinator *ta*. However, all zero-marked clauses allow the same possibilities regardless of whether they are functioning as relative or complement clauses, as do all *ta*-marked clauses.

Clauses marked with the subordinator *ta* do not allow any argument in preverbal topicalized position. This applies to all *ta*-marked clauses regardless of main clause function. In zero-marked relative and complement clauses a preverbal topicalized argument is possible, but is ergative—only actors (i.e., the subjects of transitive predications) may be topicalized, as (10.36)b.–c. illustrate for relative and complement clauses respectively. Intransitive subjects are precluded from occurring preverbally, even if unergative ([10.36]d.), as are objects ([10.36]e.–f.). The pragmatically unmarked structure is shown in (10.36)a.

(10.36)a. *ara manahagi=ni* [*o poma=i ago mheke ana*]
    I want=3SGO 2S hit=3SGO youSG dog thatN
    'I want that you hit that dog.'

  b. *ia mheke* [**ago** *n-o-ke poma=i=o*] *n-e lehe*
    theSG dog youSG RL-2S-PFV hit=3SGO=thatNV RL-3S die
    'The dog you hit is dead.'

  c. *ara manahagi=ni* [**ago** *o poma=i mheke ana*]
    I want=3SGO youSG 2S hit=3SGO dog thatN
    'I want that you hit that dog.'[64]

  d. **ara manahagi=ni* [**ago** *o mai ade*]
    I want=3SGO youSG 2S come here
    'I want that you come here.'

---

[64] The 2s preverbal agreement marker is optional and would typically be omitted here.

e. *ia   mheke   [ago   n-e-ke   kat-i=igo]   n-e   lehe
   theSG   dog   youSG   RL-3S-PFV   hit-TR=2SGO   RL-3S   die
   'The dog that bit you is dead.'

f. *ara   manahagi=ni   [*mheke ana*   o   poma=i   ago]
   I   want=3SGO   dog   thatN   2S   hit=3SGO   youSG
   'I want that you hit that dog.'

Note that although *manahagi* 'want' is potentially ditransitive, the *ago* 'youSG' in (10.36)c. is within a direct object complement clause, indexed by the third singular agreement enclitic on the main clause verb, not a direct object separate from an indirect object complement clause, as would be the case if the main clause agreement enclitic was second singular:

(10.37)   *ara manahagi=nigo **ago**   [o   poma=i   mheke   ana]*
          I   want=2SGO   youSG   2S   hit=3SGO   dog   thatN
          'I want you to hit that dog.'

As the controlled argument may not be overtly realized in relative clauses (see §10.2.4), topicalization is only possible when the subordinate actor is not the controlled argument.

10.2.2.2 Focus in relative and complement clauses

Like main clauses, both *ta* marked and zero-marked relative and complement clauses allow an argument in clause-final focus position. In main clauses a focused argument is marked with the focus particle *si*. In subordinate clauses of all types this focus particle may not occur. Instead, in relative and complement clauses a focused argument occurs in clause-final position without *si*. This occurs infrequently. More than one argument must be present in the subordinate clause. Moreover, intransitive subjects and objects occur in clause-final position unless an oblique is also present. Consequently it is typically a transitive actor that is focused in subordinate clauses, as (10.38) illustrates for zero-marked and *ta*-marked relative and complement clauses:

(10.38)a. *ara n-a   ʃakae=ni ia   ḡazu*
          I   RL-1EXCS see=3SGO theSG wood
          'I saw the stick

          *[n-o-ke   poma=i=o   ia   mheke **ago**]*
          RL-2S-PFV hit=3SGO=thatNV theSG dog   youSG
          <u>you</u> hit the dog with.'

b. *ara manahagi=ni* [*o poma=i mheke ana* **ago**]
I   want=3SGO   2S   hit=3SGO dog   thatN yousG
'I want that you hit that dog.'

c. *e teo kaike ǧazu* [*ta poma=i=o ia mheke* **ago**]
3S not.exist one   wood SBD hit=3SGO=thatNV theSG dog   yousG
'There isn't a stick for you to hit the dog with.'

d. *ara manahagi=ni* [*ta poma=i=o mheke ana* **ago**]
I   want=3SGO   SBD hit=3SGO=thatNV dog   thatN yousG
'I want that you hit that dog.'

However, relative and complement clause focusing is not limited to actors. In (10.39), for example, an intransitive subject occurs in clause-final position, following an oblique:

(10.39)   *ara manahagi=ni* [*ta mai ade* **ago**]
I   want=3SGO   SBD come here yousG
'I want that you come here.'

10.2.3 Relative clauses

Realis subordinate clauses occur as adnominal modifiers identifying or characterizing the head nominal on the basis of an event in which the participant coded by the head nominal took part, or a state that applies to that participant.

Two types of relative clauses occur. Reduced relative clauses consist only of the subordinator *ta* plus a single stative verb, and occur within the NP core. Full relative clauses are NP outer modifiers. Nothing further needs to be added here regarding reduced relative clauses other than that they may modify any nominal main clause argument. The behavior of relative clauses within NP structure is discussed in §3.3.2.2.3.6. The present section deals with full relative clauses.

10.2.3.1 Main clause arguments modified

Any main clause argument may be modified by a relative clause. In (10.40)a. the main clause actor (i.e., transitive subject) is modified, in (10.40)b. an unergative intransitive subject, in (10.40)c. an unaccusative subject, in (10.40)d. an undergoer, in (10.40)e. an oblique, and in (10.40)f. a possessor:

(10.40)a. *ia* **mane** [*n-e-ke fa-lehe=i ia zora*]
theSG man   RL-3S-PFV CS-die=3SGO theSG pig
'The man who killed the pig

n-e   korh-i=ri   keha   namhari
RL-3S catch=3PLO NSP fish
caught some fish.'

b. ***ia   mane*** [*n-e-ke   dupa=nau   ara*] *n-e   zaho   bla*
theSG man RL-3S-PFV punch=1SGO I RL-3S go LMT
'The man who hit me simply left.'

c. *n-e   totonu   blau   **tu~turi***
RL-3S be.straight LMT RD~tell

[*n-e-ke   la=i=o   ago   goino*]
RL-3S-PFV go=3SGO=thatNV youSG todayRL
'That story you told today is straight.'

d. ...*la hure=ri   **ira   tilo   tomoko***
go carry=3PLO thePL three war.canoe
'[They]...went and carried the three war canoes

[*n-e-ke   hage=ro   gudu   maneri*]
RL-3S-PFV ascend=thoseNV EXHST they
they had come up in.'

e. ...*ḡ-e-ke   mai   ñhau   ka=ira   **tañano***
NT-3S-PFV come eat LOC=thePL food
'...he came and ate from the food

[*n-e-ke   fafara=di   maneri*]...
RL-3S-PFV sacrifice=3PLO they
that they had sacrificed...'

f. ...*ira   ge=di   no-di   e=u*
thePL CNSM-3PLP GENP-3PLP 3S=be.thus
'...the food and things of

mane [*n-e-ke   kusu   au=de   ade*]
man RL-3S-PFV be.first exist=theseR here
the men who lived here first.'

10.2.3.2 Relative clause argument roles

The participant expressed by the main clause argument that is modified by the
relative clause (i.e., the coreferential argument) may have any grammatical
relation in the relative clause. It may have the same relation in both clauses, as in
(10.40)a., where the coreferential argument is an agent and transitive actor in

both clauses. In (10.40)b. the coreferential argument is a [+A] argument in both clauses, but has slightly different grammatical relations: in one it is a transitive actor and in the other an unergative subject. Similarly in (10.40)c. the coreferential participant is a [-A] argument in both clauses, an unaccusative subject in the main clause and a theme in the relative clause. Alternatively, the argument may have completely different roles and relations, as in (10.40)d.–e., where the coreferential argument is an oblique in one clause and an undergoer in the other. The fact that both these roles are not [+A] is not significant—a participant may be the [+A] argument of one clause and the [-A] argument of the other. In (10.40)f. the main clause oblique is [+A] in the relative clause (an unergative subject), while in (10.41) the [-A] main clause undergoer object is [+A] relative clause actor:

(10.41)   *ia   datau n-e   fa-lehe=i   **ia   mheke***
           theSG chief RL-3S CS-die=3SGO theSG dog
           'The chief killed the dog

           [*n-e-ke   kat-i=ni*]   *e=u*
           RL-3S-PFV bite-TR=3SGO 3S=be.thus
           that had bitten him.'

The freedom of participants to function in any role in both main and relative clauses creates the potential for ambiguity, as in (10.41). Here neither the actor nor undergoer of the transitive relative clause are overtly realized. Since the two main clause participants are also the two relative clause participants, and both are third singular, some means of distinguishing between the two participants in the relative clause is necessary. However, this means need not be linguistic.

Where no overt arguments are present in the relative clause the ambiguity is not resolved syntactically: the dog cannot be assumed to have the same role in the relative clause as it does in the main clause, as it could well have a different role (as it does in [10.41]). In situations like this, ambiguity is resolved pragmatically and semantically. In (10.41) the dog would normally be assumed to be the actor of the relative clause because dogs typically bite, and chiefs typically do not. If a semantically anomalous event was being described, the unusual role assignment would require an overt realization of the arguments, in which case constituent order would resolve the ambiguity. Equally, where either participant could readily perform either role, overt mentions allow constituent order to resolve the ambiguity. In (10.42), for example, no ambiguity is possible as the unmarked VAO constituent order dictates the reading.

(10.42)a. *ara n-a   fakae=ni ia   ḡazu*
          I   RL-1EXCS see=3SGO theSG wood
          'I saw the stick

> [*n-e-ke*   *poma=i=o*   *ia*   *datau*   *ia*   *mane-dou*]
> RL-3S-PFV   hit=3SGO=thatNV   theSG   chief   theSG   man-be.big
> the chief hit the old man with.'

b.   *ara*   *n-a*   *fakae=ni*   *ia*   *ḡazu*
      I   RL-1EXCS   see=3SGO   theSG   wood
      'I saw the stick

> [*n-e-ke*   *poma=i=o*   *ia*   *mane-dou*   *ia*   *datau*]
> RL-3S-PFV   hit=3SGO=thatNV   theSG   man-be.big   theSG   chief
> the old man hit the chief with.'

10.2.3.3 Relative clause argument role tendencies

Relative clauses modify main clause arguments of any argument role. However, unelicited data displays various tendencies. Relative clauses on main clause undergoers and intransitive subjects occur commonly; on obliques slightly less so; and on actors very infrequently. The role in the relative clause of the controlled argument shows similar tendencies: by far the most common controlled arguments are relative clause intransitive subjects. Undergoers are less common, obliques still less so, and coreferential actors are rare.[65]

10.2.3.4 Relative clause structure

The constituent order possibilities for subordinate clauses are discussed in §10.2.2. However, a constraint applies to relative clauses that does not apply to other subordinate clause types: the relative clause argument that is coreferential with its main clause head is subject to control by the head and may not be overtly realized except by agreement in the subordinate verb complex. A NP realizing the controlled argument may not occur.

As the coreferential argument is controlled, a relative clause cannot have all its arguments specified other than by agreement. In addition, relative clauses are subject to the same tendency as other clause types to realize highly activated participants by zero anaphora (see §8.3). Consequently relative clauses frequently consist of the verb complex only. Where an argument is realized, it is typically either a transitive actor or an undergoer in a clause where the head fulfills the other core transitive role, or is an oblique. In (10.43)a. the controlled argument is the object and in (10.43)b. the actor. In (10.43)c. it is an oblique.

(10.43)a.   *da-ke*   *au=gu*   *banesokeo*
         1INCS-PFV   exist=CNT   PNLOC
         'We will stay at Banesokeo

---

[65] See Corston 1996 for a lengthy discussion of these tendencies in Roviana.

> ka **nau** [n-a   tabar-i=Ø=ne   ara]
> LOC place RL-1EXCS buy-TR=3SGO=thisR I
> at the place I bought.'

b. e teo   **kaike ihei**
   3S not.exist one   whoeverSG
   'There is not anyone

   [ta=ge boka fa-lehe=i=na   ia   to~toi]
   SBD=PRS be.able CS-die=3SGO=thatN theSG RD~cook
   who can kill the fire.'

c. ḡ-e   farogoho fa teo=ri   **mane**
   NT-3S smite   CS not.exist=3PLO man
   'He killed the men

   [n-e-ke   au=ro   ka ḡilu=na   tema=na] e=u
   RL-3S-PFV exist=thoseN LOC inside=3SGP hut=thatN 3S=be.thus
   who were inside the small house.'

Since intransitive clauses have only one core argument, intransitive subjects are very rarely overtly realized in relative clauses. This is only possible where the head functions as a relative clause oblique. Equally, transitive relative clauses with both core arguments overtly realized occur very infrequently, and only in the same circumstances:

(10.44) ia   tafnu [n-e-ke   toi=ni   maneri ia   namhari]
         theSG oven   RL-3S-PFV cook=3SGO they   theSG fish
         'The oven they cooked the fish in

         n-e   dou
         RL-3S be.big
         was big.'

Relative clauses with more than one overt argument are also possible where the arguments are both obliques:

(10.45) tu~turi gabili   faaknu [n-e-ke   au=re
         RD~tell be.aggressive murder RL-3S-PFV exist=thoseN
         'the killer who lived

         ka=ia   puhi boñihehe ka gizu=na   a-hi   gai]
         LOC=theSG way heathen   LOC island=3SGP thisT-EMPH weEXC
         in the heathen time on our island'

Like controlled core arguments, controlled relative clause obliques are not overtly realized. When this occurs the entire prepositional phrase has a zero realization, even if in the main clause the coreferential argument is not also an oblique. In (10.44) a main clause unaccusative subject is modified by a relative clause in which the coreferential participant functions as an instrument. Instruments are normally realized by prepositional obliques with the preposition *ka* as head (see §6.7.1.6). However, when a main clause core argument occurs as a controlled relative clause oblique, as in (10.44), no preposition occurs in either clause. Similarly in (10.46), the main clause object controls a relative clause instrument that would otherwise be realized within a *ka* prepositional oblique:

(10.46) ...*la hure=ri   ira   tilo   tomoko*
go carry=3PLO thePL three war.canoe
'...[they] went and picked up the three war canoes

[*n-e-ke   hage=ro   gudu   maneri*]
RL-3S-PFV ascend=thoseNV EXHST they
that they had come up in.'

10.2.3.5 Relative clause recursion

Relative clauses are potentially recursive, with arguments of one relative clause themselves eligible to be modified by a relative clause. In (10.47) the object arguments of the relative clause in lines 1–2 are themselves modified by the relative clause in lines 2–3:

(10.47) *ia   ñehe   [n-e-ke   mala   totoku=di=ro*
theSG umbrella RL-3S-PFV PURP cover=3PLO=thoseNV
'the umbrella that was for covering

ira   liligomo,   ira   papaza,   [n-e-ke   au=ro
thePL warning.charm thePL turmeric RL-3S-PFV exist=thoseNV
the warning charm, the turmeric, that were

ka=ia   pau=na   hinage=na]]   e=u
LOC=theSG head=3SGP boat=thatN   3S=be.thus
in the front of the canoe'

10.2.3.6 Relative clause demonstrative enclitics

Full relative clauses optionally contain a cliticized demonstrative agreeing with the controlled argument. This demonstrative attaches to the verb complex. Where a relative clause is intransitive, the verb complex may be marked with an enclitic agreeing with the subject of that clause (unergative or unaccusative):

(10.48)a. *teo*   *ḡ-e*   *kaike*   *mane*
not.exist   NT-3S   one   man
'There was not one man

[*ta*   *kave=na*]   *ka*   *maneri*   *k=au*   *toa=na*
SBD   descend=thatN   LOC   they   LOC=exist   fort=thatN
who came out, of those in the fort.'

b. *e=u*   *teo*   *ḡ-e*   *boka*   *turi=di*   *manei*
3S=be.thus   not.exist   NT-3S   be.able   tell=3PLO   he
'He isn't able to tell

heve   *ḡlepo*   [*n-e-ke*   *torai*   *dia=re*]...
what   thing   RL-3S-PFV   definitely   be.bad=thoseN
whatever things that were very wrong...'

In transitive relative clauses the demonstrative enclitic attaches to the postverbal agreement marker. Where the controlled argument is the relative clause actor the demonstrative agrees with that argument, as in (10.49)a., where the relative clause object is plural and the actor singular. Where the controlled argument is the object, as in (10.49)b., the postverbal agreement marker and the demonstrative enclitic form a sequence that agrees with both the person and number of the undergoer, and its demonstrative category. The demonstrative may also agree with a controlled oblique. In (10.46) the enclitic *=ro* 'those (not visible)' agrees with the controlled instruments.

(10.49)a. *e*   *teo*   *kaike*   *mane*   [*ta*   *maḡra=di=na*   *naitu*   *are*]
3S   not.exist   one   man   SBD   fight=3PLO=thatN   devil   thoseN
'There is not one man who can fight these devils.'

b. *ia*   *nakodou*   *n-e*   *toi=ri*   *ira*   *kaku*
theSG   woman   RL-3S   cook=3PLO   thePL   banana
'The woman cooked the bananas

[*n-e-ke*   *la*   *hod-i=ri=ro*]
RL-3S-PFV   go   take-TR=3PLO=thoseNV
she had picked.'

No evident formal or syntactic bases motivate the presence or absence of a demonstrative enclitic. Instead the motivation appears to be pragmatic—the demonstrative is used to facilitate referent identification. Speakers have the option of employing this strategy if they judge it useful on a clause by clause basis. However, while elicited relative clauses often do not contain a demonstrative enclitic, that is not an accurate reflection of language use. Almost all unelicited relative clauses in the corpus contain a demonstrative enclitic.

10.2.4 Subordinate clauses as arguments

Subordinate clauses may function as arguments of a main clause. As events or states cannot be volitional entities, arguments realized by subordinate clauses are limited to non-volitional semantic roles. One effect of this is that argument clauses may not function as the agent of a transitive clause, or as an unergative subject. Beyond that, they may occur with any grammatical relation.

10.2.4.1 Subordinate clauses as subjects

While an argument clause may not function as agent, it may occur as the actor of a transitive predication with the semantic role of force. In (10.50) the clause *friñhe heta* 'work hard' is the actor of the transitive causative predication, and is marked with the demonstrative *ine* 'this (reachable)'. While subject clauses are typically marked with a demonstrative, this is optional, as in (10.51).

(10.50)   [*friñhe heta*   *ine*]   *n-e*   *fa babao=nau*   *ara*
           work   be.strong   thisR   RL-3S   CS   be.tired=1SGO   I
           'This working hard is making me tired.'

(10.51)   [*birho ravata*]   *n-e*   *fa lehe-ñhau=nigo*   *ago*
           sleep   afternoon   RL-3S   CS   die-eat=2SGO   youSG
           'Sleeping in the afternoon is making you hungry.'

Force clause actors have a superficial resemblance to nominalized adverbial contextual subordinate clauses (see §10.2.5.1). In (10.52)a. the initial adjunct clause is simply the context in which the speaker's thirst occurred. In (10.52)b., however, a virtually identical clause is the force actor of the main clause predication. While the subordinate clause is virtually identical in both sentences, the main clause in (10.52)a. is intransitive, with the speaker as subject, as the preverbal agreement indicates. In (10.52)b. the main clause is transitive, with a causative marked predication and the speaker as object (indexed postverbally).

(10.52)a.   [*mhoko=na ka*   *naprai nhorao*]   *n-a-ke*   *no-ḡu*   *kumai*
             sit=thatN   LOC   sun   yesterday   RL-1EXCS-PFV   GENP-1SGP   drink
             'Sitting in the sun yesterday, I wanted to drink.'

      b.   [*mhoko-no*   *ka*   *naprai*   *nhorao*]
             sit=thatNV   LOC   sun   yesterday
             'Sitting in the sun yesterday

             n-e-ke   *fa no-ḡu*   *kumai=nau*   ***ara***
             RL-3S-PFV   CS   GENP-1SGP   drink=1SGO   I
             made me want to drink.'

Clauses that function as the subject of an unaccusative intransitive predication typically express an event that the main clause comments on in terms of its state or some characteristic associated with it:

(10.53) [tetēgu namhari=ne] e bu~bluse ḡlehe
         fish(V) fish=thisR 3S RD~be.easy very
         'This catching fish is very easy.'

The use of a main clause with a subordinate clause as subject occurs frequently in exposition as a recapping device indicating the progression of events, often indicating the completion of one stage in a sequence of events:

(10.54) o la roh-i=Ø   ia   ḡuanha...
         2S go scrape-TR=3SGO theSG ḡuanha
         'You go and scrape the ḡuanha [tree]....

         [la roh-i=Ø] n-e   nhigo=u,   toke=na   fa blahi
         go scrape   RL-3S be.finished=CNT arrive=thatN CS be.tabu
         Going and scraping it is finished, [then] go back and bless [it].'

As with force subordinate clause actors, subordinate clause unaccusative subjects may or may not be marked with a demonstrative, as (10.53) and (10.54) illustrate. In most elicited sentences with a subordinate clause unaccusative subject, a demonstrative is present, while in most unelicited sentences the clause is not marked by a demonstrative.

10.2.4.2 Complement clauses

10.2.4.2.1 Complement clause grammatical relations and interclausal argument coreference

A number of verbs subcategorize for a sentential complement as either direct or indirect object. These include:

(10.55)a. *tahe*   'tell'   g. *gato*   'think about'
      b. *snakre* 'allow'   h. *manahagi* 'want'
      c. *lubati* 'allow'   i. *ḡonu*   'be insensible'
      d. *fa noto* 'cause to stop'   j. *gato-ḡonu* 'forget'
      e. *fa teo* 'cause to be not'   k. *fa nhigo* 'cause to be finished'
      f. *fa naḡr-i* 'cause to be blocked' l. *ooe*   'say'

Of these, the verbs in (10.55)a.–i. subcategorize for either one or two complements. Where only one complement occurs it may be a NP or a complement clause. Where two complements exist, the direct object is always a

NP, and the indirect object a complement clause. The verbs in (10.55)j.–l. subcategorize only for a single complement, which may be a NP or a complement clause. The semantic possibilities for direct and indirect complement clauses with these verbs fall into four groups:

TABLE 10.1. THE SEMANTICS OF DIRECT AND INDIRECT OBJECT COMPLEMENT CLAUSES

| | Bivalent clauses | Trivalent clauses | |
	Direct object complement clause	Direct object noun phrase	Indirect object complement clause
A. *tahe, snakre, lubati, fa noto, fa teo, fa naḡr-i*	**event** actor allows s.o. else to do, or tells of, thinks of, stops or blocks s.o. else doing	**participant** who is told, allowed, stopped, blocked or thought about	**event** DO is told or allowed to do, thought about doing, or stopped or blocked from doing
B. *manahagi*	**event** actor wants to do or wants s.o. else to do	**participant** who actor wants to act	**event** actor wants DO to do
C. *ḡonu, gato-ḡonu, fa nhigo*	**event** actor has finished doing or doesn't know or has forgotten how to do	-	-
D. *ooe*	-	**participant** who is spoken to	**event** DO is told about

With the verbs in group A the main clause actor is not coreferential with the subject/actor of the complement clause. The subject/actor of the complement clause may be overtly realized within the complement clause, as in (10.56)a. Alternatively, the subject/actor of the complement clause may be realized as the direct object of the main clause, as in (10.56)b., in which case the complement clause is the indirect object. In this second alternative the complement clause subject/actor is coreferential with the main clause direct object and may not be overtly realized in the complement clause.

(10.56)a. *ia   nahani n-e   fa noto=i   [aḡe teteḡu=na   **gita**]*
    theSG rain   RL-3S CS stop=3SGO go   fish(V)=thatN   weINC
    'The rain stopped us going fishing.'

   b. *manei n-e   fa noto=nau **ara***
    he   RL-3S CS stop=1SGO   I
    'He stopped me

[*ta ñhau=di=re*   *mala-ñhau* *ta*   *dia*   *are*]
SBD eat=3PLO=thoseN PURP-eat   SBD be.bad thoseN
eating that bad food.'

Group A verbs with indirect object complement clauses require coreference between the main clause undergoer and the complement clause subject/actor. The effect of this is that indirect object complement clauses do not allow an overt subject/actor within the complement clause itself.

With the verbs in group C the complement clause direct object realizes an event that the main clause actor performs. The complement clause subject/actor must therefore be coreferential with the main clause actor. As with coreferential main clause nominal direct objects in group A verbs, the coreferential argument may not be overtly realized. Consequently, with group C verbs the complement clause subject/actor may never be overtly realized:

(10.57)a. *ara* *ḡo-no-ḡu=di*
      I   be.insensible-GENP-1SGP=3PLO
      'I don't know

      [*ta*   *tahe=di=re*   *are-lau*]
      SBD tell=3PLO=thoseN thoseN-SPC
      how to tell those [stories].'[66]

    b. *n-e-ge*   *mai* *fa* *nhigo=i=u*
       RL-3S-PRS come CS be.finished=3SGO=CNT
       'He's coming and finishing

       [*lao tabar-i=Ø=na*   *banesokeo*]
       go buy=3SGO=thatN PNLOC
       buying Banesokeo.'

The desiderative verb *manahagi* behaves in the same way as both group A and group C verbs. As with group A verbs, the actor of *manahagi* may want another participant to act. This may be expressed either with a direct object complement clause containing the complement clause subject/actor, as in (10.58)a., or with a NP direct object realizing the other participant, and an indirect object complement clause realizing the event, as in (10.58)b. Again, here the indirect object complement clause subject/actor is coreferential with the main clause direct object and may not be overtly realized.

---

[66] In (10.57)a. *ḡonu* occurs in a reduced form comprising a single word with postverbal aspectual possessor marking. This reduction is discussed in §8.6.1.

(10.58)a. *ara manahagi=ni* [*da friñhe=ni kaike visi **gita-palu**]
I   want=3SGO   1INCS work=3SGO one   play   weINC-two
'I want that we two play a game...'

    b. *manahagi=ḡau **gau***
want=2PLO   youPL
'We want you all

       [*ta mala fa-lehe=i=na   naitu ao-hi*]
SBD PURP CS-die=3SGO=thatN devil thisT-EMPH
to kill this devil.'

However, *manahagi* also behaves in the same way as group C verbs, with a direct object complement clause realizing an event whose actor is the same participant as the main clause actor. Again, the complement clause subject/actor is coreferential with the main clause actor and cannot be overtly realized:

(10.59) *teo   ḡe manahagi=ni=u **gai**   [ta hage=na   ade]*
not.exist NT want=3SGO=CNT weEXC SBD ascend=thatN here
'We don't want to come up here.'

One further verb, *ooe* 'say', behaves like the verbs in group A, except in two important respects. Like group A verbs it may occur with a direct object NP and an indirect object complement clause, with the subject/actor of the complement clause coreferential with the main clause direct object and not overtly realized:

(10.60) *n-e   ooe=nau   **ara** [ta mala tazi=ni=na   sote   ana]*
RL-3S say=1SGO I   SBD PURP keep=3SGO=thatN shirt thatN
'He said to me to keep that shirt.'

However, unlike group A verbs, it appears that *ooe* may not occur with a complement clause direct object. Moreover, with *ooe* there is no restriction that the complement clause subject/actor be coreferential with the main clause direct object. As these two arguments may not be coreferential, it is possible for the complement clause subject/actor to be overtly realized:

(10.61) *o la ooe=ni   **zemesi***
2S go say=3SGO PN
'Go and tell James

       [***ara** teo   ḡe aḡe=u [gu=na   n-a   foḡra=nau]]*
I   not.exist NT go=CNT CNTX=3SGP RL-1EXCS be.sick=1SGO
[that] I'm not coming because I'm feeling sick.'

10.2.4.2.2 Main clause position of complement clauses

Complement clauses occur in the pragmatically unmarked main clause position for the argument they represent. In bivalent main clauses the complement clause occurs in postverbal position, following the actor, if that argument is also realized postverbally, as (10.59) illustrates. In trivalent clauses, the complement clause occurs postverbally, following both the actor, if present, and direct object, as (10.60), (10.61), and other examples above illustrate.

10.2.4.3 Nominalized clauses as adjuncts

Subordinate clauses may function as an oblique adjunct, governed by the preposition *ka*. In this context the clause is obligatorily marked with a demonstrative or article. Being nominalized in this way, possessor-indexing enclitics may also occur with these clauses. Oblique subordinate clauses typically mark a location of some kind. This may be an event because it is a location in a series of events:

(10.62)a. *o la fufunu* [*ka* [*n-e-ke   au=o   rei-palu ade fate*]]
 2S go begin LOC RL-3S-PFV exist=thatNV they-two here above
 'Start [the story] where they two stayed on top here.'

 b. [*ka* [*mhoko aḡe=na=na   manei*]] *nogoi*
  LOC sit   go=3SGP=thatN he   VOC
  'When he sat down, man! [lit. 'At that sitting of his…]

  ḡ-e   aḡe su=gu   ia   to~toi   ḡ-e   lehe=u…
  NT-3S go hiss=CNT theSG RD~cook NT-3S die=CNT
  the fire went ahead and hissed and started to die…'

 c. *kulu   zaho* [*ka*=[*ia   kokori   mau*
  be.first go LOC=theSG dig.taro taro
  'First go to the taro digging

  [*mala* [*ñhau   ka   toa,*] [*fa hage   ka   toa*]]]]
  PURP eat   LOC fort   CS ascend LOC fort
  to eat in the fort, to take up to the fort.'

The oblique may also represent a physical location associated with an event, either characteristic of the location, as in (10.63)a., or temporarily associated with it ([10.63]b.):

(10.63)a. *o   roh-i=Ø=u   [ka*=[*ia   hage=na   naprai*]]
 2S scrape-TR=3SGO=CNT LOC=theSG ascend=3SGP sun
 'You scrape [the tree] where [i.e., on the side] the sun rises.'

b. *ke pulo e=u*   *tana zelu,*
PFV return 3S=be.thus   then   PNLOC
'Then they went back to Zelu,

[*ka*=[*n-e-ke*   *hure=ri=ro*   *ira*   *tilo tomoko*
LOC=RL-3S-PFV carry=3PLO=thoseNV thePL three war.canoe
to where they had carried the three canoes,

[*n-e zaho kutare*]]]
RL-3S go   mud.shell
which had gone like mudshells.'

In addition to functioning as main clause oblique adjuncts, nominalized clauses occur with a number of other minor functions. This includes as possessor. In (10.64) the purpose of the coming of the chief is the possessor of the road in the main clause:

(10.64)   *n-e*   *ḡrui~ḡrui*   *la=ni=ña*
RL-3S RD~garden   go=3SGO=IMM
'They brushed

[*ka* [*ḡuku=na=na*   [*mala la mai=na*   *datau*   *ana*]]]
LOC road=3SGP=thatN PURP go come=3SGP chief   thatN
along that road for that chief's coming.'

A nominalized clause may also modify a pronoun—not as a relative clause, but in the same way that a NP may modify a pronoun (see §3.4.1.4). In (10.65) the pronoun *gai* 'we (exclusive)' (itself the object of a nominalized clausal oblique) is modified by a nominalized phrase marked with the article *ira* 'the (plural)':

(10.65)   ...*ḡ-e fa manemane=u*   [*ka* [*tuku=ḡai=na*   *gai*
NT-3S CS be.very.happy=CNT LOC wait.for=1EXCO=thatN weEXC
'...they are very happy as they wait [lit. ...at that waiting] for we

ira   [*ta*   *la zuke=i*   *ia*   *teḡe ka=ia*   *tahi*]]]...
thePL SBD go seek=3SGO theSG turtleLOC=theSG sea
the [ones] who go hunting turtles in the sea.'

10.2.4.4 Subordinate clause recursion

As a result of the range of functions open to subordinate clauses, a subordinate clause may occur embedded within another subordinate clause. Relative clause recursion has been discussed in §10.2.3.5. Embedding also occurs with argument and adverbial subordinate clauses. The range of possibilities is wide. In (10.66), for example, a nominalized clause oblique itself has a complement clause object:

(10.66) [*ka* [*gato la=i=na*   *bla ago* [*n-e   sodu=na*]]]
      LOC think go=3SGO=thatN LMT youSG RL-3S be.long=thatN
      'When you think it [the story] is long,

      fahorogoto la=i   *si=ago*
      ??   go=3SGO FOC=youSG
      you complete it all.'

10.2.5 Adverbial subordination

A number of adverbial functions may be performed by subordinate clauses. With most the clause is governed by an adjunct of the main clause. These constituents include the contextualizer nouns *gu-* and *nafu-*, the temporal local nouns *legu-* 'behind' and *ḡilu* 'inside', and the temporal locative *gilai* 'until'. Some contextual clauses, along with one adverbial clause type, the affective clause, are not governed by another constituent, but directly by the sentence head.

10.2.5.1 Contextual clauses

10.2.5.1.1 Zero-marked contextual clauses

A nominalized subordinate clause may indicate the context in which the main predication holds. In (10.67), clause 1 gives the context for the speaker's thirst:

(10.67) [*mhoko=na ka   naprai nhorao*] *n-a-ke   no-ḡu   kumai*
      sit=thatN   LOC sun   yesterday RL-1EXCS-PFV GENP-1SGP drink
      'Sitting in the sun yesterday, I wanted to drink.'

Contextual clauses of this kind are nominalized, typically by a cliticized demonstrative, and are neither realis nor irrealis, but related temporally only to the main clause event. In (10.67) the event expressed by the contextual clause has occurred, so would be coded realis as a main clause, while in (10.68) the event has yet to occur, so would be irrealis, but both are structurally identical.

(10.68) [*mhoko=na ka   naprai fufugo*] *ginai no-ḡu   kumai*
      sit=thatN   LOC sun   tomorrow FUT   GENP-1SGP drink
      'Sitting in the sun tomorrow, I will want to drink.'

Contextual clauses of this type are attested only sentence-initially.

10.2.5.1.2 Contextual clauses governed by contextualizer nouns

Two contextualizer nouns, *gu-* and *nafu*, are discussed in §4.5. As contextual nouns they function in an identical manner. However, *nafu* also has the root meaning of 'base'. As it is in the process of being grammaticalized as a contextual noun, and speakers still identify the root meaning when it occurs with its contextualizer function, it is glossed as 'base'. *Gu-*, on the other hand, occurs only as a contextualizer, and is glossed as 'CNTX'. *Gu-* and *nafu* are possessor-indexed to a constituent that provides contextual information about the event coded by the main clause. The indexed constituent (the complement of the possessor-indexing) may be a NP. However, it may also be a subordinate clause expressing an event that provides the context for the main clause event:

(10.69)a. *ara n-a   babao no-ḡu*
　　　　I   RL-1EXCS be.tired GENP-1SGP
　　　　'I'm tired

　　　　[gu=na   [n-a   friñhe heta   fakamo]]
　　　　CNTX=3SGP RL-1EXCS work be.strong always
　　　　because I always work hard.'

　　b. *teo   la bla gai   ḡ-e   aḡe fa surai*
　　　　not.exist ?? LMT weEXC NT-3S go CS ??
　　　　'We don't have much

　　　　fa mana=ri   ira   mereseni kastom...
　　　　CS spiritual.power=3PLO thePL medicine custom
　　　　strength in the custom medicines...

　　　　[nafu=na [n-e-ge   heta   ira   dokta]]...
　　　　base=3SGP RL-3S-PRS be.strong thePL doctor
　　　　because the doctors are strong...'

Clauses subordinated by *gu-* and *nafu* have identical formal characteristics as main clauses. They are not subject to the constituent structure restrictions discussed in §10.2.2, and the subordinator *ta* does not occur. Modal/subject particles occur as with main clauses (as [10.69] illustrates), and any or all arguments may be overtly realized, even when they are coreferential with main clause arguments. All main clause constituent order possibilities occur in contextual clauses. As (10.70) illustrates, arguments with any grammatical relation can occur in preverbal topic position, including actors, unergative and unaccusative subjects, objects, and obliques.

(10.70)a. *ara n-a   lao[gu=na   [zemesi n-e-ke   tore=nau ara]]*
　　　　I   RL-1EXCS go CNTX=3SGP PN   RL-3S-PFV ask=1SGO I
　　　　'I went because James asked me to.'

　　b. *ara n-a   fahega*
　　　　I   RL-1EXCS be.happy
　　　　'I am happy

[*gu=na*   [*ia*   *kue=ḡu*   *ara n-e*   *mai*]]
CNTX=3SGP theSG grandfather=1SGP I   RL-3S come
because my grandfather has come.'

c. *ke*   *nodo*   *fea*   *ke*   *mai*   *tore=i*   *kaoni*   *t=au=o,*
PFV   stop   INIT PFV   come   ask=3SGO account SBD=exist=thatNV
'Stop coming and asking for credit,

[*nafu=na*   [*ia*   *kaoni*   *ka*   *gita*   *n-e-ge*   *aḡe tehi*   *salupu*]]
base=3SGP theSG account LOC weINC RL-3S-PRS go   many pass
because credit with us has become too much.'

d. *ara*   *n-a*   *dia-nanafa*
I   RL-1EXCS be.bad-heart
'I am sorry

[*gu=na*   [*ago*   *a*   *ginai* *zaho koko=nigo*]]
CNTX=3SGP youSG 1EXCS FUT   go   leave=2SGO
because I will leave you.'

e. [*nafu=na*   [*ka=ira*   *mane-vaka* *e*   *au*   *no-di*   *fama*
base=3SGP LOC=thePL man-ship   3S exist   GENP-3PLP farm
'Because with the white man there are their farms

ka=ira   *buluka,*   *ka=ira*   *zora*]]...
LOC=thePL cow   LOC=thePL pig
of cows, of pigs...'

Clauses governed by *gu-* and *nafu* may also locate an argument in clause-final focus position. The focused argument may be marked with the focal particle *si*, as in main clauses, though the focal particle may also be omitted (as it must be in relative and complement clauses):

(10.71)a. *n-a*   *mai*   [*gu=na*   [*ginai turi tufa=nau*   *si=ago*]]
RL-1EXCS come   CNTX=3SGP   FUT   tell   affect=1SGOFOC=youSG
'I have come because <u>you</u> will tell me [the stories].'

b. *e=u*   *teo*   *ḡ-e*   *boka*   *turi=di*   *manei...*
3S=be.thus not.exist NT-3S be.able tell=3PLO he
'I can't tell them to him...

[*nafu=na*   [*n-e-ke*   *blahi*   *ka=gai*   *tu~turi are*]]
base=3SGP RL-3S-PFV be.tabu LOC=weEXC RD~tell thoseN
because those stories are tabu for us.'

Clauses subordinated by *gu-* and *nafu* may have a non-verbal predicate. In (10.72) an equative clause is governed by *nafu*:

(10.72) *n-a   no-mai   aḡe   mhemhe=ni=u   gai*
RL-1EXCS GENP-1EXCP go   be.difficult=3SGO=CNT weEXC
'We are finding it hard

         ta=ke   fa-nodo=i   fea   t=au=na   za~zaho=na=na
SBD=PFV CS-stop=3SGO INIT SBD=exist=thatN RD~go=3SGP=thatN
to stop that way [i.e., hunting] of

         teḡe   ine,   [nafu=na   [are=bla   ira   doli=mai gai]]
turtle thisR   base=3SGP thoseN=LMT thePL live=1EXCP weEXC
this turtle, because those are our life.'

Conjoined clauses may be subordinated to *gu-* or *nafu*, in which case the possessor-indexing on the contextual noun is plural, reflecting the plural contextual bases expressed by the conjoined clauses:

(10.73) *ara n-a   lao   [gu=di   [manei n-e-ke   tore=nau ara]]*
I   RL-1EXCS go   CNTX=3PLP he   RL-3S-PFV ask=1SGO I
'I went because he asked me to

         n-e=u   [ara n-a   manahagi lao]]
RL-3S=be.thus I   RL-1EXCS want   go
and I wanted to go.'

Clauses governed by *gu-* and *nafu* typically occur finally within the main clause. However, they may occur main clause-initially, as (10.70)e. illustrates.

10.2.5.2 Temporal adjuncts governed by local nouns

Two local nouns, *legu* 'behind, after' and *ḡilu* 'inside, within, during' (see §4.4.1), have temporal as well as spatial locative functions. Both typically have a nominal complement, but may have a subordinate clause as complement. In this situation the local noun carries third person possessor-indexing agreeing with the subordinated clause. When the complement is a subordinate clause only a temporal reading is possible.

Clauses that are subordinated by *legu* are nominalized by means of a demonstrative or possessor-indexing marking the subordinate verb complex. These clauses express an event that precedes the event coded by the main clause.

(10.74)a. [*legu=na*   [*toka* *kave=i*   **ana**   *gita*   *ḡazu* *ana*   *ge*]]
      behind=3SGP chop descend=3SGO thatN weINC wood thatN SEQ
      'After [that] we cut down that tree

      ḡ-o   *fike=i*   *no-u*   *ḡazu=ña*   *ago*
      NT-2S cut.firewood=3SGO GENP-2SGP wood=IMM youSG
      you can make your firewood.'

    b. [*legu=na*   [*n-e-ke*   *zaho=na* *manei*]]
      behind=3SGP RL-3S-PFV go=3SGP he
      'After that leaving of his [i.e., after he had left]

      ara *n-a*   *bula=nau=ña*
      I   RL-1EXCS feel.angry=1SGO=IMM
      I felt angry.'

Clauses governed by *legu* typically occur main clause-initially, iconically reflecting the actual temporal sequence of the events. However, this is a tendency, not a categorical restriction, as main clause-final *legu* subordinates occasionally occur:

(10.75)   *...huhurañi* *au=re*   *keha=re*   *n-e-ke=u*   *gai,*
      PNLOC   exist=thoseN NSP=thoseN RL-3S-PFV=be.thus weEXC
      '...some of us lived at Huhurangi

      [*legu=na*   [*au=na*   *ia*   *boñihehe*]]
      behind=3SGP exist=3SGP theSG paganism
      after the existence of the heathen time.'

Local nouns are typically immediately governed by the sentence head. However, they may instead be governed by an intervening preposition. This applies when the local noun complement is a subordinate clause as much as when it is a NP:

(10.76)   *ara* *n-a*   *tehi*   *ta*   *marh-i=au=re*
      I   RL-1EXCS many SBD be.in.pain-TR=1SGO=thoseN
      'I have many pains

      [*ka* [*legu=na*   [*faroho=nau=o*   *maneri*]]]
      LOC behind=3SGP smite=1SGP=thatNV they
      since they were hitting me.'

Nominalized clauses governed by *legu* allow only the pragmatically unmarked constituent order VS/VAO. No pragmatically marked constructions such as preverbal topicalization or clause-final focused arguments are possible.

The behavior of subordinate clauses governed by *g̅ilu* 'inside' is not fully understood. They do not appear to be nominalized:

(10.77) *fufunu   ka   keli-kava=o   n-e   la mai=u*
        begin   LOC be.good-earth=thatNV RL-3S go come=CNT
        'Start from the peace[until it] goes ahead [and] comes

        [ka [g̅ilu=na   [toke=i=a   ta   dia]]]
        LOC inside=3SGP arrive=3SGO=theSG SBD be.bad
        to reaching the badness.'

10.2.5.3 Temporal adjuncts governed by *gilai* 'until'

The particle *gilai* 'until' introduces a subordinate clause that expresses an event marking the end of the event expressed by the main clause. In positive main clauses *gilai* indicates that the main clause event finishes at a point in time coinciding with the occurrence of the subordinate clause event:

(10.78)a. *boro bla au   sare   nogoi [gilai [toke=i=n-e-ke=u*
          boro LMT exist thereP VOC   until   arrive=3SGO=RL-3S-PFV=be.thus
          '[They] just stay *boro*[67] there, man!, until comes

          ia   nare   mala sugitabu=na   suli   ana]] e=u
          theSG day   PURP baptism=3SGP child thatN 3S=be.thus
          the day for the baptism of the child.'

     b. *lao   [gilai [toke=i=u*
        go   until   arrive=3SGO=CNT
        'Go ahead [with the story] until [you] get to

        ka   n-e-ke   au=o   rei-palu ade]]
        LOC RL-3S-PFV   exist=thatNV they-two here
        [the part of the story where] they two lived here.'

In (10.78)a. the main clause event continues until a subsequent event occurs in a sequence of events. In (10.78)b. the main clause event continues until a point in a story at which an event in the story takes place.

In negative main clauses the subordinate clause indicates that the non-occurrence of the event expressed in the main clause lasts until the event in the subordinate clause takes place, effectively indicating that the main clause event only occurs once the subordinate clause event has happened:

---

[67] The verb *boro* refers to a period after the birth of a child when the mother and infant remain together indoors in close physical contact.

(10.79)a. *o-ti   mai   [gilai   [e   mai   manei]]*
         2S-NEG come until   3S come he
         'Don't come until he comes.'

    b. *teo   ḡ-e-ke   mai=u   manei   [gilai   [n-a-ke   toi]]*
         not.exist NT-3S-PFV come=CNT he   until   RL-1EXCS-PFV cook
         'He didn't come until I had cooked.'

With some elderly speakers *gilai* is itself governed by the preposition *ka*:

(10.80) *gu   bla   ḡ-e   au   palu mane=re,*
         be.thus LMT NT-3S exist two   man=thoseN
         'Like that those two men stayed,

    [ka   [gilai   [n-e-ge   knusu   ia   papari=na]]]
         LOC until   RL-3S-PRS be.broken theSG wood.stack=thatN
         until the wood stack is broken.'

The elderly speaker who gave the example in (10.80) consistently used *ka* in this context. Among all except the elderly, however, this usage has been completely lost, and *gilai* is governed directly by the sentence head. Nonetheless, all speakers accept the presence of *ka* with *gilai* as grammatical in every instance.

Clauses governed by *gilai* conform to the internal structural constraints described for realis subordinate clauses in §10.2.2.1.

10.2.5.4 Affective clauses

Affective adverbial clauses indicate that the main clause event occurs with the intention of affecting another participant. These clauses consist of the affective verb *tufa* with the affected participant as object. Affective clauses occur with either a modal/subject particle or the subordinator *ta*.

(10.81) *ara n-a   toḡla=di   ira   zora [tufa=di   nakoni=de]*
         I   RL-1EXCS chase=3PLO thePL pig   affect=3PLO person=theseR
         'I chased the pigs for these people.'

As discussed in §6.5.2, *tufa* may have a benefactive or malefactive reading, depending on the semantics of the main clause of the event.

10.2.6 Conditional clauses

Conditional clauses express an event or state that the main clause event is dependent on to occur. These clauses are subordinate to the main clause, and are marked with the conditional marker *la*. The conditional marker occurs immediately after the verb complex of the subordinate clause, following any postverbal agreement enclitic or incorporated undergoer:

(10.82)a. [*ta mai au la gai ade,*]*a-ke mai siko ginai*
　　　　　SBD come exist CND weEXChere 1EXCS-PFV come steal todayIRR
　　　　　'If we come and live here, later we would come and steal

　　　　　ka=ira ge-di no-di e=u
　　　　　LOC=thePL CNSM-3PLP GENP-3PLP 3S=be.thus
　　　　　from the food and things of

　　　　　mane n-e-ke kusu au=de ade
　　　　　man RL-3S-PFV be.first exist=theseR here
　　　　　the men who lived here first.'

　　　b. [*ta toi=ni la ago namhari ana,*]
　　　　　SBD cook=3SGO CND youSG fish thatN
　　　　　'If you cook that fish,

　　　　　gita teo ḡe-da siri=ni gudu
　　　　　weINC not.exist NT-1INCS smell=3SGO EXHST
　　　　　we won't smell it all.'

　　　c. [*ta korho namhari la*] *gita da ñha=di bla*
　　　　　SBD pull fish CND weINC 1INCS eat=3PLO LMT
　　　　　'If I catch fish, we'll just eat them.'

Unlike other subordinate clauses with the subordinator *ta*, the verb complex of conditional clauses may not be marked with a cliticized demonstrative, the conditional marker and demonstrative enclitics being mutually exclusive.

Conditional clauses typically occur sentence-initially, iconically realizing the temporal sequence of a prerequisite event followed by a dependent event. However, as with *legu* temporal clauses (see §10.2.5.2), this is a tendency only and the reverse order is possible, with no apparent change in meaning:

(10.83) *ḡ-e la heve e=u,* [*ta au la gau selena*]
　　　　　NT-3S go what 3S=be.thus SBD exist CND youPL PNLOC
　　　　　'How would it be if you all lived at Selena?'

Conditional clauses are frequently introduced by the subordinator *ta*. As discussed in §10.2.1, *ta* introduces irrealis subordinate clauses. Its occurrence in conditional clauses indicates that the event expressed by the clause has not happened, but may yet happen. However, to use *ta* the speaker must have a specific event in mind. Events that are hypothetical and not specific envisaged events are not marked with *ta*, nor are positive past counterfactual conditional events. Negative past counterfactual events, however, are marked with *ta*. Conditional clauses that are marked with *ta* are modally neutral, and may occur with the neutral modal/subject particle *ḡ-*, although this is typically omitted:

(10.84)　[*ta　ḡ-e　heta　la　foḡra-n-lau,*]
　　　　　SBD　NT-3S　be.strong　CND　sick=thatN-SPC
　　　　　'If that sickness is strong,

　　　　　a-ke　la=di　ḡazu　t=au=ro...
　　　　　1EXCS-PFV　go=3PLO　wood　SBD=exist=thoseNV
　　　　　I give [medicine from] those trees...'

When *ta* is not present in a conditional clause a modal/subject particle is obligatory. *Ta* does not occur when the speaker regards the conditional event as very speculative and hypothetical. There is no absolute demarcation point between future events that are regarded as sufficiently specific to be marked with *ta*, and those that are speculative and hypothetical enough for the *ta* to be omitted. In (10.85)a., for example, two speakers are debating the risks of custom stories falling into the wrong hands, and *ta* is omitted. In (10.85)b. the conditional clause has the pragmatic function of a suggestion canvassing a possibility not previously discussed:

(10.85)a.　*are　si　ara　n-a　mhagu-mhagu=di=re,*
　　　　　thoseN　FOC　I　RL-1EXCS　be.afraid-be.afraid=3PLO=thoseN
　　　　　'Those, I am a bit afraid of those,

　　　　　[*ḡ-e　lao　la　histiri=de*]...
　　　　　NT-3S　go　CND　history=theseR
　　　　　if these histories go...'

　　b.　*da　la　au=gu　rhuku　ña　gita-palu*
　　　　　1INCS　go　exist=CNT　landward　but　weINC-two
　　　　　'We are living on the shore side [in the bush],

　　　　　[*ḡe　au　la　ka　nasona　a-hi　ḡerona*]　*keli*
　　　　　NT　exist　CND　LOC　point　thisT-EMPH　PNLOC　be.good
　　　　　but if you and I live at the point at Gerona [that would] be good.'

Positive past counterfactual clauses are also not marked with *ta*. While all past counterfactual main, relative, and complement clauses are treated as irrealis, positive past counterfactual conditional clauses are treated as modally neutral:

(10.86) [ḡ-e-ke   au   **la**   manei,]   ḡ-e-la   a   fahega   ḡlehe ara
       NT-3S-PFV exist CND he   NT-3S-go 1EXCS be.happy very   I
       'If he had lived [instead of dying] I would've been very happy.'

Real events can also be expressed by a conditional clause, if the event is one that the main clause event is dependent on. In this situation a realis particle occurs:

(10.87) ara teo   ḡ-a   fahega
       I   not.exist NT-1EXCS be.happy
       'I am not happy

       ḡ-e-la   [n-e-ke   au=ro   la   manei]
       NT-3S-go RL-3S-PFV exist=thoseNV CND he
       like [I was] when he was alive.'

One negation strategy involves the negative existential verb *teo* with a sentential complement realizing the event negated (see §8.7.2). This is the strategy that applies to negative conditional clauses other than past counterfactuals. As *teo* is the verb of the conditional clause, and the following predicate is *teo*'s complement, the conditional marker follows *teo*, not the negated predication:

(10.88) [ta   **teo**   **la**   [ḡ-e   nahani=u]], ara ginai a   laoteteḡu
       SBD not.exist CND NT-3S rain=CNT I   FUT   1EXCS go fish(V)
       'If it is not raining I will go fishing.'

However, conditional negative past counterfactuals are formed using the negative particle *ti*, in a clause introduced by the subordinator *ta*:

(10.89) ara teo   ḡe   bula=nau=gu
       I   not.exist NT   feel.angry=1SGO=CNT
       'I wouldn't be angry

       [ta   **ti**-fa-dia-i=la   manei ḡlepo an-lau]
       SBD NEG-CS-be.bad=3SGO=CND he   thing thatN-SPC
       if he hadn't done that bad thing.' [lit. '…made that thing bad']

The conditional marker may mark the existential verb *au* subordinated by *ta* to form a single word clause translatable as 'if that is so' or 'since that is so'. This clause refers anaphorically to an event expressed by the preceding main clause, introducing a main clause coding an event dependent on that preceding event:

(10.90) n-e   la lehe mariñi, ka   mane=aro
       RL-3S go die PNLOC LOC man=theseT
       'He is dead from Maringe, from those men,

si=ba   no-g̱u   kaka
FOC=ALT GENP-1SGP grandparent
my grandfather.

[*t=au=la*]   *ke   nhogi   ia   lehe ka   manei e=u*
SBD=exist=CND PFV payback theSG die LOC he   3s=be.thus
Since that is so [we] will payback his death.'

10.2.7 Purposive subordinate clauses

The purposive particle *mala* marks the event expressed by a clause as being intended or purposeful. In main clauses, *mala* immediately follows the modal/subject particle and any attached tense or aspect markers, and preceding the verb (see §7.5.6). The particle occurs commonly, however, in subordinate clauses.

10.2.7.1 Main clause possibilities of purposive subordinates

Subordinate clauses with *mala* indicate the purpose of the modified constituent. Purposive subordinate clauses can function adverbially, adnominally, or as a complement clause. As adverbial subordinates they modify an entire main clause, coding the purpose of the main clause event:

(10.91)   *hod-i=Ø   ag̱e nai=ni   ka   sug̱a   tarai=ne*
         take-TR=3SGO go   put=3SGO LOC house pray=thisR
         'Take it and put it in the church

         [*mala lao ka   miziam*]
         PURP go   LOC museum
         in order to go to a museum.'

Adverbial purposive subordinates typically occur main clause-finally, as in (10.91), but they may occur initially:

(10.92)   [*mala nhigo   lao ago*]   *n-e=u   palu t=au=re*
         PURP be.finished go youSG RL-3S=be.thus two SBD=exist=thoseN
         'In order for you to finish, those two are like that...'

Where they function adnominally, purposive subordinates indicate that the modified nominal has the purpose expressed by the subordinate clause:

(10.93)   *e au   g̱lepo *[*mala hod-i=Ø   tege   ine*]
         3S exist thing PURP take-TR=3SGO turtle thisR
         'There is a thing for taking this turtle.'

Adnominal purposive subordinates are embedded within the NP, and follow immediately the head nominal. Typically these modify a main clause argument, as in (10.93), but may modify the nominal predicate of an equative construction:

(10.94) *ana*   *belo* [*mala* *tarai*]
         thatN bell PURP pray
         'That was the bell for prayer.'

Purposive clauses also occur as complements of a number of verbs including various verbs coding speech events, verbs of cessation, and the desiderative *manahagi*. They may occur as the direct object of these verbs, as in (10.95), or as indirect objects, as in (10.96).

(10.95)a. *ia*   *nahani* *n-e*   *fa* *noto=i*
          theSG rain   RL-3S CS stop=3SGO
          'The rain stopped

          [*mala* *aḡe* *teteḡu* [*ne-ke=u=o*   *gita*]]
          PURP   go   fish(V) RL-PFV=be.thus=thatNV weINC
          us going fishing as we said [we would].'

      b. *manei* *n-e*   *tahe=i*   [*mala* *tazi=ni*   *ara* *sote* *ine*]
          he   RL-3S say=3SGO PURP keep=3SGO I   shirt thisR
          'He said that I could keep this shirt.'

(10.96) *n-e*   *tahe=nau*   *ara* [*mala* *tazi=ni*   *no-na*   *sote* *ana*]
         RL-3S say=1SGO   I   PURP keep=3SGO GENP-3SGP shirt thatN
         'He told me that I could keep that shirt of his.'

10.2.7.2 Modal and tense/aspect status of purposive subordinates

As discussed in §10.2.1, relative and complement clauses normally occur with either a modal/subject particle (when realis) or the subordinator *ta* (when irrealis). Purposive subordinate clauses typically occur without either. However, in a significant minority of instances the subordinator does occur, introducing the purposive marked subordinate. In (10.97)a. line 1 *ta* introduces a purposive complement clause, in (10.97)b. an adverbial, and in (10.97)c. a relative clause.

(10.97)a. *manahagi=ḡau* *gau*   [*ta* *mala* *fa-lehe=i=na*
          want=2PLO   youPL SBD PURP CS-die=3SGO=thatN
          'We want you all to kill

          naitu *ao-hi*]   [*a*   *mala* *doli* *keli*   *au*   *gai*]
          devil thisT-EMPH 1EXCS PURP live be.good exist weEXC
          this devil so we can live on.'

391

b. ...*palu fata*   *roh-i=Ø*   *ara*
   two   occasion scrape-TR=3SGO I
   '...two times I scrape

   ḡazu a-hi   e=u,   [*ta mala siri=na   manei*]
   wood thisT-EMPH 3S=be.thus   SBD PURP smell=thatN he
   this tree, for him to inhale.'

c. *tana aḡe toke=i   ia   nare*
   then go   arrive=3SGO theSG day
   'Then comes the day

   [*ta mala aḡe friñhe=ni   ia   mala-ñhau*]...
   SBD PURP go   work=3SGO   theSG PURP-eat
   to make the food...'

Events coded by purposive subordinate clauses are typically either habitual (as in [10.93], [10.94], [10.95]b., [10.96], and [10.97]b.–c.), or located in the future within the temporal frame of the main clause (as in [10.91], [10.92], [10.95]a., and [10.97]a.). In other instances the intended event is located in the past but did not occur. All three of these event types, habitual, future, and past counterfactual, are coded as irrealis in Kokota. Purposive subordinate clauses coding all such events are also irrealis and could be expected to be marked with the subordinator *ta*. However, as intended events are typically located in the future (within the temporal frame either of speaking or of the main clause event), they are typically irrealis. The presence of both the subordinator, limited as it is to irrealis clauses, and the purposive marker, is redundant. Consequently the *ta* is typically omitted. However, in all such clauses its presence is optionally possible.

The absence of modal/subject particles in irrealis purposive clauses has a similar motivation. As noted in §7.5.2.5, irrealis particles are frequently omitted. This is particularly common when *mala* is present, as the prototypically habitual or future nature of intended events renders an irrealis particle redundant. However, they do occasionally occur. In subordinate clauses the particle and *mala* may occur in either order. In the second line of (10.97)a. the particle precedes the purposive marker. In (10.98) it follows it:

(10.98)   ...*mala e   au   histri   are-lau   ka   sikolu=ne...*
          PURP 3S exist history thoseN-SPC LOC school=thisR
          '...so those histories can stay in the school...'

Very occasionally a realis purposive subordinate clause occurs. As these clauses do not have the prototypical modal status, the modal/subject particle is obligatory. Again the particle may precede or follow *mala*:

(10.99)a. *fa puku~puku=ri*   *bla*   *ago*   *e=u*   *bla* *goi*
CS RD~be.short=3PLO   LMT   youSG   3S=be.thus LMT VOC
'You make it short, man!,

    [*mala n-e-ge*   *au*   *bo*   *turi=di=re*]...
    PURP RL-3S-PRS exist CNT tell=3PLP=thoseN
    so that these stories fit [on the tape]...'

    b. *ka=t=au=ana*   *ge*   *tafe*   *ia*   *ñehe*
    LOC=SBD=exist=thatN SEQ spring.open theSG umbrella
    'At that, sprang open the umbrella

    [*n-e-ke*   *mala* *totoku=di=ro*   *ira*   *liligomo*]...
    RL-3S-PFV PURP cover=3PLO=thoseNV thePL warning.charm
    that was for covering the warning charm...'

In (10.99)a. fitting the stories on the tape is presented as realis (and present tense), as the addressee is telling stories that are already being recorded and some of which are already on the tape. It is interesting that the realis subordinate clause is modifying an irrealis imperative main clause. This is possible because the speaker is directing the addressee to carry out a future event to conform to a present state. Example (10.99)b. is coded realis because the umbrella is already covering the items mentioned at the point in the temporal frame of the story.

The absence of an overt modal/subject particle in a purposive subordinate does not prevent the presence of a tense or aspect marking that would otherwise be suffixed to the particle, such as the perfective aspect marker in (10.100)a. and the present tense marker in (10.100)b.:

(10.100)a. *ke*   *la* *toke*   *ia*   *taem* [*mala ke* *visiti* *ka* *hugo hebala*]
       PFV   go arrive theSG time PURP PFV visit LOC PN
       'The time came [for them] to visit with Hugo Hebala.'

    b. *ña*   *e=u*   *la=i*   *bl=ago*   *kaike* *ta* *puku=na*
      but 3S=be.thus go=3SGO LMT=youSG one   SBD be.short=3SGP
      'So likewise you give one that's short

      [*mala ge* *fafra*   *nhigo*   *bla* *e=u*]
      PURP PRS be.quick be.finished LMT 3S=be.thus
      so [we] are finished quickly.'

10.2.7.3 Internal structure of purposive subordinates

Purposive subordinates need not be clauses with verbal predicates. Any kind of predicate can occur as the purpose of the modified clause or nominal. For example, in (10.101) possessive predicates have been subordinated (in [10.101]a. adverbially, in [10.101]b. adnominally):

(10.101)a. *tazi=ri*   *boboke=mu=are*   [*mala **no-ḡu**   **ara***]
          keep=3PLO inner.thigh=2SGP=thoseN PURP GENP-1SGP I
          'Keep your inner thighs for me.'

        b. *totogale*   [*mala **no-na**   *belama*]
          picture   PURP   GENP-3SGP PN
          'a photo I will give to Belama' [lit. '…intended to belong to Belama']

Purposive clauses with verbal predicates only allow the language's unmarked clause constituent structure of VAO or VS, followed by any oblique arguments. As with other clause types, it is rare for all arguments to be specified. In (10.100)b., for example, no overt arguments occur. However, an argument with any grammatical relation may occur. An unergative subject is present in (10.97)b.; an unaccusative subject in (10.99)a.; direct objects in (10.99)b.; and an oblique in (10.100)a.. Multiple arguments are possible, as in (10.98), where an unaccusative subject and two obliques receive overt mentions. As discussed in §8.3, there is an overall tendency in the language for recently mentioned participants to receive zero mentions. Consequently, as with other clause types, purposive clauses with all arguments are rare. However, as with other clause types, they do occasionally occur, as in (10.95)b., where an actor and object are both present. While any argument may occur in adverbial purposive clauses, in relative clauses of any type the controlled argument may not be overtly realized (see §10.2.3), and this applies equally to purposive relative clauses.

Although purposive subordinate clauses do not allow any of the pragmatically marked clause constituent orders, this does not preclude clauses in which an incorporated undergoer precedes the actor. As in other clause types, purposive subordinate clauses allow undergoer incorporation:

(10.102) *n-e*   *lao*   [*mala tabara viri*]
          RL-3S go   PURP buy   tobacco
          'He went to buy tobacco.'

Purposive subordination may have scope over more than a single clause. Clause chaining may occur, with the purposive marker having scope over the entire chained structure:

(10.103) *kulu*   *zaho*   [*ka*=[*ia*   *kokori mau*
          be.first go   LOC=theSG dig.taro taro
          'First go to the taro digging

[*mala* [*ñhau ka toa,*] [*fa hage ka toa*]]]]
PURP eat LOC fort CS ascend LOC fort
to eat in the fort, to take up to the fort.'

In purposive relative clauses the participant that is coreferential with the nominal head typically has a peripheral function, such as an instrument (as in [10.93] and [10.99]b.) or locative (as the temporal locatives in [10.97]c. and [10.100]a.). In fact *mala* often simply indicates that the head has a purpose that is associated in some way with the event in the subordinate clause. This association can be simply one of accompaniment. In (10.104) the song accompanies the activity coded by the purposive clause:

(10.104) *koze* [*mala se~seha niba tifaro*]
song PURP RD~climb possum before
'A song for climbing for possums in the old days.'

Adverbial purposive subordinate clauses may contain an argument that is coreferential with a main clause argument. Where that is so, the participant may have any grammatical relation in the subordinate clause.

The relation may be the same in both clauses; however, it need not be—in (10.91), for example, the main clause object participant occurs as the subordinate clause subject.

10.3 Recapping

Kokota makes frequent use of recapping strategies to link sequences of events. This occurs in all discourse types, including conversation and narration, but is employed most frequently in exposition, where for substantial slabs of text every sentence may commence with some recapping device. Recapping strategies in Kokota include the use of demonstratives, prepositional oblique demonstratives, reduced clauses, and clauses indicating completion of a recapped event.

10.3.1 Demonstrative recapping

Clause-initial demonstratives refer anaphorically to the event expressed by the preceding sentence. These demonstratives occur with the sequencer *ge*, placing the event within a sequence following the event coded by the preceding clause. Demonstrative recapping typically uses root demonstratives (see §3.1.3.1), as in (10.105). However, clausal demonstratives (see §3.1.3.3) occasionally occur (10.106). Demonstrative recapping is largely limited to exposition.

(10.105) *ge kulu friñhe=ni fea ia suḡa*
SEQ be.first work=3SGO INIT theSG house
'First [they] make the house.'

friñhe=ni   ia   suḡa n-e   nhigo=u
work=3SGO theSG house RL-3S be.finished=CNT
Building the house is finished.

an-lau   ge   kata   n-e=u   suli   ana
thatN-SPC SEQ bite   RL-3S=be.thus child thatN
That, then the child starts biting [i.e., contractions begin].

an-lau   ge   ḡ-e   lao=ña   ka=ia   suḡa
thatN-SPC SEQ NT-3S go=IMM   LOC=theSG house
That, then she will go to the house

ḡ-e   fa-doli=ni   ia   suli   e=u
NT-3S CS-be.alive=3SGO theSG child 3S=be.thus
[and] give birth to the baby.

doli   t=au=na   ia   suli
be.alive   SBD=exist=thatN theSG child
The child is born.

ao   ge   ḡ-e   hod-i=Ø   ḡ-e=u-ña   ia   suli
thisT SEQ   NT-3S take-TR=3SGO   NT-3S=be.thus=IMM theSG child
This, then they take the child.'

(10.106) *gu   maneri tifaro   n-e-ke=u=ña=ia*
be.thus they   before   RL-3S-PFV=be.thus=IMM=PRO
'They were like that in the old days.

t=au=na   si=ge   ḡ-e   au   mai=ña
SBD=exist=thatN   FOC=SEQ   NT-3S exist come=IMM

no-di   friñhe=re   maneri
GENP-3PLP work=thoseN   they
That, and then their work went ahead.'

10.3.2 Oblique demonstrative recapping

Oblique marked demonstratives occur with the locative preposition *ka* cliticized
to a clausal demonstrative (see §3.1.3.3). Like demonstrative recapping, these
oblique demonstratives locate the event coded by the sentence in a sequence of
events, following the event coded by the preceding sentence. However, with
oblique demonstratives the relationship between the events is closer in terms of
both time, and cause and effect. Demonstrative recapping simply locates one
event after another in time. With oblique demonstratives the event coded by the

sentence is presented as occurring in response to the event expressed by the preceding sentence (not unlike the English sentence-initial *at that...*).

(10.107) *ḡ-e   la mai=u   mane velepuhi, ḡ-e   au=gu   logahaza...*
NT-3S go come=CNT man   right.way NT-3S exist=CNT PNLOC
'A catechist came, he lived at Logahaza...

  n-e-ke   velepuhi=re
  RL-3S-PFV   right.way=thoseN
  and was catechist.

  ka=t=au=ao,   *hage   tarai, gu   nogoi,*
  LOC=SBD=exist-thisT ascend pray   be.thus VOC
  At this, [they] went up and prayed, like that, man!,

  hage   bo e=u   mane kokota ide=u
  ascend CNT 3S=be.thus man   PNLOC theseR=be.thus
  these Kokota people went up.'

Recapping oblique demonstratives typically do not cooccur with the sequencer *ge*; however, they may do so:

(10.108) *...la au   kuru   mai=di=re=n-e-ke=u*
go   exist be.first come=3PLO=thoseN=RL-3S-PFV=be.thus
'...[they] stopped them from coming.

  ka=t=au=ana   **sini-ge,**   *ḡ-e   tetu=ña   solomoni...*
  LOC=SBD=exist-thisT FOC=SEQ NT-3S stand=IMM PN
  At that then, Solomon stood up...'

Oblique demonstrative recapping is employed commonly in narratives.

10.3.3 Reduced clause recapping

Clauses may be partially repeated as a recapping strategy. These clauses are reduced by the omission of the modal/subject particle and any other modifier, with only the verb or verbs, and optionally one or more argument, repeated:

(10.109) *ḡ-e   hod-i=∅=ña*   *ia   rarau,   ziku=ro...*
NT-3S take-TR=3SGO=IMM   theSG arm.ring arm.ring=thoseNV
'He took the arm ring, those arm rings....

  ḡ-e   fa hage=u   ka kame=na=re   n-e-ke=u
  NT-3S CS ascend=CNT LOC arm=3SGP=thoseN RL-3S-PFV=be.thus
  He was putting [them] up on his arms.

> *fa hage   ka   kame=na=re   sini age*
> CS ascend LOC arm=3SGP=thoseN   FOC SEQ
> Put [them] up on his arms and then

> *ḡ-e   aḡe   n-e=u=ña   manei*
> NT-3S go   RL-3S=be.thus=IMM he
> he went.'

More often, the predication is marked with a 'be thus' tag clause (see §10.4):

(10.110)   *n-e   toga   aḡe=u   maneri,*
           RL-3S arrive go=CNT they
           'They arrived.

> *toga   ḡ-e=u   tana   nogoi lao hure=i   hinage=na...*
> arrive NT-3S=be.thus then   VOC   go   carry=3SGO boat=thatN
> They arrived and then went [and] carried that boat...'

10.3.4 'Completion' clause recapping

The partial repetition described in §10.3.3 occurs infrequently. A more frequently used recapping strategy employs 'completion' clauses. Completion clauses are unusual in structure. The main clause of a completion clause consists of the verb *nhigo* 'be finished'. The event that is completed is expressed by a subordinated verb complex that cannot be marked with a modal/subject particle. This verb complex is the subject of the main predication *n-e nhigo* 'it is finished', which it must precede. Thus in (10.113) *la roh-i* in line 3 and *fa blahi* in line 4 are the subjects of *n-e nhigo* in each completion clause. However, what is unusual is that the arguments of the subordinated verb complex coding the completed event typically occur after the main clause predication. Thus in (10.113) line 4, *ara* 'I' is the subject of the subordinated predication *fa blahi*. A more literal translation of this completion clause would be something like "I bless is finished...". Arguments occasionally occur immediately following the subordinated verb complex, as shown with the object *ia suḡa* in (10.105) line 2:

However, typically arguments occur after the main clause predication, as the subject in (10.113) line 4. In (10.111)a. *ia tañano* 'the food' is the object of *friñhe=ni* 'make it'. In (10.111)b. *ka=t=au=ana* 'of that' is an oblique adjunct of the predication *fa ku~kumai* 'cause to drink medicine'.

(10.111)a....*friñhe tañano, ke   la toi   mala-ñhau ka=manei*
            work   food   PFV go cook PURP-eat   LOC=he
            '...make food, cook food for him,

g-e=u=ni...   *...ḡure,   foro,*
NT-3S=be.thus=3SGO   nut.paste   coconut.paste
they do that ...nut paste, coconut paste,

ḡ-e=u=gu...   *...maneri   ḡaha   mane   e=u*
NT-3S=be.thus=CNT   they   five   man   3S=be.thus
that's what they the five men were doing....

[*friñhe=ni*   *n-e*   *nhigo*   **ia**   **tañano**   *si=ge*],
work=3SGO   RL-3S   be.finished   theSG   food   FOC=SEQ
Making the food is finished and then

n-e-ge   *mai*   *toke=ña*   *kaike* *mane=na*   *koromata...*
RL-3S-PRS   come   arrive=IMM   one   man=3SGP   PNLOC
a man from Koromata arrives...'

b.   *...ḡe*   *fa* *ku~kumai=ni*   *e=u*
      NT   CS   RD~drink=3SGO   3S=be.thus
      '...[you] make him drink [the medicine].

[*fa ku~kumai*   *n-e*   *nhigo*   **ka=t=au=ana**]
CS RD~drink   RL-3S   be.finished   LOC=SBD=exist=thatN
Making [him] drink from that [medicine] is finished,

ke   *fa* *ba~blahi*   *ḡ-e-ke=gu*   *nakoni ana...*
PFV   CS   RD~be.tabu   NT-3S-PFV=be.thus   person   thatN
[then] bless that person...'

Completion clauses occur during the narrative or expositional description of a series of events, recapping the event expressed by the preceding sentence and indicating that that event is completed. These occur in narratives to indicate that one event is carried out to completion before the next event occurs:

(10.112)   *...ḡ-e   la   fa-lehe=i=ña*   *n-e-ke=u*   *fadalao*
           NT-3S   go   CS-die=3SGO=IMM   RL-3S-PFV=be.thus   PN
           '...they went [and] killed Fadalao,

           ta=ni=na   *naitu* *t=au=ne*
           SBD=3SGO=thatN   devil   SBD=exist=thisR
           who was this devil.

           fa-lehe=i   *n-e*   *nhigo*   *sini ge   age,*   *ḡ-e*   *toke=ña...*
           CS-die=3SGO   RL-3S   be.finished   FOC   SEQ   SEQ   NT-3S   arrive=IMM
           They killed him finish and then they went back...'

Completion clauses occur often in exposition, particularly when a process involving a series of stages is being described. Each stage is typically described, then a clause indicating its completion introduces the subsequent clause:

(10.113) *o   la   roh-i=Ø*   *ia   ḡuanha*
          2S   go   scrape-TR=3SGO   theSG   inhale
          'You go and scrape the "inhale".

          ḡuanha e=ni   bla   nañha=na=na   ḡazu   t=au=ao
          inhale 3S=3SGO   LMT   name=3SGP=thatN wood   SBD=exist-thisT
          "Inhale" is just the name of this tree.

          [*la roh-i=Ø*   *n-e   nhigo*],   *toke=na   fa blahi*
          go scrape-TR=3SGO   RL-3S   be.finished   arrive=thatN   CS be.tabu
          Going and scraping it is finished, go back and bless [it].

          [*fa blahi   n-e   nhigo   ara   ge   age*],
          CS be.tabu   RL-3S   be.finished   I   SEQ SEQ
          Blessing is finished,

          ḡ-e   ḡuanha=ña   nakoni...
          NT-3S   inhale=IMM   person
          and then the person inhales...'

10.4 'Be thus' clauses

The verb (=)*gu* ~ =*u* has a broad range of functions with a semantically weak predication best translated as 'be thus'. This verb is cliticized to a modal/subject particle, often forming a single word clause, except occasionally with its quotative function, when it may occur in isolation. When it does occur in isolation it is the underlying form *gu* that occurs. When cliticized the initial /ɣ/ is deleted except when the final vowel of the host is /u/.

10.4.1 Exclamatory tag clauses

One major function of the 'be thus' clause is as an exclamatory tag marking a constituent, usually a complete clause, with a sense best translated as 'that's how it is' or 'that's how it was'. *E=u*, with a zero modal component, is formally irrealis. However, *e=u* is semantically bleached to the point where it has little more than an emphatic sense. Although it may mark irrealis clauses, as with the future event in (10.114)a., *e=u* also marks modally neutral clauses, as in (10.114)b., and realis events ([10.114]c.):

(10.114)a. *t=au=la*   *ke*   *nhogi* *ia*   *lehe ka* *suaragi* ***e=u***
       SBD=exist=CND PFV payback theSG die LOC PN   3S=be.thus
       'Since that is so [we] will payback the death of Suaragi, it's like that.'

   b. ...*ḡ-e au=gu*   *logahaza* ***e=u***
      NT-3S exist=CNT PNLOC   3S=be.thus
      '...he lived at Logahaza, it's like that.'

   c. ***n-e-ke***   *kave*   ***e=u***   *bla* *manei* ***e=u***
      RL-3S-PFV descend 3S=be.thus LMT he   3S=be.thus
      'He went down, it's like that.'

In other instances, *e=u* does mark an event as irrealis. In this case the person-indexing agrees with the subject. This applies to the full range irrealis events in main clauses, including future and habitual events, as in (10.115)a.–b., but does not apply to the irrealis example in (10.114)a., where the main clause subject is first inclusive. When used in this less semantically bleached sense, the perfective aspect marker *ke* may mark the modal/subject particle, as in (10.115)c.

(10.115)a. *mane heta*   *ḡ-e*   *aḡe=u=ña*   ***e=u***
      man   be.strong NT-3S go=CNT=IMM 3S=be.thus
      'A strong man will go [i.e., He'll be a strong man], he'll be like that.'

   b. *ḡlepo*   *t=au=o*   *si=ge,*   *age* *ḡ-e*   *mai=ña*
      thing   SBD=exist=thatNV FOC=SEQ SEQ NT-3S come=IMM
      'That thing then comes

      ḡ-e   *ñhau=gu*   ***e=u***
      NT-3S eat=CNT   3S=be.thus
      [and] eats, he's like that.'

   c. *manei ginai ñhau namhari* ***e-ke=u***
      he   FUT eat fish   3S-PFV=be.thus
      'He will be eating fish, he'll be like that.'

This less bleached use of irrealis tags is limited to third person subjects. The analogous first and second person tags **a=u* and **o=u* do not occur.

Realis marked 'be thus' clauses always have a less semantically bleached sense than that of the irrealis tags illustrated in (10.114). While these irrealis tags have a general sense of 'the way things are', realis tags emphasize that the situation expressed by the clause is the way that event or state actually is or was. Realis tags may mark realis or modally neutral clauses (as in [10.116]a.–b.), or clauses with no modal/subject particle (as in the second clause in [10.116]c.) and in

(10.116)d. When marking a modally neutral clause or one without a particle they assign realis status to the events coded by the clause:

(10.116)a. *n-e-ge   la teo   ia   nakoni **n-e=u**...*
          RL-3S-PRS   go not.exist theSG person RL-3S=be.thus
          'The people have gone to nothing...'

    b. *ḡ-e   teo   boka=i=na   **n-e=u***
          NT-3S not.exist be.able=3SGO=thatN   RL-3S=be.thus
          'They weren't able to do that, they were like that.'

    c. *n-e   rauru   manei, pru   **n-e=u**   seku=na   hinage=o*
          RL-3S seaward he   jump   RL-3S=be.thus tail=3SGP boat=thatNV
          'He went seaward and jumped into the back of the boat.'

    d. *fa kae aḡe   **n-e=u**,   teo   ḡ-e   ka=ni=u...*
          CS see go   RL-3S=be.thus not.exist NT-3S   see=3SGO=CNT
          'He looked [but] he didn't see him...'

The less semantically bleached nature of the realis tags is indicated by their subject agreement possibilities. The irrealis tag only occurs with the third person subject agreement marker *e*, regardless of the identity of the participants in the marked constituent. By contrast, the realis tags may be indexed to a participant in the marked clause, as in (10.117). In both these examples the third person tag *n-e=u* could freely occur in place of the tags shown, giving the slightly different sense 'It is/was like that' in place of 'I was/we are like that'.

(10.117)a. *ka   fata   rhue=di=ro   maneri, ga~gato=ḡu=na   ara*
          LOC occasion cry=3PLP=thoseNV   they   RD~think=1SGP=thatN I
          'When everyone cried, I thought

        *n-e-ge   lehe baiu manei **n-a=u***
          RL-3S-PRS   die PSB   she   RL-1EXCS=be.thus
          maybe she had died, I was like that.'

    b. *manei n-e   faheḡa,*
          he   RL-3S be./happy
          'He is happy,

        *ge gita da   dia-nanafa   **da=u***
          SEQ weINC 1INCS be.bad-heart 1INCS=be.thus
          but we feel bad, that's how we are.'

Realis tag clauses may carry the perfective marker *ke* and continuous *=gu*:

(10.118)a. ...ḡ-e-ge   faroh-i=Ø   manei sala **n-e-ke=u**
           NT-3S-PRS smite-TR=3SGO he   PN   RL-3S-PFV=be.thus
           '...[and] he kills Sala, he was like that.'

      b. *suaragi mane=na   kokota **n-e-ke=u***
         PN   man=3SGP PNLOC RL-3S-PFV=be.thus
         'Suaragi was a Kokota man, he was like that.'

      c. *ka fata   kae=ni-n=ara   manei,*
         LOC occasion see=3SGO=thatN=I he
         'When I saw him

         *manei n-e-ke   ñhau ge-na   namhari **n-e-ke=u=gu***
         he   RL-3S-PFV eat CNSM-3SGP fish   RL-3S-PFV=be.thus=CNT
         he was eating fish, he was like that.'

As (10.118)b. shows, tag clauses mark verbless predicates as well as verbal clauses.

Tag clauses optionally cliticize to the preceding word. The implications of this cliticization for stress placement are discussed in §2.5.5.

10.4.2 Sentence-initial 'be thus' clauses

A 'be thus' clause may occur sentence-initially, to indicate that the sentence is a comment on the content of the preceding discourse. In (10.119)a. the speaker has described two illnesses (attributed to 'devils'), and the appropriate custom medicines for each. He concludes the exposition with the sentence given. In (10.119)b. the speaker has explained at some length that an expected visitor is unwell, and has sent him in his place, and concludes with the example.

(10.119)a. *e=u*   *bla*   *za~zaho=di=re*   *palu*   *naitu*
         3S=be.thus LMT   RD~go=3PLP=thoseN two   devil
         'So they're the ways of the two devils

         ta=lase=ri=re   *ara*
         SBD=know=3PLO=thoseN I
         that I know.'

      b. **n-e=u**   *n-a-ge*   *mai* *toke* *a-hi=ña*   *ara*
         RL-3S=be.thus RL-1EXCS-PRS come arrive thisT-EMPH=IMM I
         'Thus I have come to you now.'

Sentence-initial 'be thus' clauses of this kind may be formally realis or irrealis, but only third person-indexing is possible. Irrealis 'be thus' clauses occur as exclamatory clauses, marked with the constituent modifiers discussed in §8.8:

(10.120)a. *e=u*   *bla*
          3S=be.thus   LMT
          'That's all!'

      b. *e=u*   *baiu*
          3S=be.thus   PSB
          'Maybe.' [response to proposition]

10.4.3 Quotative 'be thus' clauses

'Be thus' clauses occur with a quotative function, assigning the origin of remarks or thoughts to the sole argument of the clause. These 'be thus' clauses immediately follow a representation of the comments or thoughts. Often comments are presented as reported speech and directly quoted:

(10.121) *'ehe, keli=bo'*   ***ḡ-e=u=ña***   *manei*
          yes be.good=CNT   NT-3S=be.thus=IMM   he
          '"Yes, good," he said.'

Quotative 'be thus' clauses often dispay the immediacy particle *ña*. They are typically modally neutral, but realis and irrealis quotative clauses do occur:

(10.122)a. *'ago'*   ***n-e=u=ña***   *manei*
           youSG RL-3S=be.thus=IMM   he
           '"You!" he said.'

       b. *l=ago.*   *'ara'* ***e=u=ña***   *goio*
           go=youSG I   IRR=be.thus=IMM VOC
           'You go ahead. "I" you will say, man!'

With the quotative function only third person agreement occurs, regardless of the person of the subject, as in (10.122)b. With this function, older speakers (at least) occasionally omit the modal/subject particle, giving the verb in isolation:

(10.123) *'...teo   ḡ-o   doli=gu   e=u'*   ***gu***   *maneri...*
          not.exist NT-2S be.alive=CNT 3S=be.thus be.thus they
          '"...you will not be alive," they said...'

Quotative uses of the 'be thus' verb may be transitive, with postverbal agreement indexing the participant to whom the comments are addressed:

(10.124)a. *'kue=ḡu'*   **n-e=u=ni**   *bla...*
       grandfather=1SGP RL-3S=be.thus=3SGO LMT
       '"My grandfather!" he simply said to him...'

   b. *'fa kave=ri*   *no-u*   *rade*   *tagi-mu'*
       CS descend=3PLO GENP-2SGP arm.ring REFL-2SGP
       '"Take off your arm ring yourself,"

       n-e-ke=u=ni=u
       RL-3S-PFV=be.thus=CNT
       he was saying to him.'

Thoughts may also be quoted in the same way:

(10.125)a. *'ḡ-e-la*   *heve*   *e=u*   *ge,*   *ḡ-a*   *fa-lehe=i=ña*
       NT-3S-go what 3S=be.thus SEQ NT-1EXCS CS-die=3SGO=IMM
       '"How will I kill

       mane ana,   *ḡ-e*   *mala tai-ḡu*   *ñheñhe'e*
       man thatN NT-3S PURP REFL-1SGP be.separate
       that man, so I can be alone?"

       ḡ-e=u=ña   *manei*
       NT-3S=be.thus=IMM he
       he thought.'

   b. *'nariha'*   **n-e-ke=u=ña=ia**
       day.after.tomorrow RL-3S-PFV=be.thus=IMM=PRO
       '"The day after tomorrow," they thought.'

'Be thus' clauses are also used to assign authorship to comments or ideas without directly quoting remarks. In this situation, the 'be thus' clause is obligatorily marked with the perfective aspect marker *ke*, and with the demonstrative enclitic =*o*, indexing the comments or ideas cited:

(10.126)a. *tazi=ri*   *boboke=mu=are*
       keep=3PLO inner.thigh=2SGP=thoseN
       'Keep your inner thighs for me,

       mala no-ḡu   *ara* **n-o-ke=u=o**
       PURP GENP-1SGP I RL-2S-PFV=be.thus=thatNV
       as you said [you would].'

b. *mala fa-lehe=i=u*   ***n-a-ke=u=o***   *b=ara,*
   PURP CS-die=3SGO=CNT   RL-1EXCS-PFV=be.thus=thatNV   ALT=I
   'I thought to kill him,

   teo   bla si=boka=ḡu=na   ka   kuiti   aro-hi
   not.exist LMT FOC=be.able=1SGP=thatN LOC trick   theseT-EMPH
   but that ability of mine with these tricks wasn't able to.'

APPENDIX: ILLUSTRATIVE TEXT

World War II Reminiscences (Told by Nathanial Boiliana)

n-e-ge　　　*tor-i*　　*b=ana*　　*manei goi?*
RL-3SGS-PRS　open-TR　ALT=thatN　s/he　VOC
Has he opened it [i.e., started the tape recorder]?

au　*bla*　*n-a-ke=u*　　　　　*[goveo] banesokeo,*
exist　LMT　RL-1EXCS-PFV=be.thus　PNLOC　PNLOC
I was living in [Goveo] Banesokeo,

tana aḡe ira　*mane ta*　*zuke*　*leba.*
then　go　thePL　man　SBD　seek　labor
then the men came to look for labor.

ḡ-e-la　　*ara-hi*　*ka*　*vaka kabani-na*　　*amerika*
NT-3S-go　I-EMPH　LOC　ship　company-3SGP　PNLOC
So I was on an American company ship

aḡe　*hod-i=au*　　*banesokeo,*
go　take-TR=1SGO　PNLOC
that took me from Banesokeo,

rauru　　　*rasalo,*　*kepmasi*
go.seaward　PNLOC　PNLOC
[we] went seaward to Russell, to Cape Masi.

n-e　*la*　*au=nau*　　*sare.*　*au*　*bla*　*ge*　*au*
RL-3S　go　exist=1SGO　thereP　exist　LMT　SEQ　exist
I went and stayed there. Staying and staying

ka　*friñhe=na*　*mane amerika=re*　　*maḡra maneri.*
LOC　work=thatN　man　PNLOC=thoseN　fight　they
in the work of those American men in the fight.

gu　　　*ḡ-au-gu*　　　*rasalo e=u.*
be.thus　NT-exist-CNT　PNLOC　3S=be.thus
Like that, living on Russell.

tana nogoi mai　*ña*　*mane zapani*　*are*
then　VOC　come　IMM　man　PNLOC　thoseN
Then, man!, those Japanese men came

APPENDIX

ge hiḡri, u, gai   e=u.
SEQ flee um weEXC 3S=be.thus
and we ran away.

hiḡri lao ka   ḡluma.
flee go LOC excavation
Ran away into a cave.

ḡluma [n-e-ke   seh-i]   n-e-ke   zoh-i   maneri.
cave RL-3S-PFV climb-TR RL-3S-PFV dig-TR they
A cave they had dug.

mala lao au   muni gai   tarata au   are   ka, u,   leba=na.
PURP go exist hide weEXC group exist thoseN LOC um labor=thatN
We went and hid, we the group who were in the Labor [Company].

an-blau   n-e   lao n-e   lao tana   aḡe nhigo   sare,
thatN-LMT RL-3S go RL-3S go then go be.finished thereP
Like that, on and on, then it finished there,

mai   mane maḡra=re   ke   lao ka   korosa=na,
come man fight=thoseN PFV go LOC hole=thatN
then the soldiers came, they came to that hole,

mai   mane zapani ta   maḡra=re,
come man PNLOC SBD fight=thoseN
the Japanese soldiers came,

ke   la ruma ka   korosa=na gu
PFV go enter LOC hole=thatN be.thus
came into the hole,

ge   gai   ka   banhi t=au=ao   e=u.
SEQ weEXC LOC cave SBD=exist=thisT 3S=be.thus
then went into that cave.

ge   gai   tehi   nakoni e=u,
SEQ weEXC many person 3S=be.thus
We were many people,

tehi   mane ta   au=na   ka leba koponi.
many man SBD exist=thatN LOC labor company
many people who were in the Labor Company.

t=au-di   *rasalo, t=au-di*   *isabelo, t=au-di*   *malaita,*
SBD=exist-3PLP PNLOC   SBD=exist-3PLP PNLOC   SBD=exist-3PLP PNLOC
Some from Russell, some from Isabel, some from Malaita,

e=u   *ta fodu=re*   *gai*   *au=re*   *friñhe=re*   *gai*   *sare.*
3S=be.thus SBD be.full=thoseN weEXC exist=thoseN work=thoseN weEXC thereP
we were full of that laborers there.

gu   *bla*   *ḡ-e*   *lao*   *ḡ-e*   *lao,*
be.thus LMT NT-3S go   NT-3S go
Like that, on and on,

ke   *mai*   *vaka flalo are,*   *ke*   *hiḡri*   *gai.*
PFV come ship   fly   thoseN PFV flee   weEXC
and then those planes came, and we ran away.

ke   *dani*   *lao bla*   *ka*   *ḡluma*
PFV do.in.unison go   LMT   LOC   excavation
We all went into that hole.

t=au=ana   *lao bla.*
SBD=exist=thatN go   LMT
Like that.

gu   *bla*   *n-e*   *lao n-e*   *lao n-e*   *lao n-e*   *lao,*
be.thus LMT RL-3S go   RL-3S   go   RL-3S   go   RL-3S   go
On and on and on and on,

u   *gilai aḡe au*   *nhigo*   *ia*   *komhu*   *t=au=ana.*
um until go exist be.finished theSG year   SBD=exist=thatN
um, until that year was finished.

an-bla   *ke*   *kota-u*   *ara, ke*   *mai*   *au*   *banesokeo,*
thatN-LMT PFV go.ashore-CNT I   PFV come exist PNLOC
That, then I came back, came and stayed at Banesokeo,

ke   *mai-di=ro*   *bla*   *maneri,*
PFV come-3PLP=thoseNV LMT they
then they came back again,

vaka mala   *ke*   *hoda nakoni mala aḡe*   *au=ro*
ship PURP   PFV take   person PURP go   exist=thoseNV
a ship to take people to go

ka   leba=na   t=au=ana   rasalo   e=u.
LOC labor=thatN SBD=exist=thatN PNLOC 3S=be.thus
in that Labor [Company) at Russell.

klisu-g̠u   sare,
depart-1SGP thereP
So I left there,

mai   hod-i=au   ara banesokeo.
come take-TR=1SGO I   PNLOC
they came and took me from Banesokeo.

ke   rauru   ña   bla   ara   rasalo
PFV go.seaward IMM LMT I   PNLOC

ge   rauru   t=au-a=na   ara-hi.
SEQ go.seaward SBD=exist-1EXCS=thatN I-EMPH
I went seaward to Russell.

n-e-ge   nhigo   ia   mag̠ra e=u.
RL-3S-PRS be.finished theSG fight 3S=be.thus
The fight was finished.

n-e-ge   zaho ia   mag̠ra.
RL-3S-PRS go theSG fight
The fight had gone.

teo   g̠-e   ge   au   ia   mag̠ra.
not.exist NT-3S SEQ exist theSG fight
The fight wasn't present.

n-e-ge   'pis'   t=au=are   ka   ooe vaka=re.
RL-3S-PRS peace SBD=exist=thoseN LOC talk ship=thoseN
There was 'peace' in Pijin.

are-bla   sare   g̠-e   nhigo,
thoseN-LMT thereP NT-3S be.finished
Those there [the fighting) was finished,

tana kolola au   bla   ke   friñhe kako friñhe sug̠a friñhe,
then ??   exist LMT PFV work cargo work house work
then we just stayed there to work cargo, build houses, just work.

u,   bla   ḡ-au=gu   rasalo   e=u.
um   LMT   NT-exist=be.thus   PNLOC   3S=be.thus
Um. That's what we did on Russell.

gu   bla   n-e   lao n-e   lao n-e   lao n-e   lao   friñhe ana,
be.thus   LMT   RL-3S   go   RL-3S   go   RL-3S   go   RL-3S   go   work   thatN
Like that, that work went on and on and on and on,

friñhe suḡa   tetena,
work   house   sago
we built sago [thatch] houses,

fa   rauru   tetena   mane   aro,
CS   go.seaward   sago   man   thoseNV
those men [the people in the Kokota district] sent sago [thatch],

ḡ-e   [hoda]   mai   hoda vaka, vaka dou   ana,
NT-3S   take   come   take   ship   ship   be.big   thatN
a ship came and took it, that big ship,

hod-i=ri   ḡ-e   aḡe   rasalo
take-TR=3PLO   NT-3S   go   PNLOC
took them all [the thatch leaves/panels] and went to Russell

[gai   ta]   gai   ta   faḡoi   di=re,
weEXC   SBD   weEXC   SBD   carry   3PLP=thoseN
and we carried them,

hure   kota   t=au=re   gai,
carry   go.ashore   SBD=exist=thoseN   weEXC
we carried those ashore,

faḡoi   di=re   sara   rasalo   e=u.
carry   3PLP=thoseN   thereD   PNLOC   3S=be.thus
carried them there in Russell.

nhigo   t=au=are   tana   toka   tetu   mala   suḡa,
be.finished   SBD=exist=thoseN   then   chop   post   PURP   house
That finished, we cut posts for houses,

gu,   gai   sare   e=u,   toka   tetu   ḡahao,   fata,
be.thus   weEXC   thereP   3S=be.thus   chop   post   beam   rafter
that's what we did there, cut posts, beams, rafters,

411

gu,   ḡ-e   nhigo-u,   hafe,
be.thus NT-3S be.finished-CNT tie.thatch
that finished, we tied the thatch,

hafe   nhigo   ririñi,
tie.thatch be.finished wall
the tying finished, [then] the walls,

ririñi nhigo-u,   tana
wall   be.finished-CNT then
walls finished, then

"ade sekseni-na=o   isabela ka suḡa a-hi."   gu   maneri,
here section-3SGP=thatNV PNLOC   LOC house thisT-EMPH be.thus they
"Here, that Isabel [i.e., Banesokeo] Section in this house," they said.

gai   la au   ka   t=au=an-e=u.
weEXC go exist LOC SBD=exist=thatN-3S=be.thus
We lived in that one.

gu   bla n-e   lao n-e   lao,
be.thus LMT RL-3S go RL-3S go
Like that,

n-e   aḡe lao la mane kia=re,
RL-3S go go go man PNLOC=thoseN
those Kia men went [to another house],

ḡ-e   lao la mane hoḡrano are,
NT-3S go go man PNLOC   thoseN
those Hograno men went [to another house],

ḡ-e   lao la mane malaita=re,   mane bugotu   are.
NT-3S go go man PNLOC=thoseN man Bugotu thoseN
those Malaita men went [to another house], those Bugotu men.

gu   bla ḡ-e=u   ka   taem t=au=ana   e=u.
be.thus LMT NT-3S=be.thus LOC time SBD=exist=thatN3S=be.thus
Like that at that time.

la nhigo   tana friñhe bla suḡa=o,
go be.finished then work LMT house=thatNV
Building the house was finished,

kota   kako   are
go.ashore cargo thoseN
[then] cargo came ashore

stakim kako ka suḡa tetena ka n-e-ke   friñhe=ri   are   gai.
stack   cargo LOC house sago   LOC RL-3S-PFV work=3PLO thoseN weEXC
and we stacked the cargo in the sago thatch houses that we had built.

la fodu-i   kako-di   bla suḡa t=au=are=u.
go   be.full-TR cargo-3PLP LMT house SBD=exist=thoseN=be.thus
Those cargos filled up those houses.

sare bla nogoi ḡ-e   au   bla ḡ-e   au   bla ḡ-e   au   bla
thereP LMT VOC   NT-3S exist LMT NT-3S exist LMT NT-3S exist LMT

friñhe ana.
work   thatN
There that work just continued on and on.

friñhe ḡ-e   lao ḡ-e   lao ke   nafa, ke friñhe gu   bla
work   NT-3S go   NT-3S go PFV rest   PFV work   be.thus LMT
Work on and on and on, then we rested. [We] worked like that,

ḡ-e   lao bla ḡ-e=u   ka suḡa t=au=are   ḡilu-na
NT-3S go LMT NT-3S=be.thus LOC house SBD=exist=thoseN inside-3SGP
went like that in those houses

kaike komhu.
one   year
for a whole year.

an-bla   nhigo   tana t=au=are,
thatN-LMT be.finished then SBD=exist=thoseN
That, then those [jobs] were finished,

an-blau   nhigo-na=na   ta=ke   lao=na   maneri,
thatN-LMT be.finished-3SGP=thatN SBD=PFV go=thatN they
at that finish of it they went,

ta=ke   pulo-na   mane amerika=re   e=u.
SBD=PFV return-3SGP man PNLOC=thoseN 3S=be.thus
the American men went back.

ke   pulo   mane   amerika=ro   nhigo,
PFV   return man   PNLOC=thoseNV   be.finished
Those American men went back,

age   ḡ-e   lotum=ḡai   ña   gai   mane isabel   e=u,
SEQ   NT-3S load=1EXCO IMM weEXC man   PNLOC   3S=be.thus
[they] loaded us, we Isabel [i.e., Kokota] men,

mane   malaita e=u   mane hoḡrano   e=u,
man   PNLOC 3S=be.thus man   PNLOC   3S=be.thus
Malaita men, Hograno men,

t=au=are   ke   hoda pulo=ḡai=na
SBD=exist=thoseN PFV take   return=1EXCO=thatN

vaka   t=au=an-e=u.
ship   SBD=exist=thatN-3S=be.thus
that ship took us back.

sare   bla   ḡ-a-ke   mai   au   bla,
thereP LMT NT-1EXCS-PFV come exist LMT
There we came and just stayed,

ḡ-a-ke=u   ka   nau=de,
NT-1EXCS-PFV=be.thus LOC village=theseR
we were like that in this village;

[ḡ-e   aḡe   nhigo-u   ia]
NT-3S go   be.finished-CNT   theSG

n-e   aḡe   nhigo   ia   maḡra e=u.
RL-3S go   be.finished theSG fight   3S=be.thus
the fighting was finished.

sare   bla   ḡ-e   nhigo   ara   tu~turi=na.
thereP LMT NT-3S be.finished I   RD~tell.story=thatN
There I finish my story.

REFERENCES

Bogesi, George. 1948. "Santa Isabel, Solomon Islands." *Oceania* 18:208–232, 327–357.

Boswell, Freddy. 2002. "The genres of 'shouted speech' in Cheke Holo." *Australian Journal of Linguistics* 22/1: 35–43.

Church of Melanesia. 1965. *A Melanesian English Prayer Book with Hymns.* Honiara: Provincial Press. [has numerous subsequent revised editions]

———. n.d., *Buka Nhau Blahi Ka O'oe Kokota.* Honiara: Provincial Press.

Corston, Simon H. 1996. *Ergativity in Roviana, Solomon Islands.* Canberra: Pacific Linguistics.

Fitzsimons, Matthew. 1989. *Zabana. A grammar of a Solomon Islands language.* MA thesis: University of Auckland.

Foley, William A., and Robert D. Van Valin. 1984. *Functional syntax and universal grammar.* Cambridge: CUP.

Gordon, Raymond G., Jr. (ed.). 2005. *Ethnologue: Languages of the World.* 15th edition. Dallas: SIL International. www.ethnologue.com.

Grimes, Barbara F. (ed.). 2000. *Ethnologue: Languages of the World.* 14th edition. Dallas: SIL International. www.ethnologue.com/14/web.asp.

Hayes, Bruce. 1995. *Metrical stress theory. Principles and case studies.* Chicago: University of Chicago Press.

Lynch, John. 1974. *Lenakel phonology.* PhD thesis: University of Hawai'i.

———. 1978. *A grammar of Lenakel.* Canberra: Pacific Linguistics.

Palmer, Bill. 1997. "Notes on mood and aspect in Mandeghusu (Simbo)." In Lynch, John, and Fa'afo Pat, eds., *Oceanic studies: Proceedings of the First International Conference on Oceanic Linguistics.* Canberra: Pacific Linguistics.

———. 1998. *Ia tarai ka saigona. Ia nona ooe God ka Ooe Kokota.* Port Vila: desktop published.

———. 1999a. *A grammar of the Kokota language, Santa Isabel, Solomon Islands.* PhD thesis: University of Sydney.

———. 1999b. "Voiced sonorants—phonemes or underlying clusters?" *Australian Journal of Linguistics* 19/1:77–88.

———. 2002a. "Kokota." In Lynch, John, Malcolm D. Ross, and Terry Crowley, eds., *The Oceanic languages.* London: Curzon Press.

———. 2002b. "Absolute spatial reference and the grammaticalisation of perceptually salient phenomena." In Bennardo, Giovanni, ed., *Representing space in Oceania: culture in language and mind.* Canberra: Pacific Linguistics.

Palmer, Bill, and Dunstan Brown. 2007. "Heads in Oceanic indirect possession." *Oceanic Lingusitics* 46/1:199–209.

Ross, Malcolm D. 1988. *Proto Oceanic and the Austronesian languages of Western Melanesia.* Canberra: Pacific Linguistics.

———. 1995. "Some current issues in Austronesian linguistics." In Tryon, Darrell T., ed., *Comparative Austronesian dictionary. An introduction to*

Austronesian studies. Part 1: Fascicle 1. Berlin: Mouton de Gruyter. pp.45–120.

———. 1998. "Proto-Oceanic adjectival categories and their morphosyntax." *Oceanic Linguistics.* 37/1: 85–119.

Tryon, Darrell T. and Brian D. Hackman. 1983. *Solomon Islands languages: an internal classification.* Canberra: Pacific Linguistics.

Van Valin, Robert D. 1993. "A synopsis of Role and Reference Grammar." In Van Valin, Robert D., ed., *Advances in role and reference grammar.* Amsterdam: Benjamins.

White, Geoffrey M., Francis Kokhonigita, and Hugo Pulomana. 1988. *Cheke Holo (Maringe/Hograno) dictionary.* Canberra: Pacific Linguistics.

Whiteman, Darrell, and Gary Simons. 1978. *The languages of Santa Isabel, Solomon Islands: a sociolinguistic survey.* MS.

INDEX